Inspired

The Paranormal World of Creativity

Grant Cameron
with Katarina Castillo

Itsallconnected Publishing
Winnipeg Canada

Copyright © 2016 by Grant Cameron

Cover Produced by Eduardo Pogorelsky. Picture provided by Monica King of her two boys, Tenzin, and his younger brother Kalsang.

All rights reserved.
No part of this publication may be reproduced, distributed, or transmitted in any form or by any means, including photocopying, recording, or other electronic or mechanical methods, without the prior written permission of the publisher, except in the case of brief quotations embodied in critical reviews and certain other noncommercial uses permitted by copyright law. For permission requests, write to the publisher, addressed "Attention: Permissions Coordinator," at the address below.

Printed in the United States of America

First Printing, November 2016

ISBN-13: 978-1539674337
ISBN-10: 1539674339

Itsallconnected Publishing
445 Hudson Street
Winnipeg, Manitoba
Canada R3T OR1

whitehouseufo@gmail.com

Grant Cameron is the recipient of the Leeds Conference International Researcher of the Year and the UFO Congress Researcher of the Year awards. He became involved in Ufology beginning in May 1975 as the Vietnam War was ending when he had several personal sightings of an Unidentified Flying Object which locally became known as "Charlie Red Star."

These sightings led to a decade of research into the Canadian government's early engagement of the flying saucer phenomenon. Cameron became the leading authority on both the government program and on Wilbert B. Smith, who had headed it up. This led to almost two decades of subsequent research into the role of the President of the United States and extraterrestrial contact, much of which is available at the Presidents' UFO Website – www.presidentialufo.com, and at Cameron's blog site http://whitehouseufo.blogspot.ca/ .

Cameron has lectured widely in Canada, the United States, and Europe. He was one of the 43 witnesses who testified in front of six former members of the United States Congress (five Representatives and one Senator) in Washington, DC during the 2013 "Citizen's Hearing on UFO Disclosure." He has appeared on many television documentaries about UFOs and has been interviewed on nearly one hundred different radio programs, including frequent appearances on Coast to Coast AM.

Other books by Grant Cameron
UFOs, MJ-12, and the Government
UFOs, Area 51, and Government Informants
Alien Bedtime Stories
The Clinton UFO Storybook

Table of Contents

Introduction 1
Chapter 1. Chance vs. Pattern 8
Chapter 2. Inspiration and a Helping Hand 17
Chapter 3 Inspirations in Music 23
    Inspirations Before Rock and Roll 34
    Inspirations By Unpublished Musicians 40
Chapter 4 Inspiration by Serendipity 45
Chapter 5 Inspiration by Biomimicry 53
Chapter 6 Inspirations for Inventions 59
Chapter 7 Inspirations for Nobel Prizes 71
Chapter 8 Inspirations for Scientific Discoveries 79
Chapter 9 Inspirations for Books 88
Chapter 10 Inspirations for Movies 102
Chapter 11 Inspirations in Art 107
Chapter 12 Inspirations by Savants and Prodigies 114
Chapter 13 Inspirations from Psychics and Mediums 129
Chapter 14 Inspirations through Scientific Investigation 135
Chapter 15 Inspiration from the Third Man Factor 142
Chapter 16 Inspirations from Aliens 149
Chapter 17 - Inspirations from the Ancients 160
Chapter 18 Inspirations from Channeled Entities 166
Chapter 19 Inspirations through Automatic Writing 179
Chapter 20 Inspirations through Meditation 182
Chapter 21 Inspirations for the Dying and the Grieving 185
Chapter 22 Inspiration through Psychedelic Compounds ... 193
Chapter 23 What is the Main Message? 204

    Oneness 204

    Fear/Love 209

    The Environment 212

Chapter 24 What is the Mechanism? 217

    The Brain 218

    The Nonlocal Field 218

    Consciousness is Primary 222

    Two Brains and Two Minds 226

    Right Brain Gateway to Nonlocal Phenomena 233

    The Oneness Ghost in the Machine 244

Conclusion 250

    The End of the Physical World as We Know It 251

    Altruistic Inspirations 254

    It's All Connected 258

    A Final Note 261

Appendix 1- Songs That Were Inspired by Dreams 263

Footnotes 273

Introduction

The intuitive mind is a sacred gift, and the rational mind is a faithful servant. We have created a society that honors the servant and has forgotten the gift. We will not solve the problems of the world from the same level of thinking we were at when we created them. More than anything else, this new century demands new thinking: We must change our materially based analyses of the world around us to include broader, more multidimensional perspectives.
Albert Einstein

This book on inspirations and downloads is not what was originally intended. The book that I started to write dealt with the disclosure by some alien force telling us that we were not alone in the universe.

My investigation of this alien disclosure involved looking at stories of their influencing modern musicians to get across messages they wanted out. These downloaded musical communications included the idea that extraterrestrials are visiting the world. It also included musicians putting into their lyrics some of the same messages that appear to be given to UFO experiencers[1] and abductees such as love being the basis of everything, replacing fear with love, the concept of Oneness, and protecting the environment.

The strange reality buttressed in this download by aliens was that many modern musicians are very interested in UFOs and extraterrestrial life. It was these discoveries that inspired me to document the 20th-century musical obsession with UFOs, the message they were putting out, and why aliens might be using musicians as vehicles for their messages.

As that book neared a final first draft, the whole focus changed. It became apparent it was more important to talk about downloads and inspirations. What was happening to musicians became only a small part of the story.

The expansion away from just musicians started in response to questions following a lecture on the alien-music connection in Boulder, Colorado. Some in the audience maintained that it was the devil and evil forces that were influencing modern music. Audience members told me that my assumption of positive alien intentions was sadly misplaced.[2]

Somewhat taken aback by the criticism, and the old idea of a battle for men's minds by forces of good and evil, I had to sit back and re-examine my world view. I grew up in a home where my mother was a church organist for four decades. That inspired me to see if the composers of church hymns experienced the same downloads and inspirations as modern musicians. It turned out that they had. That meant that if the devil was behind downloads and inspirations in rock and roll, it appeared that he had also composed all the church music as well.

My research indicated that the idea that the devil was influencing music appeared to have much more to do with how we view other people's music than a behind the scenes devil pulling strings. The basic rule seemed to be that if my left brain ego doesn't like someone else's music it must be bad and include demonic elements. The ego, after all, is always going to consider itself to be the good guy on the road of truth and knowledge. Those who opposed must, therefore, be wrong or evil.

The timing of the devil's participation became an important consideration in my research. Some told me evil only entered music with the creation of heavy metal music and that rock music was okay. Having grown up in the 1960s, I knew this was wrong because I recall the claims back then that Satan was clearly a part of rock and roll.

People accused bands like the Rolling Stones, Beatles, and Led Zeppelin of creating songs where satanic messages were apparent when played backward. Even Elvis Presley, who started the whole rock and roll era, was accused of siding with the devil as he incorporated African-American rhythm into his music and in the 1950s blacks were seen to be in league with the devil. For this reason, Presley music was banned in many areas of the United States, and you could lose your job as a disc jockey for playing it.

A look farther back showed that others considered jazz and the blues satanic because the music was played in bars where drunkenness, loose women, and other sinful things could exist. The rule for satanic music became – it is never in "our" music, but is in "other people's" music.

It was during the search for the source of classical and church musician's inspirations and downloads that I started to run across claims by musicians that they were getting songs in dreams through some form of channeling process.

When I began looking at downloads of music in dreams, I began to shift away from a book on just musical downloads. What I discovered was that dreams had also led to inventions, scientific discoveries, and Nobel prizes.

Many creative endeavors seem to employ the use of inspirations and downloads. This discovery inspired me to add the topic to a lecture I gave to the Phoenix MUFON UFO group in January 2014. It was there where I first detailed how many different types of inspirations and downloads there were in various human creative processes. The snowball that became this book had started to roll down the hill.

It only took a bit more searching to manifest scores of inspirations in many fields of endeavor. The examples were everywhere. It appeared clear that people were tapping into some unconscious nonlocal reality. Secondly, it seemed that something or someone in this nonlocal reality appeared to be aiding the process.

Just when I thought I had invented the wheel, I discovered Brad Steiger and his wife Sherry reached a similar conclusion related to the 180 books on

UFOs, ghosts, and other paranormal phenomena that they have written. Steiger wrote,

> We have been engaged in UFO and paranormal research since the early 1950's, and we have come to the conclusion that throughout history some external intelligence has interacted with Homo sapiens in an effort to learn more about us and/or to communicate certain basic truths. In our book *Real Encounters, Different Dimensions, and Otherworldly Beings* (VIP, 2013) we present the thesis that the aliens, angels, spirit guides, demons, and gods or goddesses encountered by unaware, yet somehow receptive, percipients may actually be the product of a multidimensional intelligence that masks itself in physical forms that are more acceptable to humans than its true image--if image it has. We choose to define and to name this multidimensional intelligence and its multitude of manifestations as the Other.[3]

The Consciousness Connection

No collection of inspirations and downloads would be complete without some attempt to theorize where the inspirations are coming from, why people got them, and how those who received them got them.

After much study, all roads seemed to lead back to the role of consciousness and how it presents reality to us. The definition of consciousness is being aware. That's all it is, and that is all there is. Consciousness is reality as each of us sees it. All the inspirations and downloads that are a part of this book are a part of this mystery of consciousness.

Unfortunately, consciousness has been ignored by science. The reason is that it does not fit in well with the local causation material paradigm that universities indoctrinate into most scientists. This belief defines matter as the sole constituent of the universe. This teaching implies that "we are biological robots" and "consciousness and free will are illusions," and that the universe is a random, lonely, and meaningless place.

The inability to deal with the hard problem of consciousness and its mysteries is typified by scientists such as Bill Nye, who presents himself a skeptic on UFOs and the paranormal. He makes regular appearances in the media as a science commentator and paranormal debunker. During one debate he was given two minutes to explain the mystery of consciousness.

Nye, who paints himself as the guy with all the answers, quickly replied "Don't know. Great mystery."[4] All he could add to his response was a story that he had a friend who was a neurologist, and then he proceeded to tell an unrelated dog joke. He concluded his short answer with the words, "the joy of discovery. That's what drives us. The joy of what is going on, so we don't know where consciousness comes from."

This book's author, like others that have seriously looked into the mystery of consciousness unfettered by dogmatic beliefs, has come to understand that consciousness is a much bigger and more complex entity than just the brain or the mind.

Despite the claims by the materialist model that consciousness is just illusionary epiphenomena given off by a physical brain, a significant amount of research has shown something much bigger. Much of the world has come to understand that there is waking consciousness and a much more powerful unconscious mind that runs 95%+ of the functions of the human body and mind. Research done by Dr. Bruce Lipton on the unconscious mind shows that the unconscious mind operates at 40 million bits of data per second. The conscious mind, on the other hand, processes at only 40 bits per second.[5]

The chapters of this book are divided into various inspiration and download categories. Within each chapter are examples of the many times that people have received information, help, and encouragement from outside themselves by that particular inspiration or download.

I have used lists which make the incident examples easier to read. Because the examples are incident related, some people will appear in more than one chapter if they have had multiple different encounters.

Taken one by one, these various stories may be unimpressive. When the reader looks at the number of incidents in each chapter they can see a compelling argument that materialism is no longer an entirely adequate explanation of how our world works.

The last 100 years has brought tremendous changes in the attitude to consciousness despite the lack of research. People like Freud used hypnosis and psychoanalysis to expose the formally unknown, unconscious mind. This Freudian subconscious was more the mind of the mystics and dreams than it was a physical model of the brain. Now it has been confirmed through EEGs that the right hemisphere, associated with the subconscious becomes much more active when a person dreams.

Carl Jung added the idea of the collective unconscious, and the reality of synchronicity. The mind described by Jung became even more mystical and much less physical sounding. This mystical interpretation comes as no surprise given to the fact that Jung produced some of his material with automatic writing.

At the same time, science was starting to discover things that had been described by mystics throughout history. What came first was the idea that the physical world was space connected by electromagnetic fields. Ernest Rutherford in 1911 came up with the calculation that there were ten trillion (10^{13}) parts of space for every piece of matter. A couple of decades later it became known that the protons that made up the matter were also mostly space and that there were one nonillion (10^{30}) pieces of space for every piece of matter. Now with the latest model involving string theory, the subatomic particles have broken down into theoretical vibrating strings and a lot more space. The figure has now become ten sexdecillions (10^{52}) pieces of space for every piece of matter. Theoretical science had dissolved matter and the idea of the physical universe into a whole lot of nothing.

Then came the idea that elementary particles could be wave and particles at the same time which was hardly an idea supporting the fundamentalist physical world view.

Next came the discussions at the Fifth 1927 Solvay Conference on Electrons and Photons attended by 29 top physicists, 17 of who had or would win Nobel Prizes. It was in presentations at this conference that Wolfgang Pauli, Niels Bohr, and Werner Heisenberg raised the idea that consciousness might be the basis of the universe and that matter could only come into existence with an observer. This new role for consciousness arose from the results of the "double slit" experiment which showed that observation was influencing what happened in the lab.[6]

It was as Pauli described it "a situation transcending natural science." He added, "I do believe that the natural sciences will out of themselves bring forth a counter pole in their adherents, which connects to the old mystic elements."[7]

Heisenberg spelled out the new understanding of reality, "atoms or elementary particles themselves are not real; they form a world of potentialities or possibilities rather than one of things or facts."[8]

It was that conversation that sent many Newtonian physicists including Albert Einstein into a tailspin as they watched the physical world model melt before their eyes. Einstein accused Bohr of trying to introduce mysticism "incompatible to science" into physics. He described this "mystical trend of our time" as being a symbol of weakness and confusion.

Then in the 1980s, scientists ran the experiments confirming the "entangled particle" idea proposed fifty years earlier.[9] It upheld the fact that entangled elementary particles are instantly aware of what you might do to their entangled buddy who might be on the other side of the Universe. The idea of time and space and matter being bounded by the speed of light had run up against what Einstein complained as "spooky action at a distance."

The entangled particle experiment clearly showed that elementary particles are aware and conscious.[10] The research appeared to provide support for the ancient wisdom traditions that stated awareness and consciousness are the essential elements of the universe. The physical world becomes at best the creation of some aware observer because no particle will take a position in time and space without an observer. Until there is an observation, the particle does not exist.

Those materialists still married to the standard physical model of the universe heeded the calls to "shut up and calculate." Materialists knew if they didn't look behind the curtain they would not have to contend with the shattering of the physical world view they had learned in school. If they looked they would likely see what Seinfeld's George Costanza called "Worlds colliding."

This call to shut up about the philosophical implications of quantum mechanics and just build technology with the equations supposedly led to the technological world we now enjoy. That is the working hypothesis but not the full story.

This book will point out that a lot of the people taking credit for current technology were no more than observers. Many discoveries came through a download process outside the calculating mind. Other inventions, credited to conscious analytic efforts, are based on biomimicry which is only making copies of complex structures that nature creates.

What follows is an accumulation of evidence that may help provide some new building blocks for a more accurate description of consciousness and reality. I have chosen to avoid a left brained book intended to analyze and logically prove an accurate, reproducible model for inspirations and downloads.

A book based on left brained arguments would be a book written to convert the left-brained minds that rely only on reason and analysis. They are not about to accept any of my inspiration and download material. That is the nature of left-brained skeptical people. They will maintain that new ideas, inventions, songs, and art, come from rigorous logical scientific thinking and thatintuition, inspirations, and downloads are simply brain chemistry and pseudoscientific delusions.

The reason for this belief is that the left-brained rational, analytical brain has a consciousness component in it that makes up things to keep the story consistent. This left-brain component is something of a pathological liar. Neuroscientist V.S Ramachandran called it the confabulator. Neuroscientist Dr. Michael Gazzaniga, who discovered this module called it the interpreter. Harvard-trained neuroanatomist Jill Bolte Taylor calls it the storyteller.

What this element of the left brain does, when confronted with something that creates a hole in the paradigm or makes the story inconsistent, is to make up something to fill the gap or inconsistency. It makes up something like an alcoholic lying about a drinking habit.

Therefore, a book written to try and shift the paradigm is pointless, because the storyteller that helps maintain the left-brain physical model can fill the holes with BS as fast as I can produce evidence. Moreover, this storyteller will stubbornly resist any rational assessment of proof.

Gazzaniga highlighted the operation of this storyteller by working with epileptic patients where the 300 million connecting fibers between the two halves of the brain called the Corpus Callosum were cut to control seizures.

His research showed cases where the storyteller was in operation. One patient suffered from anosognosia caused by a stroke in the right parietal cortex which caused a paralyzed left arm. Because the right brain controls the left arm, the left brain is getting no input that anything was wrong. The left brain interpreter quickly came up with an explanation of why the arm was not working. Gazzaniga stated that the interpreter took over making up a tale to make inconsistent story consistent again, "When patients with this disorder are asked about their arm, and why they can't move it, they will say "It's not mine" or "I just don't feel like moving it."[11]

In another case, Gazzaniga referred to a woman with a right-brain condition that caused her to believe she was in her home and not a hospital. No amount of talk could convince her otherwise. Finally, he said to her "If you are at home, why are there elevators in the hallway?" She quickly replied, "Do you know how much it cost me to put those elevators in?" The left brain interpreter was ready with a story to explain the discrepancy in the tale.

Gazzaniga's research also showed "The left-hemisphere interpreter is not only a master of belief creation, but it will stick to its belief system no matter what." Everyone in the fields of UFO or paranormal research already knows that beliefs rarely change and that science, as Max Planck put it "advances one funeral at a time."

Chapter 1. Chance vs. Pattern

Mathematicians agree that any requisite number beyond 10^{50} has, statistically, a zero probability of occurrence. **Vance Ferrell, The Evolution Handbook**

Everyone who is seriously involved in the pursuit of science becomes convinced that a spirit is manifest in the laws of the Universe - a spirit vastly superior to that of man, and one in the face of which we with our modest powers must feel humble. **Albert Einstein**

An honest man, armed with all the knowledge available to us now, could only state that in some sense, the origin of life appears at the moment to be almost a miracle, so many are the conditions which would have had to have been satisfied to get it going. **Nobel Laureate Francis Crick who discovered the DNA structure.**

Once upon a time in a human body far, far away, there was a cell that had a vision. He told his fellow cells, "I had a vision last night. In my vision, I saw that we are all part of a bigger One, that we are all connected, and that we all have our specific roles to play."

The other cell said, "I am sorry. I am a skeptic. The prevailing science says survival of the fittest is the rule, and we are therefore all randomly created individuals. You are nothing more than a biological robot and must have been hallucinating."

In the same body at the same time, there was a brain neuron that had a vision as well. He envisioned that he and the other neurons were not just competing among themselves but that they were all part of a giant mind that could think, reason, and imagine, plus create language and images.

His buddies were not convinced, and one rational minded skeptic neuron said that this was not possible. The prevailing theory is that each neuron is simply a randomly created switch or a little biologic robot that has no meaning. Each neuron is an individual in a random meaningless universe. "You must," he told the neuron with the vision, "be hallucinating."

Then the human himself was visiting Brazil and one long night engaged in the Ayahuasca experience. He had a vision that his mind was part of a universal mind. The entities that he met encountered taught him that he was part of the ONE and that the ONE was made up of all the parts.

Coming back to his regular life, he told his friends that we are all part of the ONE. There is no separation.

But like the cell and the neuron, his skeptic friends told him of the reality of the physical world. He said that the prevailing view held by the majority of those at the National Academy of Sciences is that we are all biological robots in a random meaningless world. The rule is to get the girl, get the job, get the house, get two cars, get some kids, and try and enjoy life while it lasts because that is all there is. The one with the most toys at death wins.

As weird as this story sound it sums up the present belief by most scientists on consciousness. The story told says we are biological robots run by a randomly evolved unconscious mind. We, therefore, have no free will and our conscious of self is an illusion.

Mainstream science declares that everything we do results from a random interaction of firing neurons in our head. What we do is simply a result of what neurons are firing at the time. Stephen Hawking said the following:

> *Although we feel that we can choose what we do, our understanding of the molecular basis shows that biological processes are governed by the laws of physics and chemistry and therefore are as determined as the orbits of the planets. Recent experiments in neuroscience support the view that it is our physical brain follow the known laws of science that determine our actions, and not some agency that exists outside those laws... It is hard to imagine how free will can operate if our behavior is determined by physical law, so it seems that we are no more than biological machines and that free will is just an illusion.*[12]

A human being, therefore, according to Hawking, is nothing more than "a chemical scum on the surface of a typical planet that's in orbit around a typical star on the outskirts of a typical galaxy."[13]

There are a few scientists who have opposed this random meaningless view of the universe. One of these was Dr. Fred Hoyle, credited with the discovery of supernova and their creation of heavy elements in the universe. Hoyle stood up against the idea of randomness in the universe, and his public acknowledgment of his belief probably cost him a Nobel Prize. He was clear about his view, "You would be more likely to assemble a fully functioning and flying jumbo jet by passing a hurricane through a junkyard than you would be to assemble the DNA molecule by chance. In any kind of primeval soup in 5 or 600 million years, it's just not possible."[14]

Even Francis Crick, who came up with the discovery of the DNA double helix structure, had his doubts that the random theory was right. Speaking of DNA, he stated, "An honest man, armed with all the knowledge available to us now, could only state that in some sense, the origin of life appears at the moment to be almost a miracle, so many are the conditions which would have to be satisfied to get it going."[15]

Crick even proposed a panspermia theory claiming that aliens had deposited DNA, and there was no random evolution. He did not account for where the alien DNA had originated.

When it came to the even more impossible problem of explaining consciousness and its millions of mysteries Crick reverted to the materialist party line of a random and meaningless universe, despite his belief that DNA would be impossible through natural selection; strangely, the even more complex brain was believed by Crick to be possible by chance.

The idea of a brain producing random neuronal actions that in turn randomly dictates our every movement and thought raises many questions requiring an answer. If our consciousness is an illusion and we are merely biological robots does it mean that the 19 terrorists who were part of 911 did not choose to fly planes into the World Trade Center and the Pentagon? Is Hawking maintaining that all 19 just suddenly were all overcome with identical neurological signals that made them all join in an instantaneous impulse to highjack planes and destroy key targets? Does this random theory of the event sound sane?

In the same way, in 2011 one billion people watched the Pakistani-India final in cricket. Are Hawking and the other materialists who see humans as biological robots claiming that one billion brains did not choose to turn on the TV, but all suddenly got the impulse to turn the television on and watch the same channel on the same day and time?

In 1969 there were 4.7 billion people who watched Neil Armstrong walk on the moon. Is it possible that instead of a free will decision to view the moon landing, 4.7 billion brains all randomly fired in sync to cause everyone to turn on the TV at the same time?

The fundamental issue that needs resolving is what is the guiding force to evolution in the universe? Is it random chance or is it a pattern?

Hawking and others maintain that invoking God is not necessary to explain the origins of the universe. The laws of physics explain everything. These laws of physics explanation raise new questions - Who are the laws of physics? When were they written? Did they come from a burning bush?

Religion has its Gods and science has its superheroes. The law of physics is one of the scientific superheroes, known as laws of physics man. The law of physics man has super powers, and no one questions how he does his smoke and mirror tricks. He is like Spiderman, Spiderman, does whatever a spider can. Other scientific superheroes include placebo man, instinct man, spontaneous remission man, illusion man, genetic memory man, and the superhero of all superheroes that started it all, singularity man. To challenge any of these superheroes, or to question how they do their tricks elicits the same reply, "Shut up and calculate."

The superheroes of science that are used to explain reality sounds a lot like an old man with a long white beard sitting on a cloud, Santa Claus, Easter Bunny, or the Tooth Fairy.

This use of such superheroes is known as naming theory. When a problem is unsolvable or goes against a prevailing and firmly held belief, naming is used to handle the problem. You give the problem a name, and you can move on without any further explanation. There is no need to explain the magic trick.[16]

What has happened is that the scientists with a strong personal faith in universal randomness have confused describing with explaining. They will state that they are explaining things in the universe when they are not. All they are doing is describing events.

A key example is a human cell, which is the simplest thing in biology. When it comes to how it divides, biologists will talk about spindles forming and dividing chromosomes, but they are merely describing what the cell is doing.

In reality, there will be no explanation of how the cell sources the 100 trillion atoms required for the new cell, or how the cell can put the atoms in the right place, in the right order, give the second cell life, and do the whole process in 15-24 hours. Also ignored is the fact that this same cell will create 100 trillion cells of various types to make a human body, and find a way to replace the 50-70 billion cells that will die each day. The magic trick remains a mystery.

We know a cell can do this, and that a scientist cannot perform even the first step of the process. Science is full of many descriptions of natural processes but has no explanations.

The scientific descriptions of natural processes are much like Biblical stories. Consider the story of Moses and his rescue of the children of Israel. Moses brings with him his staff and leads everyone to the edge of the Red Sea. He hits his staff on the water, and the sea opens a dry path for the people to escape through. When everyone gets to the other end, they see the Egyptians coming through the divided sea. Moses hits his staff on the shore, and the sea closes up. Like the formation of a cell, it is a good story. The question, however, remains: How is the trick done?

How did the Universe come into being? From where did the laws of physics originate? There is no universe without them so how did these thousands of laws all emerge at the same time?

Terence McKenna spoke up about this type of mythical naming when he talked about the materialistic scientific explanation for the origin of man and the magical process described by science used to describe extraordinary natural events.

> *The dominant and virtually unchallenged myth or our origin is either that God created us in seven days along with the rest of creation or that the universe was born out of nothingness in a single moment for no reason. These are the two choices on the menu – neither terribly compelling to rationalists. Interesting to note that this scientific explanation – the universe sprang from nothing in a single instant*

however we may think of it in terms of its veracity- notice that it is the limit case for credulity. You understand what I mean?

I mean that if you can believe that – hell - you can believe anything. Sit down and try and think of something more improbable than that contention. So it's like they open up with the one-two punch and say put that in front of them. If they can swallow that then the hydrogen bond, the gene segregation or whatever will follow hard pace because the hard swallow comes first.

I maintain that it is a very odd place to look. What that's called is a singularity, and many theories require a singularity. That means to kick start the intellectual engine you have to go outside the system, and you get one free hypothesis and then once you have used that up your system has to run very very smoothly clear down to the end.

So science uses up its one free miracle with the big bang. Give me the first 10 to the high 12 nanoseconds and if I can do smoke and mirrors in that, then the rest will proceed in an orderly fashion. Now that is orthodoxy you have to understand. That's what the straight people believe.[17]

The Threat of the Extraterrestrial Question

There are an estimated 10^{78} to 10^{82} atoms in the known universe. [18] There are about one thousand enzymes in the human body, and the chance of obtaining them all in a random trial is only one part in 10 to the 40,000power[19]. The odds are so high it led scientists like S. Shklovskii, Carl Sagan, and DNA discoverer to propose alien directed panspermia theories to account for life on earth. Crick suggested that a dying civilization had sent a spaceship out that happened to hit Earth. Crick described his faith in his 1981 book *Life Itself*.

The microorganisms are supposed to have traveled in the head of an unmanned spaceship to earth by a higher civilization which developed elsewhere some billions of years ago. The spaceship was unmanned so that its range would be as great as possible. Life started here when these organisms were dropped into the primitive ocean and began to multiply.[20]

Crick first published his direct panspermia theory "quietly" in a Carl Sagan's edited space journal called Icarus. Despite Crick's Nobel Prize, his opinion is ignored as it proposes something just as unbelievable.

So why is this all important? What is so important about determining if pattern or chance govern the universe?

Centuries ago before Columbus made his trip across the Atlantic and thus dispelled the idea that the world was flat, humankind believed that man was unique and that the whole universe revolved around man – the geocentric model of the universe.

Then after Nicolaus Copernicus published *Concerning the Revolutions of Celestial Spheres,* we suddenly understood that our belief of being at the center was wrong.

Later discoveries showed that there was a common pattern in the universe. Our sun was just like all the other stars in the night sky. Then it was discovered that there was another pattern. Our sun, like others stars, is just one of many in the galaxy. Sadly we are not even at the center of our galaxy.

The pattern continued when we discovered that galaxies were not unique. The present estimate is 100 billion galaxies in the visible universe. These discoveries, however, did not diminish man's ego in believing he was the only intelligent life in the universe.

Then in 1994 the first exoplanet was discovered, and another pattern arose. Rather than planets being random accidents as preached by Neo-Darwinism, it became apparent that they too were part of a pattern. They were everywhere and indicated that perhaps every star had planets.

The appearance of a vast number of UFOs starting in World War II hinted at another pattern. It appeared from the thousands of different types of beings reported that like stars, galaxies, and planets, advanced life forms were part of the design of the universe.

Most significantly the creatures described were very much like us. This similarity contradicted the idea of random evolution. It seemed impossible that after billions of years of random mutations that the result all over the universe would look pretty much the same; two arms, two legs, upright, with a head complete with two eyes, ears, and a mouth.

If the odds of the creation of one cell being by a random evolution were 10 to the $40,000^{th}$ power,[21] an alien similar to us would mean then a second random evolution at odds of 10 to the $40,000^{th}$ power times 10 to the $40,000^{th}$ power.

If that is not enough, Albert Rosales, who runs Humanoid Sighting Reports & Journal of Humanoid Studies,[22] has recorded more than 18,000 reports of alien sightings consisting of maybe 1,000 different aliens. One is left to believe a change at 10 to the $40,000^{th}$ power multiplied against itself 1,000 times or the more obvious conclusion that advanced humanoid life in the universe is part of a pattern of the formation of galaxies, stars, planets, carbon, hydrogen and probably everything else found on Earth.

The defenders of randomness fought back against this apparent new pattern in the Universe. One scientist declared confidently that advanced life could not happen a second time stating in defense of our geocentric uniqueness, "If it hadn't been for an asteroid wiping out the dinosaurs even we would not exist."

The UFO appearances raised a new challenge to the chance hypothesis. That was because the random theory assumes a physical world and nothing outside of the physical.

If a multitude of alien species are coming here, they are defying the idea that nothing can exceed the speed of light in a physical world. This distance dilemma means that either aliens aren't here, or the physical universe concept is flawed.

The scientific community has chosen to deny the ET stories to protect their belief in the physical world. If they were to accept the stories, it would mean that most of what they believed was wrong and that is a no go.

It is a no go because it is all about belief. Scientists will claim that they are only interested in the evidence, but they aren't. Most choose to live in a fact-free world where everything they believe is correct. Scientists who agree that there is something outside the physical would keep quiet about it. If they don't, they risk their careers.

From time to time, an idea will be in a person's head and then suddenly slips away. Where does the idea go? It unmistakably slips away. Most everyone has had that feeling. An example is when you awake from a dream, only to watch it leave like water going down a drain. You yell "No stop" in your head, but it still leaves.

It is going somewhere and if so where?

Sometimes the memory is recovered by going back to the place where you first had the idea. Sometimes it is right there but can't be accessed for some reason. People describe that experience as having the memory on the tip of the tongue.

In the same way, people through recorded history have reported that ideas have entered their head, and they don't know where the ideas arose. Often, the idea is something the person didn't learn or experience, which would indicate the brain is not where the idea originated.

At times, the idea is an actual talent like mathematical calculation, musical ability, or artistic talent and the door to the information stays open for life.

The present basic scientific belief structure is that these types of inspirations and downloads are not possible. The accepted theory is that the mind is like a computer and cannot output anything not imputed at an earlier time. We are as Richard Dawkins maintains biological robots created by random chance in a long evolutionary process of random genetic mutations. This evolutionary story, however, never mentions the fact that the fundamental evolutionary theory – survival of the fittest – was itself an inspirational download received during a fever by Russell Wallace.

When people like Wallace report inspirations or downloads, scientists use naming theory to protect their belief in chaotic randomness. They will use words like instinct, artificial schizophrenia, and genetic memory to explain information that appears suddenly to someone who clearly didn't learn it.

Many times science ascribes a human body's information and skills to the unconscious mind. This naming is an attempt to answer many very complex operations called which are in turn named automatisms.

How does the body breathe on its own?

How does the body regulate blood pressure?

How does the heart beat for 100 years without forgetting to beat or deciding to take a 15 minute coffee break?

How does a cut or bone heal on its own?

How does the body digest food and send the proper nutrients to the correct location?

How do the thousands of modules that make up the brain gather all the input the body is receiving and turn it into an instantaneous appearance of reality?

How does the body know how to replace almost 500,000 cells per second or 50 billion cells of varying type that die each day in the body? Just as important how does it know when to make new cells? Who is in charge of determining which cells get made and getting them to the proper location?

Who organizes the 100 trillion bacteria that work with the body to do everything from fight disease to digest food? The body would be dead almost instantly with this cooperative effort by bacteria that outnumber human cells 10 to 1.[23]

Who collects a memory from the past when we seek it? Does the thing managing the memory also have a memory as it has to know where it stored the memory? Does that memory have a memory?

The conscious mind processes about 16-40 bits a second. The unconscious mind is estimated to be processing 40 million bits a second, up to and maybe as high as 400 Gbits/sec. The conscious mind can only remember 3-4 items[24] and the subconscious mind can remember an almost endless number of things. Estimates for unconscious storage capacity are as high as 2.5 petabytes.[25] How does this unconscious mind with no known physical properties do what it does and how did it learn? Is this all done through random events by the body? If memory collection and management are orderly, who is providing the order, and how does order arise from chaotic randomness?

The answer usually given is that it is an "automatic process" which the body learned to do. It had millions of years to learn. This theory, however, leads to the question of how breathing, cell replacement, blood pressure, digestion, and healing occured on day one. Most of these functions would have to work without fail from minute one. When did it learn?

The automatisms of the body are accepted as fact and explained away through naming theory. Science has learned to incorporate them into a meaningless world of chance.

If someone claims that they experienced an automatism consisting of spontaneous writing, invention, drawing, music, mathematics, or painting then they are instantly considered delusional or deceptive.

The consciousness in the materialistic belief system is simply a product of random brain processes. The idea that something could come from outside is, therefore, impossible. Unfortunately for the materialistic belief system, phenomena and supporting structures do exist as the following chapters will clearly show.

Chapter 2. Inspiration and a Helping Hand

My entire scientific career has been a meditation on my dream. **Albert Einstein, speaking of his dream of racing a sled through the universe.**

Where do brand-new human ideas come from anyway? **Nobel Prize Winner Charles Townes**

"The Lost Chord" is a song composed by Arthur Sullivan in 1877 after getting it in a dream. He could only remember part of the melody he heard – thus, the song title mentioning the lost chord. This song was also one of the first songs ever to be recorded on the phonograph in the 1880s.[26]

The big unanswered question is where does inspiration come? From where do musicians get their new music? From where do inventors, artists, and scientists get their new ideas? Where do prodigious savants get the ability to do massive calculations faster than computers with no schooling or play music without a single music lesson? What about the information given to people who channel spirits or aliens, or mediums talking spirit guides of the dead? Are all these groups able to tap into some nonlocal part of reality just discovered?

The public perception of discovery and invention is of scientists who are toiling in laboratories all over the world using their five senses and reason to come up with all that we have come to know as modern technology. This paradigm is at some odds with the evidence.

The first problem with this model is that scientists don't typically invent things. This observation was pointed out by the former President of the Ivy League Engineering Penn State University, Dr. Eric Walker, who stated that scientists can fill libraries full of information, but it is not until you bring in an engineer that anything of use gets built for the public. It is engineers and not scientists who have constructed the modern technological world.

The second problem with the model is that the evidence shows a lot of inventions came either through 1) sheer accident 2) by duplicating a process seen in nature and 3) inspirations and downloads coming from somewhere outside the individual's conscious mind.

Plato seemed to have already picked up on this concept over 2000 years ago when he said, "Science is nothing but perception." In more recent history Charles G. Sampas stated, based on an earlier use of the idea by Sir Winston Churchill, who came to the same conclusion, "Men occasionally stumble over the truth, but most of them pick themselves up and hurry off as if nothing had happened."[27]

Morton Myers M.D. spelled out the accidental part of inventions in a book he wrote on medical discoveries called *Happy Accidents: Serendipity in*

Modern Medical Breakthroughs. The principle he identified seems to apply to not just medical but all discoveries and inventions. Myers wrote,

> *Many of the most important breakthroughs in modern medicine have routinely come from unexpected sources in apparently unrelated fields, have often been the work of lone researchers or close-knit teams operating with modest resources and funding, and have depended crucially on luck, accident, and error...The scientific reality very rarely reflects this reality. The dominant convention of all scientific writings is to present discoveries as rational driven and to let the facts speak for themselves.*[28]

The final problem with the idea of the use of reason as the source of discoveries and inventions is that many novel concepts came from sudden inspirations and downloads. These are rarely spoken about in the scientific literature because of the implication that there might be something beyond the reasoning of the conscious mind.

The public, less bound by the strict scientific materialistic paradigm, is more willing to accept the idea that inspirations and downloads occur. Many people have had an inspiration moment in their life sometimes called a eureka moment (Greek for "I've Got it."). Research shows that there are meditative moments when people describe the inspiration occurring.[29]

The TOP female eureka-moments:	The TOP male eureka-moments:
1. Driving 13.8%;	1. Showering 12.9%;
2. Sleeping 10.6%;	2. Sleeping 8.4%;
3. Waking up 9.8%;	3. Walking 8.0%;
4. Working out & jogging 8.1%;	4. Before sleeping 7.1%;
5. Walking 8.1%;	5. Working out & jogging 6.7%;
6. Showering 8.1%	

Back in ancient Greece Socrates claimed to have a daemon or a "divine something" that came in the form of a voice to warn him about mistakes, and spoke wisdom to him from afar. Ancient Greeks did not believe that creativity came from within the person. *Eat Pray Love* author Elizabeth Gilbert described her research on inspiration saying, "people believed that there was this divine attendant spirit that came to a human being from some sort of distant and unknowable source for distant and unknowable reasons."[30]

In the same way, the Romans believed that ideas came from outside the person. Gilbert said they "called that disembodied creative spirit a genius. The Romans did not think that a genius was a particularly clever individual. They believed that a genius was this magical divine entity who was believed to live literally in the walls of an artist's studio, kind of like Dobby the house elf, and who would come out and sort of invisibly assist the artist with their work and would shape the outcome of that work."[31]

The switch to the present day concept that ideas and creativity come only from the individual arose in during the Renaissance. It was decided, according to Gilbert, to put the personal ego at the center of the Universe above all Gods. "There was no more room," said Gilbert, "for mystical creatures who take dictation from the divine. And it's the beginning of rational humanism, and people started to believe that creativity came completely from the self of the individual. And for the first time in history, you start to hear people referring to this or that artist as being a genius rather than having a genius."

Dissociative States

Many of the inspirations and downloads appear to occur in a dissociative state according to research done by Dr. Stanley Krippner. According to Krippner, many inspirations seem to happen "when the person is distracted, absorbed in another activity, in a state between sleeping, asleep, totally concentrating something entirely different to the exclusion of ordinary, in a blank state that sometimes occurs between finishing one activity or act of attention and taking up another, or in an altered state induced by meditation, creative activity, drugs, illness, or being in love."[32]

The hypnagogic state is one of the dissociative states mentioned by Krippner. It is the state of consciousness between being awake and being asleep. Many, like Brian Weiss, M.D., have talked about the potent condition. "The hypnagogic state is considered by many to be a genius state, without boundaries or any limitations."[33]

Many of the present scientific ideas and inventions owe their genesis to people who knew how to tap into the hypnogogic state. Hypnagogic states are reportedly highly creative. They are also extremely productive, packing a high density of ideas into a short period.

An early example of this was Emanuel Swedenborg, who appears to have perfected special breathing techniques which enabled him to achieve 'hypnagogic' states. He was responsible for the first ideas on galaxy formation, brain physiology, anatomy, and modern concepts such as pulsars, neurons, and split-brain theory, pineal gland as "seat of the soul," "island universes" (recently confirmed by the Hubble Telescope), planets in the solar system originated in the solar mass, came near to discovering how the lungs purify the blood, the importance of pituitary gland, the technology to transport boats 40 miles over land, and produced concept drawings of a submarine and a glider aircraft.

Another person who used the hypnagogic state was the prolific inventor Thomas Edison. Despite the fact that he claimed "Genius is one percent inspiration and ninety-nine percent perspiration" it was apparent he knew the technique of tapping into an outside genius or daemon.

Edison had developed a hypnagogic state to aid his inventions. What he did was to sit in a chair with steel balls in each hand. His hands rested face down over the end of the chair. Edison would then use relaxation and meditation to enter into the hypnagogic state between sleep and wakefulness.

As he entered into the state, he would fall asleep, and the ball bearing would fall out of his hand into steel bowls that he had placed on the floor. The ensuing sound would wake him up, and he could quickly write down what was in his head. Edison would then repeat the process over and over again, going in and out of the hypnagogic state. He would quickly journal what came to him and filled 3,500 notebooks in his life. When all was said and done, Edison had filed 2,332 patents for inventions.

Some of the top Edison inventions included the electrographic vote recorder, the automatic telegraph, electric pen, phonograph, carbon telephone, commercial electric light, electric lighting system, electric generator, carbon rheostat which produced louder telephones and dimmer lights, fuel cell technology, universal stock printer, an ore separator, moving pictures, alkaline battery, and cement.

Salvador Dali also used Edison's trick. While taking naps during the day, he would sit in a chair holding a large key over a metal plate. When Dali fell asleep, the key would fall and hit the plate. Like Edison, he would record what was in his mind. Most of Dali surrealistic paintings would come from his dreams.

Others who it was believed used this technique have included Aristotle, the Greek philosopher; Robert Desnos, the French surrealist poet; Isaac Newton, the English scientist; the German composer Beethoven; and American writer Edgar Allan Poe who talked about the "fancies" he experienced "only when I am on the brink of sleep, with the consciousness that I am so."[34]

Music

The inspiration process is common in music, indicating it may be the norm. In 2005 at the University of Florence Valeria Uga, Maria Chiara Lemut, Chiara Zampi, Iole Zilli, and Piero Salzarulo published a paper called Music in Dreams[35] in which they set up a controlled study of the phenomena.

They employed two groups, musicians, and non-musicians. They found that musicians dreamed of music twice as much and "nearly half the recalled music was non-standard, suggesting that music can be created in dreams."

The scientific materialist would claim revelatory experience in music as just biological robots stringing together random words combined with random musical notes. It would be just an apparent melody in the random background noise of the random universe.

The explanation harkens back to Fred Hoyle's illustration of the tornado in the junkyard, where tornados over time go through a junkyard and over time built a bunch of radios. Those radios in turn somehow found power to operate and now are broadcasting millions of different song melodies with lyrics that teach and inspire the other radios that were also created by the same many tornados.

The materialistic theory is possible just as it is possible for a person to win the Power Ball lottery a billion times in a row. It is possible but not highly unlikely.

Nevertheless, statistics are still a big part of science. The odds can be 3.5 trillion to one, but many scientists will still go with the odds claiming there is still a statistical chance.

Even the idea of consciousness itself is considered a random process of evolution that "emerges" through a complex enough brain. The idea is that conscious animate objects can arise from unconscious inanimate objects that have become complex.

The idea is sort of like taking a rock and piling more rocks on top of it. Once the pile gets big enough, consciousness will suddenly emerge.

When the emergence theory became indefinable as a credible model, science came up with a new paradigm that evaded having to use the emergence idea. The new concept was that the mind was merely a byproduct of the brain and that self-consciousness was simply an illusion.

Rutgers University philosopher Jerry A. Fodo described the brain consciousness theory shortfall saying, "Nobody has the slightest idea how anything material could be conscious. So much for our philosophy of consciousness." [36]

Dr. Stuart Hammeroff, Professor of Anesthesiology and Psychology Studies, and Associate Director of the Center for Consciousness at the University of Arizona commented on the idea that the mind is the brain, and we are therefore biological robots. "Extraordinary claims require extraordinary proof, said Hammeroff. 'Now the problem is that the people defending the conventional theory to consciousness that mind= brain=computer behave as if they have proof, and we don't and they've got bull shit."[37]

The biggest musicians of all times would say something much different when it comes to the mind being simply the brain.

When a musician is composing new music, he may have an idea of what the theme of the songs will be, but when it comes to the song he/she has to wait for the tune and the lyrics to come into his/her head. It is at that point that inspiration takes over. "The best songs that are written write themselves," said Michael Jackson. "You don't ask for them; they just drop into your lap… I don't force it. I let nature take its course. I don't sit at the piano and think, 'I'm going to write the greatest song of all time.' It doesn't happen. It has to be given to you. I believe it's already up there before you are born, and then it drops right into your lap."[38]

This inspiration would explain how many of the greatest musicians of the 20th century could neither read nor write music which would represent a left brain rational, analytical process. "The more analytical you become about music, the farther you move from art," said Doug Marks, who is noted as the man who taught more people to play the guitar than anyone else with his Metal Method Instructional tapes. "You move from right brain to left brain. When I write, I seldom think about the key, scales, or the proper chords. I just simply write what's in my mind." [39]

Many of the great musicians merely waited for the song to appear in their heads which would indicate a right brain subconscious tapping of music created somewhere else.

Many of the top musicians have talked about the process. They have mentioned that hard work must go in before the inspiration comes. Arnold Schoenberg, the famous Austrian composer, put it this way, "Alas, human creatures, if they be granted a vision, must travel along the long path between vision and accomplishment; a hard road where driven out of Paradise, even geniuses must reap their harvest in the sweat of their brows."[40]

Many have also described the weird almost mystical aspect of writing the song. It is this mystical element acknowledged by the proponents who say that all Rock and Roll music is evil. Their contention is that Satan is initiating this altered state when the song is downloaded. God, higher spirits, and aliens could not be involved because Rock and Roll ais corrupt and therefore must have an evil source.

Many musicians have talked about receiving songs in dreams. There has even been a study of this phenomena by Dr. Irving Massey. He pointed out that strangely "music is the only faculty that is not altered by the dream environment, whereas action, character, visual elements and language may all be modified or distorted in dreams." Massey added that music in dreams does not become fragmented, chaotic or incoherent, neither does it decay as rapidly as do the other components of dreams on our awakening. The music dream download experience is unique and unexplained.

Chapter 3 Inspirations in Music

I ain't never wrote nothin. Those songs was float'n in the air and I just pulled them down. **Bob Monroe, the father of modern bluegrass music**.

If I knew where the good songs came from, I'd go there more often. It's a mysterious condition. It's much like the life of a Catholic nun. You're married to a mystery. **Leonard Cohen**

In spiritual literature, there are many claims that there is a hall of music where earthly musicians get musical downloads. Henry Edwards (1893-1976) for example described that music was telepathically transmitted from the music room in the Hall of Learning into the minds of musicianal artists.

This idea may seem far-fetched until one realizes that most of the greatest musicians of the 20th century could not read or write music. The list of musicians include Elvis Presley, Bob Dylan, All four of the Beatles, Michael Jackson, Barbra Streisand, Jimi Hendrix, Keith Richards, Eric Clapton, Jerry Garcia, Jimmy Page, Pete Townsend, Kurt Cobain, Tori Amos, Thom Yorke, BB King, Stevie Ray Vaughan, Irving Berlin, Famed composer Danny Elfman, Kanye West, Phil Collins, Tom Moello guitarist for Rage Against the Machine, Tony Ionni of Black Sabbath, Marvin Gaye, Adrian Smith from Iron Maiden, Angus Young from AC/DC, Eddie Van Halen, Slash of Guns and Roses, Kurt Vile and Indi legend, and Jackie Gleason whose orchestra produced 20 record albums. Music was therefore not something that they were trained to create via music lessons.

Edgar Cayce stated that music in the material world was a reflection of the music of the spheres. When a musician begins to compose, he taps into these realms of nonlocal consciousness. Cayce recommended music for deeper meditation stating it was a bridge from the finite to the infinite.

Leaving out where the music might be coming from, there is absolutely no doubt that musicians get downloads of music from somewhere. If it were not for the music claimed to have been downloaded, some of the most popular music of all times would not exist.

Here are a few examples of the inspiration behind the writing of some of the favorite songs of all times. Many of these came in dreams, which is significant because dream music appears to be the only element of dreams that is <u>not</u> distorted by the dreaming process. The music heard is clear without the usual fragmentation, chaos, or incoherence commonly associated with dreams, indicating that they may have been lucid dreams.

As the following list shows (a fuller more complete list will be part of a book just on music), the occurrence of inspired music goes back for centuries and includes professional and non-professional musicians alike.

Jon Anderson and Rick Wakeman - from the British band Yes wrote the song "Madrigal" about UFOs. The lyrics and melody came in a few minutes in a "flow of consciousness."

Jon Anderson - Asked if he had ever had a song come in a moment of inspiration, like during a dream, Anderson replied, "Yes, it happens all the time actually. I remember vividly in 1971 I woke in the middle of the night. I always kept a cassette machine next to the bed, and I just sang the song into the cassette machine. We were actually on tour. I sang this song, and I put the tape away and forgot about it for a couple of years, and then I found it and listened to it and the words were word for word exactly correct. I didn't have to change a thing. The words were pure and correct. It is the song I called "O'er." It's on a record somewhere – over the green mountains and over the green valleys."[41]

Joan Baez - "It seems to me that those songs that have been any good, I have nothing much to do with the writing of them. The words have just crawled down my sleeve and come out on the page…"[42]

David Bowie - In 1972 Bowie had a dream in which his father appeared to him telling him that he only had five years to live. The message was that there was to be an environmental disaster such as shown by aliens to experiencers. At that point, Bowie produces the song "Five Years." It becomes the opening track to the album *The Rise and Fall of Ziggy Stardust and the Spiders from Mars*. In the song, there is an aired announcement that the world will end in 5 years' time because of a lack of natural resources. The song then proceeds to describe the frenzied aftermath of the announcement.

Bradford Cox - Front man for band Deerhunter stated, "I'm basically the audience for my own music. Because I don't write things consciously, I don't set out to write things, it's all automatic writing, like the music and the chords and the lyrics and everything. So when I listen to it, I'm sort of analyzing it the same way that somebody who gets the record and listens to it for the first time.[43]

Karyn Crisis - Front woman for the experimental metal band Crisis has much to say about the inspirational process in music. "On tour, I always had premonitions about how shows would go…and I always felt this sensation when I was singing, whether it was on stage or in the studio or in rehearsal where there was something bigger than myself, moving my voice through me. I would call it summoning, and it would be very frustrating for my band mates because whenever we had to write songs, I felt like I have never written a song in my life. I don't know how to write the lyrics or write vocals. But once I sort of got my mind out of the way which for me taking a word out of a thesaurus and get into it. The singing became what happens in a meditative state. My vocals would write themselves in my mind…they would be created in my clairvoyance clairaudient space and I would have to figure out how to sing that live. So often I was writing material that was right out of my vocal range, but when it came time to sing them, the range was there...I was very aware of these forces that I considered bigger than myself, more knowledgeable and more talented than myself."[44]

Burton Cumming - Cumming was the lead singer of the Canadian band The Guess Who - Cummings talked about how their greatest hit "American Woman" came to be. The song went on to be # 1 on the US charts for three weeks.

The date was 1968. Burton Cummings was backstage in Mississauga, Ontario, Canada during a break in the show and was negotiating with a fan for some old records from another band. As they are talking, the rest of the band begins the second show with a riff. Cummings raced back on stage.

"I run inside," Said Cumming, "and run up onto the stage and just grab a microphone and started singing whatever came into my head. It was all stream of consciousness at the moment stuff ... all that stuff about war machines and ghetto scenes, colored lights can hypnotize ...it was all just spur-of-the-moment. And nobody would have ever heard it again, but there happened to be a kid bootlegging the show that night...So it was all an accident; I guess the music Gods were smiling on us. The music Gods probably sent that kid with the cassette machine."[45]

During the show, they see the kid with the cassette tape recorder, seize it, and when they play the tape, there is the song "American Woman." Without the tape, there would never have been a song that was #1 for three weeks in the USA."[46]

Donovan (Donovan Philips Leitch) - Scottish songwriter and singer stated: "With songwriting, it all comes out in one flash. Then you work it, and then you craft it." Later Donovan made a claim, "I believe I'm a reincarnated poet from an old tradition."

Yelena Eckemoff - Eckemoff spoke about dream inspired music saying, "I often hear music in my sleep. Many times I woke up hearing the tune that I liked, and several times I made myself get up, find a pencil and notepaper and write it down. Some other times I was too sleepy to get up and was trying to memorize the music I heard, but most likely I would not remember in the morning. There are several compositions on my CDs that I borrowed from my dreams. One, in particular, comes to mind. I woke up like at two in the morning hearing some persistent tune, got up and went to my piano room where I remained the rest of the night and wrote the entire piece (it was "Quasi Sonata" from my CD Forget-me-not). Another memorable encounter was when I clearly heard the tune in my dream that I still remembered when I woke up, but I did not have time to write it down in the morning, and then I forgot about it. To my surprise, I dreamed about it again the next night, and the next day, I sat at the piano and played it as if it was already done. This was the tune "Pep" from my latest CD, *A Touch Of Radiance.*"[47]

Kevin Estrella - Estrella is the man behind the Instrumental Rock Band

"Pyramids on Mars." His song "Dream Division" came to him in a dream. American instrumental rock guitarist Joe Satriani was playing the song. "Or at least," said Estrella, "he was playing it though the soundboard already pre-recorded."[48] When he awoke, Estrella realized that Satriani had never played the song. He quickly recorded the song.

Patty Griffin - Grammy award-winning folk singer and 2007 Americana Music Association's "Artist of the Year" award winner Patty Griffin said, "It's always amazing to me that songs show up (laughs). I've practiced writing songs for a long time. I still am practicing writing songs. I'm not really sure how it works. That's a very good way to put that; it is amazing (laughs)…You know there is something mystifying about it. When I sit down to write, I try to feel what I want to sing. That's how they show up. When they're really strong and written quickly…the words and music arrive together. That's very strange, but that's how it works."[49]

Harlan Howard - Howard, a country and western singer thought he could not take credit for his hit song "The Blizzard." "The pencil kept on moving, and I didn't know where it would end. Did some great songwriter in the sky use me as a medium?"[50]

Jimi Hendrix - Hendrix got the idea for his song "Angel" from a dream he had where his mother came down from heaven to take him with her. He recorded the piece on July 23, 1970 - just a few months before his death on September 18, 1970.

Michael Jackson - "The songwriting process is something very difficult to explain because it's very spiritual. It's, uh…You really have it in the hands of God, and it's as if it's been written already - that's the real truth. As if it's been written in its entirety before you were born and you're just really the source through which the song come. Really! Because there is…they just fall right into your lap in its entirety. You don't have to do much thinking about it. And I feel guilty having to put my name, sometimes, on the songs that I - I do write them - I compose them, I write them, I do the scoring, I do the lyrics, I do the melodies, but still, it's a... it's a work of God."[51]

Michael Jackson - "I wake up from dreams and go, "Wow, put this down on paper. The whole thing is strange. You hear the words; everything is right there in front of your face."

Jay Greenburg - The young musical prodigy who had composed five symphonies by age five and had the London Symphony record the fifth stated, "the music just streams into my head at lightning speed, sometimes several symphonies running simultaneously. My unconscious mind directs my conscious mind at a mile a minute."[52]

Billy Joel - Billy Joel got a lot of song ideas in his dreams and often struggled to remember them when he woke up. For his song, "A River of Dreams" however, he woke up with the song in his head but tried NOT to write it down. He explained on The Howard Stern Show in 2010: "I thought, who the hell am I to try to pull off this gospel song, so I took a shower to wash this song away. I sang it in the shower and knew I had to do it."

Bill Joel added, "Many of my songs I dream fully realized. I dream that I am in the control room, listening to something on the speakers, and it is this piece of music that I have not written yet.... This has happened so frequently that I can wake myself up and remember substantial parts. I don't know whether my subconscious has been working overtime writing these songs without my help and then revealing them to me, or whether they're transmitted to me by some kind of muse or angel, or whether there is a difference between the two.... They're lucid to the extent that I realize I'm dreaming and wake myself up to write the song down."[53]

Carole King - King was a prolific singer-songwriter with over 25 solo albums in 50 years. Her highlight album was the 1971 masterpiece *Tapestry*, which was one of the bestselling records of all time. It outsold The Beatles' Sgt. Pepper's Lonely Hearts Club Band album and included the iconic "You've Got a Friend." Speaking of that song Kind said, "That song was as close to pure inspiration as I've ever experienced. The song wrote itself. It was written by something outside of myself through me… It happens from time to time in part. That song is one of the examples of that process where it was almost completely written by inspiration and very little if any perspiration."[54]

Ed King - Saw Solo 1 and Solo 2 in the song "Sweet Home Alabama" in his dream. He recorded note it for note. Producer Al Kooper did not want it in because it was in the wrong cord, but the band members wanted it in saying "he saw the solo in a dream." The whole Southern mysticism thing really kind of fell in, said King, "played in my hands, because I'm not that big into Southern mysticism, you know? I'm from Southern California. But I figured, well, it meant enough to them that I saw it in a dream that it has to be used."[55]

John Lennon - "When the real music comes to me – the music of the spheres, the music that surpasses understanding – That has nothing to do with me because I am just the channel. The only joy for it to be given to me and to transcribe it, like a medium."[56]

John Lennon - 1974 - The song "Dream #9" came in a dream. Lennon stated, "I just sat down and wrote it, you know, with no real inspiration, based on a dream I'd had." Lennon's one-time girlfriend May Pang said, "This was one of John's favorite songs because it literally came to him in a dream. He woke up and wrote down those words along with the melody. He had no idea what it meant, but he thought it sounded beautiful. John arranged the strings in such a way that the song really does sound like a dream."

John Lennon - "I felt like a hollow temple filled with many spirits, each one passing through me, each inhabiting me for a little time and then leaving to be replaced by another." [57]

John Lennon - "There was something wrong with me, I thought because I seemed to see things other people didn't see. I thought I was crazy or an egomaniac for claiming to see things other people didn't see. As a child, I would say, 'But this is going on!' and everybody would look at me as if I was crazy. I always was so psychic or intuitive or poetic or whatever you want to call it, that I was always seeing things in a hallucinatory way."

"It was scary as a child because there was nobody to relate to. Neither my auntie nor my friends nor anybody could ever see what I did. It was very, very scary and the only contact I had was reading about an Oscar Wilde or a Dylan Thomas or a Vincent van Gogh -- all those books that my auntie had that talked about their suffering because of their visions. Because of what they saw, they were tortured by society for trying to express what they were. I saw loneliness…Surrealism had a great effect on me because then I realized that my imagery and my mind wasn't insanity; that if it was insane, I belong to an exclusive club that sees the world in those terms. Surrealism to me is a reality. Psychic vision to me is a reality. Even as a child, when I looked at myself in the mirror or when I was 12, 13, I used to literally trance out into alpha. I didn't know what it was called then. I found out years later there is a name for those conditions. But I would find myself seeing hallucinatory images of my face changing and becoming cosmic and complete. It caused me to always be a rebel. This thing gave me a chip on the shoulder; but, on the other hand, I wanted to be loved and accepted. Part of me would like to be accepted by all facets of society and not be this loudmouthed lunatic musician, but I cannot be what I am not."[58]

Ray Manzarek - Manzarek is a founding member and keyboardist of The Doors from 1965 to 1973. He stated, "when the Siberian shaman gets ready to go into his trance, all the villagers get together... and play whatever instruments they have to send him off [into trance and possession].... It was the same way with The Doors when we played in concert.... I think that our drug experience lets us get into it... [the trance state] quicker....It was like Jim [Morrison] was an electric shaman, and we were the electric shaman's band, pounding away behind him... pounding and pounding, and little by little it would take him over....Sometimes he was just incredible. Just amazing. And the audience felt it, too!"[59]

Paul McCartney - McCartney wrote about the writing of his 1984 song "No Values." I dreamt this song. I dreamt that I was with The Rolling Stones. They were all there, Mick; Bill, Charlie, Keith. Mick was up front. I woke up and said to myself, 'I really like that song that they do.' Then I thought, 'Hey, wait a minute, there is no Rolling Stones song called No Value. They don't do that song.' My brain just created it. So I thought, 'Well, there it is. I've got this new song called "No Values." But I won't be telling Mick; he'll probably claim the copyright."

Paul McCartney - 1965 - The song "Yesterday" came in a dream. The song has the most cover versions of any song ever written and, according to record label BMI. Artists performed it over seven million times in the 20th century. McCartney stated, ""I woke up with a lovely tune in my head. I thought, 'That's great, I wonder what that is?' There was an upright piano next to me, to the right of the bed by the window. I got out of bed, sat at the piano, found G, found F sharp minor 7th -- and that leads you through then to B to E minor, and finally back to E. It all leads forward logically. I liked the melody a lot, but because I'd dreamed it, I couldn't believe I'd written it. I thought, 'No, I've never written anything like this before.' But I had the tune, which was the most magic thing!"[60]

Paul McCartney - In 1969 as McCartney had a serious personal situation trying to keep the Beatles together he was visited by his mother, Mary, who had died in 1956 from cancer when McCartney was 14. Her words are comforting him "to let it be" became the song by the same name. McCartney recalled the dream, "One night during this tense time I had a dream I saw my mom, who'd been deceased ten years or so. And it was so great to see her because that's a wonderful thing about dreams: you actually are reunited with that person for a second; there they are, and you appear to both be physically together again. It was so wonderful for me, and she was very reassuring. In the dream, she said, 'It'll be all right.' I'm not sure if she used the words 'Let it be' but that was the gist of her advice, it was, 'Don't worry too much, it will turn out OK.' It was such a sweet dream I woke up thinking, Oh, it was really great to visit with her again. I felt very blessed to have that dream. So that got me writing the song "Let It Be." I literally started off 'Mother Mary', which was her name, 'When I find myself in times of trouble', which I certainly found myself in. The song was based on that dream."[61]

Joni Mitchell - Mitchell was a folk-jazz artist described in one biography as having her own muse: "Joni Mitchell's own strongest creative impulses come to her in a somewhat unusual way. She deeply believes in a male muse named Art who lends her his key to what she airily calls the 'Shrine of Creativity.' I feel like I'm married to this guy named Art, I'm responsible to my Art above all else."[62] In 1974, Joni Mitchell told the press of a male spirit who helps her write music. "Joni Mitchell credits her creative powers to a 'male muse' she identifies as Art. He has taken so much control of not only her music, but her life, that she feels married to him, and often roams naked with him on her 40-acre estate. His hold over her is so strong that she will excuse herself from parties and forsake lovers whenever he 'calls." [63]

Alanis Morissette - "A lot of the songs were written in 15-30 minutes, very stream-of-consciousness, as though it was being channeled through us."[64]

Yoko Ono - Ono said, "I am sure there are people whose lives were affected because they heard Indian music or Mozart or Bach. More than anything, it was the time and the place when the Beatles came up. Something did happen there. It was a kind of chemical. It was as if several people gathered around a table and a ghost appeared. It was that kind of communication. So they were like mediums, in a way. It's not something you can force. It was the people, the time, their youth and enthusiasm… The Beatles themselves were a social phenomenon, not that aware of what they were doing. In a way - as I said, they were like mediums. They weren't conscious of all they were saying, but it was coming through them.[65]

Jimmy Page - 'I spent all my time listening to these records and trying to learn them, and I think it was almost like this force came out and grabbed me, and I just got pulled right into it. Playing the guitar was obviously what I was meant to do in life."[66]

Carl Perkins - Perkins is the man who wrote the lyrics to Elvis Presley's song *Blue Suede Shoes* came to songwriter Carl Perkins in a dream. In an interview with Gadfly Online Perkins stated, "I was playing at a place called the Roadside Inn. I heard this boy tell the girl he was dancing with 'Watch out, don't step on mah suedes' and I looked down at his feet, and he had on this pair of blue suede shoes. It kinda stuck to me." The incident stayed on his mind all night, and when he woke up in the morning, he immediately began writing down the lyrics on an old brown paper potato sack, the only piece of paper he had around the house.[67]

Mike Pinder - Pinder was the lead singer for the Moody Blues. In the early days of the band, Pinder spoke about the source of many of the bands lyrics; "Lyrics were placed into the public domain from somewhere else."[68]

Reg Presley - The lead singer for The Troggs was watching a TV show featuring the Joy Strings Army band in England. Even though he was not religious, he was overcome with emotion, and the words and tune to *Love is All Around* started to flow into his head. He produced the song and in the days when the Beatles ruled the British music scene *Love is All Around* sat in the number one spot for 15 weeks. Decades later it was the theme song to the movie *Three Weddings and a Funeral* when it returned to the top of the charts.[69]

Mike Reno - Loverboy lead singer talked about the writing of the song *All I Ever Needed* that came to him in a dream complete with music and lyrics. At the time, he was working with David Foster.

> He asked me to come down to do the backing tracks for his solo album. And while we were there, he asked me to come over early one day and see if we couldn't write a song and that night I had a dream. I dreamt all the lyrics, and I woke up and wrote them down and I hummed into my tape recorder the melody. And I went over, and he said, "Do you have any idea what we can do?" and I started him off on this thing. And he started playing it, and it developed in about an hour into that song.[70]

Johnny Rzeznick - Rzeznick of the Goo Goo Dolls told Katie Couric back when she was with the TODAY Show on NBC that the lyrics to the song

"Better Days" came to him while he was at his house and that they seemed to "fall out the sky."

Richard Rodgers - "It took about as long to compose it as to play it." (said about "Oh, What a Beautiful Morning," the opening song in "Oklahoma!")

Todd Rundgren - Rundgren became associated with bands such as Nazz, Utopia, The New Cars, Meat Loaf, Ringo Starr & His All-Starr Band, Edgar Winter, Mark Klingman, Daryl Hall, Hello People, Tame Impala, The Tubes, Grand Funk Railroad, and The Band. Rundgren spoke about how "Bang the Drum All Day," a song featured in many sports arenas, commercials, and movie trailers, was downloaded in a dream.

> *When I started immersing myself in a suit of musical and conceptual ideas, I began actually to dream fully completed songs. They may be completely unrelated to everything else I'm doing. It isn't necessary during the recording process. Bang the Drum was something that just popped into my head one night I don't know how that song I dreamed I was called Bang the Drum all Day, but the musical part of it was fairly complete. The title lyrics must have been in there too. Songs like that I can't deny them. In other words, I have to finish them, & I have to put them on the record, even if they don't sound like they belong to me. If a song comes to you completely realized that it's really your muse at work if it comes you completely realize that, and you don't know what it's about, and you have to figure it out you think, where did that come from? Well, it came from inside me somewhere. So there must be something in me, yet another thing that I have to uncover and examined in order to fully understand myself.*[71]

Stereophonics - Stereophonics lead singer Kelly Jones reported the song "I won't believe Your Radio" came in a dream where Ringo Starr and George Harrison were sitting on a curb singing the song to him.[72]

Mike Scott - Scott from the Waterboys stated, ""I was six or seven when I noticed the music in my head. It was there in the classroom, on the football pitch, at the dinner table, when I went to sleep and when I woke up. And it's continued ever since."[73]

Ringo Starr - Starr spoke about the making the album *Rain*. "I feel as though that was someone else playing. I was possessed!"[74]

Rolling Stones - Keith Richards - On May 6, 1965, Clearwater, Florida while on their first US tour. According to a St. Petersburg Times article, about 200 young fans got into an altercation with a line of police officers at the show, and The Stones made it through just four songs as chaos ensued. That night, Keith Richards woke up in his hotel room with the guitar riff and lyric "Can't get no satisfaction" in his head. He recorded it on a portable tape deck, went back to sleep, and brought it to the studio that week. The tape contained his guitar riff followed by the sounds of him snoring.

Rolling Stones - Keith Richards - "We receive our songs like inspiration, like at a séance. People say they write songs but in a way you are more the medium. I feel that all the songs are floating around, and it is just a matter of being like an antennae, of whatever you pick up. So many uncanny things have happened to us. A whole new song appears from nowhere in five minutes, the whole structure and you haven't worked at all."

Michael Stripe - R.E.M. - Some of the lyrics to "It's The End Of The World As We Know It" came to R.E.M. lead singer Michael Stipe in a dream. In 1992 he revealed to Q Magazine that "The words come from everywhere. I'm extremely aware of everything around me, whether I am in a sleeping state, awake, dream-state or just in day to day life. There's a part in "It's The End Of The World As We Know It" that came from a dream where I was at Lester Bangs' birthday party, and I was the only person there whose initials weren't L.B. So there was Lenny Bruce, Leonid Brezhnev, Leonard Bernstein... So that ended up in the song along with a lot of stuff I'd seen when I was flipping TV channels. It's a collection of streams of consciousness." [75]

Marc Storace - vocalist with heavy metal band Krokus - "You can't describe it [playing rock music] except to say it's like a mysterious energy that comes from the metaphysical plane and into my body. It's almost like being a medium...." [76]

Pete Townshend - Townshend from the band The Who heard music in his head as a child. He wrote, "The tide was high, and it wasn't safe to row, so the men fitted an ancient outboard motor to the stern and fired it up. As we swept past the Old Boathouse at Isleworth once again, I began to hear the most extraordinary music, sparked by the whine of the outboard motor and the burbling sound of the water against the hull. I heard violins, cellos, horns, harps and voices, which increased in number until I could hear countless threads of an angelic choir; it was a sublime experience. I have never heard such music since, and my personal musical ambition has always been to rediscover that sound and relive its effect on me." [77]

Townshend would later write an Internet novella called *The Boy Who Heard Music* which became a rock opera that would fictionalize his story.

The story takes place in 2035 and Townshend is now an older musician named Ray High, who is in a mental institution looking back on his life. It covers a period in the life of three children as they grow up to form a band based on the concepts of High.

High is the narrator of the story living in an alternate plane of existence called "In the Ether." The three young children have various gifts. There is Gabriel, who "could hear music," Josh, who "could hear voices," and Leila, who "could fly." The three live in the same neighborhood but are of different religious faiths: Gabriel is Christian, Josh is Jewish, and Leila is Muslim.

It was in *The Boy Who Heard Music* novella that Gabriel described the music he had experienced as a child, "Not like the music I heard in church. I heard it in the air, between the stars and the trees. It was sometimes like singing, sometimes like grand orchestras playing Beethoven's symphonies. It was always very beautiful. There is a difference between the inspired composer and the skilled orchestrator. A good orchestrator can sit with sheets of manuscript and, as the arrangement develops, can read the notes and actually hear a phantom orchestra in his head. But an inspired composer hears music in his mind so complex, so diverting, that any attempt to write it down seems facile. What this kind of visitation produces in the subject is a desire to rediscover what has been heard before."

Tom Waits - American singer and songwriter who composed for Bruce Springsteen, The Eagles, and Rod Stewart told author Elizabeth Gilbert of one instance of inspiration.

> *But then he got older, he got calmer, and one day he was driving down the freeway in Los Angeles he told me, and this is when it all changed for him. And he's speeding along, and all of a sudden he hears this little fragment of melody, that comes into his head as inspiration often comes, elusive and tantalizing, and he wants it, you know, it's gorgeous, and he longs for it, but he has no way to get it. He doesn't have a piece of paper, he doesn't have a pencil, he doesn't have a tape recorder.*
>
> *So he starts to feel all of that old anxiety start to rise in him like, "I'm going to lose this thing, and then I'm going to be haunted by this song forever. I'm not good enough, and I can't do it." And instead of panicking, he just stopped. He just stopped that whole mental process, and he did something completely novel. He just looked up at the sky, and he said, "Excuse me, can you not see that I'm driving? Do I look like I can write down a song right now? If you really want to exist, come back at a more opportune moment when I can take care of you. Otherwise, go bother somebody else today. Go bother Leonard Cohen."*[78]

Ryan Wang - 5-year-old piano prodigy who played Carnegie Hall when asked how he remembered all the music he plays after only 18 months of playing, "It's just in my memory. I love it, and sometimes it just goes through my fingers."[79]

Bill Ward - Ward of Black Sabbath - "I've always considered that there was some way where we were able to channel energy and that energy was able to be, from another source, if you like, like a higher power or something, that was actually doing the work. I've often thought of us just being actually just the earthly beings that played the music because it was uncanny. Some of this music came out extremely uncanny." [80]

Hank Williams - "If a song can't be written in 20 minutes, it ain't worth writing."[81]

Gary Wright - Wright, himself, once claimed that the music and lyrics for his signature 1976 hit *Dream Weaver* seemed to flow out of him "as if written by an unseen source." Wright wrote the song in one hour, and it made it to #2 on the Bill Boards chart. The song featured only keyboards, drums, bass and a soaring synthesizer. Best lyric: "Fly me high through the starry skies; maybe to an astral plane; across the highways of fantasy; help me forget today's pain." Wright described the song as 'it was a kind of fantasy experience... a Dream Weaver train taking you through the cosmos."

Angus Young - Young was the guitarist for the band AC/DC. He said, "It's like I'm on automatic pilot. By the time, we're halfway through the first number someone else is steering me. I'm just along for the ride. I become possessed when I get on stage." [82]

Led Zeppelin - No one in the band knows where the song "Stairway to Heaven" originated. Robert Plant stated 'Pagey had written the chords and played it for me. I was holding the paper and pencil, and for some reason, I was in a very bad mood. Then all of a sudden my hand was writing our words. I just sat and looked at the words, and then I just about leaped out of my seat."[83]

Inspirations Before Rock and Roll

The idea for this chapter came in looking into the claim made by many that inspiration within rock and roll was coming from drugs/alcohol or demonic/evil spirits.

To evaluate the demon theory I decided to go back and review whether or not there was inspiration in classical music which is viewed by many as real music. This "good" music is the basis for much of the music of the Christian churches. If inspirations and downloads part of the music process they should occur over the entire history of music creation.

What I found is that the belief that drugs, alcohol, and dark forces are the source of rock and roll inspiration does not stand up in light of the evidence.

The one thing that did seem to change from rock and roll to the classical music of the 18th, 19th and 20th century is that there was much more use of the words by classical composers of spirit, soul, or God as the source of the inspiration. Modern music tends to use phrases such as unconscious mind, séance, inspiration, or channeling.

To both groups, the inspirations and downloads are mysterious and real, and in both cases, some dissociation takes place to allow the information to be received.

Consider, for example, one of the key stories that have been brought up to illustrate Satan's role in modern music – the fact that Robert Plant's lyrics for Len Zeppelin's "Stairway to Heaven" came through a process of automatic writing.

Stanley Krippner in his book *Broken Images: Broken Selves* described how Mozart used a similar dissociation technique to Plant's automatic writing of "Stairway to Heaven."

Mozart explained how he applied the rules of counterpoint, adapting his inspired ideas to different instruments, until his composition stood "almost complete and finished in my mind, so that I can survey it, like a fine picture or beautiful statue, at a glance. Nor do I hear in my imagination the parts successively, but I hear them, as it were, all at once." This process he says, "takes place in a very pleasant lively dream."

What Mozart transcribed to paper differed from what he heard in his "lively dream." The writing was automatic - "for whatever may be going on around me, I write, and even talk, but only of fowls or geese of Gretel or Baerbel, so some such matters." In other words, he employs what Janet called the "method of distraction" for invoking the "second self." He would occupy his conscious mind with trivia, such as geese or girls while his hand transcribes the music. All this, wrote Mozart, was "the best gift I have my divine Maker to thank for."[84]

Another key story of using automatic writing to write the lyrics to a song came from the story of the composition of the words to "The Battle Hymn of the Republic" which seems wholly unrelated to the devil.

Julie Ward Howe, who was a writer, created the song. It was during a trip that she had heard Union Soldiers moving by her hotel window with their methodical stomping sound. It made her think of a promise she had made to a church Reverend to write an inspiration camp song for the Union Soldiers. So far she had come up with nothing.

It was November 19, 1861, and Howe went to bed with the sound of the marching soldiers in her head. In the pre-dawn hours she awoke and faintly recalled what happened. She sat at her desk in the dark with her eyes closed and her hand started to write. The verses were quickly moving into her head. It ended, and she went back to bed.

In the morning, she found the lyrics on her desk for the "Battle Hymn of the Republic." Only four words changed in arriving at the final version.[85]

These stories may be enough to convince the reader that inspirations and downloads have happened to all music and not just drugged up Rock and Roll stars. If they aren't, then here are a few more examples that tell the same story of downloads and inspirations in music.

Ludwig Beethoven - "I must accustom myself to think out at once the whole, as soon as it shows itself, with all the voices, in my head."[86]

He used sketchbooks to write down his ideas when they flew into his head before he forgot them.

"Music is a higher revelation than all wisdom and philosophy."[87]

"Music is the one incorporeal entrance into the higher world of knowledge which comprehends mankind but which mankind cannot comprehend."[88]

"Music is the mediator between the life of the senses and the life of the spirit."

"Tones sound, and roar and storm about me until I have set them down in notes."[89]

Louis Hector Berlioz - Berlioz spoke of his musical inspiration,

> *Two years ago, at a time when my wife's state of health was involving me in a lot of expense, but there was still some hope of its improving, I dreamed one night that I was composing a symphony, and heard it in my dream. On waking the next morning, I could recall nearly the whole of the first movement, which was an Allegro in A minor in two-four time (that is all I now remember about it). I was going to my desk to begin writing it down when I suddenly thought: 'If I do, I shall be led on to compose the rest.' My ideas always tend to expand nowadays; this symphony could well be on an enormous scale.*
>
> *I shall spend perhaps three or four months on the work (I took seven years to write Romeo and Juliet), during which time I shall do no articles, or very few, and my income will diminish accordingly. When the symphony is written, I shall be weak enough to let myself be persuaded by my copyist to have it copied, which will immediately put me a thousand or twelve hundred francs in debt. Once the parts exist, I shall be plagued by the temptation to have the work performed. I shall give a concert, the receipts of which will barely cover one-half of the costs--that is inevitable these days. I shall lose what I haven't got, and be short of money to provide for the poor invalid, and no longer able to meet my personal expenses or pay my son's allowance on the ship he will shortly be joining." These thoughts made me shudder, and I threw down my pen, thinking: "What of it? I shall have forgotten it by tomorrow!" That night the symphony again appeared and obstinately rang in my head. I heard the Allegro in A minor quite distinctly. More, I seemed to see it written. I woke in a state of feverish excitement. I hummed*

the theme to myself; its form and character pleased me exceedingly. I was on the point of getting up. Then my previous thoughts recurred and held me fast. I lay still, steeling myself against temptation, clinging to the hope that I would forget. At last, I fell asleep; and when I next awoke, all recollection of it had vanished forever.[90]

Johannes Brahms - Brahms, a 19th-century symphony composer and arranger, made many claims about receiving his musical inspiration from somewhere else. At times when composing, Johannes Brahms felt he was "in tune with the Infinite." Although he believed that his inspiration came from God, the fact that he admitted having to be "in a semi-trance condition... with the conscious mind... in temporary abeyance,"[91]

Three weeks before his death Brahms wrote, "When I feel the urge, I begin by appealing directly to my Maker... I immediately feel vibrations which thrill my whole being...the ideas flow in upon me, directly from God, and not only do I see distinct theme's in my mind's eye, harmonies, and orchestration. Measure by measure the finished product is revealed to me when I am in those rare and inspired moods. I have to be in a semi-trance to get such results - a condition when the conscious mind is in temporary abeyance and the subconscious is in control, for it is through the subconscious mind, which is part of the Omnipotence, that inspiration comes. I have to be careful; however, not to lose consciousness otherwise the ideas fade away…"[92]

"Straightaway the ideas flow in upon me, directly from God and not only do I see distinct themes in my mind's eye, but they are clothed in the right forms, harmonies, and orchestration. Measure by a measure, the finished products is revealed to me when I am in gold rare, inspired moods. "[93]

Anton Bruckner - wrote large-scale symphonies. The most famous of his works is the opening of the Seventh Symphony, which came to him in a dream. In the dream, he met an old musician friend, Ignaz Dorn. Dorn either whistled or played the melody to Bruckner on a viola, and told Bruckner it would make him famous.[94] It became his greatest musical successes.

Frederick Delius - "I, myself, am entirely at a loss to explain how I compose - I know only that at first I conceive a work suddenly through a feeling."[95]

Edward Elgar - wrote the central theme for his *Cello Concerto* after waking up from dental surgery.[96]

Rudolph Friml - an Operetta composer, described his experience: "I sit down at the piano, and I put my hands on the piano, and I let the spirit guide me! No, I'd never do the music. I never compose it; O no no! I am a tool. I am nothing. I am being used. It comes from someone, a spirit perhaps, using me."[97]

George Gershwin - Gershwin described how, while riding on a train from Boston and under pressure to complete *Rhapsody in Blue*, he "suddenly heard, even saw on paper, the complete construction of the Rhapsody, from beginning to end."[98]

George Frideric Handel - Composer Handel talked of an altered state that came on him while composing, "Whether I was in my body or out of my body as I wrote it I know not. God knows."[99] Handel followed his dreams to help him compose his famous *Messiah*, especially the last movement.

Arthur Honegger - Speaking of musical inspiration, "It is a manifestation of our unconscious which remains inexplicable to us…an impulse for which we are no, so to speak, responsible."[100]

Elisabeth Lutyens - Lutyens' mother told her to "let the composer rest" so she could take care of her family. Lutyens wrote back, "If artists could let their art rest and didn't suffer from the divine discontent which demands expression like labor demands a confinement, there would never have been any art at all…It is an urge as strong as the urge to love, labor, or have children, which will always surmount all vicissitudes."[101]

Gustav Mahler - Mahler claimed, "I don't choose what I compose it chooses me." He also spoke of being stymied for weeks in trying to finish a composition, "I made up my mind to finish the Seventh, both andantes of which were then on my table." He labored for many weeks and then entered a row boat to start his trip home believing he had completed his whole summer of work. "At the first stroke of the oars," Mahler wrote the theme (or the rhythm and character) of the introduction to the first movement came into my head - and in four weeks the first, third and fifth movements were done."[102]

Wolfgang Mozart - "When I am ..... Completely myself, entirely alone... or during the night when I cannot sleep, it is on such occasions that my ideas flow best and most abundantly. Whence and how these ideas come I know not nor can I force them."[103] Mozart also appeared to have the same flows of consciousness reported by modern musicians. He reportedly wrote his last symphony, the celebrated *Jupiter* in sixteen days, and the overture to Don Giovanni the morning of the premiere of the opera while suffering a hangover. Mozart was able to get on a train and a few hours later get off with a whole opera composed in his head.

Marta Ptaszynska - The Helen B. and Frank L. Sulzberger Professor of Music and the Humanities, Marta Ptaszynska wrote *Hymn of the Universe* in 2008 for the rededication of the organ and carillon at Rockefeller Memorial Chapel stated, "Sometimes I wake up in the middle of the night, and I will hear the whole structure of a piece, and then I have to notate it quickly. These are moments that pass quickly by, like the wind."[104]

Giacomo Puccini - Puccini believed that his grand opera *Madame Butterfly* was "dictated to me by God. I was merely instrumental in putting it on paper."[105]

Maurice Ravel - Ravel stated that his most delightful music "Came during his dreams."

Lewis Redner - Redner, who composed the music for "Oh Little Town of Bethlehem," received the music in a dream while struggling to write the song the night before Christmas Eve. Redner got up and wrote down the melody. When he presented it to Philip Brooks, the pastor who wrote the lyrics, he said, "I think it was a gift from heaven."[106]

Arnold Schoenberg - Schoenberg spoke of the reverence and trust in his musical inspirations, "One must be convinced of the infallibility of one's own fantasy, and one must believe in one's own inspiration."[107]

Robert Schumann - On February 17, 1854, a choir of angels sang to Robert Schumann in a dream. In the middle of the night, he woke from the dream and rushed to his desk to write down what he had heard. The angels singing would become the basis of his "Ghost Variations," a work which seems to wander between waking and dreaming states.[108]

Dmitri Shostakovich - Russian composer Shostakovich carried a piece of German shrapnel around in his brain for the last 34 years of his life following WWII and used it to help him compose music. Each time he leaned his head to one side he could hear the music. When he straightened his head, it would stop.

Jean Sibelius - Finnish composer Sibelius said, "When the final shape of our work depends on forces more powerful than ourselves, we can later give reasons for this passage or that, but taking it as a whole one is merely an instrument. The power driving us is that marvelous logic which governs a work of art. Let us call it God."[109]

Richard Strauss - Strauss described his musical inspiration saying "all the ideas were flowing in upon me, the entire musical, measure by measure, it seemed to me that I was dictated to by two wholly different Omnipotent Entities."[110] Strauss also described the feeling of "be aided by more than an earthly power."

Strauss talked about using his unconscious mind to figure out things during his sleep. "My experience has been this. If I am held up at a certain point in my composition at night and cannot see a profitable way of continuing in spite of much deliberation, I close the lid of the piano or the cover of my manuscript book, and I go to bed, and when I wake up in the morning - lo and behold! I have found the continuation."[111]

Igor Stravinsky - Stravinsky called dreams his psychological digestive system. "*The Octet* (Octet for Winds) began with a dream, in which I saw myself in a small room surrounded by a small group of instrumentalists playing some attractive music . . . I awoke from this little concert in a state of great delight and anticipation and the next morning began to compose."[112]

The basis of Stravinsky's *A Soldier Tale* comes from a dream. He dreamt of a young gypsy sitting by the roadside and playing a fiddle to her child with long sweeps of the bow. The small boy loved it and applauded. In the Symphony (played by the Soldier after he regains his fiddle); the score includes the instruction "with the full length of the bow."

Pyotr Ilyich Tchaikovsky - Tchaikovsky was the 19th century composer who produced the *Nutcracker* and the *1812 Overture*. He spoke of inspiration, saying, "I sit down to the piano regularly at nine o'clock in the morning, and Mesdames les Muses have learned to be on time for that rendezvous," [113] and "It is already a great thing if the main ideas and general outline of a work come without any racking of brains, as the result of that supernatural and inexplicable force we call inspiration."[114]

Tchaikovsky stated, "She (the Muse) leaves me only when she feels out of place because my workaday human being has intruded. Always the shadow removes itself and she reappears…In a word, an artist lives a double life….Sometimes I look curiously at this productive flow of creativeness which entirely by itself, separate from any conversation I may be at the moment be participating in, separate from the people with me at the time, goes on in the region of my brain that is given over to music."[115]

Tchaikovsky wrote of the discovery of a new inspiration of music. "I would try in vain to express in words the unbounded sense of bliss that comes over me when a new idea opens up within me and starts to take on a definite form. Then I forget everything and behave like one demented. Everything inside of me begins to pulse and quiver: I hardly begin the sketch before one thought begins tumbling after another. There is something somnambulistic about this condition. 'On ne s'entend pas vivre.' It is impossible to describe such moments."[116]

Richard Wagner - Wagner's opera *Tristan and Isolde* came in a dream. Also, Wagner speaking of his opera *Rheingold* stated, "Returning in the afternoon, I stretched myself, dead tired, on a hard couch, awaiting the long-desired hour of sleep. It did not come; but I fell into a kind of somnolent state, in which I suddenly felt as though I were sinking in swiftly flowing water. The rushing sound formed itself in my brain into a musical sound, the chord of E flat major, which continually re-echoed in broken forms; these broken chords seemed to be melodic passages of increasing motion, yet the pure triad of E flat major never changed, but seemed by its continuance to impart infinite significance to the element in which I was sinking. I awoke in sudden terror from my doze, feeling as though the waves were rushing high above my head. I at once recognized that the orchestral overture to the Rheingold, which must long have lain latent within me, though it had been unable to find definite form, had at last been revealed to me. I then quickly realized my own nature; the stream of life was not to flow to me from without, but from within. I decided to return to Zürich immediately, and begin the composition of my greatest poem."[117]

Inspirations By Unpublished Musicians

Inspirations in music come to all musicians and not just the ones who make it big. I once had a long conversation with an unpublished musician from the Philadelphia area that was getting downloads and had put together six albums of music where she had done both the lyrics and the melody.

What follows is a list of some of the musicians I have found who were not famous but who had received a song through some download purpose.

Dr. Anthony Cicoria - Cicoria, is an orthopedic surgeon specializing in orthotics, prosthetic supplies, and sports medicine. After being hit by lightning while talking on the phone, he developed the ability to play and compose music with no training other than a year of piano at seven years old. During the lightning experience, his heart stopped, and he could see his lifeless body. A nurse revived him while waiting to use the phone.

Following his near death lightning experience, he began to want to hear piano music which was contrary to his usual taste for rock and roll. Shortly after the experience Cicoria woke up in the middle of the night with a dream where he was wearing a tuxedo and playing a piano symphony that he had composed in a large concert hall that he can clearly remember. This piece he was playing came to dominate his life, and he began to work on it. When completed it was 26 pages, three movements and twenty-five minutes long. He has composed the symphony called *Fantasia* and the "The Lightening Sonata" which have been played publicly in many locations.

Maria Cuccia - Cuccia from Commack, Long Island, is the founder and President of Elijah Records, began studying piano at the age of seven. She majored in music education at the University of Rhode Island and opened a piano studio in 1987 on Long Island, New York where she not only teaches piano and keyboards to students of all ages but records music as well. In 1992 Maria had a series of out-of-body experiences in which she saw a child named Elijah.

Eight years before that she had a miscarriage at three months. The fetus had a strong heartbeat. The failure produced a sac but no fetus.[118]

It felt like a movement through time and space. She was shown some children outside a window and one particular child. They said his name was Elijah. The being around her said, "There are things we want you to do, and you are to remember the name, Elijah." Next day she kept hearing. This is Elijah. He is your son.

She went to psychiatrists and priests for an answer but got nothing. She felt violated.

One of the things that Cuccia heard is that "she must write music." She told them that she did not write music but heard: "We will guide you."

She went into meditation, and she started to hear melodies, but not piano melodies. "Not the way I was trained with the way that I played the piano. These were different types of melodies. It was different types of sounds. There was no exact rhythm or tempo."

Cuccia stated that people started showing up in her life, and soon she was producing CDs of meditation music. That led to producing other artists under the record label Elijah Records. Cuccia ran the company for 17 years till 2009.

To cope with the experiences, Maria discovered the healing powers of meditation. Inspired by her meditations, Maria recorded her first meditation CD in 1993, using minimalist synthesizer arrangements and repetitive instrumental keyboard phrasing, which has been, and still well received by many yoga and tai chi teachers, as well as massage therapists.

Doug Auld - An artist from New York City, who has had many experiences and later became good friends with experiencer Chris Bledsoe. Before meeting Bledsoe, he felt inspired to write a song. He opened up to me after I went public with an ET connection to modern music and first alerted to me by Bledsoe.

"Grant," he wrote, "I felt its time I should send you this. Please don't feel obligated to like. It's just that I wrote it in 2012 prior to my meeting Chris, you and this music ET connection concept. I recorded it all on garage band, and it's in early stages, I play all the instruments, and my singer is Kalindi. It is best to have some decent headphones and read the lyrics to the music."

Boulder Experiencer - This girl as a teenager opened for Pat Boone in Nashville. She has been a lifetime experiencer and was regressed twice by Budd Hopkins. She reported one particular song that could be considered a download. The song was called The Heart. Her professional musician son, who I have met, is also an experiencer and has written a couple of songs that a UFO experiencer could relate to.

RW Sanders - Sanders is one of the many musicians who found himself enveloped in the UFO world as a writer and research. He related a story that sounds very much the same as all the great musicians of the last century.

> *My own songs I've written have largely come in the form of a download. And often it happened simultaneously with my songwriting partner, Dr. Jeff Cortazzo. We often wrote finished songs in simply as long as it took us to write it down, and play it. Maybe twenty minutes. :)*
>
> *Probably half my songs came when I suddenly awoke from sleep and wrote them down. The only problem is that one must grab the guitar and also play the music, to imprint it until morning in your mind. I often kept a small recorder, though usually didn't use it as the songs were most always still in my head next morning.*
>
> *I began doing this with both songs and poetry at around puberty."*

As well as these most alien related musical related inspirations there are others involving savants that are much more dramatic.

In the work of Dr. Darold Treffert, the leading authority in the world on savants, he refers to people who had an aha moment when they could suddenly play after not being able to play in the past despite practicing.

One of Treffert examples was an Israeli man K.A. who suddenly picked up savant type music skills with an absence of injury or neurological disability. In his letter to Treffert, the man wrote,

> *A most amazing thing happened to me about two years ago at age 26½. While sitting in front of a piano at my friends' wine store at the local mall, just playing the keys, trying to figure out what's what and who's who, all of a sudden I felt things 'come together in my head.' It's a little hard to describe what went on in my head. Among other things, I suddenly (just like that) realized what the major scale was, what its chords were, and more importantly, where to put my fingers on the keyboard in order to play a certain part of the scale. The final ingredient in my gift, I noticed, was the ability to instantaneously recognize harmonies of the scales in songs I knew and reproduce them on the piano, as well as a somewhat less strong ability to reproduce melody by quickly figuring out how high or low the next note is, i.e. interval recognition.*
>
> *Suddenly, at age 26½, after what I can best describe as a 'just getting it' moment, it all seemed so simple. I started playing every song I knew from memory right there. Suddenly people around and my friends stopped what they were doing, looked at me, and said 'whoa.....look at him play!!!' They, as well as I, were amazed at how just a few moments ago I was playing random chords on the keyboard, when all of a sudden I started playing like I had been a well-educated pianist. In a second case, Treffert referred to J.D., who despite an IQ of 135 was not able to learn the guitar. Then at the age of 16, he suddenly acquired the ability to comprehend all the intricate rules of musical structure.*[119]

Another savant with talent coming from somewhere else is Leslie Lemke whose grandmother woke up in the middle of the night to find blind and severely mentally impaired Leslie flawlessly playing Tchaikovsky's Piano Concerto No. 1. Leslie had heard the song earlier in the day on TV. Lemke only has to listen the music once to play it again correctly.

Ellen Boudreaux is a blind, autistic savant with exceptional musical abilities. She can also play music perfectly after hearing it just once. She had no musical training but has a repertoire of thousands of songs she can play.

A third person in the same category is Derek Paravicini, a blind British musical savant. His disabilities were so severe he cannot tell his right from the left hand. He can, however, play any song he has heard. He can also change the key and play the song in a different style of music.

David Stinnett - UFO Researcher David Stinnett had a musical download. He told me in 2013, "It was about six years ago. I was exhausted and passed out on the couch in the afternoon. I woke up a few hours later with a complete song...lyrics and music chord changes and all...chord changes I've never used. Showed my music partner and he said: "where'd you come up with those chord changes?" I didn't have an answer... They were just "there." I wasn't crazy about the song, but the chord change turnarounds were something I never used.

Chapter 4 Inspiration by Serendipity

A discovery is said to be an accident meeting a prepared mind. **Albert Szent-Györgyi**

The skepticism with which experts nearly always greet these revolutionary discoveries confirms that the available knowledge has been a handicap." **W.I.B. Beveridge, medical historian Cambridge University**

Most people have had at least one experience in which unintentional action or inadvertent observation, or perhaps even simple neglect, led to a happy outcome. **Dr. Morton A. Myers**

A study of inventions in the modern world shows a high number of inventions that arose through sheer accident or serendipity. The word serendipity was coined by Horace Walpole in 1754 and means a "fortunate happenstance" or "pleasant surprise."

In the world of serendipity inventions the engineer, doctor or scientist was trying to develop one product and accidently created something entirely different that became a popular and money making success. The process could be called serendipity or the attainment and discovery of something valuable that was not intended. One example of this is Dr. Morton Myers, who wrote *Happy Accidents: Serendipity in Modern Medical Breakthroughs, Accidental Discoveries* about accidental discoveries in medicine. He pointed out the important role of serendipity in the development of psychotropic drugs, "Serendipity, not deductive reasoning, has been the force behind the discovery of virtually all psychotropics." (Meprobamate, chlorpromazine, LSD, Valium, and antidepressants.)[120]

Because of the money involved with patents and ownership, sometimes credit is not given where credit is due. Myers described the lack of discussion about accidental discoveries this way, "The scientific reality very rarely reflects this reality. The dominant convention of all scientific writings is to present discoveries as rational driven and to let the facts speak for themselves…It banishes any hint of blunders and surprises along the way."[121]

Like inventions and discoveries that come with inspirations, downloads, or through biomimicry the mind of the inventor or discoverer usually has to be aware enough to value or notice that something of significance has occurred. Nobel Prize Winner Paul Flory on the occasion of winning the Priestley Medal put it this way:

> *Significant accidents are not mere accidents. The erroneous view is widely held and is one that the scientific and technical community has done little to dispel. Happenstance usually plays apart, but there is much more to*

the invention than the popular notion of a bolt from the blue. Knowledge in depth and in breadth are virtual prerequisites. Unless the mind is thoroughly charged beforehand, the proverbial spark of genius, if it should manifest itself, probably will find nothing to ignite.[122]

Many will maintain that accidental inventions are just accidents have no significant meaning or message. This view is a result of the belief in a random meaningless world where the accident is the only rule.

Many things go against the random world view, but two key ones that apply here.

1) There are many examples of synchronicities in the world. One of the more famous in the UFO community is the story of researcher Jacques Vallee, who was studying a cult by the name of The Order of Melchizedek. He is unable to come up with much. He arrives in Los Angeles and takes a taxi into the city. He asks for a receipt and finds out that the taxi cab driver's name is Melchizedek. He checks the phone book only to find that this is the only person with that name among the millions of individuals. Minutes after Colin Wilson writes up the story in his book "From Atlantis to the Sphinx: Recovering the Lost Wisdom of the Ancient World" he takes his dog for a walk. When he returned home, he saw an unfamiliar book from his extensive book collection on a spare bed. He opens it to see what the book is about, and the book opens to a page titled "The Order of Melchizedek." If synchronicities are a reality, does this mean that the universe cares about who Vallee gets for a taxi cab driver, but it does not take any role in the discovery of penicillin, angioplasty, the phonograph, photography or thousands of other inventions that have changed the world?

2) One of the more common reported paranormal phenomena reported is precognition where psychics or remote viewers see events in the future. Remote viewers, in fact, claim it is just as easy to remote view the future as the present. If precognition is a reality, the idea of inventions being random accidents must be discounted.

Scores of examples exist for inventions and scientific discoveries that came by complete chance. Here are some of the most prominent.

Jocelyn Bell - Neutron stars - Bell was a Ph.D. student who in 1967 was using a new radio telescope technique for finding quasars. What she discovered in addition to quasars was an important signal at regular 1.3-second intervals. Her supervisor Anthony Hewish and herself thought it may be a signal from an extraterrestrial civilization. Researchers later identified them as spinning neutron stars which are the remains of supernova explosions. Hewish got the 1974 Nobel Prize, and Bell got nothing for the discovery.

Harry Coover - Crazy Glue - In 1942 Dr. Harry Coover of Eastman-Kodak Laboratories created cyanoacrylate for a new precision gun sight which he considered a total failure. The substance stuck to everything it touched. So it was forgotten. Later it was a material used for airplane canopies and the stuff again was getting stuck to everything. In 1958, a full 16 years later, the product was called super-glue and was being sold in stores.

Bernard Courtois - Iodine - Courtois was a French business person who was making potassium nitrate used in ammunition. He obtained his product by burning seaweed that washed up on shore, burn it, and extract the potassium from the ashes.

   The discovery of iodine came one day when workers added too much acid to clean the tank used for the extraction. A large cloud of smoke billowed up, and dark crystals appeared on the surface. He called it iodine after the Greek word for violet. Iodine is plentiful in seaweed.

George Crum - Potato Chips - Crum was a chef in a diner in Saratoga, New York. One of the customers, railway magnate Cornelius Vanderbilt repeatedly sent back the fries he had been served complaining that they were too thick and soggy. Crum was frustrated and decided to play Vanderbilt's game and cut the potatoes paper thin to make a point. Vanderbilt was initially upset but when he finally tried one he loved them and soon they were on the restaurant menu. From there they went onto the shelves of stores around the world.

Louis Daguerre - Photography - In working on a way to get the paintings to paint themselves. Daguerre discovered that iodine vapor made a shiny silver plate sensitive to light. However, he could not get anything more than a faint picture when using his camera. It was not until in 1839 that he left a developed plate in a cabinet where tiny drops of mercury from a broken thermometer had caused mercury vapor and a translucent mirror-like image on the plate.

Charles Dotter - Angioplasty - Dotter discovered the technique accidently in 1963 while doing an examination of a patient with an artery obstruction in the pelvis. During the exam Dotter accidently jammed the catheter into the obstruction and it cleared. He used the mistake to develop Balloon angioplasty which involves mechanically widening narrowed or obstructed arteries or veins using a balloon on a guide wire. The balloon is moved to the arterial obstruction and then inflated to a fixed size.

Jennifer Doudna - Gene Editing - Doudna was at the University of California who invented a tool for editing genes that she called CRISPR/Cas9. She got the inspiration when she and her colleagues were trying to find out how body bacteria fight the flu. What she discovered is that weird repetitive RNA sequences tucked in the genomes of bacteria known as CRISPRs can search out and identify invading viruses. They, in turn, have a particular protein Cas9 that can cut open the DNA of an invading virus and efficiently kill the virus. It came as a surprise. "I certainly didn't set out to discover a genome editing tool by any stretch of the imagination," said Doudna.[123]

Thomas Edison - Phonograph - While experimenting to improve the design of his telegraph transmitter he noticed a sound coming from the equipment that sounded like human speech. He began the search to see if he could record human speech. He started with a needle attached to the telephone receiver diaphragm and moved to a stylus on a tinfoil cylinder where he recorded and played back, "Mary had a little lamb."

Frank Epperson - Popsicle - At 11 years old, Epperson was trying to make soda pop by mixing soda water powder and water, but left his invention on the porch with the stir stick in it overnight where it froze. In the morning, he found the frozen mixture with the stir stick in it. Fifteen years later he remembered the event, filed a patent and made the first popsicles with fruit flavors.

Constantin Fahlberg - Saccharin - Fahlberg failed to wash his hands after working in his lab and while eating discovered something sweet on his hands. He went back and tasted all the chemicals that had been worked on that day. It became Saccharin, the artificial sweetener.

Alexander Fleming - Penicillin - When Fleming examined some bacterial cultures that had become contaminated with mold he noticed that the bacteria in the glass dish had died. He immediately saw an avenue toward killing bacteria - the epoch-making discovery of what would become penicillin.

Dr. Leslie Gay and Paul Carliner - Dramamine - These two allergists used Dramamine to treat hives. One day a patient reported that the drug had cured her of travel sickness. That is one of the uses for the drug.

Wilson Greatbatch - Pacemaker - Greatbatch mistakenly picked a 1-megaohm resistor instead of a 10,000-ohm resistor out of a box to use on a heart-recording prototype. The mistake produced a signal that sounded for 1.8 milliseconds, and then paused for a second - a dead ringer for the human heart.

Dr. William Stewart Halsted - Surgical gloves - before the use of surgical gloves used in operations, surgeons would spray carbolic acid on their bare hands before operating. At John Hopkins Hospital Dr. William Halsted had a problem with this technique. The problem was that his lover was a nurse in his operating room, and she got dermatitis from the carbolic acid. In an attempt to keep her in the operating room Halsted approached Goodyear Tire and Rubber to make rubber gloves that his girlfriend could wear during the operation. One of Halsted's assistants began the gloves and soon it was standard practice at John Hopkins. Now everyone wears sterile surgical gloves.

Julian Hill - Nylon fiber - Hill, while working on plastic polymers pulled a stick out of a jar of plastic polymer one day while his boss was out and discovered that he had drawn out what appeared to be a thread. He and his colleagues had a tug-of-war with the thread in the hallway to see how far it would go before it broke. They found that the stretching of the fibers made them even stronger.

Albert Hofmann - LSD-25 - The drug lysergic acid diethylamide was created in 1943 to obtain a stimulus to the circulatory and respiratory system. Hofmann described the accidental ingestion of the chemical and the discovery of its psychedelic properties in his diary. "Last Friday April 16, 1943 I was forced to stop my work in the laboratory in the middle of the afternoon and to go home, as I was seized with a particular restlessness associated with a sensation of mild dizziness....As I lay in a dazed condition...there surged upon me an uninterrupted stream of fantastic images of extraordinary plasticity and vividness and accompanied by intense, kaleidoscopic-like play of colors. This condition gradually passed off after two hours."[124]

Ice Cream Cone - The invention came at the St. Louis World's Fair in 1904. An ice cream stand was running out of dishes for its ice cream, and the neighboring stand selling Zalabia, which is a thin Persia waffle was not doing well. The Persian waffles were rolled into cone shapes to help out the ice cream vendor and the ice cream cone was born.

Richard James - Slinky - James was working during WWII on springs for the US Navy when one of the springs fell off the work bench. It hit the floor and then quickly righted itself. It inspired the toy.

Alec Jeffreys - DNA Profiling - Jeffreys described the moment the weekend cells were broken open and their DNA extracted attached to film with radioactive probes to help identify repeated sections of DNA. When he first pulled the film out on Monday, his first reaction was, "What a mess." As Jeffreys unfolded the story, "My life changed on Monday morning at 9.05 am, 10 September 1984. What emerged was the world's first genetic fingerprint. In science, it is unusual to have such a 'eureka' moment. We were getting extraordinarily variable patterns of DNA, including from our technician and her mother and father, as well as from non-human samples. My first reaction to the results was 'this is too complicated', and then the penny dropped and I realized we had genetic fingerprinting."[125]

Will Keith Kellogg - Corn Flakes - While trying to come up with a new menu item for the vegetarian diet at the Battle Creek Sanatorium Kellogg was working with boiled wheat. Instead of putting the sticky mass of grain through the rollers he left it overnight and then stuck the dry bulk through the rollers. It came out in broken flakes, and corn flakes were born. Mail order was used to sell it before being put in stores.

Antonio Meucci - Meucci invented the "speaking telegraph" in 1849, but initially it had nothing to do with the telegraph or telephone. Meucci had set up an experiment to cure migraine headaches. He placed a metal plate in the patient's mouth attached to a battery. Meucci then wired that to another plate putting that in his mouth. When he turned on the power, he heard the patient yell in pain, but it came not only through the air but through the wire that connected the two units. It led to the patent that Alexander Bell (who he once worked with) would file twenty-seven years later. In 2001 the US Congress gave official recognition to Meucci for the invention.[126]

Alfred Nobel - Dynamite - Nobel, the man who put up the money for the present day awarding of Nobel prizes made his money from inventing dynamite. Nobel was the owner of a nitroglycerin factory in the 1860s. This explosive was very unstable. One day Nobel dropped a vial of the volatile chemical, but he did not explode. Examination showed there was sawdust in the chemical which stabilized it. Nobel realized the potential adding kieselguhr as a further stabilizer and dynamite was the result.

Dr. George Papanicolaou - Pap Smear - Papanicolaou was working on vaginal smears of animals during their sex cycle. When he moved his research to humans, he happened to get the fluid sample of a woman suffering from uterine cancer. The cancer cells were very easy to see on the smear. Papanicolaou was amazed saying, "The first observation of cancer cells in the smart of the uterine cervix gave me one of the greatest thrills I ever experienced during my scientific career." He developed the pap smear test which helped to end one of the deadliest forms of cancer for women.

John Pemberton - Coca Cola - Pemberton originally tried to make a medicine that would help the nervous and exhausted to relax. When he and his assistant tried it, they found that it tasted sweet and delicious. When his assistant made the second batch of medicine, he accidently used carbonated water instead of plain water. When Pemberton tried it, he decided to sell it as a drink. The rest is history.

Dom Pierre Perignon - Champagne - Perignon was in charge of the Benedictine Champagne Abbey wine cellars in France in 1697. The in-bottle fermentation over two years in the cooler Champagne region was producing bubbles in the wine which was considered poor winemaking. Perignon tried to eliminate the bubbles but couldn't. Fortunately the aristocratic crowds from the French and English courts that drank it loved it, and bubbly Champagne began its production. The English, however, claim to have invented bubbly wine 35 years earlier. The British inventor was a Gloucester doctor called Christopher Merret when he began experimenting with adding sugar to wine. He reported in a paper to the Royal Society how "our wine-coopers of recent times add vast quantities of sugar and molasses to wines to make them drink brisk and sparkling."

Roy Plunkett - Teflon in 1938 - Plunkett, a DuPont chemist, had hoped to create a new non-toxic variety of chlorofluorocarbons for refrigeration. He had developed about 100 pounds of what he called tetrafluoroethylene (TFE). Plunkett was using small tanks to store the chemical. One morning he came in and opened the valve to obtain some TFE only to discover nothing came out. The tank weighed the same, so Plunkett cut the tank open to see where the gas had gone. What he found was white flakes lining the inside of the reservoir. The waxy material had four unique properties: that led Plunkett to send it on to the DuPont Central Research Department 1) It was evaluated to be one of the slipperiest substance known to man, 2) it was non-corrosive, 3) chemically stable, and 4) had an extremely high melting point. These properties were deemed interesting enough that the study of the substance transferred to DuPont's Central Research Department where it became Teflon.

Wilhelm Roentgen - X-Ray - Roentgen was experimenting with a cathode ray tube when he noticed that a piece of fluorescent cardboard was lighting up from across the room. He searched for the source of the light and realized that the cathode emitter was passing right through a dense screen in the way of the cardboard. He experimented with the strange unknown rays and found that they moved through things. He called them x-rays and his wife's hand was the first thing to be x-rayed. Her reaction was that in seeing the bones of her hand she had just witnessed her death.

Spencer Silver - Post-it Notes - Silver was a researcher for 3M who was trying to create new stronger glue. What he produced was a weak type of glue. Four years later a colleague of Silver was having a problem with slips of paper being used to identify pages in his hymnal while in choir practice. He recalled the weak glue that Silver had produced and found that he could mark the pages with bookmarks and then remove the marker without leaving any residue on the hymnal pages. In 1977 3M started production of Post-it Notes with the weak glue and the money started rolling in.

Patsy Sherman - Scotch Guard - Sherman was a 3M engineer assigned to work on the project development a rubber material resistant to jet aircraft fuel deterioration. During the process, Sherman spilled one of the compounds she was using on her tennis shoes and found that nothing would take it off. It seemed to resist water, alcohol and oil. She used the accident to develop a protective spray for fabric and Scotch Guard was born.

Percy Spencer - Microwave oven - Spencer was a Raytheon electrical engineer who was working on a microwave-emitting magnetron used in radars. He suddenly noticed that a chocolate bar in his pocket had begun to melt. Understanding that the cause was the microwaves, he realized the cooking potential of microwaves and designed an oven. His first experiment to verify was he believed was happening was turning corn into popcorn.

Leo Sternbach - Sternbach was the director of medicinal chemistry for Hofmann - LaRoche and was working on the development of a new "psycho sedative" drug. He had prepared 40 new compounds which all came up negative as muscle relaxants and sedatives. They suspended the program for two years. In 1957 Sternbach was cleaning up his laboratory bench when a colleague pointed out a crystalline compound Sternbach was about to throw out had never been tested. A couple of days later after it left for tests, he got the call that the compound had extraordinary properties. The mixture became known as Librium.[127]

Pfizer - Viagra - The 1993 testing of sildenafil citrate for angina was a failure but produced an entirely unexpected discovery. They discovered that the drug returned penile erectile function to the penis. It became the fastest selling drug in the world.

Arno Penzias and Robert Wilson - Micro-Wave Background Radiation - These two radio astronomers kept picking up a low-level radiation signal from their antennae. They cleaned the equipment thinking it might be bird dropping, but the noise continued. Later they determined that the signal was the low-level background from the big bang as predicted mathematically years earlier. The two researchers shared the 1979 Nobel Prize in Physics.

Chapter 5 Inspiration by Biomimicry

One thing I have learned in a long life - that all our science, measured against reality, is primitive and childlike. **Albert Einstein**

Ninety-nine parts of all things that proceed from the intellect are plagiarisms, pure and simple; and the lesson ought to make us modest. But nothing can do that. **Mark Twain**

What has been will be again, what has been done will be done again; there is nothing new under the sun. Is there anything of which one can say, "Look! This is something new?" It was here already, long ago; it was here before our time. **Ecclesiastes 1:9-10**

Inspiration by Biomimicry is getting inspiration for new inventions by studying how nature structures things. Some refer to it as bio-inspiration. In biomimicry, the engineer simply copycats what nature has already created. He files a patent for the process of describing the natural procedure or structure. Many organizations how have departments that study nature looking for inspiration for inventions.

Even Christian groups attacked in the 19th and 20th century for believing in God's design as opposed to random evolution are now fighting back. They point out, quite successfully, that most of the modern inventions claimed by secular science as their handiwork, are simply copies of God's creation that have been around for a long time. One group called The Evolution of Truth summed it up saying "Ever get the feeling someone is saying 'Been there. Done that…We invent nothing. We simply discover.'" They are probably right. The long list of examples on their website include the following items,

> *Camera (lens, focus, iris, film)/Eye (cornea curves to focus, iris, retina), Microphone/Eardrum, Amphitheatre shape /Outer ear shape, Pump/Heart, Valves/Heart Valves, Plumbing and hydraulic systems/Circulatory system, Communication and telephone cables/ Spinal cord and nervous system, Ball joint/Shoulder joint, Windshield wiper/ Eyelid, Wiper fluid Tears, Mortar and pestle/ Molar teeth, Woodwinds /Voicebox, Computer program/ DNA, Bubble level/Inner ear tubes for balance, Construction crane /Arm and hand, Honeycomb reinforcements /Bee's Honeycomb, Solar panel (energy from light)/Leaf, Fishhook (reverse barb design)/Bee stinger, Light stick (light from chemical reactions)/Firefly, glow worm, deep sea creatures, Airplanes /Birds, Radar/Bats and dolphins, Blu-blocker sunglasses/Orange oil in eagle eyes to improve acuity,*

Suction cups/Octopus, Inboard Propulsion (boats)/Squid, Anesthetics/Venoms and poisons, Swim fins, paddles/Webbed feet (frogs, ducks), Water cooled systems/Sweat glands and perspiration, Core aeration for health of lawns/Worms, insects and moles, Hypodermic syringe/Snake fangs and mechanism used by viruses to inject into cells, Antibiotic medicines/Immune system, Hydraulic shock absorbers/Knee joints, Dust filter/Nostril hairs, Magnets/Lodestone, Internet Connected neurons in brain, Mirror/Reflection on water, Water filtration techniques Same filtering techniques as found in nature and swamps and rivers /charcoal, Sponge (synthetic)/Sponge, Satellite/Moon, silt, Smoke detectors/Noses, Cup/Cupped hands, Fishing net/Spider's web, Fires set to aid heat in agriculture/Naturally occurring forest fires, Shock absorbing helmet/Woodpecker skull, Snowshoes/Penguin's feet, Frames of Buildings/Skeleton of living organisms, Medicine/Herbs, Evolution of civilization and technology/Evolution of the universe and life, Beaver dams/Water dams, Pliers, tongs Lobster/crab claws, Fur coats/Fur coats, Vitamin pills/Fruits and vegetables.[128]

A look back through various inventions shows clearly that many inventions were the process of only studying nature and duplicating what their observations.

ACE inhibitors (Lisinopril, Ramipril) - Researchers discovered these essential blood pressure medications after studying victims in Brazil who died from low blood pressure after being bit by the deadly jararaca snake. The venom of the snake lowered blood pressure.

Peter Agre - Agre was awarded the 2003 Nobel Prize in part for his discovery of a memory protein called aquaporin that allows the passage of water through the cell wall. Agre stated that the development "really fell into our lap."[129] A Danish company called aquaporin is now using this idea to help desalinate water.

Fred Baur - Pringles Potato Chips - Baur noticed that wet leaves, when stacked, retain their shape and do not break. Dry leaves are fragile and break. The process used, therefore, was to stack the chips and then bake them. The result was shipping containers that took up less space and suffered no breakage.

Biomatrica - Biomatrica is a San Diego company that has developed a process that allows vaccines to be stored or transported without refrigeration. They copied the process used from Tardigrades, which are millimeter-long cousins of arthropods, which use a process called anhydrobiosis which can dry out for up to 120 years, and be revived by water.

Brinker Technology - This company filed a patent on an invention that mimicked the ability of the human body to stop a cut from bleeding. They applied the technology to seal leaks in pipes and duct work that otherwise would be very expensive and difficult to seal. The three patents U.S. Patent #s 7,856,864, 7,810,523 and 8,061,389 base themselves on a sensor that goes through the pipe, like blood platelets, looking for leaks and sealing them.

Clarence Birdseye - Frozen food - Birdseye got the idea in 1912 for frozen food by watching Labrador ice fishermen pulling fish from the water that instantly froze in the bitter cold. The fish stayed fresh and did not turn to mush like slowly frozen food. He figured how to freeze fish quickly and keep the product frozen on the way to the store, creating a new industry.

Coumadin - This important drug, discovered in the early 1930s, is used to stop blood clots in humans. A Wisconsin farmer found many of his cows dying with distorted abdomens and no explanation. When no vet would come to tell him what was going on, he loaded one of his dead cows and some sweet clover the cow had been eating and drove to the University of Wisconsin where he angrily deposited the cow in the lobby of the Chemistry building. After a couple of days, the smell got so bad that a veterinary pathologist was called in in preparation for disposing of the animal. The pathologist discovered the cow had died from anemia or bleeding in the stomach and intestine caused by a mold in the clover that stopped clotting. The scientists filed for a patent, and the product became the rat poison WARFARIN. Later is was decided that the product might be good to stop clots in humans so they mixed it in small doses with aspirin, called it Coumadin. It became the main drug used to avoid blood clots in susceptible patients.

Eastgate Centre - A building in Harare, Zimbabwe has been built with no heating and cooling system beyond a system copied from mound termite technology. Professor Torben Lenau at the Technical University of Denmark described the building this way, "Termite mounds have constant humidity and temperature inside, regardless of the climatic conditions outside. It is controlled simply by air exchange," says Lenau. "Cooling is achieved by opening certain ventilation channels, and the same principle is used in the Eastgate building. Warm air is expelled and replaced with cooler air is drawn up from below ground."[130]

Frank Fish - Fish designed turbine blades that added bumps to the leading edge. They reduced drag and noise and boosted power by 20%. The idea was copied from the design of the warty ridges, called tubercles on the front edge of the fins of humpback whales.

Geckskin™ - According to this company, the adhesive "is so powerful that an index-card sized piece can hold 700 pounds on a smooth surface, such as glass, yet can be easily released, and leaves no residue." The adhesive was designed based on geckos which can walk upside down on the ceiling from grip provided by millions of microscopic hairs on the bottom of their toes that could theoretically hold 250 pounds per gecko. They can change instantly the direction of the fibers called setae; the grip breaks instantly when needed.

Joseph F. Glidden - Glidden got the idea for metal barbed wired after he noticed that people planted thorny plants around their property to keep their cattle inside their properties.

Michael Gratzel - Photosynthesis cells - The idea for the cells came from Michael Gratzel who studied natural sciences to answer the question "how did nature come up with photosynthesis?" He wanted to figure out if it was possible to imitate the process. The dye used in the process Gratzel developed uses the dye color from natural fruit like raspberries to capture the light and convert it to energy. The cells cost half what silicon solar cells cost. They cover the second glass plate with tin oxide and graphite and iodine solution. The dye gathers light producing positive and negative charges producing an electrical current.

GreenShield - GreenShield is a fabric finish made by G3i based on the "lotus effect" which allows it to stay clean. The lotus (Nelumbo nucifera) is a leaf that processes the ability to cause water and even honey to bead and just roll off the leaf even though the surface isn't smooth at all. The leaf surface has a myriad of microscopic crevices which traps a maze of air and which forces the liquid to roll off taking dirt particles with it.

Paul Robert-Houdin – Light and Sound shows – Robert - Houdin created the first "light-and-sound show in 1953 based on lightning and thunder that he had seen in a major storm in 1939.

Hippopotamus Sweat - The Hippopotamus sweats a highly efficient 1 in 4 sunblocks. As well as a highly efficient sunscreen, it is an antiseptic, insect repellant, and anti-fungal. Because three out of four sunscreens are not as effective as claimed, scientists are now trying to synthesize a product from it and change the smell which is highly offensive. [131]

Edward Jenner - Smallpox vaccination - Jenner got the idea for a smallpox vaccination from hearing a dairymaid Sarah Nelson brag that she could not get smallpox because she had gotten cowpox while milking cows. Jenner used his son Phipps as the experimental subject.[132] It worked. People with cowpox were immune to smallpox.

Light emitting diodes - Scientists were able to increase the brightness of light emitting diodes by copying the process used by Photuris fireflies to light their bellies. Sharp and jagged scales increase the intensity.

George de Mestral - Velcro - Mestral came up with probably the most well-known invention taken from watching how nature works. On a hunting trip in 1948, he found himself covered with cockleburs which were very hard to remove. Wondering how burrs were able to attach and stick so well, he spent time studying the burr carefully to see how it operated. He noticed the hooked needle-like objects that stuck out and were able to loop in and under the threads of his clothes. He suddenly got an idea to create a hook and loop invention for fasteners. It took some time to come up with the materials that would work but Velcro quickly developed. The use of Velcro by NASA in outer space made the idea a household name.

Mark Miles - Mirasol - The technology has been developed by micro-electromechanical and materials processing engineer Mark Miles at Qualcomm MEMS Technologies. He created the first full-color, video-friendly e-reader prototype based on the way butterfly wings gleam in the bright light. The technology, known as Mirasol, reflects light rather than transmitting light out with a standard computer or e-reader. Miles got the idea for the invention while reading an article on how Morpho species butterflies generate color in their wings, not by pigment but from "structural color." The butterfly harbors "a nanoscale assemblage of shingled plates, whose shape and distance from one another arrange themselves in a precise pattern that disrupts reflective light wavelengths to produce the brilliant blue." [133] This pattern was more energy efficient for the butterfly and turned out to be an energy saver for e-readers as well requiring on 10% of the energy of the old technology.

Joseph Montgolfier - Hot Air Balloon - It was Montgolfier who first had the idea of flying a hot air balloon when he observed clothes drying over a fire form pockets that billowed upwards, and by watching paper embers being lifted up the chimney by a fire. He believed that the smoke contained the power to lift, and he called it Montgolfier Gas. His first balloon flight aided by his brother took place in 1783.

Eiji Nakatsu - Nakatsu, an engineer for a Japanese train company, came up with the design for the high speed train. He did this by watching birds. Nakatsu solved problem of the loud gunshot sound that could be heard for one quarter of a mile away from high-speed train that would build up massive air pressure when going through a tunnel and then emerging into a reduced pressure. Nakatsu designed a 50-foot long nose for the train based on the beak of a kingfisher bird which produces almost no ripple in the water when it dives down into the water to catch fish.

Joseph Paxton - Large glass architecture - Paxton got the idea of building massive buildings by observing the structure of a giant water lily he had grown for his daughter. He had the lily in a heated pool inside a greenhouse. The plant became too big for the pool and building. He is trying to figure out how to make larger greenhouse Jenner came across the idea of building what in 1856 became the world's largest greenhouse when he happened to look at the bottom of the leaf and saw the vein structure.[134]

Stars and Stripes - The sailing vessel Stars and Stripes was winning the Olympic Gold Medal and America's Cup based on a technology called riblets. The technology was a copy of a microscopic pattern on sharks called dentricles which reduce drag and do not allow algae and other elements to accumulate on the shark. Officials banned technology in 1987.

Wiley Post - Flight suits - The idea for flexible joints in astronaut flight suits came from flying daredevil Wiley Post in 1934 when he observed a tomato worm moving across a leaf. Its flexible joints allowed it to easily move in every direction. The joints of the worm inspired his design of a flight suit with flexible joints.

Chapter 6 Inspirations for Inventions

The pattern of independent multiple discoveries in science is in principle the dominant pattern, rather than a subsidiary one. **Robert Merton**

When the time is ripe for certain things, they appear at different places in the manner of violets coming to light in early spring. **Farkas Bolyai, to his son Janos, urging him to claim the invention of non-Euclidean geometry without delay.**

Within a matter of hours, that image came, and I just said, 'AHA!' I very rarely make my decisions in such a definite way. That one just went 'Bam!' and I just said, 'Boy, that's it. That just fills all kinds of different needs.' **Douglas Engelbart is talking about the inspirational download of the modern computer in December 1950.**

My method is different. I do not rush into actual work. When I get a new idea, I start at once building it up in my imagination, and make improvements and operate the device in my mind. When I have gone so far and to embody everything in my invention, every possible improvement I can think of, and when I see no fault anywhere, I put into concrete form the final product of my brain. **Nikola Tesla**

    It is inventions that advance the world. It is inventions that allow new ideas to enter the world, and bring with it change and a better lifestyle.

    The question that remains is where do inventions originate? Do they come from reasoning and the five senses, or is there something beyond the five senses that tunes into another place where the invention information is stored?

    Two essential items can are apparent when looking at inventions. 1) The stories of inspirations and downloads are evident. These are listed below. 2) Maybe even more impressive in the history of inventions is that multiple people were making simultaneous inventions. These items indicate that the invention was in the air at the time, and that enabled inventors to turn into it and bring it into the physical world. Here is a chart that illustrates this amazing fact of history.

    It has led to serious scholarship articles being written to ask, are inventions inevitable, and if the credited inventor had died in infancy would the invention have still happened without much delay?[135]

Invention	Inventors	Date
Cotton Gin	Joseph Eve, Eli Whitney, John Barcley	1788, 1793,1795
Cosmic Background Radiation	Arno Penzias and Robert Wilson, Robert Dicke and Jim Peebles	1965
Astronomical Red Shift	Georges Lemaître Edwin Hubble	1927, 1929
Railway electrical application	Davidson, Jacobi, Lilly, Davenport, Page Hall	1830s, 1942
Wagner–Fischer algorithm	Published independently six times	1968-1975
Telegraph	Charles Wheatstone, Sir William Fothergill Cooke, Edward Davy, and Carl August von Steinhiel	So close the UK Supreme Court refused to award patent
Telephone	Alexander Graham Bell, Elisha Gray	Same day 1876
Light Bulb	Thomas Edison and 23 Other people	1878, 1879
Telescope	Hans Lipperhey, Sacharias Janssen, Thomas Harriet, Galileo Galilei, Lippershey, Della Porta, Diggs, Johannides, Metius, Drebbel, Fontana.	1558, 1571, 1608
Microscope	Johannides, Drebbel, and Galileo	1610
Pendulum clock	Burgi, Galileo, Huygens	1575,1582, 1656
Leyden jar	Von Kleist and Cuneus	1745,1746
Micro-organism infection	Fracastoro and Kircher	1546
Circular Slide Rule	Delamain and Oughtred	1630,1632
Printing	Gutenberg and Coster	1420,1443
Sewing Machine	Thimmonier, Howe, andHunt	1830, 1846, 1840
Planet NeptuneDiscovery	John Couch Adams and Urbain Leverrier	1846
E=MC2	Einstein, Henri Poincaré, Olinto De Pretto, and Paul Langevin	1900,1905, 1906
Radioactivity	Henri Becquerel and Silvanus	1896

Invention	Inventors	Date
	Thompson	
Thorium radioactivity	Gerhard Carl Schmidt and Maria Skłodowska Curie	1898
Sperm-Egg Fertilization	Oskar Hertwig and Hermann Foi	1876
Function of Pancreas	Purkinje and Pappenheim	1836
Sunspot Discovery	Galileo (Italy) Scheiner (Germany) Fabricius (Holland) Harriott (England)	1611
Lightning and Electricity	Thomas Francois D'Alibard Benjamin Franklin	1752
Electric Motor	Dal Negro, Henry, Bourbonze, McGawley	1830,1831,1835
Induction Coil	Callan and Ruhmkorff	1836, 1851
Water electrolysis	Nicholson, Carlisle, and Ritter	1800
AC Motor	Tesla, August Haselwander and C.S. Bradley, Mikhail Dolivo-Dobrovsky	1886, 1887, 1888-91
Transformer	Ganz company in Budapest, William Stanley, Gaulard and Gibbs design, Tesla, Károly Zipernowsky, Miksa Déri and Ottó Bláthy.	Late 1870s, 1882, 1885
Balloon	Montgolfier, Rittenhouse-Hopkins	1783
Airplane	Wright Brothers, Gustave Albin Whitehead	1901,1903
Phonograph	Charles Cros and Thomas Edison	1877
Microphone	Hughes, Edison, Berliner, and Blake	1877, 1878
Stratosphere Discovery	Richard Assmann and Léon Teisserenc de Bort	1902
Jet Engine	Hans von Ohain, Secondo Campini, Frank Whittle	1939,1940, 1941
Steam Boat	Fulton, Jouffroy, Rumsey, Stevens, and Symington.	1786,1788
Oxygen	Carl Steele, Joseph Priestly, Antoine Lavoisier	1773,1774,1777
Oxygen Liquefaction	Cailletet and Pictet	1877

Invention	Inventors	Date
Helium	Pierre Jansen, Norman Lockyer	1868
Lutetium	Georges Urbain (France) Baron Carl Auer von Welsbach (Austria)	1907
Epinephrine	Friedrich Stolz and Henry Drysdale Dakin.	1904
Periodic Table	Dmitri Ivanovich Mendeleev following year Julius Lothar Meyer published his independently constructed version.	1869, 1870
Chloroform	Samuel Guthrie (United States), Eugène Soubeiran (France) and Justus von Liebig (Germany)	1831
Cadmium	Friedrich Strohmeyer, K.S.L Hermann	1817
Beryllium	Friedrich Wöhler, A.A.B. Bussy	1827
Platinum	Antonio de Ulloa and Charles Wood	1740
Boron	Davy and Guy-Lussac	1808, 1809
Ceria	Hisinger, Berzelis and Klaproth	1803, 1804
Aluminum Processing	Charles Martin Hall and the French scientist Paul Héroult	1886
Decimal Fractions	Rudolf, Stevinus and Burgi	1585, 1603, 1592
Prime Number Theorem	Jacques Hadamard and Charles de la Vallée-Poussin	1896
Calculus	Isaac Newton, Gottfried Leibniz, Pierre de Fermat	1666, 1675
Evolution	Charles Darwin, Alfred Russel Wallace	1840, 1857
Law Conservation of Energy	Joule, Thomson, Colding, Helmholz	1847
Variability of satellites	Bradley and Wargentin	1746, 1752
Planetary perturbation theory	Lagrange and LaPlace	1808
Inner Saturn Ring Discovery	Bond and Dawes	1850
Size of Molecule	JJ Loschmidt and William Thompson	1865
Laryngoscope	Babington, Liston, and Garcia	1737, 1829,

Invention	Inventors	Date
		1855
Stereoscope	Wheatstone, Elliott	1839,1840
Electromagnetic Induction	Michael Faraday (England), Joseph Henry (U.S.)	1831
Polio Vaccine	Hilary Koprowski, Jonas Salk, and Albert Sabin	1950-1963
Typewriter	Agostino Fantoni, Pellegrino Turri, Pietro Conti di Cilavegna, William Austin Burt	1802,1803, 1823, 1829
Bessemer Process	William Kelly (U.S.) Sir Henry Bessemer (U.K)	1851,1855
Mobius Strip	August Ferdinand Möbius, Johann Benedict Listing	1858
Phosphocreatine Discovery	Grace and Philip Eggleton (UK), Cyrus Fiske and Yellapragada Subbarow (US)	1927
Photography	Louis Jacques Mandé Daguerre and Joseph Nicéphore Niepce, William Henry Fox Talbot	1827
Sound Film	Joseph Tykociński-Tykociner, Lee De Forest	1922,1923
Thermometer	Group called Accademia del Cimento, Galileo Galilei, Cornelis Drebbel, Robert Fludd, Santorio Santorio.	1617-1638
Pap Smear Test	Georgios Papanikolaou and Aurel Babeş	1923, 1927
Mevastatin	Akira Endo (Japan), a British group	1973
Higgs Boson	Francois Englert, Robert Brout, Peter Higgs, Gerald Guralnik, C.R. Hagan, Tom Kibble	1964
Bohlen–Pierce musical scale	Heinz Bohlen, Kees van Prooijen and John R. Pierce.	1972,1978,1984
Black Holes	John Mitchell, Pierre-Simon Laplace	1783
Color Photography	Cros and Du Hauron	1869
Molecular Theory	Avagadro, Ampere	1811,1814
Trolley Car	Van Doeple, Sprague, Siemens and Daft.	1881,1884,1888
Logarithms	John Napier, Joost Burgi	1614,1618

Invention	Inventors	Date
Universal Computing Concept	S.C. Kleene and by Alonzo Church	1936
Universal Computing Computer	Alan Turing, and Emil Post	1936
Packet Switching	Paul Baran, Donald Davies	Early 1960s
Integrated Circuit	Jack Kilby in 1958 and half a year later by Robert Noyce	1958
Laser	Charles Townes, Gordon Gould, Joe Weber, Nikolai Basov, Aleksandr Prokhorov	1952, 1957
Atom Bomb	Leó Szilárd,[30] Józef Rotblat	1933 -
Reverse transcriptase enzymes	Howard Temin and David Baltimore	1970
Computational complexity theory	Stephen Cook (US)and Leonid Levin (USSR)	1971,1973
Asymptotic freedom	David Gross and Frank Wilczek, and by David Politzer	1973
J/ψ meson	Burton Richter and Samuel Ting	Nov 11, 1974
Television	Philo Farnworth, Kenjiro Takeyanagi, Vladimir Zworykin	1924

In addition to the pattern that many or even most inventions were multiple discoveries, there is a pattern that many or most significant inventions came in through inspirations or downloads. This model applies in particular when viewing significant inventions such as the telephone, television, the computer, and the Google search concept.

Here is a list of devices that came through inspirations and downloads. These run completely contrary to secular science which would say that all inventions came through the five senses and reason.

Michael Barnsley - Barnsley developed the construction of software that allowed the compression, and hence clarification, of photographic images that were fuzzy, such as those taken from satellites. The solution came in a dream, which Barnsley described,

> *The discovery of how to automatically calculate the collage of an arbitrary picture came to me in a dream. (In it) I saw how you could straighten out the switchboard, how all the wires would come untangled and be nicely connected and how you would join all the wires from big blocks to little*

blocks in the grid. I woke up in the morning, and I knew I had discovered the total secret to fractal image compression. How to automatically look at a digital picture and a) how to turn it into a formula, and b) an entity of infinite resolution. So the goal is now to be able to capture this fire of Prometheus, this fractal wonder, put it in a box and being able to make this available to everyone.[136]

Alexander Graham Bell - Bell was the person credited with inventing the telephone even though one other person tried to file a pattern for the telephone on the same day. Bell's download came as he sat in a wicker chair in a cupola area where a large tree had blown down. It was here, on July 26, 1874, in a place Bell called his dreaming place that he suddenly got an answer to the how to make sound travel alone a line at lightning speed. It had to do with vibrations. Bell quickly sketched the idea on a piece of paper.

Hans Berger - Berger was the inventor of the EEG machine. The invention came from a direct telepathic experience between Berger and his sister. During military service in the 1890s, he had an accident where his horse reared and threw him in the path of a horse-drawn cannon. Berger was unhurt but shaken.

At the same time this happened, his sister had a telepathic impression that he was in danger and insisted that their father send a telegram to Berger's regiment. The telegram had such an impact on Berger that he was determined to build a machine that could record and document telepathy. He wrote, "It was a case of spontaneous telepathy in which at a time of mortal danger, and as I contemplated certain death, I transmitted my thoughts, while my sister, who was particularly close to me, acted as the receiver."

Chester Carlson (1906-1968) - Carlson, inventor of the Xerox photocopying process, thoroughly believed that he received the knowledge necessary to create his breakthrough photocopying method from the spirit realm.

Carlson donated significant sums for paranormal research to Duke University's Parapsychology Laboratory and the American Society for Psychical Research (for which he served as a trustee). Carlson not only made annual donations to the University of Virginia to fund the work of Ian Stevenson, who was doing work tracking young children who claimed to have lived past lives. In 1964, he made an unusually generous donation that helped fund one of the first endowed chairs at the University.

Philo T. Farnsworth - Farnsworth was a farm boy from Rigby, Idaho. At age 14 had a vision while plowing a field. His vision included "using a lens to direct light into a glass camera tube, where it could be analyzed in a magnetically deflected beam of electrons, dissected and transmitted one line at a time in a continuous stream."[137] The vision came as he plowed his potato field. He looked down at the tracks left by his disc harrow and envisioned electrons creating a similar pattern to form a picture. He drew his idea on the blackboard for his school teacher. Six years later in 1930, he successfully demonstrated the modern television, the size of a postage stamp.

Galileo Galilei - Galileo received the inspiration for the pendulum from watching a priest swing an incense burner in Pisa Cathedral. He timed the swings according to his pulse and realized it was regular. He later designed a pendulum clock which his son drew a plan for as Galileo was then blind. The first pendulum clock did not get built untill 14 years after Galileo died.

Elias Howe - Howe had a dream that led to the invention of the sewing machine. He was trying to duplicate the actions of a seamstress with a regular needle with a point on one end and a hole on the other end. It wouldn't work.

Then one night he dreamed that natives captured him. They told him they would execute him by morning if he did not complete the sewing machine invention.

As morning approached in the dream, the natives were closing in on him thrusting their spears back and forth menacingly as they got closer to him. When they got close enough, Howe realized that their spears had holes going through the points of the spears, from one side to the other. A hole...at the pointed end of the spear...moving back and forth, back and forth...

At that point, he awoke and realized that he had dreamed the solution. He ran to his shop and drilled a small hole in the pointed end of the needle instead of the back end, put thread through the hole, pushed it through the cloth, used another threat below the fabric...and he had invented the sewing machine. The problem was solved, and the rest is history.

Gordon Gould - Although he wasn't credited, Gould may have been the inventor of the laser. Strangely, the idea for the laser "came in a flash" of inspiration in 1957 exactly like Townes, credited with the invention.[138] Gould spent an entire weekend producing nine pages of calculations and then had the documentation notarized at a neighborhood candy store. Townes claimed his inspiration came to him in 1957 as well. Although Townes and two Soviet physicists shared the Nobel for the invention, Gould eventually was awarded the patent and the millions in royalties that went with it.

Alan Huang - Huang, an engineer with Bells Labs, had a dream of using optical laser circuits to replace conventional circuitry. The result was laser computers. The invention became optical computers, whose circuits run on light rather than electricity. Huang described the history of events:

> *I started to have computer dreams - about once a week. They're like [what you see] at halftime in a football game. Groups of people are marching along, and other groups march through them. But in the dreams it's not real people, it's sort of fluctuating colors merging, all these things marching along and through each other. And there are two groups of things, one thing sort of like instructions and the*

other sort of like data. The question in computing is whether instructions and data can merge and not tie up in a knot. In my computer dreams, these things marched around but kept winding up in a knot."

"Then one day I woke up, and I'd had a computer dream, but this time the people didn't march and get stuck in a huge pile. It had worked, and that bugged the hell out of me. I thought, 'Oh, my God, maybe there's a solution.' So I spent a month and a half looking for it - and the solution turned out to be similar to how I had merged McDonalds' and Burger King's hamburger processing. - It involved making all the devices and communication routes absolutely regular, like Buckminster Fuller's tessellated structures. This regularity at first looks inefficient because you can do it more simply, but on complicated problems it winds up more efficient because you spend less time housekeeping, keeping track of the data. Now you can take any particular computer problem and find a way to fold it to fit into the super-regular structure. I call it computer origami. It was the kind of thing I love to do, get myself into a situation where I don't understand what's going on, like, 'Toto, I don't think we're in Kansas anymore,' and then work my way out, and this time it was my dream that inspired me. Before, I didn't have the incentive to push it that far, but since it worked out in my dream, I started looking and found it. I believe in my subconscious. That's one thing scientists have to learn to go with."[139]

Phil Martens - Martens, was a designer with Ford who had a dream to reduce the high cost of building cars in America by standardizing among various Ford car lines. The idea he got was "Copy with pride. That's our mantra." The idea became for vehicle design teams to share designs and technologies among similar vehicles.

New Dimensions in Medicine - According to Silva instructor Ken Obermeyer, a researcher from New Dimensions in Medicine, had come to take a Silva Mind Course to help him develop an artificial artery that would not be rejected by the human body. Obermeyer stated that after the training, the researcher "awakened sometime during the night and wrote out a formula," then went back to sleep. "When he awakened in the morning, he saw the formula, went into the laboratory, put a sample together and found that the human body would accept his plastic.[140]

Larry Page - Page was one of the co-developers of Google. He got the idea for "downloading the entire web onto computers" during a 1996 dream. He told the graduation class at Michigan State, "You know what it's like to wake up in the middle of the night with a vivid dream? And you know how, if you don't have a pencil and pad by the bed to write it down, it will be completely gone the next morning? Well, I had one of those dreams when I was 23. When I suddenly woke up, I was thinking: what if we could download the whole web, and just keep the links and... I grabbed a pen and started writing! Sometimes it is important to wake up and stop dreaming. I spent the middle of that night scribbling out the details and convincing myself it would work. Soon after, I told my advisor, Terry Winograd, it would take a couple of weeks to download the web – he nodded knowingly, fully aware it would take much longer but wise enough to not tell me."[141]

David Parkinson - Parkinson was a Bell Laboratories technician who dreamed he was in Europe sitting close to an Allied artillery piece. What was significant was that this gun shot down every German plane. Parkinson wrote: "After three or four shots one of the men in the crew smiled at me and beckoned me to come closer to the gun. When I drew near, he pointed to the exposed end of the left trunnion. Mounted there was the control potentiometer of my level recorder. There was no mistaking it. It was the identical item."

He proposed the idea to Bell. The M9 gun was the result. It was very effective just like in the dream. "In one week in August of 1944, the M9's were credited with destroying 89 of 91 V-1 rockets launched from the Antwerp area toward England."[142]

Andrija Puharich - Puharich, a medical scientist and holder of more than 50 patents, gave his opinion about these strange inspirations: "I am personally convinced that superior beings from other spaces and other times have initiated a renewed dialogue with humanity.... While I do not doubt [their existence]... I do not know... what their goals are with respect to humankind."

Floyd Ragsdale - When it came to making Kevlar vests for the Gulf War, unfortunately for DuPont and the soldiers, the manufacturing machine kept breaking down. Engineers could not figure out what was going wrong. The problem was costing the company an estimated $700 an hour.

The problem was solved when one night an engineer, Floyd Ragsdale, had a dream that he was part of the production machine. Ragsdale saw water spraying all over the place, along with hoses and springs. When he woke up, he realized that the hoses must be collapsing and that springs would help keep them open.[143]

From a former NASA engineer who had an experiment on the International Space Station and sold his company for millions, "I clearly don't know where my first couple of patents came from. It felt like a memory one morning a few hours after I had gone to work. I knew it was profound, but I couldn't figure out how I learned this information. It changed my career at that moment all for the better. The thing with me though is I've never had an experience that I know of. I've not been regressed through hypnosis and maybe I should. I've only had a few dreams that felt very real and of them was a person standing at the foot of my bed in a white robe, but I never saw his face.

Ray Stanford - Stanford stated that he had received instruction for the Hilarion Accelerator, which would allow spiritually competent subjects to teleport physically from one place to another, or back in time. He received this from the Brothers.

Another invention he claimed to have received would "isolate a person from outside electromagnetic fields while enclosing him in a very high-energy electrostatic field. The Brothers say that the effect achieved would be very much like that which happened to Moses on top of Mt. Sinai.... Physically, the only thing that could have caused it was (that) the major electrolyte of the body ATP, was energized. This is one of the things we hope to do with this device - energize the ATP and enhance the process of consciousness."[144]

Nikola Tesla - Tesla was walking with a friend through a Budapest park when the solution to the rotating magnetic field flashed through his mind. Tesla referred to the vision as a polyphase - multiple magnetic fields or alternating motor. The motor had two rotating magnetic fields out of phase with each other. When one magnetic field stopped, the other would take over. It is considered one of the top 10 inventions of all times. According to some accounts, he was able to start and stop the vision of the motor, checking problems, and making adjustments. With a stick, he drew a diagram in the sand explaining to his friend the principle of the induction motor. Tesla described the event as follows:

> *The idea came like a flash of lightning and in an instant, the truth was revealed. I drew with a stick on the sand, the diagram shown six years later in my address before the American Institute of Electrical Engineers, and my companion understood them perfectly.*
>
> *The images I saw were wonderfully sharp and clear and had the solidity of metal and stone, so much so that I told him, 'See my motor here; watch me reverse it.' I cannot begin to describe my emotions. Pygmalion seeing his statue come to life could not have been more deeply moved. A thousand secrets of nature which I might have stumbled upon accidentally, I would have given for that one which I had wrested from her against all odds and at the peril of my existence..."*

James Watt - Watt who invented the steam engine described the eureka moment saying, "It was on the Green of Glasgow. I had gone to take a walk on a fine Sabbath afternoon. I had entered the Green by the gate at the foot of Charlotte Street - had passed the old washing-house. I was thinking upon the engine at the time, and had gone as far as the Herd's-house, when the idea came into my mind, that as steam was an elastic body it would rush into a vacuum, and if a communication was made between the cylinder and an exhausted vessel, it would rush into it, and might be there condensed without cooling the cylinder... I had not walked further than the Golf house ... when the whole thing was arranged in my mind."[145]

William Watts - In 1782 Watts discovered the modern method to produce buckshot for guns in a dream.

Eli Whitney - Whitney had a dream of the cotton gin where wires placed in a spinning drum would pull the cotton fibers through a comb that was too small for the cotton seeds top pass through.

Chapter 7 Inspirations for Nobel Prizes

The intellect has little to do on the road to discovery. There comes a leap in consciousness, call it intuition or what you will, and the solution comes to you, and you don't know how or why. **Albert Einstein**

I believe in intuitions and inspirations...I sometimes FEEL that I am right. I do not KNOW that I am. **Albert Einstein**

Winners of Nobel prizes have also reported inspirations and downloads. The indication is that the nonlocal transmission of information has occurred at the highest level of discovery recognized by western society.

Nobel Prize laureates have acknowledged this important aspect of innovation as evidenced in the following conversation that appeared in a BBC documentary. The conversation took place between Richard Feynman and Fred Hoyle.

Feynman shared the 1965 Nobel Prize with two other physicists for "for their fundamental work in quantum electrodynamics, with deep-ploughing consequences for the physics of elementary particles."

Hoyle, on the other hand, should have won at least one Nobel in 1983 for the central idea in modern astrophysics that all chemical elements get created inside stars by nucleosynthesis. The Nobel, however, was given to the scientist who confirmed Hoyle theory - William Fowler. Fowler and Hoyle produced their work in 1957 but in 1983 only Fowler received the Nobel. It was often brought up that Hoyle lost out on a Nobel because he had earlier criticized the Nobel committee about their selection of an earlier Nobel Prize awarded for the discovery of the pulsar.

Hoyle and Feynman discussed the strange occurrence of inspiration in scientific discovery, and both confessed that although they had both experienced it, they had no explanation or control over it.

Hoyle: You try all sorts of things, and you are hopeful about them. Have you had a moment when you have had a complicated problem where quite suddenly the thing comes into your head, and you are absolutely sure you have to be right?
Feynman: Oh Yes.
Hoyle: This is great!
Feynman: Oh God oh God. And then you try to figure out what the conditions were so you can do it again. For example, I worked out the theory of helium once, and I suddenly saw everything. I had been struggling for two years, and I suddenly saw everything. I remember everything about it. It is psychologically funny. You can remember the color of the paper you were writing on and the room. Isn't that true? Then you wonder what the psychological condition was. Well, I know at that particular time I just

looked up and said, "Wait a minute. It can't be quite that difficult. It must be very easy, so I will just stand back, and I'll just tape it. Bonk bonk, and there it was.

So how many times since then I am walking on a beach, and I say, "It can't be that complicated," and I tap it, tap tap, and nothing happens. The delights are great but...

Hoyle: It's that missing bit in the brain. It suddenly lights up and...

Feynman: I have thought about it because some man suggested that I think about that because if I could figure out what condition to be in for good ideas, I would be much more efficient and happy so I have often paid attention to what the condition is and have never found any correlation with anything.[146]

Here are a number of Nobel Prizes that were inspired by dreams or claimed spirits. These inspirations and downloads support the fact that some of the biggest ideas that have structured the modern world came from somewhere else.

Bob Dylan - Bob Dylan once said he was struggling to channel consciously what formerly came to him subconsciously. Listed as the # 2 musical artist of all time by *Rolling Stone Magazine*, Dylan wrote his 1962 song "Blowing in the Wind" in ten minutes one afternoon[147]. This quick creation is a common characteristic of many of the greatest songs of all times. Michael Des Barres, a member of Led Zeppelin and many other bands, stated that anything he ever wrote that became successful was always written in under five minutes.[148]

Dylan is on record as saying that the protest song, which he insisted wasn't a protest song came out of "that wellspring of creativity." Speaking of his early song creations, he stated that they "were magically written." [149] The first time he performed them, he couldn't read his personal handwriting and ended up have to adlib new lyrics.

In an interview with 60 Minutes Dylan was asked about the writing of his 1964 song "It All Right Ma." "It came out of that wellspring of creativity I would think," Dylan stated, "Try and sit down and write something like that. There's a magic to that, and it's not Siegfried and Roy kind of magic. It's a different penetrating kind of magic. I did it. I did it at one time." He added he doesn't think he can do that kind of magic anymore. "I don't know how I got to write those songs...those early songs were like almost magically written."

Asked why he still does the tours, Dylan said, "I don't take it for granted. It goes back to the destiny thing. I made a bargain with it a long time ago, and I am holding up my end." Asked what the bargain was, Dylan replied, "To get where I am now."

60 Minutes asked with who he made the agreement. Dylan chuckled and said, "With the chief commander in this earth and the Earth we can't see." [150]

Albert Einstein - 1921 - After years of working to figure out the general theory of relativity, the solution came to Einstein suddenly in a dream "like a giant die making an indelible impression, a huge map of the universe outlined itself in one clear vision." During his dream, we went on a toboggan ride at the speed of light that causes the heavens to bend. He described it this way,

> *I was sledding with my friends at night. I started to slide down the hill, but my sled started going faster and faster. I was going so fast that I realized I was approaching the speed of light. I looked up at that point, and I saw the stars. They were being refracted into colors I had never seen before. I was filled with a sense of awe. I understood in some way that I was looking at the most important meaning in my life.*[151]

Meditating upon that dream, Einstein eventually worked out his extraordinary scientific achievement, the principle of relativity, and was later awarded the Nobel Prize. He knew however that the vision had provided the basis for his ideas. "I knew I had to understand that dream," said Einstein, "and you could say, and I would say, that my entire scientific career has been a meditation on my dream."[152]

Neils Bohr - 1922 - Bohr worked on many designs to try to figure out what the structure of an atom was. According to three MIT researchers one evening during a dream, he saw the nucleus of the atom, with the electrons spinning around it "hissing around on tiny cords," just like our solar system with the sun and planets. Experiments confirmed the dream information.

The discovery of the quantum atom model also came to Bohr in a dream. He dreamt that he was at a horse track, and a voice was narrating to him how electrons stayed in orbit without collapsing into the nucleus. He was instructed that the horses had to stay in their lanes and that if they moved from one lane to the other, they must either speed up or slow down before changing lanes. This idea became the concept of fixed and distinct orbits of the quantum atom where electrons can jump orbits only when they absorb or emit a photon at the appropriate wavelength. This idea would win him the Nobel Prize in 1922.

Frederick G Banting - 1923 - Insulin and Nobel Prize. Banting was inspired to look for a cure after his mother passed away from diabetes. Others had linked the decrease to a problem with insulin, but they could not figure out the full connection and how it worked. Banting was unsuccessful until one night he went to sleep and dreamt of an experiment that would give him the results that he needed.

Melvin Calvin - The Nobel Prize in Chemistry for 1961 was awarded to Melvin Calvin "for his research on the carbon dioxide assimilation in plants." He described how in a moment of relaxation, the entire idea came to him.

"One day I was sitting in a car when my wife was on an errand. While sitting at the wheel of the car, the recognition of the missing piece occurred just like that - quite suddenly. Suddenly also in a matter of seconds, the complete cyclic character of the path of carbon dioxide became apparent to me. It all occurred to me in a matter of thirty seconds."

Francis Crick - Crick was the discoverer of the double helix DNA molecule and winner of the 1962 Nobel Prize in Physiology or Medicine. Secular scientists like Crick have maintained that the five senses and reason are what advance science. In this case LSD, however, it appeared to be the muse that led Crick to the discovery of the structure of DNA.

According to the *Mail on Sunday* in 2006 Crick had told a young biochemist Richard Kemp (who went on to produce a pure form of LSD before being raided by police) "that some Cambridge academics used LSD in tiny amounts as a thinking tool, to liberate them from preconceptions and let their genius wander freely to new ideas. Crick told him he had perceived the double-helix shape while on LSD."

When the newspaper asked Crick about the claim that his Nobel Prize had come with the help of LSD, Crick replied, "Print one word of it and I will sue." They printed it despite the threat.[153]

Dennis Gabor - 1971 - Inventor of the hologram. The invention came to Gabor during his work in trying to resolve the limitation posed by spherical aberration when it came to seeing an atom in the electronic microscope. His inspiration came in 1947 while he was sitting on a park bench watching people play tennis. Gabor called it "my luckiest find yet." His idea was to take an electron picture distorted by lens imperfections and correct it by optical means.

Werner Heisenberg - 1926 - Won the 1932 Nobel Prize for his role in the creation of quantum mechanics theory. His main contribution to the theory was one of the two organizing principles of quantum mechanics - the uncertainty principle (attempting to measure one attribute such as velocity or position may cause a second attribute to become less measurable). The theory came to him during a walk behind the Bohr Institute in Copenhagen after midnight. "I remember discussions with Bohr which went through many hours till very late at night and ended almost in despair. When at the end of the discussion I went alone for a walk in the neighboring park I repeated to myself, again and again, the question, can nature possibly be as absurd as it seems to us in these atomic experiments?" In a sudden insight, it became apparent to him what the position of the electron meant. He raced back to his apartment to write up the mathematics to describe it.

Rudyard Kipling - Kipling, who was the youngest-ever recipient of the Nobel Prize for Literature, spoke of receiving inspiration from a personal daemon, "Mine came to me early when I sat bewildered among other notions...(it said) 'Take this and no other.' I obeyed and was rewarded....My Daemon was with me in the Jungle Books, Kim, and both Puck books, and good care I took to walk delicately, lest he should withdraw. I know that he did not, because when those books were finished, they said so themselves with, almost, the water-hammer click of a tap turned off....When your Daemon is in charge, do not try to think consciously. Drift, wait, and obey."[154]

Otto Loewi - 1936 - Neurotransmission - Dr. Loewi won the Nobel Prize for his experiments that provided a framework for chemical synapse neurotransmission which is used daily on such medical techniques as managing drug therapy in Parkinson disease, inhibiting cholinesterase in myasthenia, or dilating the eye for an ophthalmoscopic exam.

Loewi described what happened,

> *"The night before Easter Sunday of that year (1920) I awoke, turned on the light, and jotted down a few notes on a tiny slip of this paper. Then I fell asleep again. It occurred to me at six o'clock in the morning that during the night I had written down something important, but I was unable to decipher the scrawl. The next night, at three o'clock, the idea returned. It was the design of an experiment to determine whether or not the hypothesis of chemical transmission that I had uttered seventeen years ago was correct. I got up immediately, went to the laboratory, and performed a simple experiment on a frog's heart according to the nocturnal design. Its results became the foundation of the theory of chemical transmission of the nervous impulse."*[155]

Kary Mullis - Mullis was the winner of the 1993 Nobel Prize in chemistry for his invention of a process that allows scientists to classify DNA genetic code fragments such as from a crime scene, mummified body, or wooly mammoth frozen in a glacier, and then reproduce it in vast quantities. The download came as Mullis was driving at night to his cottage in the Anderson Valley in North California. The "revelation" came when he was not looking for it "through an improbable combination of coincidences, naiveté, and lucky mistakes."[156] Later Mullis stated that "LSD had helped him develop the polymerase chain reaction." Mullis would also then openly talk about the fact that he and his daughter were experiencing alien abduction experiences. In Mullis's case, he encountered a glowing green raccoon (a standard screen image used by aliens during abductions) at his cottage which was followed by six hours missing time.

Mother Teresa - In 1946-47 Mother Teresa stated she received four visions. They led her to her work with the poor, orphans, and elderly in India and eventually the Nobel Peace Prize in 1979.

Between September 1946 and October 1947, Mother Teresa was given her four visions. In the first she saw the painful plight of the poor. They were reaching out to her for help.

In the second vision, Mother Teresa saw the same crowd of the poor...and the mother of Jesus was there in the midst of them. Mother Teresa was kneeled by Mother Mary who said to her, "Take care of them...they are mine...bring them to Jesus...carry them to Jesus...fear not...teach them to say the rosary...the family rosary and all will be well...fear not...Jesus and I will be with you and your children."

The same crowd of poor appeared in the fourth vision, but covered with darkness. In the midst of the crowd of poor that seemed unaware of His presence, was Jesus on the Cross. Mother Mary stood before him. Jesus spoke to Mother Teresa, "I have asked you...she, My Mother has asked you. Will you refuse to do this for me...to take care of them, to bring them to me?"[157]

Mother Teresa later confessed to Jesuit priest Father Celeste Van Exem about a third vision where she told Jesus to get lost - that Jesus was asking "too much." She added: "I can hardly grasp even half of what it is that you want. Go, Jesus, and look for a soul that is worthier and more generous."[158]

Jesus told her he had picked her because she was not perfect. He said he wanted, "Indian nuns, missionaries of charity" who could be the "fire of my love among the poorest of the poor, the sick, the dying, the children in the streets. I want you to bring the poor to me."

Mother Teresa began her Indian mission the next year - 1948. She never discussed her visions during her life fearing that a cult would form around her.

This rejection of a job being turned down from a higher directive in apparition has a direct parallel to a story in ufology.

In January 2007 Chris Bledsoe had an awakening experience along with four others that made him aware of the fact that he had been abducted, and that he had made a promise to the aliens before birth to bring a message to the world.

In his 2008 regression with Dr. Michael O'Conner Chris hinted that the being had chosen him:

> *Why me? All my life? My son's life. Promise. All be strong for them. I know. I know. Tell them not to worry. Hard. OK. I love my family. I'll calm down. Why? Why? Why was I chosen? Where are we?*
>
> Dr. O'Conner asked, *"are they telling you why you're chosen?"* Chris replied, *"Uh-huh.* O'Conner then asked, *"What reason was that?"*
>
> *"Since birth,"* replied Bledsoe. *"Before birth. It's possible. Everything is possible. They're my Guardians.*

Every time I get sad, they are here. I know I was sad. Promise. Promise."

The regression led to a documentary by the Discovery Channel, which did not go well in the Bible belt area of North Carolina where he lived. He was completely ostracized by everyone he knew, and he decided never to talk about it again.

Then in February and October 2012 Bledsoe had two more encounters this time with what he calls the "Shining Lady." The aliens had taken him to her. In both meetings, she said the same thing, "Chris you have a burden, and it is yours to carry." The burden was the message, and the message was that his job was to talk about his experience despite the reaction of those around him. At that point Bledsoe again went public with what had happened to him and the four other witnesses.

Charles Townes - 1964 - Charles Townes developed the MASER principles which led to the invention of the laser, and a Nobel Prize awarded in 1964. Townes recalled that the idea to use light instead of microwaves which were being utilized by the MASER came in an inspired moment on a park bench.

I worked on it and worked on it, and nothing worked. I woke up early in the morning, went out in the park, sat on a park bench worrying about it, thinking, "Why haven't we been able to get any ideas?" I said, well we tried this, tried that, and... Ooh, wait a minute! Atoms and molecules can do this... Oh, I think I see a way of using them to do it -- to have them do it for us. So, I had this sudden realization that we could do it. It was a great moment for me. I quickly pulled out a pen and wrote down some notes and equations. "Yeah," I thought. "It looks like it will probably work."[159]

J. Robin Warren - H. pylori - Warren was one of the two doctors who discovered H. Pylori, a bacterium that causes ulcers in the stomach which was discovered despite significant opposition in the medical community. In his Nobel Prize winning speech, Warren stated, "It came out of the blue. I happened to be there at the right time."

James Watson - co-discoverer of the structure of DNA, came upon the double helix image for the DNA molecule through an LSD altered state of consciousness of a spiral staircase.

William Butler Yeats - Yeats won the Nobel Prize in 1923 for literature. Although he did not win because of it one of his most famous plays, Catherine Ni Houlihan came from a dream that Yeats had in 1902. He also had done extensive experiments in automatic writing with his new wife that resulted in his metaphysical book *A Vision*. His wife held the pen, and there were 450 sessions held where he produced 3627 pages from 8672 questions asked that Yeats studied carefully to formulate theories about life and history.[160] ""If I had not made magic my constant study I could not have written a single word of my Blake book, nor would Countess Kathleen ever have come to exist," wrote Yeats. "The mystical life is the center of all that I do and all that I think and all that I write."[161]

Chapter 8 Inspirations for Scientific Discoveries

I did not arrive at my understanding of the universe through my rational mind. **Albert Einstein**

The day science begins to study nonphysical phenomena, it will make more progress in one decade than in all the previous centuries of its existence. **Nikola Tesla**

The seed which ripens into vision may be the gift of the Gods, but the labor of cultivating it so that it may bear nourishing fruit is the indispensable function of arduous scientific technique." **Morris R. Cohen**

The story of scientific discoveries has the same telltale accounts of inspirations and downloads moments quite separate from information gathered by the five senses. It illustrates a model where the left brain collects the data through much hard work but is the right brain that has the password to the nonlocal holographic store of knowledge and brings back the scientific discovery.

The scientific establishment has suppressed the story of these tales of scientific inspiration.

An example of this was the development of the theory of evolution where Alfred Russell Wallace, who came up the idea of the "survival of the fittest," differed with Darwin over whether natural selection could explain everything. He was also openly supportive of the spiritualist movement of the time. He wrote Darwin, "'Natural Selection could only have endowed the savage with a brain a little superior to that of an ape, whereas he actually possesses one but very little inferior to that of the average members of our learned societies...we must, therefore, admit the possibility, that in the development of the human race, a Higher Intelligence has guided the same laws of variation, multiplication, and survival] for nobler ends." [162]

When Darwin received this, he scribbled "No" in the margin, underlined it three times and added many explanation marks beside it. He wrote Wallace saying that natural selection could explain it all and warned Wallace about the damage his ideas were creating, "I hope you have not murdered too completely your own and my child."

Darwin gained control over the theory, and the concept of random selection has been a doctrine of faith for scientists ever since. The ideas of Wallace who came up with most of the theory of evolution have disappeared from the history of the discovery.

Then there was the story Sigmund Freud, who in 1922 published an article "Dreams and Telepathy" and a full-length article titled, "Psychoanalysis and Telepathy." He planned to read this defense of telepathy at the 1922 International Psychoanalytic Congress of 1922.

That was until cornered by Ernest Jones, founder of the British Psychoanalytical Society, who warned him about the damaging repercussions his paper would have on the whole fledgling psychoanalytic movement. Freud was won over, and the article did not see print until 1941 after Freud died.

Again in 1924 Freud prepared to support telepathy after being very impressed with a report on telepathic experiments prepared for the Society for Psychical Research by Oxford professor Gilbert Murray. As he prepared himself to support thought-transference publically and provided the support of psychoanalysis to the matter, he was again confronted by Jones. Once again he was convinced of the damage that would ensue and withdrew his support of Murray's work.[163]

The stories vindicate the father of quantum physics who stated, "A new scientific truth does not triumph by convincing its opponents and making them see the light, but rather because its opponents eventually die, and a new generation grows up that is familiar with it."

The Downloads

Probably the most famous of all scientific discovery stories is Sir Isaac Newton and his discovery of gravitational theory when she saw an apple fall in his mother's garden. The story was voiced many times such as by William Stukeley, who wrote the Memoirs of Sir Isaac Newton's Life in 1752. The idea came to Newton in a sudden moment of inspiration.

> *After dinner, the weather being warm, we went into the garden and drank the, under the shade of some apple trees...he told me, he was just in the same situation, as when formerly, the notion of gravitation came into his mind. It was occasion'd by the fall of an apple, as he sat in contemplative mood. Why should that apple always descend perpendicularly to the ground, thought he to himself..."*[164]

Perhaps the next biggest scientific discovery - the theory of evolution - came through the same sudden download process. It happened in February 1858 by Russell Wallace who was suffering from a raging fever. He recorded the event.

> *I was suffering from a sharp attack of intermittent fever, and every day during the cold and succeeding hot fits had to lie down for several hours... Then it suddenly flashed upon me that ... the fittest would survive. ... I became convinced that I had at length found the long-sought-for law of nature that solved the problem of the origin of species. ... I waited*

anxiously for the termination of my fit so that I might at once make notes for a paper on the subject. The same evening I did this pretty fully, and on two succeeding evenings wrote it out carefully in order to send it to Darwin.[165]

Wallace sent the inspired idea to Charles Darwin, who shamelessly ripped off the idea as something he arrived at through reason as pointed out by more and more writers such as Roy Davies.[166]

Many scientific discoveries have come from close observation of how the universe does things. In this case, the innovations came from a back-engineering process of reproducing something that was already in place.

The copy process is a familiar story in modern science. An example is the claim that nitinol, night vision technology, fiber optics, and the transistor got developed by back-engineering material recovered in the 1947 UFO crash near Roswell, New Mexico.

In a similar story, Ben Rich, the former President of Lockheed Skunk Works stated in a 1993 speech to the engineering alumni at UCLA, that Lockheed now had the technology to take ET home because engineers had discovered mistakes in the equation.

When Dr. Barry Taff asked him during the question period if the technology had been developed or acquired, Rich said "what do you think?

Taff stated, "Acquired."

"You may be right," replied Rich.

Most of the scientific community has rejected the idea that some modern technology may be technology from aliens. Most of the same scientists have also rejected inspiration as a source of new discoveries and techniques. The theory put forward by the dialectical materialism is that the only two ways to attaining knowledge were through the five senses and reason.

When Max Planck entered the University of Munich in 1875, a Professor Philip Jolly urged him not to take science as everything had already been discovered.

In 1923 physics Nobel Prize winner Robert A. Millikan was told much the same thing in 1894 when he roomed with four graduate students who were taking the new live field of the social sciences. "I was ragged continuously," recalled Millikan, "for sticking to a 'dead subject' like physics."

Lord Kelvin continued to demonstrate the ego of science when he stated, "There is nothing new to be discovered in physics now. All that remains is more and more precise measurement."[167]

He was followed shortly after by Michelson, who stated in 1903 "The most fundamental laws and facts of physical science have all been discovered, and these are now so firmly established that the possibility of ever being supplemented in consequence of new discoveries is exceedingly remote."[168]

What follows is a list of ideas and inventions that defy this explanation of the invention. What these examples will show is that invention may not be a left brain rational exercise. It may, in fact, be a brain action where the idea or invention downloads if from somewhere outside the brain.

Andre-Marie Ampere - Ampere was the man who formulated the law of electromagnetism, called after him Ampère's law that describes the magnetic force between two electrical currents mathematically. Ampere described one of his inspirational downloads, "I gave a shout of joy…it was seven years ago that I proposed to myself a problem which I have not been unable to solve directly, but for which I found by chance a solution, and knew it was correct, without being able to prove it."[169]

Louis Agassiz - One of the fathers of modern fish fossils had a dream about one fish captured inside a rock that he was afraid to try and excise. His wife described what happened,

> *Weary and perplexed, he put his work aside at last, and tried to dismiss it from his mind. Shortly after, he wakened one night persuaded that while asleep he had seen his fish with all the missing features perfectly restored. But when he tried to hold and make fast the image it escaped him. Nevertheless, he went early to the Jardin des Plantes, thinking that on looking anew at the impression he should see something which would put him on the track of his vision. In vain--the blurred record was as blank as ever.*
>
> *"The next night he saw the fish again, but with no more satisfactory result. When he awoke, it disappeared from his memory as before. Hoping that the same experience might be repeated, on the third night, he placed a pencil and paper beside his bed before going to sleep.*
>
> *Accordingly, towards morning the fish reappeared in his dream, confusedly at first, but at last with such distinctness that he had no longer any doubt as to its zoological characters. Still half dreaming, in perfect darkness, he traced these characters on the sheet of paper at his bedside. In the morning, he was surprised to see in his nocturnal sketch features which he thought it impossible the fossil itself should reveal. He hastened to the Jardin des Plantes, and, with his drawing as a guide, succeeded in chiseling away the surface of the stone under which portions of the fish proved to be hidden. When wholly exposed it corresponded with his dream and his drawing, and he succeeded in classifying it with ease."[170]*

Rene Descartes - claimed that the dreams he had on November 10, 1619, revealed to him the basis of a new philosophy, and the scientific method. Most importantly his discovery of analytical geometry was inspired by the second of the three mystical dreams which occurred that day, after a feast on Saint Martin's Eve. The discovery of analytical geometry was particularly important as it provided the basis of calculus that has helped to describe the physics of the universe.

Dr. J. Norman Emerson - Emerson was a senior professor at the University of Toronto and the founding vice-president of the Canadian Archeological Association. He often used a psychic to make archeological discoveries. "It is my conviction," Emerson told the 1973 gathering of the archeological elite, "that I have received knowledge about archaeological artifacts and archaeological sites from psychic information from a psychic informant who relates this information to me without any evidence of the conscious use of reasoning." [171] The man who provided the information which would uncover the history of many Indian tribe histories in Canada was George McMullen. Later another psychic was employed named Sheila Conway.

Carl Friedrich Gauss - Gauss, a German, was coined "greatest mathematician since antiquity," and stated, "As a sudden flash of light, the enigma was solved....For my part, I am unable to name the nature of the thread which connected what I previously knew with that which made my success possible."[172]

Jacques Hadamard - Hadamard made major contributions in number theory, complex function theory, differential geometry and partial differential equations. He said this of his burst of creative insight, "On being very abruptly awakened by an external noise, a solution long searched for appeared to be at once without the slightest instant of reflection on my part...and in a different direction from any of those which I had previously tried to follow."[173]

Friedrich Kekule - Kekule was a prolific scientist who claimed that "three-fourths of modern organic chemistry is directly or indirectly the product of his theory. Much of his theory came in dreams, and he had two dreams in 1865 that inspired him to make two significant scientific discoveries in organic chemistry. In one dream he saw a snake swallowing its own tail. He awakened and drew what he had seen which was the circular ring shape of the benzene molecule. He didn't win the Nobel Prize as they were not be awarded at that time but three of the first five Nobels in chemistry were awarded to students of his - Hoff in 1901, Fischer in 1902 and Baeyer in 1905. He described the dream,

> ...I was sitting writing on my textbook, but the work did not progress; my thoughts were elsewhere. I turned my chair to the fire and dozed. Again the atoms were gamboling before my eyes. This time, the smaller groups kept modestly in the

> background. My mental eye, rendered more acute by the repeated visions of the kind, could now distinguish larger structures of manifold conformation; long rows sometimes more closely fitted together all twining and twisting in snake-like motion. But look! What was that? One of the snakes had seized hold of its own tail, and the form whirled mockingly before my eyes. As if by a flash of lightning I awoke; and this time also I spent the rest of the night in working out the consequences of the hypothesis.

In an earlier dream, he had discovered the tetravalent nature of carbon, the foundation of structural organic chemistry.

> I fell into a reverie, and lo, the atoms were gamboling before my eyes! Whenever, hitherto, these diminutive beings had appeared to me, they had always been in motion; but up to that time, I had never been able to discern the nature of their motion. Now, however, I saw how, frequently, two smaller atoms united to form a pair; how a larger one embraced the two smaller ones; how still larger ones kept hold of three or even four of the smaller; whilst the whole kept whirling in a giddy dance. I saw how the larger ones formed a chain, dragging the smaller ones after them, but only at the ends of the chain....The cry of the conductor: "Clapham Road," awakened me from my dreaming; but I spent part of the night in putting on paper at least sketches of these dream forms. This was the origin of the Structural Theory.

In yet a third dream, he came up with the theory that is the basis of all organic chemistry - there exist bonds between atoms. He described the reverie that occurred on a horse-drawn street bus, this way,

> I feel into a reverie and Lo! The atoms were gamboling before my eyes...I saw how, frequently, two smaller atoms united to form a pair, how a larger one embraced the two smaller ones; how a still larger one kept hold of the three or even four of the smaller; whilst the whole kept whirling in a giddy dance. I saw how the larger ones formed a chain, dragging the smaller ones after them.[174]

Dimitri Mendeleyev - Mendeleyev created the entire periodic table from a dream. He had fallen asleep while playing chamber music in the next room. The vision showed him the relationship of the chemical elements to the themes and phrases in music. When he awakened, he was able to write out for the first time the entire periodic table, and make predictions for future elements not yet discovered. Also, the table produced had the items listed by atomic weight which was still unknown. "In a dream I saw a table where all the elements fell into place as required," wrote Mendeleev, Awakening, I immediately wrote it down on a piece of paper."[175]

Eadweard Muybridge - Muybridge was an eccentric, creative, and obsessive scientist of the late 19th century who became that way after a head injury suffered in a stage coach accident. Today Muybridge might be considered to be an acquired savant where the left frontal lobe is injured, and the creative right side takes over without any rational questioning mind to fight off. Muybridge became famous for an innovative idea to figure out the running motion of a horse - whether or not all legs are off the ground at the same time during the galloping motion, or was one foot always planted. Muybridge developed photographic techniques to record the minute movements of a horse while in motion. These photographs made him famous.

Henri Poincare - was a celebrated mathematician who pioneered chaos theory and mathematical methods that are still employed in studying elementary particles. Poincare was trying to discover some general method by which to solve a whole group of equations. The answer came in a dream. When he awoke, he found several sheets of paper on a table by the bed on which he had worked out a complete solution to the problem.

On the development of Fuchsian functions, Poincare wrote, "For fifteen days I strove to prove that there could not be any functions like those I have since called Fuchsian functions. I was then very ignorant; every day I seated myself at my work table, stayed an hour or two, tried a high number of combinations and reached no results. One evening, contrary to my custom, I drank black coffee and could not sleep. Ideas rose in crowds; I felt them collide until pairs interlocked, so to speak, making a stable combination. By the next morning, I had established the existence of a class of Fuchsian functions, those which came from the hypergeometric series; I had only to write out the results, which took but a few hours."

And on one thorny mathematical problem he wrote, "One morning, walking on the bluff. The idea came to me, with brevity, suddenness, and immediate certainty....Most striking at first is this appearance of the sudden illumination, a manifest sign of long, unconscious prior work. The role of the unconscious work in mathematical invention appears to be incontestable."[176]

Srinivasa Ramanujan (1887-1920) was an Indian mathematical genius who made substantial contributions to the analytical theory of numbers and worked on elliptical functions, continued fractions, infinite series, and for proving over 3,000 theorems in his lifetime. On his deathbed, he created a formula that was verified almost a hundred years later that could explain the behaviors of black holes.[177]

Michio Kaku said of Ramanujan, "Srinivasa Ramanujan was the strangest man in all of the mathematics, probably in the entire history of science. He has been compared to a bursting supernova, illuminating the darkest, most profound corners of mathematics, before being tragically struck down by tuberculosis at the age of 33.... Working in total isolation from the main currents of his field, he was able to re-derive 100 years' worth of Western mathematics on his own."[178]

All of this inspiration, according to Ramanujan came in dreams from a Hindu goddess, named Namakkal. Ramanujan explained one such dream, "While asleep I had an unusual experience. There was a red screen formed by flowing blood as it were. I was observing it. Suddenly a hand began to write on the screen. I became all attention. That hand wrote a number of results in elliptic integrals. They stuck to my mind. As soon as I woke up, I committed them to writing..."[179]

One such formula given to Ramanujan is used for checking the accuracy of Supercomputers and in calculating the value of π to one billion places.

$$\frac{1}{\pi} = \frac{2\sqrt{2}}{9801} \sum_{k=0}^{\infty} \frac{(4k)!(1103 + 26390k)}{(k!)^4 396^{4k}}$$

Even stranger is the fact that his mother had a vivid dream in which the family Goddess, the deity of Namagiri, commanded her "to stand no longer between her son and the fulfillment of his life's purpose" as Ramanujan was preparing to go to England.[180]

Nikola Tesla - Tesla reported a condition in which blinding flashes of light would appear before his eyes, often accompanied by visions. Often, the visions were linked to a word or idea he might have come across; at other times, they would provide the solution to a particular problem he had encountered. Just by hearing the name of an item, he would be able to envision it in realistic detail. Tesla would visualize an invention in his mind with extreme precision, including all dimensions, before moving to the construction stage, a technique sometimes known as picture thinking. He typically did not make drawings by hand but worked from memory. Beginning in his childhood, Tesla had frequent flashbacks to events that had happened previously in his life.

Vicki - a girl, blind from birth, had two NDEs. In the second one, she reported she had been downloaded with knowledge about everything including languages, "I had a feeling like I knew everything... and like everything made sense. I just knew that this was where ... this place was where I would find the answers to all the questions about life, and about the planets, and about God, and about everything.... It's like the place was the knowing.... I don't know beans about math and science.... I all of a sudden understood intuitively almost things about calculus, and about the way planets were made. And I don't know anything about that.... I felt there was nothing I didn't know."[181]

Jon Von-Neumann - Von-Neumann was a brilliant man with an eidetic memory. He slept only four hours a night and had discovered a way to work while asleep. He gave himself problems to solve before sleeping. At 4 am, he would race to write down what his unconscious mind had revealed. He reported "he was working on a proof that set theory is consistent. The next night he dreamed again and got very near to completion. It is a mercy; he said that he did not dream on the third night; otherwise, he would have confidently proved what Godel later showed to be untrue."[182]

Chapter 9 Inspirations for Books

He'll be famous - a legend - I wouldn't be surprised if today was known as Harry Potter Day in the future - there will be books written about Harry - every child in our world will know his name!" **A line on page 15 in the very first Harry Potter book which 12 publishers turned down as not marketable.**

Show up, show up, show up, and after a while, the muse shows up too. **Novelist Isabel Allende**

"So when I heard that story (Tom Waits song inspiration), it started to shift a little bit the way that I worked too, and it already saved me once. This idea, it saved me when I was in the middle of writing *Eat, Pray, Love*, and I fell into one of those, sort of pits of despair that we all fall into when we're working on something, and it's not coming, and you start to think this is going to be a disaster, this is going to be the worst book ever written. Not just bad, but the worst book ever written. And I started to think I should just dump this project. But then I remembered Tom talking to the open air, and I tried it. So I just lifted my face up from the manuscript, and I directed my comments to an empty corner of the room. And I said aloud, "Listen you, thing, you and I both know that if this book isn't brilliant, that is not entirely my fault, right? Because you can see that I am putting everything I have into this, I don't have any more than this. So if you want it to be better, then you've got to show up and do your part of the deal. O.K. But if you don't do that, you know what, the hell with it. I'm going to keep writing anyway because that's my job. And I would please like the record to reflect today that I showed up for my part of the job." **Elizabeth Gilbert, whose book *Eat Pray Love* remained on " Sellers list for 187 weeks.**

Most people have had the dream of being a published author. Many have made some try at it finding out quickly that it is easier said than done. To others, like the nine-year-old daughter of Nobel Laureate George Wald, the Harvard neurobiologist who won the Nobel Prize in 1967 for his work with pigments in the retina, writing comes easier; at least for a few moments of inspiration. As Wald told the story is an essay, "Life, and Mind in the Universe" his daughter and son were playing in her room when the son picked up a piece of paper off the floor. He told her it was a good poem and showed it to Wald and his wife. It read:

If you ever get to infinity
You will find me there
For tomorrow, I will climb
The elementary stair.
I will climb to the very top
Open up the door
Look at all the ages
Lying on the floor.

Wald saw it as much more than a good poem but more as a mysterious inspiration.

> *To me, that is not just a good poem; it is a revelation. How could a little, middle class, nine-year-old American girl, living a carefully nurtured life, going to a select private school - how could such a child write such a poem? And that was it: there never was another like it, and I doubt that there ever will be. I don't really understand how that poem happened, but I think that at that time in her life an intuitive wisdom which distilled into those words was connected with what we should like to be connected, but have lost contact with and would have to work hard and change very much to reestablish it.*

As with musical, inventions, and scientific discovery downloads, many of the principal authors of the 20th Century have reported receiving direction from aliens, spirits, guides, or through entities met in near-death experiences (NDEs), or in dreams.

Breton and Philippe Soupault wrote the first automatic book, *Les Champs Magnétiques* in 1919, while Breton wrote the *The Automatic Message* in 1933.

Like the downloads and direction given to musicians, inventors, and scientists the process seems to be an activity of creative right-brained individuals who have somehow tapped into something akin to a universal consciousness, global internet, Akashic record, or some nonlocal entity that is passing the information to the author.

Even before the understanding of the right-brain unconscious mind, writers like Graham Wallas in his book *The Art of Thought*, spoke about what he called the incubation stage that was necessary for inspirational ideas. He stated it was a process of "relaxing the conscious cognition."

Some writers such as Sasha White the author of *Wicked* and other novels even use this knowledge of tapping into the nonlocal. White employs it all the time to write her books. "I lie down and close my eyes and think," said

White, "What would happen next? Then that's when the ideas come. The trick is remembering the ideas when you wake up."

Brenda Ueland talked about trying to tap into this hypnagogic state in her classic book *If You Want To Write*. She suggested that writers start writing at their desk as soon as they wake up before the ideas flow away. Ueland opines turning on the computer should come first.

The technique is the same one used to record dreams. Dr. Russell Targ, who co-directed the CIA work into remote viewing, stated that you must write down your dreams before the movement of the major muscles in the body quenches the dream.

Here are some of the many authors who have reported being helped by something or someone outside of themselves.

P.M.H. Atwater - Atwater is one of the foremost authorities in the world on near death experiences. She has authored 12 books on the subject, and she has lectured around the world. Her interest in the subject arose from three near death experiences that she had during complications related to a pregnancy in 1977.

During the third near death experience, she heard a voice that gave her instructions to write three books on the subject of near-death experiences. This is what Atwater clearly recalled happening:

> *"Then a voice spoke. I was used to guides and guardians and angels and all those kinds of voices. It wasn't that kind of voice. It was a voice so big. Let me describe how big, big big big big big. That voice filled the entire universe and all of creation. That's how big that voice was. And that voice said to me, and I quote, 'test revelation.' You are to do the research, one book for each day. It did not name book 1. It did name books 2 & 3, future memory is book 2. It showed me what all this meant and what was to be in each book. It did not tell me did how to do work or how long it would take."*

Richard Bach - Bach wrote the book *Jonathan Livingston Seagull*: In 1959 Bach heard what he called a "disembodied voice" whisper the title of the book. It was not the first time he experienced a "voice" giving him instruction. He had heard a voice while flying that told him to "PULL UP." The incident saved his life. He immediately wrote the first few chapters of the work before running out of inspiration. Bach shelved the half-finished manuscript until eight years later. It was then that he had a dream about the now-famous titular seagull, which enabled him to complete what has become one of the most profound and philosophically moving novels ever written. The book spent 38 weeks on The New York Times Best Sellers list.

L. Frank Baum - Baum wrote the *Wizard of Oz* from an instant inspiration download according to his grandson who relayed the story to Jean Houston.[183] On the way into his Chicago home, he was overwhelmed by a flood of images that would become the book. "Suddenly," wrote Baum, "this [one] story came in and took possession," he later marveled. "The story really seemed to write itself....I grabbed a piece of paper that was lying there."[184] On another occasion, he stated, "It was pure inspiration. It came to me right out of the blue."[185]

Allison Brennan - Brennan, a New York Times bestselling author, said, "The most common experience for me is solving plot problems in my dreams."[186]

Charlotte Bronte - *Jane Eyre* - Part of the eponymous character's personal arc stems from her highly detailed dreams, both asleep and diurnal slips in and out of consciousness. Though she may not have necessarily pulled inspiration from her personal dreams, Charlotte Bronte wielded the standard literary device of prophetic, unconscious mind visions, carefully taping their real-life hallucinatory, stream-of-consciousness structure.

John Bunyan - Though no definitive answers exist regarding whether or not John Bunyan launched the classic *Pilgrim's Progress* because of his dreams, he certainly pulled plenty of inspiration from their structure. So while nobody knows for certain, the fact that he so diligently paid attention to how they operated to pen his unearthly prose still earns him a place on this list.

Suzanne Clarke - *Jonathan Strange & Mr. Norrell* was a novel that won the 2005 Hugo Award for Best Novel and was #3 on The New York Times Best Sellers list. Clarke spoke of its origin, "I had a kind of waking dream ... about a man in 18th-century clothes in a place rather like Venice, talking to some English tourists. And I felt strongly that he had some magical background - he'd been dabbling in magic, and something had gone badly wrong."[187]

Judy Carroll - Another author who got instructions to write books is Judy Carroll, who received instruction by aliens to write three books, "Human by Day: Zeta by Night," "Looking through the Eyes of Love," and "The Zeta Message: Connecting All People in Oneness." Carroll talked about the third upgrade in her life by the aliens in 1995 that led to the instruction,

"The third upgrade in June 1995 included detailed instructions in the writing of these books for the purposes of relaying information on ET/human contact from their perspective to present their side of the story but also my side as a lifelong experiencer/participant and my subsequent journey of awakening."[188]

Samuel Taylor Coleridge - *Kubla Khan* - One of the most famous examples of dream-inspired literature, the famous poem - printed in the book *Christabel* - wafted into Coleridge's brain from a combination of sleep and opium. One of his most beloved works, he described it as a "fragment" rather than a whole, though most critics these days analyze it as the latter.

Karyn Crisis - Former lead singer for the band Crisis, Karyn has now written a couple of books. "These I have gotten from my (soul) guide, so I don't sit down at the computer, and I have never considered myself a writer. So the idea of writing a book is something that my mind finds very stressful, but when my spirit guides wanted me to write these books…I would just sit down at my computer, and all I would have to do is type. Sometimes they would want to keep me typing for hours. I don't edit any of the things. I don't go back and change anything except typos, so it's a very interesting process of them wanting me to write this information."[189]

Pearl Curran - In 1913, Curran, then a 31-year-old homemaker, was playing with an Ouija board when a message came across, "Many moons ago I lived. Patience Worth my name. Wait, I would speak with thee. If thou shalt live, then so shall I. I make my bread at thy hearth. Good friends, let us be merry. The time for work is past. Let the tabby drowse and blink her wisdom to the fire log."

The spirit Patience Worth claimed to have lived between 1649 and 1694. Worth began to download an incredible four-million-word collection of books and poetry exhibiting, "phenomenal memory, phenomenal speed, and phenomenal complexity of mental operations."[190] The collection of writings received praise from the *Hartford Courant, Los Angeles Times*, and the *New York Times*. William Marion Reedy, a literary critic considered The Sorry Tale to be a new classic of world literature. Patience Worth was listed as one of the outstanding authors of 1918 by The Joint Committee on Literary Arts of New York. The prestigious Braithwaite anthology listed five of her poems among the nation's best published in 1917, and the *New York Times* hailed her first novel as a "feat of literary composition." Stephen Braude, a professor of philosophy at the University of Maryland stated, "What is extraordinary about this case is the fluidity, versatility, virtuosity and literary quality of Patience's writings, which are unprecedented in the history of automatic writing by mediums." [191]

Curran gave her last channeling session November 25, 1937, where Patience said she was at the "end of the road." Although Curran was not sick, she developed pneumonia and died eight days later at the age of 54.

Philip K. Dick - was another author that Brad Steiger identified as someone who was getting help from somewhere else. Dick was the fictional author whose works led to the movies *Blade Runner, Total Recall, Minority Report, A Scanner Darkly, Paycheck,* and *Next*. Dick believed that he was one of the Star People described by Brad Steiger in his book *Gods of Aquarius: UFOs and* the *Transformation of Man* released in 1976.

Steiger identified the Star People as "individuals who feel that they bear within their gene awareness that is acquired by extraterrestrial interaction with humans in prehistoric or ancient times and who have now been activated by DNA memory to fulfill a mission of assisting others in their spiritual and advancement."

Steiger was told this by Dick in 1977 a year after the publication and added that in 1974 "he was shown in a vision, 'more properly, an inner hologram,' the cover of my book, *Revelation: The Divine Fire* (Prentice-Hall, 1973). A feminine voice told him that this book would help him to understand what was occurring to him. He was also told by the voice to get in touch with me."

Dick told Steiger that he was writing a similar book on the Star People concept called *Valis* (released in 1981) but that it would be fiction. "I wish to hide behind the veil of fiction," he told Steiger. "I can claim that I made the whole thing up. The revelations that I received were so astounding that it has taken me five years to arrive at a place where I will even put forth the concept as fiction."

Mary Ann Evans - According to her husband, the 19th-century writer's best work, was something that was "not herself." It took possession of her, and she felt that her personality to be "merely the instrument which this spirit, as it were, was acting."[192]

Elizabeth Gilbert - Author of the phenomenal selling "Eat Pray Love," said, "I'm not the pipeline! I'm a mule, and the way that I have to work is that I have to get up at the same time every day, and sweat and labor and barrel through it really awkwardly. But even I, in my mulishness, even I have brushed up against that thing, at times. And I would imagine that a lot of you have too. You know, even I have had work or ideas come through me from a source that I honestly cannot identify. And what is that thing? And how are we to relate to it in a way that will not make us lose our minds, but, in fact, might actually keep us sane?" [193]

Joseph Heller - Author of "Catch-22" - "I was lying in bed in my four-room apartment on the West Side when suddenly this line came to me: 'It was love at first sight. The first time he saw the chaplain, someone fell madly in love with him.' I didn't have the name Yossarian. The chaplain wasn't necessarily an army chaplain - he could have been a prison chaplain. But as soon as the opening sentence was available, the book began to evolve clearly in my mind - even most of the particulars…. The tone, the form, many of the characters, including some I eventually couldn't use. All of this took place within an hour and a half. It got me so excited that I did what the cliché says you're supposed to do: I jumped out of bed and paced the floor. That morning I went to my job at the advertising agency and wrote out the first chapter in longhand…. I don't understand the process of imagination - though I know that I am very much at its mercy. I feel that these ideas are floating around in the air, and they pick me to settle upon."[194]

Lisa Hendrix - Hendrix is the author of "Immortal Outlaw" and other Novels. She stated, "If I can wake slowly, with no interruptions or urgent need to get up, and just drift for a while, my mind comes up with the most marvelous things which I then jot down." [195]

Carl Jung - Jung wrote the book *The Seven Sermons to the Dead written by Basilides in Alexandria*. According to his account:

> It began with a restlessness, but I did not know what it meant or what "they" wanted of me. There was an ominous atmosphere all around me. I had the strange feeling that the air was filled with ghostly entities. Then it was as if my house began to be haunted....
>
> *Around five o'clock in the afternoon on Sunday the front doorbell began ringing frantically...but there was no one in sight. I was sitting near the doorbell, and not only heard it but saw it moving. We all simply stared at one another. The atmosphere was thick, believe me! Then I knew that something had to happen. The whole house was filled as if there were a crowd present, crammed full of spirits. They were packed deep right up to the door, and the air was so thick it was scarcely possible to breathe. As for myself, I was all a-quiver with the question: "For God's sake, what in the world is this?" Then they cried out in chorus, 'We have come back from Jerusalem where we found not what we sought.' That is the beginning of the Septem Sermones."* In three evenings Jung had completed the book and the haunting ended as quickly as it started.[196]

Jack Kerouac - "Book of Dreams" - Everything readers need to know about this novel comes straight from the title. Beat poster boy Jack Kerouac kept and published a book comprised entirely of his dreams, spanning from 1952 to 1960 and starring characters from many of his other works.

Steven King - King, who is one of the top horror novelists of all times used dreams repeatedly to get plots for new stories. He told Naomi Epel in an interview for her book *Writers Dreaming*, "I've always used dreams the way you'd use mirrors to look at something you couldn't see head-on, the way that you use a mirror to look at your hair in the back. To me, that's what dreams are supposed to do. I think that dreams are a way that people's minds illustrate the nature of their problems. Or maybe even illustrate the answers to their problems in symbolic language."

Akeane Kramarik - Considered a poetry prodigy as well as a painting prodigy, Kramarik has written two books of poetry and stated that it comes without thinking of the words - an unconscious download at the rate of three pages every five minutes.

> *It was about that time (age 7) that I began to write poetry. I was seeing these words everywhere. I was seeing these profound sentences, and I wanted to write them…*

> *I was looking at my paintings and I just wanted some sort of description but in such a way that makes more sense and makes more meaning to it so I just closed my eyes and it just happened. All of a sudden I see words flying through my head and I just starting picking words and putting them together. That's how poetry came about. Slowly I developed them into sentences and then paragraphs and then books.*
>
> *Even now when I look at a painting I cannot find any kind of description – I cannot think of anything because it is too powerful or it was lacking something – I go to my poetry, and I read over hundreds and hundreds of pages of poetry and most of the time it would be meant to be, and I would find a poem that was perfect for the painting. It just happens unconsciously.*[197]

Steven King - *Misery* started as a novel and became a bestselling movie. King fell asleep on a flight into London and dreamt of a tale where a girl finds and kills her favorite author. Upon awakening, King was so anxious to capture the story of his dream that he sat at the airport and frantically wrote the first 40-50 pages of the novel.

Kewaunee Lapseritis - Lapseritis stated, "In writing my first book *The Psychic Sasquatch and the UFO Connection* for three days when I was working about 12 or 14 hours a day on that particular chapter in the book an ET in another dimension stood beside me and told me what to write."[198]

D.H. Lawrence - Most of D.H. Lawrence's more lilting, dreamlike works such as *Women in Love* could qualify for inclusion here. However, *Fantasia of the Unconscious* so perfectly maps out such experiences and explains their importance and inspiration in such great detail it edges out any other competing works.

Dianna Love - Love, *New York Times* bestselling author of *Phantom in The Night* and other novels, said of the *Phantom* book, "I woke up in the night and saw the whole scene."

H.P. Lovecraft - It probably comes as little shock to anyone even tangentially familiar with the work of horror master H.P. Lovecraft that the man pulled his inspiration from the vivid nightmares he suffered most nights. Any novel or short story featuring the Great Old Ones especially drew from the corners of his unconscious mind.

Reiko Matsuura - *The Apprenticeship of Big Toe* - Though available in English and enjoying cult rather than mainstream attention, the novel of a woman who wakes up with a penis for a toe became a bestseller in its native Japan. Her incredibly original premise meant to explore gender identity and relations, came to her through a most unusual dream she eventually adapted into a favored work of fiction.

Marshall McLuhan - McLuhan was the author who predicted the internet 30 years before it occurred - "the medium is the message," "15 minutes of fame," and "tune in, turn off, and drop out," was considered the most famous English teacher of the twentieth century.

McLuhan believed that he was getting help from the Virgin Mary, not just in an inspiration sense, but in real conversations." He told one associate the story in private. "He alluded to it very briefly once, almost fearfully, in a please don't laugh-at-me tone. He didn't say, 'I know this because the Blessed Virgin Mary told me,' but it was clear from what he said that he was interrogating her about his ideas and that one of the reasons he was so sure about certain things was that the Virgin had confirmed his understanding of them."[199]

Shirley MacLaine - Actress Shirley MacLaine has also written many books. She talked about a figure she encountered that aids her. "I saw a form of a tall, almost androgynous human being," wrote MacLaine. She asked who the figure was and got the answer "I am your higher self."

MacLaine replied "Oh, my goodness. Are you really there?"

"Yes," it replied, "I have always been here. I have been here with you since the beginning of time. I am never away from you. I am you. I am your unlimited soul. I am the unlimited you that guides you and teaches you through each incarnation."[200]

Stephanie Meyer - *The Twilight Series* - In June of 2003 Meyer woke up from an intense dream about two lovers. The man is a vampire, and the girl is a human. The books went on to sell 17 million copies.[201] The books became movies.

Grant Morrison - Leading DC Comic book artist and editor *of Heavy Metal Magazine*, Morrison talked openly about where the ideas for his *Invisibles* comic book series came from; a 1994 alien abduction during a trip to Katmandu. "They took me out of my body. I wasn't in my body anymore…I'm out of my body and these f**kers ask me where do you want to go. The first thing I said was Alpha Centauri, which is the first thing you would say of course. It was f**king real. The whole thing was moving. There were three suns exactly as we are told it is supposed to move astronomically. I'm there, and I say to them, 'What the hell's going on here as you might.' They say, 'We've come to tell you this stuff so you can put it in your work and explain it to the world.' Why do they always say that to everyone? Why do they always go out and tell everyone to go out and tell everyone to go out and tell the world what going on and everyone and everyone tells us the same shit?"[202]

Frederich Nietzsche - In his autobiography *Ecce Home* Nietzsche spoke of having used inspiration when his writing *Thus Spoke Zarathustra*. "The notion of revelation describes the condition quite simply, by which I mean that something profoundly convulsive and disturbing suddenly becomes visible and audible with indescribable definiteness and exactness. One hears - one does not seek; one takes - one does not ask who gives: A thought flashes out like lightning, inevitably without hesitation - I have never had a choice about it....Everything occurs with volition, as if an eruption of freedom, independence, power, and divinity."[203]

Edgar Allan Poe - Most of his works stemmed from troubled nightmares.

Fernando Pessoa - Pessoa was considered one of the most significant literary figures of the 20th century and one of the greatest poets in the Portuguese language. In March 1916, Pessoa suddenly started having mediumistic experiences where he used automatic writing. He also experienced "astral" or "ethereal visions." He reported being able to see "magnetic auras" similar to radiographic images.

J.K. Rowling - Rowling, having sold 400 million books in 69 languages and 200 countries, stated, "I haven't got the faintest idea where my ideas come from, or how my imagination works" and further stated that Harry Potter came "fully formed" into her head, during a four-hour delayed train journey in 1990 from Manchester to London after she had awakened from a nap. "I simply sat and thought," for four hours, and "all the details bubbled in my brain, and this scrawny, black-haired, bespectacled boy who didn't know he was a wizard became more and more real to me."[204] In an interview with Oprah Winfrey Rowling described what happened:

> *I wrote compulsively through my late teens and into my twenties, but I had never really found the right thing. Then I was on a train, and I was 25, and it came. What came was – boy doesn't know he is a wizard and goes to wizard school bang bang bang. That was it, and that was like touch paper, and I was on this delayed train from Manchester to London, and my head was just flooding with what's at this wizard school!! There were four houses, and there are ghosts. There are house ghosts. What do they teach? What subjects do they teach? What do they learn? Who are the teachers? And I had no pen! But that was it. I don't think I had ever felt so excited. I thought "I would love to write that." I had never thought about writing for children. I had never thought about aiming anything at that age group. Yet it was the thing I was meant to write. I had always been fascinated by folklore. I loved a kooky word."*[205]

Rowling also stated, "I do remember one day writing "Philosopher Stone" which became "Sorcerer Stone," walking away from the café where I had been working, and I had this moment where I suddenly thought - it was like another voice was speaking to me. The voice said, 'The difficult thing is going to be getting published. If it is published, it will be huge.'"

Wilbert Smith - Smith ran the Canadian government investigation on flying saucers from 1950-54. He wrote an entire book called *The New Science* that he stated had come from aliens telling about the construction of the universe. He wrote on the opening page, "Assembled by W.B. Smith from data obtained from beings more advanced that we are."[206]

Kerrelyn Sparks - Sparks, a romance author, stated she had used the hypnagogic state many times in writing her books. "I've seen whole scenes in those last drowsy moments before I fall asleep or wake up."[207]

Brad Steiger - the author of 180 books on the paranormal, talked about incidents where people got help or inspiration as being a normal creative process. He equated it to the shamanic experience traditions which were at the basis of all the great religions.

Speaking of his experience, Steiger talked about *Revelation: The Divine Fire*, written in the 1960s and aided by a robbed figure he and his wife Sherry came to call Elijah.

> This was channeled in a sense that it was a robed figure that appeared beside the bed... I got up and tried to hit it. There's a robed figure there waving his hands in the air. I thought how did you get in here and what have you meant to do? Then a voice said not to be afraid, and I am sure the voice said 'we won't hurt you."
>
> It's difficult for me to shut off because of an insomniac but I fell asleep, and when I had awoken I had the outline of a book - who I should interview who I should call, and what I should do with it.
>
> Then the next night I was thinking is this going to replicate itself, and strangely enough, what came down the hall was this greenish light that was buzzing like a metallic bumblebee. It came into the room, and it became this robbed figure again. I had the complete outline again flashed out more than before, but not that I heard. This had to be seconds, but when I awakened, I had these pages and pages and pages. So that is the book that over the years people will come up to me after lectures and so forth. It will say to me that came at a time when I needed it. The teaching therein was exactly what I needed. Even celebrities and movie stars would call I'd say I was having trouble with my children at that time, and that helped me.
>
> I don't feel any less and author. I had some help with that. The spirit guide angel, entity, what everyone may want to call it was in the shamanic tradition. Sherry and I called him Elijah. We don't know what to call him.
>
> She met him, and we think it was exactly the same time. She was in meditation. He eyes saw a robed figure in sandals walking away from here, and she heard Elijah Elijah Elijah.

We never call upon him. That is the shamanic tradition. You don't call upon your spirit guide for help. You just try to have a receptive attitude at all times to get the information that's being directed towards you...the entity has only appeared twice to me after that.

Whitley Strieber - The title of Strieber's book *Communion* came from a channeling his wife had while sleeping one night. The voice that came from his wife stated that the book should not be called "Body Pain" which is what Strieber wanted to call it. The voice said Whitley should call the book *Communion* because that is what it is. The book led to half a million letters from people to Whitley about their abduction experiences.

Ruth Stone - Stone wrote 13 books of poetry and won the 2002 National Book Award for Poetry told author Elizabeth Gilbert of her creative moments with poems.

She told me that when she was growing up in rural Virginia, she would be out working in the fields, and she said she would feel and hear a poem coming at her from over the landscape. And she said it was like a thunderous train of air. And it would come barreling down at her over the landscape. And she felt it coming because it would shake the earth under her feet. She knew that she had only one thing to do at that point, and that was to, in her words, "run like hell." And she would run like hell to the house, and she would be getting chased by this poem, and the whole deal was that she had to get to a piece of paper and a pencil fast enough so that when it thundered through her, she could collect it and grab it on the page. And other times she wouldn't be fast enough, so she'd be running and running and running, and she wouldn't get to the house and the poem would barrel through her, and she would miss it and she said it would continue on across the landscape, looking, as she put it "for another poet." And then there were these times -- this is the piece I never forgot -- she said that there were moments where she would almost miss it, right? So, she's running to the house, and she's looking for the paper and the poem passes through her, and she grabs a pencil just as it's going through her, and then she said, it was like she would reach out with her other hand and she would catch it. She would catch the poem by its tail, and she would pull it backward into her body as she was transcribing on the page. And in these instances, the poem would come up on the page perfect and intact but backward, from the last word to the first.[208]

Urantia Book - According to the Urantia book website, "the papers were authorized by high deity authorities, and written by numerous super mortal personalities." The contact people's names remain secret because the "revelators do not want any human being - any human name - ever to be associated with *The Urantia Book*."[209] The 2,000-page book was channeled starting in 1911. The papers of the book "physically materialized" in four sections ending in 1935.

H.G. Wells - *Twelve Stories and a Dream* and *A Dream of Armageddon* - Some claim that many of H.G. Wells' other classic science-fiction work likely sprouted partially from his dream life. As the title describes, this harrowing work speculates on the dangerous directions in which mankind's technology could ultimately lead. "It is possible to believe that all the human mind has ever accomplished is but the dream before the awakening." And "We all have our time machines, don't we?" Those that take us back are memories....And those that carry us forward are dreams."

E.B. White - *Stuart Little* - One of the most memorable and beloved characters from children's literature sauntered into E.B. White's unconscious mind in the 1920s, though he didn't transition from notes to novel until over two decades later. From there, the tiny boy with the face and fur of a mouse became a classic that continues to delight both adults and kids even today.

William Wilson - Bill Wilson was not only the co-founder of Alcoholics Anonymous but also the man who wrote the *12 Steps and 12 Traditions* which is the key manual used by A.A. members. What is not known is that Wilson wrote the 12 Steps book with the help of an Ouija board and a 15th-century monk by the name of Boniface.[210] Wilson's wife wrote about her husband ability to bring in nonlocal entities, "Saturday was the scheduled day for these psychic adventures. 'Bill would lie down on the couch. He would get these things. He kept doing it every week or so. Each time, certain people would 'come in.' Sometimes, it would be new ones, and they'd carry on some story.'"[211]

In a letter to a Roman Catholic priest Rev. Ed Dowling, Wilson wrote of his first encounter with Boniface, "One turned up the other day calling himself Boniface. Said he was English and a Benedictine missionary. Had been a man of learning, knew missionary work and a lot about structures. I think he said this all the more modestly, but that was the gist of it. I'd never heard of this gentleman, but he checked out pretty well in the Encyclopedia. If this one is who he says he is - and of course there is no way of knowing...."[212]

Francisco de Paula Candido Xavier - Xavier was a Brazilian medium who had his first experience with automatic writing in 1927. He was nominated twice for the Nobel Peace Prize. He finished his first channeled book in 1932 called *A Collection of Poems from Beyond the Grave*. He went on to write 412 books channeled from a collection of spirits and the dealt with the subjects of religious teachings, novels, poetry, theater, and works of philosophy and science. His books sold 50 million copies, and all the profits went to charity.

Chapter 10 Inspirations for Movies

In the same way that professional musicians seem to be getting inspirational downloads, there appear to be downloads of songs from various sources to people who are not professional musicians and these end up in major Hollywood movies.

Many directors are aware of the dream as inspiration. Steven Spielberg states that his greatest inspirations come in dreams. It is not surprising then that he calls his studio Dreamworks pointing back to the Freudian idea of dream work.

One of best stories that illustrate how this music process happens comes from an unknown source. Catherine Lanigan tells the story in her book *Devine Nudges*.

Lanigan had no musical training spelling out that the only instrument she ever learned to play was the radio. It was while working on the film project *Adventures of Lillie and Zane: The Secret of the Seven Stones,* Lanigan thought it would be a good idea to create a song for the main character "but not a single word ever manifested either in my brain or on paper."

During this time she awakened suddenly at 5:00 by a voice that told her "Cathy, Wake Up."

She got up and began to perspire, as the voice said, "Write the song."

"What song?" asked Cathy.

"Go upstairs now. Do not go back and sleep. Write the song."

"I...I don't have a song. I know of no song..."

"Do it," commanded the voice.

Cathy raced to her computer upstairs with no idea of what would happen. Twenty minutes later she had the lyrics to a trail of fabulous, visual, and melancholy words telling a story of true love.

"One thing needs to be stated very clearly," wrote Cathy, "I didn't write this song. It was given to me. It was a great celestial, angelic gift for me to give to the world and whoever will hear it."[213]

She told her friend Dan about what had happened, and he asked to write the melody even though he had not written music for years. He reported back, "I have your music for you. It was the strangest thing. It just flowed, and I haven't written music in years. You have to hear this. It sounds very special."

Then there are the stories where people come up concepts and movie ideas like the dream inspired movies, Avatar, and Terminator, which were major commercial successes. Often lawsuits are filed, but other people inspired by the same ideas claim that the ideas were so close that they had to have been stolen. One example of this came from a UFO experiencer who told me of her movie download experience.

> *I wrote a story for a university writing class right after my mother died in 2004 that in many respects mirrored the Avatar story James Cameron wrote. I found out recently that he didn't announce he was making that movie until 2005, even though he had been working on the story in the years before talking about it publicly. Funny thing was, in Avatar, the dying human's consciousness, in the end, enters the Avatar as his next incarnation as a blue Navi and in my story, about blue beings whose bodies glistened like they were lit up, on a planet with two moons, a female was being prepared to have her consciousness veiled in order to incarnate in a human body for the Earth experience. It ends with her saying goodbye to everyone she knows and then being born on Earth in a hospital as a baby. Ha! A human becomes Blue, and a Blue becomes human! Guess the public needed the former message this time around, lol.*

Here is a list of the many movies that were inspired by various forms of inspiration and download.

Ingmar Bergman said that he received many of his movies images from dreams.[214]

Craig Campobasso - Campobasso is a Hollywood producer and casting director. He spoke of a couple downloads he has received while doing his regular Hollywood job.

> *I was twenty-six years old; I had just finished "Amazing Stories." I had my own amazing story occur where I woke up into not only spirituality but universal spirituality. I was being visited in the dream state by Master Teachers, and they were feeding me energy modules of information that would go into my cells and all of these ideas and awakenings in me. My first awakening actually happened when they fed me gold light and I literally and I'm not kidding, I was casting, I had an office on Sunset Boulevard in a beautiful office overlooking the entire city, and I would have actors come in my office, and I would see somebody I recognize and I would recognize the beauty of who they are on the inside and what their path was... I sat down and started writing, and I wrote a 400-page book about all of these experiences that I was going through.*[215]

Val Thor, an alien who had reportedly been in the Pentagon as a guest of the United States for three years in the 1950s, visited Campobasso. The visit occurred on the first day that Campobasso was writing the script for the movie on Val Thor called *Stranger at the Pentagon*. Campobasso stated," He came to me in the dream state and showed me the whole path of the movie and everything before it and that he was the one who was guiding it and I've never had to worry about anything. It's like magic appearing you know. It's incredible."[216]

James Cameron - Cameron was the director of *Avatar*. He spoke about employing his ability to vivid dream in the movie, "when we're kids we dream of flying and I certainly did, and still have a lot of flying dreams and I thought that if I can connect to an audience, to a kind of collective unconscious in almost the Jungian sense, then it bypasses all the politics and all the bull."[217]

Paul Davids - Davids is a writer producer and director in Hollywood. He has produced many films and documentaries but is best known for his Showtime production of *Roswell*. Davids got what he believed was a message from his dead friend Forrest J. Ackerman who had been the editor of *Famous Monsters of Filmland*. The message led to Davids writing and directing a documentary *The Life after Death Project*.

Walt Disney - As mentioned in the chapter on psychedelics Disney took Mescaline (Peyote Linklater talked about using his ability to lucid dream in his movie making such as the movie Waking Life. "I always did it just kind of naturally a little bit") starting in 1936 after visiting Black Mountain College in North Carolina in 1935. The result was the 1941 movie *Fantasia*.

Richard Linklater - Linklater stated, "I never really thought about it much, but these dreams would happen, and I would be aware I was in a dream. As I started to make this movie, I started doing all the research; I knew it to be a phenomenon, and it confirmed a lot of my own experience."[218]

Chris Nolan - Nolan's movie *Inception* was inspired by lucid dreams that Nolan would have after waking up and going back to bed. He would try and manipulate the dreams which he found "frustratingly elusive."

Mary Shelley - Shelley wrote the original book which became the movie - *Frankenstein*. Following the death of her and Percy Bysshe Shelley's daughter at only 12 days old, the heartbroken Mary Wollstonecraft Godwin dreamt of the child coming back to life after massaging her near a fire. She wrote of it in the collaborative journal. It later grew into one of the most iconic, influential horror novels of all time.

> *When I placed my head upon my pillow, I did not sleep, nor could I be said to think... I saw -- with shut eyes, but an acute mental vision -- I saw the pale student of unhallowed arts kneeling beside the thing he had put together. I saw the hideous phantasm of a man stretched out, and then, on the working of some powerful engine, show signs of life, and stir with an uneasy, half-vital motion. Frightful must it be; for*

supremely frightful would be the effect of any human endeavor to mock the stupendous Creator of the world.

...I opened mine in terror. The idea so possessed my mind, that a thrill of fear ran through me, and I wished to exchange the ghastly image of my fancy for the realities around. ...I could not so easily get rid of my hideous phantom; still it haunted me. I must try to think of something else. I recurred to my ghost story -- my tiresome, unlucky ghost story! O! if I could only contrive one which would frighten my reader as I myself had been frightened that night!

Swift as light and as cheering was the idea that broke upon me. 'I have found it! What terrified me will terrify others, and I need only describe the specter which had haunted me my midnight pillow.' On the morrow, I announced that I had thought of a story. I began that day with the words, 'It was on a dreary night of November', making only a transcript of the grim terrors of my waking dream.[219]

Robert Louis Stevenson - *The Strange Case of Dr. Jekyll and Mr. Hyde* - Stevenson described dreams as occurring in "that small theater of the brain which we keep brightly lighted all night long." As with most of H.P. Lovecraft's terrifying tales, this horror classic also sprang into existence because of its writer's graphic nightmares. In this case, a "fine bogey tale" tormenting him as he slept grew into one of the most famous and genuinely scary English-language novels ever penned. Stevenson described that his best writing came from characters that took on an independent life of their own and seemed to move around and speak for themselves unaided. During his dreams, Stevenson stated that he would sit in a stage box and watch the "little people" unfold plots as he watched.[220]

He referred to his little dream helpers as Brownies. "…and for the little people, what can I say they are but just my Brownies, God bless them! Who do half my work while I am fast asleep, and in all human likelihood, do the rest for me as well, when I am wide awake and fondly suppose that I do it for myself."[221]

William Styron - Styron wrote the book *Sophie's Choice*, which became a 1982 American drama film directed by Alan J. Pakula. Meryl Streep starred as the main character Sophie, for which she won the Academy Award for Best Actress. The film was also nominated for Best Cinematography, Costume Design, Best Music, and Best Adapted Screenplay The plot that opens the book introducing Sophie as a character came in a dream Styron had one afternoon.

Andy and Lana Wachowski - Both men, are lucid dreamers who drew on this dream state to create a virtual reality world in the movie *The Matrix*. The concept is that people mentally enslaved, not recognizing that they are merely "dreaming."

Denise Williams - Williams, an independent Hollywood producer, got an intuitive message one day to find a medical intuitive. She found one working in a metaphysical bookstore in Los Angeles and within minutes of meeting the woman asked what Williams did. She said that she was a Hollywood film producer.

The woman said, "I have to tell you this story. I think it would make a great film" She said that she had talked to other producers, and no one would listen.

She told Williams the story of John Mack, who had at that time only been dead a year. Williams said the story gave her goose bumps. The woman had been a patient of John Mack. Williams began to research the story and was overcome with the stories.

Chapter 11 Inspirations in Art

If the doors of perception were cleansed, man would see everything as it is: infinite. **William Blake**

Pure psychic automatism by which it is intended to express, either verbally or in writing, the true function of thought. Thought dictated in the absence of all control exerted by reason, and outside all aesthetic or moral preoccupations. **André Breton, the founder of the Surrealist movement.**

In the 16th century, Raphael (Raffaello Sanzio da Urbino) was considered one of the three great masters of the period along with Michelangelo and Leonardo da Vinci. Raphael attributed his ability to depict angelic scenes to inner visions.

There are a number of different types of inspiration download effects in the world of art. Some of the inspirations involved automatic drawing which was developed by surrealists and pioneered by André Masson. Artists who were placed in this category included Joan Miró, Salvador Dalí, Jean Arp and André Breton. Even the late etching and lithographs in the 1960s by Pablo Picasso seemed to express automatic drawing. The types of automatism include surrealist automatism and mediumistic automatism which is inspired by ghosts and spirits. Most artists who acknowledge it would say automatism expresses the creative force in the art of what they believe is the contained in the unconscious.

The idea of getting art from the unconscious is so common that L. Gamwell documented over 1,000 pieces of dream-inspired art from the 20th century in his book "Dreams 1900-2000: Science, art, and the unconscious Mind."[222]

What is very significant and unusual about many of the automatism painters is that they drew or painted in the dark, produced huge volumes of works at incredible speed, used the wrong hand or both hands at the same time, and did weird things like paint the picture upside down or started in one corner and worked out instead of from the middle.

Lastly, according to Kristine Stiles, the France Family Professor of Art, Art History, and Visual Studies at Duke University, dissociative behaviors are quite common in Performance Art, and many artists "are interested in, or state they possess, various forms of nonlocal consciousness traditionally associated with psychic phenomena."[223]

Some examples of inspiration and download in art include:

Florencio Anton - Anton stated that he began his mediumship with spirit people at the age of eight. He began with spirit voices, then automatic writing, and then dead artists started working through him. Anton gave demonstrations for 20 years producing over 5,000 paintings by over 100 artists, never repeating a painting.

John Bartlett - Bartlett produced automatic writing in part written in Latin and Middle English of Glastonbury Abbey bring out exacting architectural details that were unknown at the time. He worked from the top left of painting downward. He produced 8 drawings of the way the Abbey would have looked and did them with his left hand even though he was right-handed.

Rita Berkowitz - Spiritually related - Berkowitz has been doing spirit drawing since 1985. Draws the spirit of dead people, and then compares the drawing to pictures provided. She has had cases where she drew people who were not known yet to have died.**William Blake** - Spiritually related - Blake sketched visiting spirits as if they were sitting posing for him. If the spirit left, Blake would stop painting until the spirit returned. He called his sketching "intoxicating." He claimed he had visions of angels his whole life, claiming that one had taught him to paint at a very early age.

In an 1803 letter, Blake described downloading poems "from immediate dictation…without premeditation and even against my will" which he got from "his friends in Eternity."[224]

Chris Bledsoe - UFO and spiritually related - Chris Bledsoe had a UFO abduction experience in January 2007 outside the city of Fayetteville, North Carolina. Among the many things that changed in his life after the event was the strong desire to paint. Despite the fact that he had never drawn or painted, following the event Bledsoe went out and picked up canvasses and paints. He began to paint flowers and hummingbirds with extreme precision. Asked why the hummingbird he stated that the "Guardians" had told him that the bird was the "keeper of the forest" and was very important.

Lloyd Canning - UFO - Canning recalls what he thinks was his first abduction in 2005 when he was buying a used car. A few days later he felt compelled to paint. He gets a download once a week and paints. "When the visions are coming on it feels like a load of anxiety, building up and up sometimes for days. Then all of a sudden I have a clear vision in my mind of what I have to paint. Ever since that first sighting, I have these crazy visions that just come over me. When they happen, it's like I don't have a choice. I just have to paint them."[225]

Ithell Colquhoun - Automatism - Colquhoun was a British surrealist painter. In 1939, after meeting three keys artists of the Surrealist who were using the unconscious to produce paintings, Colquhoun made the move to do the same thing. She named the process "mantra," from the Greek meaning "divine inspiration." She became extremely interested in the spiritual realm. Her method in her art and writings relied on the practice of automatism, magical techniques and visionary walks called "drifting."

Cindy Davidson - <u>UFO and spiritually based</u> - Davidson is a Winnipeg artist that suddenly got the impulse to paint. Believes it has some sort of alien connection.

Luiz Gasparetto - Does channeled paintings from 44 different artists (Picasso, Renoir, Toulouse-Lautrec, Gaugin, Modigliani, Van Gogh, Rembrandt, Tissot, Manet, Monet, and Matisse) working <u>in the dark</u>. Each painting takes about 5 minutes, and while he paints he answers questions put to the artist who is channeling the painting to him. He has produced at least 6,000 high-quality drawing sometimes done with both hands producing two different drawings by two different artists at the same time.

"The music plays inside of me. It is clear that my sensitivity is far from me. It is bigger. Everything that is in that field is inside of me. So the spirits approach and I feel the spirits. I can feel their personalities; I can see them and hear them. When they think what they want to do my body responds of what they think."[226]

Marjan Gruzewski - <u>Mediumship</u> - Gruzewski produced full daylight paintings of scenes from the spirit world, historical events, and dead people he did not know. Many of the dead people canvases included grinning and weird faces. He could paint <u>in the dark,</u> but these were not as good as the daylight pictures.

Susannah Harris - Harris painted a painting upside down <u>while blindfolded</u> in two hours.

Frederica Hauffe - The Seeress of Prevorst (Frederica Hauffe) drew complicated geometrical designs <u>in the dark</u> while bedridden for 10 years. She was clairvoyant, made predictions, and exhibited a wide range of psychic phenomena. At one time she spoke only in verse for three days.[227]

"She threw off the whole drawing," wrote Dr. Justinus Kerner as described in *Die Seherin von Prevorst* (1829), "in an incredibly short time, and employed, in marking the more than a hundred points into which this circle was divided, no compasses or instruments whatever. She made the whole with her hand alone and failed not in single point. She seemed to work as a spider works its geometric diagrams, without a visible instrument. I recommended her to use a pair of compasses to strike the circles; she tried, and made immediate blunders."

David Huggins - Huggins, a New York City artist, has been a UFO experiencer since he was 8 and maybe earlier. He didn't know what to do with his experiences when he became aware of them in the late 1980s. The aliens told him, "David, do paintings." He has produced a whole collection of his encounters with Crescent, a female alien, and he became the father of almost sixty hybrid children. He wrote a book on his experiences called *Love in an Alien Purgatory* which features many of the paintings.

Aleane Kramarik - <u>Spiritually based</u> - Kramarik started having visions as a young child. "At 3.5 to 4 years old I started to see these visions and dreams of these different worlds, different dimensions," said Kramarik. As part of the vision, she reported that she had talked with God. She was told she should paint, and she would be helped.

To prove her encounters to her mother, she started drawing these visions he told her about, things that would happen in the future, and these things came true. She also drew the many faces she had seen in the visions. "I drew probably a hundred over 2-3 days," said Akeane. "They were mostly about faces. There were so many faces that I was seeing....It was a mixture of everything. It was voices and colors and shapes. Sometimes I would literally see the future. I would see some things. I would see the past. It was just a combination of everything. It happened when I was sleeping walking, doing dishes. It just varied. It came to me. It was mostly in color, but a percentage was voices, hearing things. It was sounds of nature, or it could be sounds of various space elements, or someone talking in a smooth voice. It was very hard to explain what I was hearing and seeing. My mother started to notice that I was drawing the walls and the tables.[228]

"Right after I sketched them, I don't know why, but they all the visions would fade away of that particular image. If I didn't put it down on paper, I would forget it the next day. It was all meant to be that I had to put it down or else it would be forgotten."

The visions got more complex showing scenarios in different stars and galaxies. At age six, Akeane moved from sketching to painting. By 8, she had painted her now infamous painting of Jesus. It was the painting where Akeane couldn't find a model for that would match her vision. After two years of searching she prayed for a day and the same day a seven-foot tall man matching the vision showed up at the front door looking for work. Later Colby, a four-year-old who had had a near-death experience and reported that he had gone to heaven identified Akeane's painting as the Jesus he had seen.

By 9, the brilliance of her painting skill had landed her on the Oprah show. Now 20 years old, some of Akeane's paintings have been appraised at up to five million dollars.

In one of the main visions that have inspired many paintings, Akeane physically disappeared for a number of hours.

> *When I was five and a half years old, I was in my room, and suddenly I just blacked out. My physical body – my eyes turned black – I don't have any viewing of my physical eyes. The last thing I remember is my body parting from above. My soul started lifting up higher and higher, and I started splitting into thousands of pieces going through thousands of doors.*
>
> *Meanwhile, it appears that I was missing for 7 or 8 hours. My mom and dad called the police. There were people dogs and at least 12-15 policemen searching the house, the*

property, and the whole neighborhood and no one could find me. It was in the newspaper, and it was a traumatic experience for my parents.

I had no recollection of what happened. All I remember is my body being glued to different doors with different experiences and lives. After my whole experience, I don't know how I came into the hallway of my house and walking up to my mom, and I remember being so so exhausted with the lives I have been living, and my mom is crying. It was a real emotional experience.

From that point on I think my whole family started seeing the whole world differently. It was definitely a different chapter, point in my life that shaped who I am...it is definitely a learning experience for me. I know that it is a mission for me to teach people, to show people, but it is also a better understanding of who I am and who were are as human kind. It goes back to the meaning of life and the purpose of it.

As far as I remember in my experiences I had this message come to me saying through all my images and the paintings I have completed there are puzzles in each one of them that if a person understands them, they will understand the meaning of what life is.

Even looking back on my work I am trying to decipher what the message really is. It is definitely a challenge for me as a person, but I am very glad that I have something that I can show to people to give them hope and inspiration.

Augustine Lesage - Spiritually based - Lesage was a French miner, automatism painter, and produced his first work in 1918 at the age of 35 after attending some séances. In a span of 10 years he produced 57 canvases, the conceptions of which are harmonious and suggest an innate genius for color. He always began at the top of the canvas and worked his way down. Lesage, who believed himself to be the reincarnation of an old Egyptian painter, experienced an inner prompting before he began to paint. In 1926, the Society of French Artists exhibited some of his works.

Matthew Manning - Spiritually based - Manning was haunted at his home in Shelford, England by very strong poltergeist phenomena from the age of 11 and into his college days. Manning stated "heavy beds were moved, and knives, nails, electric light bulbs and other objects were sent flying through the air. Showers of pebbles and pools of water manifested, and strange lights appeared on walls."[229]

While at college, Manning experienced automatic writing while doing an essay which led to communications from dead individuals some writing in languages unknown to him, including Italian, German, Greek, Latin, Russian, and Arabic.

Next manning began to produce psychic art resembling that of Thomas Bewick, Thomas Rowlandson, Aubrey Beardsley, Paul Keel, Henri Matisse, and Picasso.

José Medrado - Medrado was a Brazilian trance medium, painted 10 paintings from masters in one hour, twenty minutes at the Arthur Findlay College exhibition in the U.K. in 2008.

John Ballou Newbrough - Newbrough was a New York City dentist who was clairvoyant and clairaudient. His own psychic gifts were remarkable. He could paint in total darkness with both hands at once.[230]

Heinrich Nusslein - Nussein was a German automatist of the 1920s who in two years painted 2,000 pictures of his visions. The small works took three or four minutes and the largest works in 30 or 40 minutes. They were painted in total darkness. One reviewer described his paintings "His pictures are remarkable in part because of the fantastic vistas rich with colossal archaic edifices, or images reminiscent of blurred colored photographic portraits. The strong complementary colors underline the unrealistic character of the images and further transpose it into a sphere beyond the natural."[231]

Coral Polge - Polge was a psychic artist who produced 60,000 sketches of spirits. She claimed that she started off as a skeptic about psychic things. She felt he had a guide helping her and drew him. Later she found a self-portrait the man had done while alive. He turned out to be Maurice Quentin de La Tour, a French painter & pastellist who was born 1704 and died in 1788. Polge believed that her role was to bring the spiritual and material world together in perfect balance. Before she died in 2001, she produced a book called *Living Images: The Story of a Psychic Artist* illustrating her 54 years of psychic drawings.

Marguerite Burnat-Provins - From 1914 on, Birnat-Provins produced some 3,000 painting based on visions. She called the collection Ma Ville (My Town). She spoke of the visions, "I endure them, cringe as I feel them coming and simply cannot help drawing them."

In her 1915 painting Frilute le Peureux (Frilute the Timorous) was one where she felt as if the creatures of her dream life came to her and "dictated" her paintings of them.

Alma Rumball - Spiritually based - Alma was called the mystic of Muskoka, Ontario. She painted normal artwork such as flowers and trees until sometime in the 1950s when everything changed. It all started with a vision in which she encountered Christ with a panther at his side. He told her "she must draw, and she must write." For the next 25 years till her death in 1980, she did just that.

The other great inspiration behind the paintings was Aba Pasha who was Rumball's spirit guide and who Rumball stated was her constant companion. He spoke to her and directed her. The work she produced, was according to Rumball (like Akiane Krumarik) a reproduction of visions she was being given.

The work that she produced was identified by Michael Greenwood at York University as surrealist psychic automatism and stated that Alma was the best example of it since William Blake.

Rumball stated that she wasn't actually the one that was producing the painting but that it was automatically done by "the hand." Her hand would hold the pen or brush and "the hand" would just start painting. It would move effortlessly around the paper and even choose the colors.

The hundreds of paintings that Rumball produced often consisted of swirling multicolored masses filled with what were later identified by Kalu Rinpoche, spiritual advisor to the Dalai Lama as 7 of 20 Tibetan deities "in perfect position with appropriate identifying features" and Tibetan symbols. This was despite the fact that Rumball did not believe in reincarnation and didn't like the idea. One can only imagine what she thought the day the hand wrote across one painting, "Alma Came To Earth As Joan of Arc."

At one point she drew 100 drawing that dealt with Atlantis, complete with downloaded writing and warning that the same thing might be revisited unless people headed God's laws. Atlantis was, however, another subject Rumball didn't really believe strongly in.

Rumball was a strong Christian, who believed in the inspired word of God, but that did not stop her from producing paintings highlighting the Kundalini and body Chakras. Her writings go on to tell about the Queen of the Universe and the Queen of Atlantis. Some of this appeared to go against her Christian upbringing, and she burned many pieces in fear of God's punishment.

Rumball claimed that the pen would move on the paper and that she was just there watching. Sometimes the pen would go right off the paper and start painting on whatever was outside the painting.

Austin O. Spare - Spare was an English psychic artist and was supported by Aleister Crowley who proclaimed Spare's work as 'a message from the Divine.' Spare subsequently submitted several drawings for publication in Crowley's Thelemite journal, *The Equinox*. His 1907 self-portrait portrait of an Artist was later bought by Led Zeppelin guitarist Jimmy Page.

Ionel Talpazan - Romanian-born Talpazan has been acclaimed for his paintings of spaceships in the NY Times, Wired, Newsweek, Raw Vision, and Art Forum. His paintings are of flying saucers and outer space based on his personal experiences with extraterrestrial life.

Talpazan is self-taught who believes he has created more than 1,000 works of art inspired by his visions and ideas about UFOs and their travel throughout the universe. Talpazan told author Daniel Wojcik "that he has 'sacrificed his life to the UFO,' and his ultimate goal is to reveal the mysterious technology and hidden meanings of flying saucers to the people of planet Earth."[232]

Chapter 12 Inspirations by Savants and Prodigies

It is fascinating to me that music, mathematics, and art are considered the pinnacle of human creativity requiring high intelligence, dedicated practice, and focus, but is that true? Savants smash that. **Dr. Allan Snyder, Director of the Center of Mind at Sydney University.**

Kim Peek, the inspiration for Rain Man, possesses one of the most extraordinary memories every recorded. Until we can explain his abilities, we cannot pretend to understand human cognition. **Darold A. Treffert, MD and Daniel D. Christensen**

Savants are untrained and untrainable, illiterate and uneducable...few can read or write....Yet each has apparently unlimited access to a particular field of knowledge that we know they cannot have acquired...Ask... [mathematical] savants how they get their answer and they will smile, pleased that we are impressed but unable to grasp the implications of such a question....The answers come through them, but they are not aware of how - they don't know how they know....The ones sight-reading music can't read anything else, yet display this flawless sensory-motor response to musical symbols....The issue with these savants is that in most cases, so far as can be observed, the savant has not acquired, could not have acquired, and is quite incapable of acquiring, the information that he so liberally dispenses. **Developmental psychologist, Joseph Chilton Pearce**

The mystery of savants is one of the clearest forms of inspiration that has no apparent physical brain mechanism. It clearly indicates the possibility of a nonlocal mind. "In a way, savants are the great enigma of today's neurology," said Prof. Joy Hirsch, director of the Functional M.R.I. Research Center at Columbia University.

Researcher Jane Duckett of the University of Texas at Austin called for an "extensive theory revision" already back in the 1970s to understand the abilities of savants. Despite this call and the potential for learning how these "probably innate" abilities work, the area has been basically ignored except by a few researchers who operate with almost no funding.

The history of savants goes way back as was pointed out by savant expert Dr. Diane Powell. She pointed to the case of Zerah Colburn was born in Vermont in 1804. At the age of 5, his father discovered his son's ability to do mathematics. "He was asked the square root of 106929, and before the number could be written down, he immediately answered 327. He was then required to name the cube root of 208,336,125, and with equal facility and promptness he replied 645....One of the parties requested him to name the factors which produced the number 247483, which he immediately did by mentioning the two numbers 941 and 263."[233]

There are savants like Rain Man played in the movie by Dustin Hoffman, who are able to count 246 toothpicks on the ground in a single glance. There are musical savants with no musical training can replay and remember for life songs they have only heard once. There are savants who exhibit pure telepathic abilities for numbers, sentences, made up words, and foreign languages. There are savants who can do calculations as fast as computers, or produce the day of the week for a date thousands of years in the future or past, and at the same time cannot tell you what 4 x 7 will equal.

Savants usually exhibit brain injury or brain birth defects. A list of some of the people who have suffered from brain conditions such as Asperger's and Synesthesia shows that many of the great musicians and thinkers in history had these conditions. It leads to the theory that much music and discovery may have come from brains that were just simply wired differently from the average human.

Synesthesia	Asperger's	Asperger's
Leonard Bernstein	Craig Nicholls	Bill Gates
Billy Joel	Dan Aykroyd	Al Gore
Alexa Joel	Albert Einstein	Bob Dylan
Van Halen	Alexander Graham Bell	Alfred Hitchcock
Tony DeCaprio	Benjamin Franklin	John Denver
Duke Ellington	Bertrand Russell	Jim Henson
Franz Liszt	Bobby Fischer	Isaac Asimov
Lady Gaga	Carl Jung	Glenn Gould
Nikola Tesla	Abraham Lincoln	Howard Hughes
Justin Chancellor	Friedrich Nietzsche	Charles Schulz
Harvey Gittleman	Henry Ford	Andy Warhol
Richard Feynman	Ludwig van Beethoven	Robin Williams
Max Heath	Isaac Newton	Vernon L. Smith (Nobel
Elvin Jones	Mark Twain	Emily Dickenson
Manu Katche	Michelangelo	George Bernard Shaw
Brooks Kerr	Nikola Tesla	Gustav Mahler
Kaki King	Thomas Edison	Socrates
Andrew Legg	Thomas Jefferson	Marie Curie
Gyorgy Ligeti	Wolfgang Mozart	Charles Darwin
Olivier Messiaen	Vincent Van Gogh	

The inspirations and downloads that come to savants are important for two reasons.

Savants all suffer from brain damage that seems to involve the left hemisphere either through birth defect or injury. Brain injuries appear to have triggered some of the top psychics and savants of the last century. Peter

Hurkos, considered by some as the top psychic ever, received his psychic abilities after falling off a ladder in 1941 and sustaining a head injury. Edgar Cayce considered the best psychic in America, received his amazing abilities after being hit in the head with a baseball. Daniel Temmett, the synesthesia savant who can do massive calculations including Pi flawlessly to 22,514 places, suddenly got his gift after having seizures at four years old. Tony Cicoria, who was hit by lightning, gained a sudden interest in music and was flooded with music that seemed to come from nowhere. Within months, he spent all his time composing and playing piano music. These brain injuries create what is known as an acquired savant, and allows a possible road to understanding what is happening and where such inspirations and downloads come from.

More importantly, the amazing paranormal abilities of savants are different from the abilities of others who have claimed amazing abilities in that prodigious savants are 100% accurate. There is no error. which implies that they have a clear, direct connection to wherever they are getting their information from. Identifying the path could allow everyone to access these amazing talents.

These talents indicate that the mind is nothing more than a receiver and that the savant's brain damage simply allows the savant to log in to some sort of universal internet or hologram where everything is stored. The brain damage is in effect their password.

Some researchers like Dr. Allan Snyder at the University of Sydney's Center of Mind have even done successful experiments which work off the idea of the damaged savant brain. What Snyder did was inhibit the dominant left hemisphere. He did this by sending a series of electromagnetic pulses (known as transcranial magnetic stimulation or TMS) into the left frontal lobe. In 40% of test subjects, this produced a strange savant-like intelligence in drawing, proofreading, and mathematics. The savant-like abilities were being caused by shutting down part of the brain just like brain damage does in savants.[234]

Dr. Diane Powell, a Johns Hopkins-trained neuroscientist who has researched savants made statements backing up Dr. Snyder's contention that when it comes to the brain, sometimes less is more. Dr. Powell stated, "Some people have conditions such as autism that shift the balance between local and nonlocal processes by knocking out the functioning of the neocortex. The rest of us can decrease this classical dominance by such mind-quieting practices as meditation."

The shutting down of part of the brain still does not fully explain where the inspirations and abilities are coming from. The classical idea of memory is a network of 100 billion neurons, with each neuron having an average of 50,000 connections with other neurons. The classical model goes on to claim that learning arises when we select and reinforce specific connections and pathways in this network.

With the savant, however, there doesn't appear to be any learning process. Mathematical savants can do calculations faster than computers without ever having gone to school. Musical savants can play any song they ever heard or compose music without ever having had a music lesson. Artistic savants can paint at the highest levels without any training.

Therefore, the information they are coming up with cannot be stored in the brain as there was never any training to put the information in the brain. The savant experience seems to support the idea more fully that the brain is a receiver like a radio, TV, or computer that is suddenly able to pick up signals from outside the brain that have always been there but were not accessible to the normal left dominant brain.

Another key talent possessed by many savants is an autobiographical memory. This is a very rare talent held by only a few people in the world. These people are able to tell you events in their life from a certain point of childhood or since suffering an injury. Not all the people are savants.

These people are able to tell the weather for any day, what they did or had to eat on a certain day, or like the case of savant twins Flo and Kaye, remember what their favorite game show host was wearing on any particular day in the past.

If there are seven people in the world with the talent, it would be safe to assume that their brain is tuning into something that others are not able to tap into, as opposed to believing that these seven represent some new element that is unique to the rest of the universe.

The development of hypnosis has helped to confirm that everyone's mind records and catalogs everything we see and do. A person can be regressed and will be able to remember things long since forgotten.

Part of the job of the mind appears to be to pull out of consciousness memories and things that are unnecessary for daily living. It is necessary and like a normal event in a person's mind. In the case of people with autobiographic memory, the wiring of the brain or a brain injury has stopped the natural process of deleting unnecessary events from the past.

Like many savant talents, autobiographical memory also fits well into the concept of the akashic record, A-field, noosphere, all-self, ground of being, universal consciousness, and zero point field, which would be part of the holographic field that makes up the universe.

Jason Padgett, an acquired savant, spent 3 years alone in his house dealing with OCD and how everything looked the same. He spent his time on the internet looking up material on geometry. "It was so beautiful seeing things like that. There is this underlying geometry to every single thing....The Universe has opened up to me."

Is Padgett hallucinating or does his perception now see the world as it is? The latter would seem to be the case.

Padgett describes that when he sees the world with no smooth continuous motion, "It is like hitting pause on your television and watching frame by frame by frame so that you see whole discrete images that are coming towards you...when it moves, every image is attached to a grid structure. I picture it geometrically. All the points on it can be fixed to a smaller and smaller lattice structure - like space-time is a lattice structure itself, and it works the exact same way. The smaller the movement, the smaller the lattice structure."

The questions immediately arise. Did Padgett's injury make him crazy or awaken him to an underlying principle of the universe that we are missing because we can't see it? Has Padgett been given an inspirational download that stays on 24/7, and which allows him to see deeper levels of reality? Can we learn from him?

The case of Andrew illustrates the ability of a savant, with a severely limited ability to communicate, to be able to link telepathically with the mind of one of his parents.

The story comes from Teresa, whose 10-year-old son, Andrew, exhibited strong telepathic abilities,

> *From very early on my son would act out my - and others' - worst fears. I would be at someone's house and think in my mind, "I hope he doesn't pull down the drapes." No sooner could I finish my thought, and he would walk over to the drapes and swing on them like Tarzan. I was infuriated because I knew he could somehow hear my fear. I truly came to terms with abilities of audio clairvoyance (ability to hear others' internal dialogue).*
>
> *At times, Andrew would get excited and have a tantrum. My husband would tell him to chill. Andrew took this phrase and changed it to "Kill kill." It would scare me. This child had very limited abilities to speak, and for him to walk around chanting "Kill kill" could not be good.*
>
> *One day at camp, the young man shadowing Andrew had spoken of attention-getting behaviors. I had just always seen Andrew as reacting to his environment; I didn't see him as trying to get attention. So on the drive home, I began to review in my head about what that would look like – as he was trying to get attention? I thought about how Andrew would say "Kill Kill!" – was he trying to get attention this way? The conversation occurred completely in my head. Andrew suddenly sat up in the back seat and laughed, and said the words, "Chill Chill" for the first time.*
>
> *This was a pivotal moment for Andrew and me.....All of a sudden it was much clearer for me. Now I understand him on a much deeper level. Most of my communication with him is intuitive...Most of the time he does not know where*

these messages are coming from. We do lessons - not in math and reading but in how to acknowledge and attend to the messages he is receiving...I see his abilities not as supernatural, but just natural. Andrew somehow has direct access to the flow of intuitive communication."[235]

Ellen Boudreaux - Boudreaux had the ability like many musical savants to play any song after hearing it only once and knew so many songs it was impossible to stump her with a song she did not know. She was blind and made a chirping song as she walked which allowed her to walk around without running into anything. Perhaps her most impressive ability was that although blind from birth, Boudreaux was able to tell the time at any time of the day or night to the minute after her mother let her listen to the time lady on the phone at age 8.

Tony Cicoria - Dr. Tony Cicoria was an orthopedic surgeon who was hit by lightning after getting off a pay phone in a park at age 42. He had a near death experience where he floated blissfully over his body as a nurse performed CPR. "Suddenly, over two or three days, there was this insatiable desire to listen to piano music," said Cicoria, which was funny because although he had a few music lessons as a child he had "no real interest." He started to listen to Chopin. He bought record after record and suddenly he had the desire to play the piano. He got a piano and struggled to teach himself to play.

Then he started to hear the music in his head. It started in a dream with him playing on stage. He awoke and tried to write down the music he could still hear in his head. Asked if these were, hallucinations Cicoria said no they were inspirations. It's like frequency, a radio station, if I open myself up, it comes. I want to say, 'It comes from Heaven,' as Mozart said."[236] Cicoria would play starting at 4:00am and then after work, making his wife upset.

He had become very spiritual after the NDE reading everything he could get on the subject. He had a whole library now on Tesla and high voltage electricity. He could see auras around people.

Alonzo Clemons - As a child, Clemons suffered a head injury that left him severely mentally disabled and unable to talk. However, he could accurately sculpt beautiful clay animals with his hands without even looking at the animal. Later he began to sculpt statues that included people with animals.

Zacharias Dase - Dase was a 19th-century mathematical savant who suffered from epilepsy from early childhood:

He multiplied and divided large numbers in his head, but when the numbers were very large, he required considerable time. Schumacher once gave him the numbers 79532853 and 93758479 to be multiplied. From the moment in which they were given to the moment when he had written down the answer, which he had reckoned out in his head, there elapsed 54 seconds. He multiplied mentally two numbers each of 20 figures in 6 minutes; 40 figures in 40 minutes; and 100 figures in 83/4 hours, which last calculation must have made his exhibitions somewhat tiresome to the onlookers. He extracted mentally the square roots of a number of 100 figures in 52 minutes.[237]

One of the amazing abilities Dase had was the ability to count items almost instantaneously.

He had one ability not present to such a degree in other ready reckoners. He could distinguish some thirty objects of a similar nature in a single moment as easily as other people can recognize three or four. The rapidity with which he would name the number of sheep in a herd, of books in a bookcase, of window-panes in a large house, was even more remarkable than the accuracy of his mental calculations.

This ability may not have been a logical left-brain function, but rather a right brain telepathic ability, as illustrated by the story told about Dase counting peas. Dase "who would instantly call out '183' or '79' if a pile of peas was poured out, and indicate as best he could - he was also a dullard - that he did not count the peas, but just 'saw' their number, as a whole, in a flash."[238] (See Sacks Twins for an identical story.)

Jay Greenberg - Greenberg is a musical prodigy considered by instructor Samuel Zyman at the Julliard School of Music to be the best in 200 years. His parents reported that he started to draw cellos on paper at the age of two even though the parents did not play and there were no instruments in the house.

At the age of three, they decided to take him to a music store to see a cello. They ended up purchasing a miniature cello which Jay picked up and played. From day one he demonstrated that he instinctively knew the rules of music. By five, Greenberg had composed five symphonies, and nine by the time he was 15. One was 190 pages long and was recorded by the London Symphony orchestra.

Greenberg stated that the music just streams into his head at lightning speed, sometimes several symphonies running simultaneously. "My unconscious mind directs my conscious mind at a mile a minute."[239] He can process multiple symphonies going at the same time while he is going about his daily routine. He simply notates what he is hearing. He almost never makes corrections.

Like many other reports of musical downloads, the material comes very quickly. Jay stated that a symphony called "The Storm," which he was commissioned to write for the New Haven Symphony orchestra was written in only a couple hours, and he wrote every piece for every instrument. Greenberg told 60 minutes that "he doesn't know where the music comes from, but it comes fully written like from an orchestra in his head." He doesn't change the music or add instruments. As Greenberg described it, the instruments "just come in when they want."

Akiane Kramarik - Kramarik is one of the only double prodigies (art and poetry) in the world. "The earliest memory that I can recall was at 4 or 4 ½ years old one day, said Kramarik. "I started having strange and amazing visions. There were voices following me and guiding me through the galaxies, and I asked 'Who are you?' And I started calling him God. I would like to say both me and God are completely in control of everything. He tells me an idea, and I can just take that idea, and I can just take that idea and make it better and polish it and just put it into paints. He is like my personal teacher."

Leslie Lemke - Lemke was blind and suffering from severe mental defects from birth. He didn't learn to walk till 15. At 16, his adopted mother found him at the piano in the middle of the night playing Tchaikovsky's Piano Concerto No. 1. He became one of the savants that could play anything he had heard only once. Lemke became famous and toured the country.

Flo and Kay Lyman - The Lyman twins are known as the Rain Man Twins. The savant girls are able to tell what day of the week any date in history fell on. They are able to tell what the weather was like, what they had for dinner each day, and what games show hosts were wearing for every day of their life.

Franco Magnani - Acquired savant - Magnani experienced a temporal lobe seizure at which point he started to have dreams of the Tuscan village of Pontito where he was born. The dreams of pre-Nazi Pontito were vivid enough that they were described as "like holograms." Magnani also became consumed with painting. He taught himself to paint and produced hundreds of painted views of Pontito so photographically precise he became known as the memory artist. This was despite the fact he had not been in the town for 30 years. Three-dimensional holograms would appear in front of Magnani during his waking state inspiring his next painting. This actually happened once when Oliver Sacks, who studied him extensively, was visiting.

A sudden painting obsession also came over UFO experiencer Chris Bledsoe after his UFO abduction experience in 2007. He lacked the brain injury found in many savant cases and had never painted, but following his experience, he suddenly he felt compelled to go out and buy painting supplies. He produced numerous painting including many with hummingbirds feeding on flowers.

Bob Milne - Milne is a ragtime piano player who can do many incredible things such as playing a tune with one hand, while at the same time playing another tune with his other hand, as if carrying on a conversation.

His biggest mind talent is his ability to listen to four symphonies at the same time. The test to see if he could do it was run by neuroscientist Kirstein Betterman at the Penn State University.

Milne was given four symphonies to listen to by different composers a couple days before the test. While lying in an MRI machine, Milne was given the command to start the first piece in his head. After 15 seconds, a message came on the screen to continue listening to #1 and start the second piece. 10-15 seconds later, he was asked to start the third symphony in his head, and 10-15 seconds later, the command to start #4.

A while later, the screen message told Milne to stop all four pieces and one by one he was asked to sing where he was in each piece. He was to the note on all four pieces.

The control subject, a conductor for a symphony orchestra, could do one piece but was completely lost once he started the second symphony in his head.

Jason Padgett - Padgett is an acquired savant. He was attacked outside of a karaoke bar and received a severe brain injury. Padgett sees reality synesthetically as fractals describable by equations and is able to draw them. Since the incident, he sees mathematics in everything and even dreams about mathematics. He has produced drawing for equations such as $E=mc^2$, Planks Blackhole, and Pi.

Kim Peek - Peek is the person that the movie *Rain Man* was based on. He was known as a mega-savant and considered to have the best memory of anyone who has ever lived. He was affected by severe brain damage at birth. Peek read 12,000 books and knew everything about the books. Peek could read two pages at a time in three seconds. His right eye read one page, and the left eye read the other page. He memorized things from the age of 16 months.

Sacks Twins - John and Michael, known as the Sacks Twins, were savant twins that psychiatrist Oliver Sacks met in 1966 in a state hospital. The two had IQs of 60 and could do no mathematics but were able to come up with prime numbers from numbers in the order of 7-20 digits. They could also do calendar calculations, and recite back 300 digit numbers with ease. Sacks concluded, "The twins seem to employ a direct cognition - like angels....They see directly a universe and a heaven of numbers."

Although they could not do logical left brain mathematics like 7 x 4, they were exhibited right-brain telepathic type abilities, such as giving the day of the week for any date in history, and being able to instantly count immense figures.

The twins were the basis of the famous toothpick scene in the movie *Rain Man* where a waitress drops a box of toothpicks on the floor Raymond Babbitt instantly declares there are 246 toothpicks. This event is based on an even more spectacular event involving the Sacks Twins.

Oliver Sacks witnessed a box of matches fell from the table. As the matches fell, the twins simultaneously called out 37, 37, 37 and 111 when the matches hit the floor. Sacks counted the matches, and there were 111. Dr. Sacks described it as follows:

> *A box of matches on their table fell, and discharged its contents on the floor: '111,' they both cried simultaneously; and then, in a murmur, John said '37'. Michael repeated this, John said it a third time and stopped. I counted the matches - it took me some time - and there were 111.*
>
> *'How could you count the matches so quickly?' I asked. 'We didn't count,' they said. 'We saw the 111.'*
>
> *'And why did you murmur '37', and repeat it three times?' I asked the twins. They said in unison, '37, 37, 37, 111'.*
>
> *And this, if possible, I found even more puzzling. That they should see 111 - '111-ness' - in a flash was extraordinary....But they had then gone on to 'factor' the number 111 - without having any method, without even 'knowing' (in an ordinary way) what factors meant. Had I not already observed that they were incapable of the simplest calculations, and didn't 'understand' (or seem to understand) what multiplication or division was? Yet now, spontaneously, they had divided a compound number into three equal parts.*
>
> *'How did you work that out?' I said, rather hotly. They indicated, as best they could, in poor, insufficient terms - but perhaps there are no words to correspond to such things - that they did no 'work it out', but just 'saw' it, in a flash. John made a gesture with two outstretched fingers and his thumb, which seemed to suggest that they had spontaneously trisected the number, or that it 'came apart' of its own accord, into these three equal parts, by a sort of spontaneous, numerical 'fission.' They seemed surprised at my surprise - as if I were somehow blind; and John's gesture conveyed an extraordinary sense of immediate, felt reality. Is it possible, I said to myself, that they can somehow 'see' the properties, not in a conceptual, abstract way, but as qualities, felt, sensuous, in some immediate, concrete way? And not simply isolated qualities - like '111-ness' - but qualities of relationship?*[240]

Orlando Serrell - Like the famous American psychic Edgar Cayce, after being hit in the head with a baseball at age 10, Serrell developed abilities to instantly do calendar calculations[241] and remember the exact weather for every day following the accident.

Daniel Tammet - The model that best explains what is happening with savants is outlined by Dr. Diane Powell, who has worked with many autistic savants in an effort to explain their unusual abilities. "When I was looking more and more at these savant skills, the people who were able to express what they are experiencing, they say that they are not dividing it in their head. They say that the answer just pops into their consciousness, and they don't know how they get it. I thought that sounds so much like psi. Maybe that is what it is." [242]

An example of this is the explanation Daniel Tammet gives for his mathematical savant skill. Tammet has synesthesia where he sees color, shape, texture, and taste when he experiences numbers. He gave an example of how he multiplies two complex numbers together and how the answer downloads into his mind. When he sees the numbers 53 and 131, he sees distinct shapes associated with the numbers.

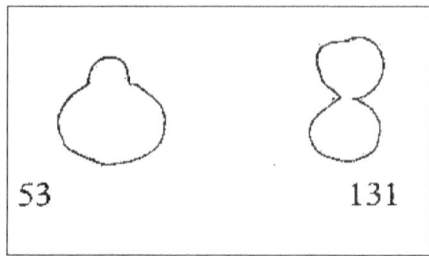 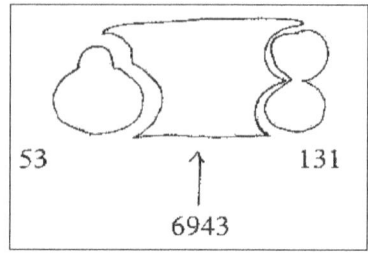

As soon as he makes the decision to multiply them together, a third shape appears which fits neatly between the two other shapes like a piece in a jigsaw puzzle. That shape has a number associated with it 6943 which Tammet recognizes. It is the answer.

Tammet is quite clear in what happens in his head. The answers to the complex math he is asked to do pops into his head like a right-brain visual download. He does not do any left-brain calculating.

Tammet had epilepsy seizures at four along with autism. He can learn a language in a week, and did learn Icelandic in one week after being challenged to do so by a documentary film producer. In another public challenge in front of cameras, he recited Pi to 22,514 places. Tammet became known as Brain Man. He states that like other people with synesthesia he perceives all numbers up to 10,000 with shape, color, texture and feel.

Vishal - Vishal is an eight-year-old Indian savant who "knows without studying." He published his first book when he was six called *Meadow of Moods*. He is in conversation with a leading genetics scientist about tracing the fragile X in chromosomes to avoid autism even before the assembly of DNA in future generations. He is researching Algae fuel authenticated by Professor at Indian Institute of Technology. He has corresponded with researchers such as Abhishek Shivakumar (a research scholar at Sweden's

KTH University) about strategies for harnessing nuclear energy, creating renewable energy from organic material, and traveling to Mars.

Swami Vivekananda - Vivekananda had memory ability like Peek and Von Neumann. He reported memorizing 10 Volumes of an encyclopedia in days. He reported that he did not read word by word, but line by line, or paragraph by paragraph.

John Von Neumann - Von Neumann was a mathematician who at 6 could divide two eight-digit numbers in his head; by 8 he had mastered calculus; by 12 he had read and understood Borel's Theorie des Fonctions. He reportedly could remember everything he had ever read word for word including page numbers and footnotes.

Ryan Wang - Wang is a four-year-old Chinese boy that is able to play at a master level after only one year. He played Carnegie Hall at five.

Steven Wiltshire - Wiltshire didn't speak his first words till he was five. The two words he spoke were pencil and paper. At 11, he was taken on a 45-minute helicopter ride over London and was able to draw a complete reproduction of the city on a 16-foot long canvas. His detail was so accurate that he even had the right number of windows and floors in each building correct. Later he did the same feat drawing Rome, Tokyo, Dubai, and New York City after flying over for only 45 minutes in a helicopter. It was this ability that gave him the name the "human camera."

Like the other download grouping, precognitive dreams have played a part in Wiltshire's life. His teacher tells the story of a flight from England into New York City. Wiltshire the day before had a recurring dream that he would be invited into the cockpit as they flew over the Manhattan skyline coming into the airport. Just as they approached the city a flight attendant approached Wiltshire and just like in the dream he was led to the cockpit.[243]

How does it work?

Darold Treffert, considered perhaps the foremost authority on savants believed that the savants could do things that they had not learned and attributed this to genetic memory and that it is all contained within a local physical world.

Treffert is aware of the nonlocal claims "from reliable witnesses" of savants having paranormal abilities including extrasensory perception as he pointed it out in a 1988 review article in a journal on savant syndrome. For his mentioning of the subject, he received criticism. "Thus," wrote Treffert, "my merely reporting that there were such reports engendered censure from the scientific community."

It may be this fear of censure and expulsion from the "boys club" that has led Treffert to arrive at very conservative conclusions about the savant mechanism which are not supported by much evidence.

The main theory that Treffert has adopted is the genetic memory theory. "Whether called 'ancestral,' 'genetic,' or 'racial' memory or referred to as 'intuitions' or 'congenital gifts,' the genetic transmission of skills and knowledge is convincing demonstrated, I believe, in the prodigious savant and child prodigies."[244]

Genetic Memory

Genetic memory assumes that there are mathematical talents that are passed physically from generation to generation and then like a bell curve where some people are not athletic and run slow whereas some are very athletic and run fast, the savants are doing some complex algorithm calculations to arrive at their answers. The assumptions being made are based on evolutionary religious faith positions.

The genetic theory has problems on many fronts.

Many of the savants had no family history of talent in the savant's area of expertise. An example of this comes from the case of Eddie, a young five-year-old musical savant who was a key subject in the University of Illinois study into musical savants.[245] Dr. Leon Miller reported that "At the time that Eddie was first seen by me, no formal music lessons had been attempted, and there was no piano in the house. None of the other members of the family plays an instrument, and there is no history of musical talent in the family."[246] When there is no history in many cases the gene theory becomes wanting.

The assumption that "unconscious inculcated algorithms" are being used has a couple of obvious problems. The first is that it is simply naming theory - giving an unknown a name and thereby somehow resolving the mystery. Nothing is resolved and the word "Unconscious inculcated algorithms" could easily be replaced with God, Santa Claus, or the Easter Bunny. Even the idea of consciousness arising from the brain is simply called "emergence" with not the slightest evidence to back up how this happens.

Second, there is a serious problem in that the algorithms being proposed are probably the most complex left-brained function that can be performed by a person. Yet, the one thing that we know about autism, savants, and prodigious savants, is that the left brain is damaged and severely compromised. In many cases the more compromised the left brain is, the better the talent. The idea that a damaged left brain is doing things that a healthy left brain can't do is very counterintuitive.

Kim Peek is a prime example. Except for memorizing things and having the musical savant talent, he could do nothing requiring his left brain. Yet he was considered a mega-savant and perhaps the most talented savant ever.

Dr. Elliot Sherr, who performed standardized neurological tests on Peek, spoke about his left-brain functions. "One of the things that were particularly obvious was for Kim to follow instructions," said Sherr. "I think he had a very hard time both focusing as well as following directions."

Rita Jeremy, who administered a standardized intelligence test, stated Kim had trouble with tasks that required new thinking and for which he could not call upon facts in his memory. When he had to do something where he had to figure something out, he had great difficulty.[247]

The concept that people have great difficulty figuring things out is at great odds with their being able to figuring out the most complex mathematical problems with mysterious godlike algorithms that have allegedly been genetically passed on. Jeremy stated that with Peek "things that were novel were difficult."

Another big problem with the genetic theory is that the researchers are speaking on behalf of the savants instead of going to the savant to find out how these calculations are done and what it might mean.

Most of this is because the many savants are so left-brain compromised that they cannot carry on a conversation, let alone describe what is going on in their head as they come up with answers faster than a computer. They sometimes even providing answers that stump a computer, as happened with Indian prodigious savant, Shakuntala Devi, when she calculated the 23rd root of a 201-digit number in 50 seconds. The powerful government Univac computer that was up against her in the challenge could not answer the question. It had to be reprogrammed to make the calculation and even then it took 12 seconds longer than Devi.

The acquired savants present new problems for the genetic memory. Acquired savants are people who suddenly pick up savant-like characteristics after sustaining head injuries such as hitting their head in a swimming pool or being struck by a baseball. Does the genetic theory state that genes have been damaged in such accidents causing the savant abilities? One of the key related theories proposed to explain savantism is that the excess capacity in the right brain is rewired to compensate for damage in the left hemisphere. Does this happen instantly in acquired savants? How does evolution explain this ability of the brain for instantaneous healing?

The genetic theory has never been fully explained. Some savants like Kim Peek have Google-like memories. Does it mean that memories are being stored in the genes and are accessed by the brain? Where are the laws of music stored in the genes and how does the mind of the savant tap into this?

There is a good understanding of the role of genes in the human body, and the role has nothing to do with memory. Genes are simply a playbook that give instruction for the formation of proteins.

Alonzo Clemons is an acquired savant who suffered a head injury at the age of 3. It left him with "serious cognitive disability, very limited speech and vocabulary and an IQ of 40. One of his key talents is to be able to mold a lifelike 3-D clay sculpture of an animal or animals with one look at a picture. He goes through an amazing process where he spends 45-50 minutes molding the animal with his hands is an armaturing process, using a self-fashioned wire framework to create real life motion in the animal. Does the genetic theory for savants claim that the armaturing process is contained in the genetic memory?

Then there is the homerun example provided by former Harvard psychiatrist Diane Powell, who talked about one savant who reproduced the periodic table without ever having seen one. "Darold Treffert examined this autistic savant, and here he is, a child who has never gone to school because frequently they cannot go to school. They can function. Sometimes they cannot even add... Treffert thought 'I would like to show that this child can do some information that he has not been exposed to.' He asked him to draw the periodic table, and he did. He drew it accurately, and he even drew in the letters that are used for the different elements and these are for the Latin names for the elements. Then he drew in the atomic numbers and weights. That is a lot of information for a child just to produce, so where does that come from?"[248]

Tammet can do Pi because Pi represents a part of the universe and has a standard structure to it, like the mathematics behind gravity, the speed of light, and electromagnetic fields.

A lot of it has to do with memory, and that goes back to Karl H. Pribram in the 1950s, and his holonomic model of brain processing is described in his 1991 book *Brain and Perception*.

The basic idea proposed by Pribram, supported by the work of physicist Dr. David Bohm and hologram inventor Dennis Gabor, is that processing in the brain can occur in a nonlocalized manner

The Sacks Twins knew which months since the year 2000 did Wednesday fall on the third day of the month, and what years since the year 1900 did April 21 fall on a Sunday, but they couldn't multiply 4 x 7 and couldn't say how much change they would get if they bought a three dollar shirt with a ten dollar bill. It is evident that The Sacks Twins did not possess a mathematical calculation gene.

Genetic Memory or Morphogenetic Field?

Chapter 13 Inspirations from Psychics and Mediums

We must learn to understand and internalize the nonlocal nature of what reality comprises. To put it simply, psi is a manifestation of our and the universe's nonlocal (nondual) nature. **Dr. Russell Targ**

Unless there is a gigantic conspiracy involving some 30 University departments all over the world and several hundred highly respected scientists in various fields, many of them originally hostile to the claims of the psychical researchers, the only conclusion the unbiased observer can come to must be that there does exist a small number of people who obtain knowledge existing either in other people's minds, or in the outer world, by means as yet unknown to science. **Professor Eysenck, the Psychology Chair at the University of London, and Director of Psychology at the Maudsley and Bethlehem Royal Hospitals**

In remote viewing, it is necessary to quiet the mind and give up the idea of guessing and analysis…the Buddhists call it giving up conditioned awareness when you are describing an object. **Russell Targ, Remote Viewer**

There are probably thousands of books written on psychics and mediums and their ability to obtain information from nonlocal sources. This chapter will only discuss a few.

No discussion of psychics would be complete without a discussion of the scientific testing done in the 1970s and 1980s by the American and Soviet governments. It was the work done in the Soviet Union that inspired the CIA, DIA, NASA, USAF, and Army. Millions of dollars were spent and the conclusion regarding extra sensory perception ("ESP") by the two men that headed up the American research, Dr. Hal Puthoff, and Dr. Russell Targ, was that "the scientific evidence for it is now overwhelming, and modern physics has the means and tools to embrace it. Such abilities have many names: Psi, metaphysics, clairvoyance, and ESP - the last being the most familiar."[249] Following are some of the more dramatic results from the 23 years that the scientific investigation was funded by the United States government.

Two key subjects in the scientific remote viewing research, Pat Price (the psychic) and Hella Hammid (the control who had never done anything psychic before), were to find contract monitors hiding in randomly chosen places in the San Francisco Bay area. Both were able to get accurate descriptions of churches, harbors, playgrounds, building, and parks where the monitor was hiding. Price located the monitor on 7 of the 9 attempts on his first try (odds of 1 in 100,000). This means that if the monitor had been kidnapped, Price would have found him 7 of 9 times on his first guess.

Hammid surprisingly was even better getting 5 or 9 targets on her first try and the other four on her second guess (1 in 1,000,000). She had no complete misses. Later, a psychic named Ingo Swann was able to develop a protocol where the controlled remote viewing was able to be taught to ordinary people.

The recovery of a TU-22 Tupelov supersonic bomber that the Soviets had converted to an intelligence platform which had crashed in Africa needed to be recovered. Remote viewers at both Wright-Patterson AFB and SRI accurately located the plane in a river a number of miles away from where the CIA had been searching.

After Targ had left SRI, he continued his work on psi and was able to begin a whole new industry based on controlled remote viewing. He and many of the others who had been trained in government program went on to develop precognition skills that were used to make money in the stock market and in the gaming industry. Some examples:

In 1982 Targ and his Delphi group used associated remote viewing to forecast the price of silver. (In associated remote viewing, objects are used as right-brained visual targets to associate with up a little to a lot, or down a little to a lot). The test hit nine weeks in a row, and the group made $120,000. The whole episode was documented by *NOVA* and written up on the front page of the *Wall Street Journal*.

The next year the group tried again but were unsuccessful because they were betting twice a week and the remote viewer was not getting feedback between predictions. Once the problem was determined the test was run again, and 11 or 12 predictions were correct, and a lot of money was made.[250]

Dr. Hal Puthoff used the same technique to raise $26,000 (his percentage of what the $260,000 that was made) for a school that was being built.

Fredrick Bligh Bond and John Alleyne - Mediumship - Fredrick Bond was an English architect who at the turn of the 20th century was considered an acknowledged authority on the history of church architecture. In 1908 the Church of England appointed him as director of excavations at Glastonbury Abbey.

Bond was highly successful at rediscovering the nature and dimensions of a number of buildings that had once occupied the abbey site. His method however was to use John Alleyne as a psychic to communicate with a dead monk from the abbey who had lived 400 years earlier, and the latter told him where to look. It was perhaps the first case of psychic archeology. In 1919 Bond published *The Gates of Remembrance*, which told how he had rediscovered the abbey sites using psychics. This led to his being fired in 1921 by the church.

Bond later became the subject of a major CBC documentary called The Ghosts of Glastonbury which reviewed the claims about the rediscovery of the abbey.[251]

Dr. Douglas Cottrell - Cottrell is known as the Edgar Cayce of Canada. He operates as a trance clairvoyant, where he goes into a trance and remembers nothing after the session. His son operates as the person who takes the questions and records what has happened.

Cottrell describes what he does as quantum meditation where the ego rational (left brain) mind is subdued and the subconscious contemplative Eastern mind is allowed to access the mind of the person asking the question, or it is able to read the information it needs from the akashic record.

Cottrell has downloaded two books through this trance method, *Secrets of Life* and *The Complete New Age Health Guide*.[252]

Pearl Curran - In 1913 Curran was using an Ouija board which suddenly relayed a message from a 17th-century spirit who wrote 'Many moons ago I lived. Again I come - Patience Worth my name." When it was all over Curran had produced "thousands of poems, six novels, and reams of philosophical musings that apparently transcended the abilities of the medium in her ordinary state…and elicited the highest praise from critics of the *Hanford Courant, Los Angeles Times,* and *The New York Times.* The writings were full of obsolete, archaic, and dialectical words, as well as recondite and obscure historical facts quite outside Curran's normal knowledge."[253] This was all done at incredible speed and in different styles.

Edward Kelley and Dr. John Dee - Mediumship - These two men were 16th-century alchemists who claimed to have communicated with angels using a language called Enochian. Kelley referred to the language as

"Angelical," the "Celestial Speech," the "Language of Angels," the "First Language of God-Christ," the "Holy Language" or "Adamical."

The communication of the twenty-one lettered alphabet started on March 26, 1583, when Kelley reported visions in a crystal sphere.

Kelley's alchemical writings were published as *The Alchemical Writings of Edward Kelley* (1893). Kelley was a self-declared spirit medium who worked with John Dee in his magical investigations. Besides the professed ability to summon spirits or angels in a crystal sphere, Kelley also claimed the secret of transmuting base metals into gold.

John of God - Disembodied spirits - John is a medium spiritual healer who lives in Abadiânia, Brazíl, where he runs the Casa de Dom Inácio de Loyola ("The Casa"). He can neither read nor write. He is probably the most famous spiritual healer alive today.

He did a rare interview with Oprah Winfrey. Dr. John Alexander reported on his visit to see John of God presenting his report to the Society for Scientific Exploration.

John of God reportedly uses "more than thirty other primary healing entities" to perform the many psychic healing that have made him famous.

Carl Jung - Jung was able to predict the rise of Hilter long before he came on the scene, "If somebody is clever enough to see what is going on in people's minds, in their unconscious minds, he will be able to predict. For instance, I could have predicted the Nazi rising in Germany through the observation of my German patients. They had dreams in which the whole thing was anticipated, and with considerable detail. And I was absolutely certain - in the years before Hitler came in the beginning; I could say the year..1919 - I was sure that something was threatening in Germany, something very big, very catastrophic. I only knew it through the observation of the unconscious."[254]

Charles Leadbeater - Psychic - Another interesting psychic inspiration came in one particular project set up by the Theosophical Society in India, which carried out a microscopic psychic examination, called *Occult Chemistry*, on the inner structure of elements on the periodic table. The two prodigious psychics involved in the project were Charles Leadbeater and Annie Besant. In 1895 Besant started publishing papers on their finding in 1895. Of great interest was research published in 1907 by the other psychic, Charles Leadbeater, who did a psychic viewing into a block of paraffin wax ($C_{25}H_{50}$) and described two different types of hydrogen being present. He said one was hydrogen with mass one (ordinary hydrogen) and the other with mass 3 (tritium) which would not be discovered until 1934 when Ernest Rutherford proposed it. Leadbeater had given it the name occultium. They also described three other items twisted together which sound like the present idea of quarks.

What was more significant is that hydrogen isotopes were unknown in 1907. The first mention of the possibility of isotopes was made by Frederick

Soddy in 1913. He received a Nobel Prize for the idea in 1921 even though Besant and Leadbeater had published it in a 1908 book called *Occult Chemistry* complete with a drawing of tritium. The isotope of hydrogen would not be discovered till the 1930s.[255]

Bennett Mayrick - Spirit Guides - Mayrick whose healing abilities inspired Dr. Bengston guides and the development of protocols for the Bengston Healing Method claimed that he was receiving inspiration and help from spirit guides that followed him around. They were described a "stereotypically humanoid in shape, without facial features, hands, or legs, as if they were wearing diaphanous sheets too opaque to see through." [256]

Mayrick had incredible psychic skills including being 100% accurate in an 8-person intuitive diagnosis experiment set up by Bengston. Bengston had people sign their names and place them in an envelope at the reception desk of a major hospital. Later, when they were collected, Mayrick, by just holding the envelope, was able to diagnose their illness without error. Later Bengston reported that the "Fellows" followed him around, even when Mayrick was not around.

Judith Orloff - Orloff is able to do "intuitive diagnosis" or read a stranger's medical state from a distance. Dr. Targ, who learned how to make this remote diagnosis, states that it works on the same principles of remote viewing and can produce the same accurate results. This type of remote psychic ability was made famous by the psychic Edgar Cayce, who did 9,400 such readings in the early 20th century.

Nandana Unnikrishnan - This is an important case as it hints that the telepathy of savants may be of a higher quality (in line with savants' perfect abilities in music, math, or whatever their skill is) than the telepathy reported in non-savant people. Nandana is a nine-year-old United Arab Emirates savant who can read her mother's mind as well as her emotions. Dr. Darold Treffert, the world expert on savants, stated that of 319 savants, 1% reported of savants reported ESP or Psi abilities. Child psychiatry specialists at the Sunny Specialty Medical Center in Sharjah, United Arab Emirates, certified "the strength of Nandana to read her mother's thoughts, desires and intentions."[257]

A test done involving a Grade 2 level poem was written and given to Nandana's mother, Sandhya, who read the poem in her mind; Nandana was asked to type what she saw in the laptop provided to her.

The Khaleej Times newspaper ran their own test before making the story public. They reported in part:

> *In our test, Sandhya was first given a note. It read "044050799 – the office number of Khaleej Times." As soon as she read it in her mind, Sandhya sat with Nandana across a table. The computer was kept in such a way that the*

keyboard faced the daughter, and the monitor faced the mother.

When her mother asked her to start typing, Nandana started keying in the numbers without even constantly looking at her mother. As she typed 044050799, it became evident to us that the child can actually read her mind! We were witnessing something unseen and unheard of.

When Nandana successfully completed the first test, we decided to try her telepathic skill. This time, the note given to her mother read: "Can I have some warm water please?"

The result came out as a sentence without any space between the words and with some minor spelling mistakes in between. But, it was still as amazing as the first instance.

To determine how the child would react when the mother is away, we sent Nandana to the bedroom and asked Sandhya to think about an object. When she decided the object as "biscuit" and told us that, without letting Nandana hear it, we called Nandana to the living room. Sandhya was then sent to the bedroom.

When Nandana's father Unnikrishnan asked her what the object was, the child was initially reluctant to say anything. Then her mother prompted her from inside, saying aloud, "say what it is Nandana." Looking very shy, the child leaned on her father and started pronouncing the word slowly. "bis...ki..t," she said.[258]

Nandana could type the entire poem and also reproduce a 6-digit number that the mother was given to think about. This is a very high level of telepathy. Diane Powell discusses other savant cases that involved telepathy:

> George was able to tell when his parents would pick him up at school, even though they provided him with no warning and the more typical scenario was for him to take the bus. Michelle has several episodes of clairvoyance, one of which was when she told her father that he had replaced a watch that had fallen out of the bathroom. She said this shortly after it happened and without any way that she could have known. Ellen was a blind musical savant who could predict her Christmas presents one week in advanced without any clues. Another savant dreamed that her father died from a heart attack the day before he died that way.[259]

Chapter 14 Inspirations through Scientific Investigation

Sometimes when I go to sleep, I am stuck with a terrific bog that I can't fix, and in my dreams, I see myself programming. When I wake up, I have figured out the solution. **14-year-old computer prodigy Santiago Gonzalez**

In 2006 former President Jimmy Carter gave an interview to GQ Magazine where he talked about the psychic investigations that had been done by the American government. The revelation came in reply to a question about the UFO cover-up,

Carter: *Well, in a way. I became more aware of what our intelligence services were doing. There was only one instance that I'll talk about now. We had a plane go down in the Central African Republic - a twin-engine plane, small plane. And we couldn't find it. And so we oriented satellites that were going around the earth every ninety minutes to fly over that spot where we thought it might be and take photographs. We couldn't find it. So the director of the CIA came and told me that he had contacted a woman in California that claimed to have supernatural capabilities. And she went into a trance, and she wrote down latitudes and longitudes, and we sent our satellite over that latitude and longitude, and there was the plane.*

GQ: *That must have been surreal for you. You're the president of the United States, and you're getting intelligence information from a woman in a trance in California.*

Carter: *That's exactly right.*

GQ: *How did your scientific mind process that?*

Carter: *With skepticism. Whether it was just a gross coincidence or…I don't know. But that's one thing that I couldn't explain."*

The story that Carter told was not completely accurate as the whole subject of what happened is still classified, and in his telling of the story, Carter had changed the type of plane that was recovered. The plane was not a small twin engine plane. Why would the top intelligence people be alerted to find some small plane? Years later the remote viewing officials that found the plane described the story more accurately. The plane being searched for was a Tupolev 22 Russian supersonic bomber, codenamed Blinder, which had been transformed into an intelligence platform. The plane had crashed in Zaire and American intelligence scrambled to find the plane before the Russians, as the plane would represent the leading edge Soviet intelligence technology, along with all the code books. Because it crashed in the jungle, American spy satellites were unable to find the target.

Both the CIA remote viewing program at the Stanford Research Institute and the USAF remote viewing program at Wright-Patterson Air Force were given the classified assignment of remote view the location of the missing Russian spy plane.

The officials running the CIA program chose remote viewer Gary Langford from the dozen or so remote viewers in the program. Langford had exhibited the ability to view high technology targets, and he had the technical knowledge to be able to describe what he was picking up.

The targeting session took 10 minutes. Langford was identifying that the plane was in a river, and he could only see part of the tail sticking up out of the water. He was less clear on describing exact location and roads in the area, so the session ended, and the information was sent back to the Pentagon so they could search the Zaire river region.

At Wright-Patterson, the classified remote viewing plane target was given to a woman by the name of Frances Bryan. She was shown a picture of the TU-22 and told it had gone down in Africa. Like Langford at SRI, she quickly saw a plane in a river but was able to be much more detailed about the surrounding area. The head of the program there, Dr. Dale Graff, wrote up the information Bryan had provided, along with Langford's description and cabled it to the CIA station chief in Kinshasa. It showed an area 70 miles west of where the CIA believed the plane had gone down. Later Jimmy Carter would tell the end of the story referring to Bryan's classified session, "She went into a trance, and when she was in the trance, she gave some latitude and longitude figures. We focused our satellite cameras on that point, and the plane was there."

In his diary, Carter was quite specific about how well remote viewing had worked and how he had been briefed on it April 11, 1979, "We've had several reports of parapsychology working...both we and the Soviets use these parapsychologists on occasion to help us with sensitive intelligence matters, and the results are unbelievable. The proven results of these exchanges between our intelligence services and parapsychologists raise some of the most intriguing and unanswerable questions of my presidency. They defy logic, but the facts were undeniable." [260]

Solid evidence exists for psi, and it goes way back into history, and there seems to be three categories.

1. **Head Injuries or brain/birth defects.** Like the inspirations of talents given to savants, there is a link between some psi abilities and brain injuries or birth defects.

Peter Hurkos - Considered by some as the greatest psychic in the world, Hurkos gained his great psychic abilities after falling off a ladder in 1930, and sustaining a head injury, resulting in coma.

Edgar Cayce - The great America psychic Edgar Cayce picked up his psychic talents to diagnose disease after he was hit in the head with a baseball.

Joe McMoneagle - One of the best remote viewers in the CIA's remote viewing program, McMoneagle in 1970 had a near death experience in the Army where he collapsed in the doorway of a restaurant, went into convulsions swallowing his tongue, and then stopped breathing. After being revived and having recovered, he started having spontaneous out-of-body experiences and spontaneous knowledge about things he ordinarily would have no way of knowing.

Studies that have been done with people who claim to be psychic seem to back up the idea that part of the brain is being shut off or quieted when the paranormal activity is going on, "psychic-sensitive people… experienced more head injuries and serious illnesses than the controls. Sixty-six percent showed evidence of right hemisphere and right temporal lobe dysfunction. Mystical experiences showed a trend toward being related to non-dominant hemisphere (usually right) dysfunction."

2. **People who get help** - The psychic Edgar Cayce had a message when he was thirteen that he was going to be helped in life. While out in the country reading his Bible he reported that an angel-type figure appeared and asked, in a voice that sounded like music, how she might help him. Cayce said he would like to help people. The next day at home Cayce's father was trying to teach him to spell without any success. It got so bad that his father lost his patience and hit Cayce knocking him off the chair and onto the floor. Thirty minutes later he still could not spell, and he was knocked to the floor again. Cayce, while lying on the floor, reported that he clearly heard the woman's voice again giving him an instruction saying, "If you sleep a little, we can help you."

He begged his father to let him sleep a minute, and that he would then know the answer. His father left the room and returned thirty minutes later finding his son asleep with his head on the book. When his father woke him, he found that Cayce apparently knew every lesson in the book and could repeat each one word for word. He continued through his whole life being able to sleep on a book and learn all of its contents.

As previously discussed, Peter Hurkos was a Dutchman, who manifested ESP after recovering from a head injury and coma caused by a fall from a ladder at age 30.

ESP is generally associated with a decrease in frontal lobe function (disinhibition) and increases or decreases in right temporal lobe function (similar to seizure phenomena).

Many UFO experiencers report increased psychic experiences after reported abductions. These experiences would run the whole gamut of psi, such as mental projection, clairvoyance, death warnings, dowsing, ability to do energy healing, mediumship, channeling, precognition, psychokinesis, remote viewing and telepathy. Asked at the 2014 UFO Congress what the percentage might be, Yvonne Smith, one of the most prominent abduction hypnotherapy regressionists replied, "Oh, about 99.9% report increased psychic experiences."

This high percentage was also supported by the results of a small study done by Peter Hough, who found that of 26 abductees, "A high 88 percent revealed they experienced minor premonitions."

The finding indicates that abductees have been inspired or helped to develop these psychic abilities. Following is a list of some such accounts.

Chris Bledsoe - Bledsoe had an abduction experience in January 2007 in North Carolina with four witnesses. Except for a short period in late 2008, Bledsoe kept quiet about what he had experienced. In 2012, he was inspired to talk again and gave a lecture to the MUFON group in Ashville, North Carolina.

During that lecture, he was heckled. While trying to figure out how to handle the situation, Chris said a message suddenly appeared in his head to tell the audience that there would be an earthquake in Baja California on September 25, so he said it out loud. Then the same voice said to tell the audience that there would be a natural disaster that would affect the outcome of the 2012 election, so Chris told them this.

On September 25, 2012, there were three earthquakes off the coast of Baja California. The first was 6.2, the second 4.2 and the third 4.8. As for the second prediction, Hurricane Sandy slammed into the east coast of the United States just 7 days before the election. It left polls in the dark, and special arrangements had to be made to get the vote.

Daniel (not real name) - Daniel is a prominent Canadian businessman who was involved in an abduction at West Hawk Lake, Ontario with seven other prominent individuals. None of the men have gone public with their abduction-type experience.

As Daniel tells the story, the aliens he encounters are what he calls the shims. The beings have no apparent sex. They are a combination of shes and hims – thus shims. Daniel has been taken many times in an abduction that is more like an out of body experience than a physical abduction. The shims have told him things to prove to him that they are who they say they are. One of the experiences that he relayed to an associate of mine was that he was told there would be a plane flying out of Rio de Janeiro flying to France. The plane would crash into the sea, and everyone would die. Days later, on June 1, 2009, it happened, just as predicted.

My associate was so taken when he saw the story on CNN that the next time Daniel was in his office with 6 other individuals he taped the meeting. Daniel was asked if he had received any other premonitions. He stated that he had. The encounter happened while he was scuba diving in the Caribbean. He was suddenly pulled and found himself with the shims. He protested to them that he was underwater and that he was going to die. They told him not to worry, that they had taken care of it.

They moved him above a body of water and showed him a scene of a slick of ugly material floating on the water. They told him this would be the biggest environmental disaster in history.

That was the story that was taped. Four days later the gulf BP oil disaster occurred. My associate told everyone that he had taped the meeting and provided everyone with a copy of the prediction of a disaster before it had occurred.

Carl Jung - Jung, a key 20th century psychologist stated, "All my works, all my creative activity, has come from those initial fantasies and dreams which began in 1912, almost fifty years ago. Everything that I accomplished in later life was already contained in them, although at first only in the form of emotions and images." [261] Jung listened carefully to Philemon, who he considered his daemon or spirit guide, "…Philemon and other figures of my fantasies brought home to me the crucial insight that there are things in the psyche which I do not produce, but which produce themselves and have their own life. Philemon represented a force that was not myself. In my fantasies, I held conversations with him, and he said things which I had not consciously thought. Psychologically, Philemon represented superior insight."[262]

Connie Parent - In 1977, Connie had a close encounter UFO experience in Steinbach, Manitoba, Canada, and can diagnose disease by seeing a person or their picture. She predicted future events such as a Utah mine disaster which killed 16 men and a major high-speed train collision in China. She states the future is like being on the internet 24/7.

Stan Romanek - In July, 2013, Stan Romanek sat in a plane that was going to be taking off from La Guardia airport. He suddenly grabbed his wife Lisa's hand and exclaimed, "Something has happened to a plane." For a number of minutes, he sat agitated and on edge. Ten minutes later an announcement came over the intercom from the pilot. Their take-off would be delayed as there was a crash on the runway. It turned out that an inbound Southwest Aircraft from Nashville had crashed on the runway.

Charles A. Schwartz - distant or remote viewing - Schwartz used remote viewers to do archeological digs. Schwartz was successful at finding Cleopatra's Palace, Mark Anthony's Palace, and the Lighthouse of Pharos, one of the seven wonders of the ancient world. Schwartz also found a buried building in the city of Maria, the remnants of one of Christopher Columbus's caravels from his fourth voyage, an American brig in the Caribbean, the talking idol of Cozumel, and the Library of Alexandria (awaiting excavation).

Schwartz also led up a detailed scientific experiment called Project Deep Quest which was set up to establish three key elements. The whole experiment was filmed, and Ann Kale, a senior scientist at Jet Propulsion

Laboratories, the then head of Earth Applications Satellite Research Group, was a witness and in control of all the experimental records.

Could psychics find an undiscovered shipwreck that had not been previously listed in the catalog kept by the Department of Land Management? Could they then identify how it had gone down and what items were on the ship? The results of a 1977 experiment were positive.

A wreck was identified by 7 of the 11 remote viewers used in the experiment. They identified a location a couple hundred yards long in a 150,000 square mile area off Santa Catalina Island off the coast of California. The sailing ship that had a small steam engine on the deck was identified as predicted with "the steam winch, the aft helm with the wheel down and the shaft pointing up along with the large (5 by 6 by 7) stone block" that had been identified by Hella Hammid, one of the viewers. Thomas Cook at the Department of Land Management confirmed that the site had never been listed on the 53 wrecks that had previously been located off Santa Catalina.

Then a submarine with remote viewers was taken below the level of being able to use ELF or any other waveform to communicate. The test was to see if remote viewing was electromagnetic in nature. If so, the viewers would fail their viewing at the sub's depth. Their ability to view, however, was not diminished.

On the first day of the experiment Ingo Swann and Hella Hammid identified the locations of Dr. Puthoff and Dr. Targ in Palo Alto. The targets were generated by a computer. In the one target randomly picked it was a great tree on the edge of a cliff. And one of the remote viewers said "There's this great big tree, and they're climbing in the tree." It was a direct hit.

Then in another target experiment Ingo Swan said, "They're hiding in a shopping mall. There are big glass windows, and there are people all around. There's red tile on the floor. There's this big turning wheel." It was a direct hit and proved that these aspects of consciousness were not electromagnetic and that we are not like walkie-talkies.

Global Consciousness Project - The Global Consciousness Project was set up at Princeton University to look for meaningful correlations in random data. The idea was to test for correlation with possible interconnected human consciousness on a global scale.

The system used random number generators spread around the world. If there was no interconnected consciousness, the machines would continue to produce a random pattern of ones and zeros.

As described on the project's website, "When a great event synchronizes the feelings of millions of people, our network of RNGs becomes subtly structured. We calculate one in a trillion odds that the effect is due to chance. The evidence suggests an emerging noosphere or the unifying field of consciousness described by sages in all cultures."[263]

Roger Nelson, who runs the project, stated that the theory he likes best can be described as a field theory producing the variations in the RNGs during big events like the 911 attack. The field would not be electromagnetic but more like a field of information. "Sometimes, said Nelson, people talk about a consciousness field." That is his favorite and the information from the Global Consciousness Project actually favors some sort of field theory.[264]

Max Planck Institute for Human Development Guitar Study - Researchers Johanna Sänger, Viktor Müller and Ulman Lindenberger at the Center for Lifespan Psychology, Max Planck Institute for Human Development, Berlin, Germany, conducted a study on guitar players looking at the ability of a group of guitarists to synchronize their brains.

The research was reminiscent of research that was done by Dr. David Bohm in the 1950s at the Berkeley Radiation Laboratory with plasmas. The experiments showed that the individual electrons, instead of acting chaotically and randomly, as would be the case if the Universe has no underlying intelligence, acted as if they were part of an interconnected whole. The electrons in the plasma assumed the nature of a self-regulating organism as if they held inherent intelligence.

In the same way, at the Max Planck Institute it was predicted there would be no coherence of interconnectedness between the brains of the 12 pairs of guitar players who took place in a study.

In the study, 12 pairs of guitarists played a modified Rondo in two voices by C.G. Scheidler while their brains were being scanned. What the scans showed is that the guitarists' neural networks would synchronize not only during the piece but even slightly before playing. It was as if their minds could read each other and synchronize.

In technical terms, the study reported it this way,

> *Indicators of phase locking and of within-brain and between brain phase coherence were obtained from complex time-frequency signals based on the Gabor transform. Analyses were restricted to the delta (1–4 Hz) and theta (4–8 Hz) frequency bands. We found that phase locking, as well as within-brain and between-brain phase-coherence connection strengths, were enhanced at frontal and central electrodes during periods that put particularly high demands on musical coordination... We conclude that brain mechanisms indexed by phase locking, phase coherence, and structural properties of within-brain and hyper brain networks support interpersonal action coordination (IAC).*[265]

Chapter 15 Inspiration from the Third Man Factor

Another source of inspiration and help from an outside source comes in what had been referred to as the "third man factor." In these reported experiences, an unseen presence such as a "spirit" or "entity" provides comfort or support during traumatic experiences, great stress, or in a life-and-death struggle.

This factor has occurred with single individuals and more importantly with multiple witnesses, which is important because it eliminates the skeptical idea that it might be a psychological phenomenon. The hallucination belief fails in two key respects: 1) The idea of a hallucination is just a word placed on something that doesn't fit into our belief about collective reality. There is no concrete proof that such a thing as a non-existent hallucination exists. 2) A claim of mass (multiple people) hallucinations is totally unsupported by any scientific evidence. Claims that multiple people imagine something is counterintuitive because what multiple people perceive is how we define what is real in the world. Trying to make the case that a group or the whole world is hallucinating something that threatens our world view is bordering not on science but psychotic behavior.

In my UFO research career, even I have run across a third man story. A friend of mine who was interested in UFOs was teaching young elementary school children.

He relayed to me that back in the early 1970s he was driving in the mountains of British Columbia on narrow roads with steep drop-offs, unlike the present day wider roads with guardrails on every cliff edge.

On a dark rainy night, my friend had gone off the cliff and although I don't recall how far the car dropped, I recall it was a fair distance down onto a railway track below. He was injured, and realized that he had to climb up the mountain and reach the road to survive, and so he began the long steep climb on slippery rock face.

As he began to make the climb he suddenly realized that there was man helping him do the climb. Oddly, he did not talk to the man nor thought it unusual that this man had suddenly appeared to help him in the climb.

After a great deal of pain, time, and suffering my friend finally made it to the top. He took a second to gather himself and then turned to thank the man for his help. There was no one there. He stood on the dark highway alone. It was a story that still mystifies him, and after relaying the story to me, I had nothing I could contribute.

There are scores of these stories of third man rescue, companionship, and disappearance when the crisis is over. Many of them have been documented as guardian angels stories, such as the collection by Catherine Lanigan in her books *Divine Nudges* and *Autobiography of My Guardian Angel: Divine Words from Above to be Read by Humankind.*

Among the stories told in her books Lanigan tells the story of a mysterious reverend who rescues a woman that was traveling through a rough part of town and then disappears as soon as he brings her to a service station. There is also the story of Patricia Galanti in Texas who told of being in a major car accident and rescue people who used the Jaws of Life to get her out of the car. The rescue people told her she was lucky she turned off her car as it had been leaking gas. Galanti told them a woman had told her through the shattered window to turn it off, to which the rescue people told her no one could have told her that as the cars were together at the point where the window was.

There was also the story of Lynn Anderson from Miami Florida, who drove into a ravine and before she passed out from her injuries heard a voice that told her to turn on the car lights. Later two hunters in the area saw the car lights and rescued her. It was only after telling the tow shop about her rescue that Anderson found that, according to the tow shop, the battery had been disconnected in the crash and the lights couldn't have been on.[266]

More importantly, there are two stories of people who were prevented from being hit at a railway crossing when they failed to see the train. In one of these cases, a man appears mysteriously on the track forcing the driver to stop, and in the other a girl is pushed off the track and down into the ditch. In both cases, the witnesses believed they would have been dead without those interventions, and in both cases the being that saved them was nowhere to be found once the train was gone.[267]

A similar story of being warned before an accident was told by Milton Forbes. The incident happened in his town of Ottumwa, Iowa. Forbes reported that he was in doing grocery deliveries and had returned to his truck, where he threw an empty box into the back of the truck. He jumped into the truck, started the motor and was preparing to rush to the next delivery stop.

"I froze stone cold," said Forbes. 'Time stood still, and I heard a voice say, 'Check the front of the truck.' I immediately turned off the engine, walked around to the front, and gasped. Right there was a small boy on his tricycle. He was leaning against my bumper, looking up at me with a smile. Chills of terror ran through me. I could have killed the tyke. But something had stopped me."[268]

These train and car stories are important because they also directly counter the explanation of sensory illusion or hallucination caused by loneliness, fear, injury, extreme physical exertion or monotony, or medical conditions attributed to low blood glucose, high altitude edema, or cold stress. In the third man train stories the experiencers did not realize anything was wrong till the experience was over.

Following is a list of some of the people who have also reported third man help and inspiration.

Anne Cooley - Multiple witness case - This is a bizarre case which has a crossover to the world of UFOs because it involves what is referred to in ufology as Men in Black ("MIB"). MIBs stand out as being very strange. Many in the early years of ufology are just like the man Anne encountered, who was dressed in clothes that had gone out of style decades ago. Anne was a single mother working as a cashier in a restaurant when she found out she had breast cancer.

A few days before her cancer surgery an MIB walked into the restaurant dressed like he had come out of the 1940s. He asked Anne if she believed in angels. Anne stated that she was aware of the Biblical passage about entertaining angels unawares, to which the man replied, "You are not alone. We are here to help you."

Anne looked around to see if anyone else had heard the weird comment and when she looked back the man was gone. She asked the other cashier who had talked to the man if she saw him leave but this woman was just as taken by what had happened. They both looked for him without success.[269]

Ron DiFrancesco - DiFrancesco was a worker at the World Trade Center during 911 event. He was the last to escape the south tower before it collapsed.

DiFrancesco worked on the 84th floor and after plane hit, he was forced to lie down to avoid a raging fire and thick smoke on the 79th floor. Suddenly a male voice called him by his first name. "Somebody lifted me up. I was led to the stairs. I don't think somebody grabbed my hand, but I was definitely led." The voice told him, "Hey you can do this."

As he proceeded down the stairs, he encountered a downed wall and a fire. He heard the voice tell him to run through the fir, so he covered his head with his forearms and did as he was told for what he believed was about three floors. He was singed but alive. At the 76th floor, the presence disappeared.

DiFrancesco eventually made it down and out the church street exit seconds before the tower collapsed. He attributed his survival to divine intervention. "It was a higher being rather than an internal being," he said. "Maybe it was an angel. I didn't see the face of God, but I know somebody came and helped me."

Peter Hillary - The son of Edmund Hillary had a third man experience during an expedition to the South Pole in November 1998, retracing Scott's final Antarctic journey.

The third man in Peter's case was his mother who had died 20 years earlier. 'The voice was insistent but encouraging and was accompanied by a vivid sense of physical presence…It was like she'd come out there to keep me company,' he said.

Voytek Kurtyka and Robert Schauer - multiple witness encounter - Kurtyka spoke of their encounter with the third man while climbing Gasherbrum IV in 1985:

"What was possibly the most amazing thing about this is that both Robert Schauer and I had (it) at the same time. It was so striking, so tangible, this sense of a third person, that at one moment I tried to talk about it with Robert, and the moment I started, I could not express myself. I just said something like, 'Robert, I would like to tell you something, but it is very strange.'

'I know what you mean,' he said. 'You sense him, the third person.'

'Yes, do you?'

'Yes.'"[270]

Charles Lindbergh - On his first trans-Atlantic flight after the 22 hours of flight, Lindbergh was visited by third men. He referred to them as "Disembodied beings speaking with human voices….Emanations from the experiences of ages, inhabitants of a universe closed to mortal men…like the gathering of family and friends after years of separation, as though I've known of them in some past incarnation. I live in the past, present and future, here and in different places, all at once…" Here is how Lindbergh described the experience in his book *The Spirit of St. Louis:*

On a long flight, after periods of crisis and many hours of fatigue, mind and body may become disunited until at times they seem completely different elements, as though the body were only a home with which the mind has been associated but by no means bound. Consciousness grows independent of the ordinary senses. You see without assistance from the eyes, over distances beyond the visual horizon. There are moments when existence appears independent even of the mind. The importance of physical desire and immediate surroundings is submerged in the apprehension of universal values.

For unmeasurable periods, I seem divorced from my body, as though I were an awareness spreading out through space, over the earth and into the heavens, unhampered by time or substance, free from the gravitation that binds to heavy human problems of the world. My body requires no attention. It's not hungry. It's neither warm nor cold. It's resigned to being left undisturbed. Why have I troubled to bring it here? I might better have left it back at Long Island or St. Louis, while the weightless element that has lived within it flashes through the skies and views the planet. This essential consciousness needs no body for its travels. It needs no plane, no engine, no instruments, only the release from the flesh which circumstances I've gone through make possible.

Then what am I – the body substance which I can see with my eyes and feel with my hands? Or am I this realization, this greater understanding which dwells within it, yet expands through the universe outside; a part of all existence, powerless but without the need for power; immersed in solitude, yet in contact with all creation? There are moments when the two appear inseparable, and others when they could be cut apart by the merest flash of light.

While my hand is on the stick, my feet on the rudder, and my eyes on the compass, this consciousness, like a winged messenger, goes out to visit the waves below, testing the warmth of the water, the speed of the wind, the thickness of intervening clouds. It goes north to the glacial coasts of Greenland, over the horizon to the edge of dawn, ahead to Ireland, England, and the continent of Europe, away through space to the moon and stars, always returning, unwillingly, to the mortal duty of seeing that the limbs and muscles have attended their routine while it was gone.[271]

Doug Scott and Douglas Haston - multiple witness encounter - On a 1975 ascent of Everest both Scott and Haston reported to the expedition's medical officer that they had "a curious sensation of a third person that had been sharing the snow hole during the night."[272]

Diane Richard - multiple witness encounter - Richard was driving with her two children through an intersection when she was hit in the passenger door by a car driving through the red light. The accident caused her arm to hit and shatter the driver's side window forcing her to pass out. She awoke to a woman in purple opening the passenger side door and climbing into the car. He said that everyone would be alright and wrapped Diane's arm in a tourniquet using her sweater. Then she climbed into the back seat, calmed the two boys down and used Diane's cell phone to phone her husband.

As she completed the call, the firemen arrived announcing that they would get everyone out, and then they would call her husband. Diane said a lady had just done that to which the fireman replied, "Which lady?"

Diane explained what had happened as they got her out and placed her on a stretcher to which the fireman said no one had been at the scene, and she must have imagined it. Furthermore, no one could have gone in the rear passenger door as it was smashed in. Diane protested asking who had bandaged her arm and phoned her husband. The question was answered by her son who said. "The lady." He had also seen her.[273]

James Sevigny - In 1983, Sevigny fell 2,000 feet in an avalanche off a mountain in a remote part of the Canadian Rockies. He awoke and found his back broken in two places, his knees were broken, and he had internal bleeding. His partner was killed in the fall. He curled up waiting to die when he hear a voice, "No, you can't give up. You have to live. You have to get your jacket on. You have to get water."

Sevigny heard the voice that reminded him of a woman over his right shoulder. He said, "It was like if I would sneak up to you and put my nose a quarter of an inch from your neck. It was that kind of physical sensation."

He did as he was told. He said, "I didn't question it. I didn't think about it. I did exactly what the voice said."

The presence encouraged not to give up as it led him back to his campsite. When he arrived, Sevigny saw three people skiing nearby and called for help, at which point the presence disappeared.

Sevigny was moved by his experience. "It made me cry," he said. "It was so powerful. I just couldn't tell many people... "If it wasn't for the Third Man, I would be dead. There's no way that I would have the strength to get up and walk across that valley and do the things I did to survive."[274]

Stephanie Schwabe - Schwabe was a cave diver who was diving in a cave off South Bahama Island in August 1997 when she lost the guideline which would lead her back to the entrance. As she began to panic figuring that she might die, she suddenly heard the voice of her late husband and diving partner, Rob Palmer.

At the height of her desperation and sadness, everything changed. "I suddenly felt flushed, and it seemed like my field of vision had become brighter," she stated. Then she heard her husband calming her and telling her she would survive. She slowly rescanned the cave and spotted the white rope. The second she saw it the presence of her former husband was gone. [275]

Sir Ernest Henry Shackleton - A multiple witness case - Shackleton was a famous British explorer who led three expeditions to explore the Antarctic. Shackleton reported that he and two or the others on one expedition were joined by an incorporeal being on the third leg of their 1914-1916 Antarctic journey. Saying, "during that long and racking march of thirty-six hours over the unnamed mountains and glaciers of South Georgia, it seemed to me often that we were four, not three."[276] I said nothing to my companions on the point, but afterward, Worsley said to me: "Boss, I had a curious feeling on the march that there was another person with us." Crean confessed to the same idea. On this point, being interviewed by the Daily Telegraph (February 1, 1922), he said: "None of us cares to speak about that. There are some things which can never be spoken of. Almost to hint about them comes perilously near sacrilege. This experience was eminently one of those things."

Frank Smythe - Smythe was a climber who in 1933 came within 1,000 feet of the top of Mount Everest. Had he made it he would have been the first to reach the summit. He described his encounter with the third man in his diary. The experience was so real that he pulled out a piece of Kendal mint cake at one point, broke it in half, and turned around to give the other half to a companion. But there was no one there: "All the time that I was climbing alone, I had a strong feeling that I was accompanied by a second person. The feeling was so strong that it completely eliminated all loneliness I might otherwise have felt. It even seemed that I was tied to my 'companion' by a rope, and if I slipped 'he' would hold me. I remember constantly glancing back over my shoulder."

Henry Stoker - A multiple witness case - Stoker, a British Naval Officer, and two others escaped a Turkish prisoner-of-war camp in 1916 and crossed 350 miles of rugged terrain to reach the coast. Stoker reported that he had been joined by a fourth man and that he was comforted by the presence. Because the group had almost no food, they became hungry, thirsty and dispirited. Later in discussion with those who were with him he discovered that they also had experienced the fourth man. [277]

Chapter 16 Inspirations from Aliens

We've come to tell you this stuff so you can put it in your work and explain it to the world. **Grant Morrison on how he was influenced to put alien-inspired ideas into his comic books.**

There are surprisingly a lot of cases in this category of aliens downloading information especially in the area of spirituality, mathematics, science, free energy devices and other inventions.

Most of these inspirations from the aliens come through telepathy. Unlike humans who have almost no control over telepathy, the aliens seem to have complete control over the ability. That is the main element that makes them different from us.

In the presence of aliens, however, humans do have telepathic ability. This cross-species communication ability is important because it shows minds are probably part of one collective element like gravity or energy. It also links aliens and humans into some bigger collective as opposed to our idea of separation where we are here, and the aliens are "out there." The ability to use telepathy is a matter of knowledge.

In a survey of 2,000+ experiencers done by the Foundation for Research into Extraterrestrial Encounters (FREE) it was shown that 41% of those that responded to question 54 replied yes. Question 54 dealt with downloads:

> Do you believe that you possess information about advanced technologies, advanced physics or other scientific information that you've never read or learned in your normal environment?[278]

These are very significant and large numbers. A 1991 omnibus survey done by the Roper organization showed that 2% of the American population, now pegged at 320,738,520, answered the question in a way to indicate that they were experiencers. That means 6,414,770 people just in the United States. If 41.73% of these were receiving downloads of technical, mathematical, and scientific information, it would mean there are 2,676,883 people in American getting information downloads from aliens.

The immediate questions become why are so many people being given this advanced knowledge? How long has this been going on?

Like all other areas of inspiration/download the right brain may be the key element in the process, as it is known that the people who claim to interact with aliens are generally right brained, creative people.

There are many in the literature. One that I personally was told about involved one of the top neuroscientist researchers in the country. It was pointed out to me that she was an experiencer and that she gave some credit for some of her discoveries to her experiencer status.

This is also an area that researchers, government, and businesses have expended a fair bit of time and money on. In government circles, there is a whole field of research on military abductions where it appears government military forces are reabducting experiencers to find out from them what the aliens told them or what type of technical information they might have been given.

The Aerospace industry is another group that has had a definite interest in contactees. Douglas Aircraft, for example, ran a UFO research program from 1967 to 1969 after engineer Dr. Robert Wood said if they didn't for business gain solve how alien technology worked, their competitor, Lockheed, would. The Douglas program was financed to the tune of $500,000. Part of the program involved regressing experiencers to see if they had received any technology during their encounters with aliens.

Following are some of the more prominent stories of downloads received by people from aliens.

Darryl Anka - Anka, Paul Anka's cousin, is the channel for the extraterrestrial entity, Bashar. Anka says that the downloads he gets come in pictures and when he is by himself he can get direct downloads that he does not have to interpret to the audience. On one occasion he asked for the answer to how Bashar and his spacecraft got here. Anka stated that the actual download took a fraction of a second, but it took him three hours to write out what he had been told.[279]

Connie - Connie is one of the many experiencers who has received mathematical formulas and other scientific concepts as part of her lifetime experiences. She described the situation to me:

> I have had only a few dreams during the summer where I remember math, science, psychic healing (lady with white hair and her assistant), space and rewinding time as well as a refresher course on "super helix 8," (the first super helix 8 was two years ago).
>
> The math formulas, numbers and symbols being shown to me (someone was teaching me) had symbols I didn't recognize. After awakening during the night after one of these math dreams, I felt like I was having so much fun learning. I wrote the clearest part of the equation down that morning.
>
> The "e" symbol is based on Latin characters using set membership, set theory and mathematical logic (I had to look this up; I didn't understand the symbol).
>
> I had the numbers written down properly, but oddly, I can't find them. This is best I can remember.

The square roots squared on each side cancel each other out leaving the same number of 23759, duplicated. I don't understand how the "e" fits in, but I suppose if I could remember the rest of the equation it might explain things better. The way it seems to me is: 23759 is not an element of 23759.

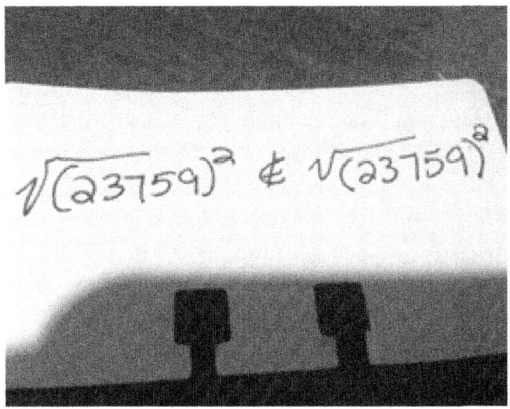

Gabrielle Giet - Giet is an intuitive from the west coast of Canada who is getting downloads from a group of spirit guides and a council of aliens who started the experiment on Earth and are referred to as "the others." Giet described the type of material she is receiving, "I have been given medical information for the purpose of curing the human population of all disease, bold statement I know, but if you knew what I knew this is what you would be saying, as well. Currently, I am in the process of patenting a living biomedical bandage made of human components that will flip the medical world upside down according to the some of the world specialists who have reviewed it. This bandage repairs skin rapidly, leaving no scars."[280]

German Mother and Painter - This German mother of young children is an experiencer with no science background. She stated, "Physics still spills out of my head all the time… Physics and plasma dynamics are something I know too much about."

Renario Hernandez - Hernandez is the founder of FREE, a major support group for UFO experiencers. He is an IRS attorney in Miami Florida whose wife in 2012 suddenly started seeing large UFOs the size of a stadium, following a mysterious healing of their dog that she attributed to an object that appeared in the living room. After a number of these stories from his wife, Hernandez decided to see if he could send out a message and see one of these huge crafts his wife was seeing. Fifteen minutes into the experience a UFO the size of Wembley Stadium, appeared over his neighbor's house, which his daughter and friends observed with him.

Realizing that there was some sort of consciousness connection, he began reading books on consciousness, quantum physics, UFOs, and NDEs. He became so consumed to find an answer to what he had seen that he was only sleeping two hours a day.

Hernandez contacted me as he had heard me talking about UFOs and consciousness, and we e-mailed back and forth. I then told him that I would be in Florida near where he lived, and doing a lecture on consciousness and UFOs. Hernandez said that he would come and bring his wife.

Both showed up attended my lecture. It was the first and only UFO conference Hernandez has attended. His wife did not want to talk about her experience indicating that her husband "talks too much about UFOs." She seemed at peace with what had happened to her and placed it in a religious context.

Both attended the experiencer session where people can talk about their encounters in a safe room. Hernandez described the events and how he believed there was a consciousness connection. Then three days after the conference, Hernandez received a download:

> *I am driving down a congested highway in downtown Miami, 8:30 in the morning in the middle of a traffic jam, all of a sudden I got what I call an ET telegram. It was both a voice that popped into my head, and I saw a video that surrounded it...The video basically said that I have to do an organization that is going to be presenting to the world the relationship between ETs, the spirit world, and quantum physics. The video that I saw was sort of like that video of the Price is Right wheel...where you spin around, and all these colors flash around saying "Oh you have won $200 dollars, or $300 or whatever. What it was in my case was inside this wheel where different types of paranormal topics – out of body experiences, remote viewing, mystical meditations, mystical travel, ETs, telepathy, teleportation, on and on with all these paranormal...and what was holding everything together was quantum physics.*[281]

Within hours, he has started to put together a group called Foundation for Research into Extraterrestrial Encounters. Key people like Dr. Rudy Schild at Harvard and Dr. Edgar Mitchell, the 6th man to walk on the moon, agreed to be scientific advisors. Many of the key people in the fields of UFOs, quantum physics, NDEs, and consciousness are now advisors.

Hernandez has stated that he had received many downloads since that time which have helped him put together this key organization, as if he is getting help and direction from the aliens.

Audrey Hewins - Like Hernandez, Hewins runs a major experiencer support group in Maine, hosts a yearly conference for experiencers, and has a radio show that deals with the UFO experience.

Hewins recalled that, "In 2004 I had a near death experience where I was pulled into the Ocean, by a rip-tide but saved by a blond being with amazing eyes.....He appeared very human looking, but he called me by name. That was what I consider the beginning of my 'Spiritual Awakening.'"

Then, like Hernandez, she started to review inspirations and downloads to begin a support network for experiencers. Hewins stated, "On November 6th, 2006 I was visited in my home in Oxford Maine by a beautiful glowing female humanoid being with AMAZING EYES. She told me I was ready to begin my work and that I was to start a group to help and guide other experiencers and to name this group Starborn Support. She told me that someday the world would know who Starborn Support was, that we would help MANY, and that someday in the future all involved would become ambassadors to the planet. I started this group the very next day, and having no clue what to do I simply opened a MySpace page and used my cell phone number as a hotline for those who have had ET contact, and were looking for help and support."

Then exactly like Hernandez she received a vision with audio that involved a wheel, "Several days after the encounter on Nov 6th with the female being, I had another experience. This time, I had a vision. It played like a movie in my head and was both an audio and visual message. During this experience I was shown a wheel, this wheel lay like a table and surrounding it were at least a dozen different types of beings. They were all looking at the wheel. On the wheel were many types of symbols, and writing."

Hewins followed the instructions she was given and now provides support to experiencers all over the world.

Manitoba Contactee - As told by one of the business investors who was dealing with the contactee in Manitoba, the contactee said he had dreamed the invention and was an experiencer. While out berry-picking on July 31, 1974, he had been abducted with two of his cousins, aunt and Grandma, in the Interlake area of Manitoba. The Manitoba contactee stated to the business investor that:

> *He [the contactee] was working on a fairly large battery type thing that was the size of a very large suitcase. They were able to be hooked up in sequence, and you could connect as many as these units together as you like. They could charge and discharge at the same time and from multiple sources such as a wind generator, grid energy, solar panels, etc. They could charge at night when energy in California energy prices was cheaper and readied to*

discharge during peak hour timeframes. If a house had 8 of these hooked up, they would act as a backup power supply that could run essential items if grid power was lost at a critical point in time. These units could also be part of the grid power supply. Utilities could control these with a keystroke over the internet.

In a weird synchronicity, the inventor was in the businessman's office when the subject of UFOs took place. As the businessman described the event:

> *Halfway through our discussion he walked into my office one day while I was working on something at my desk. That morning I had discovered a person named Rael in France and he had been abducted and asked to write a few books on true history and such. I had downloaded them, and one of these books was on my desktop and was on a page which showed some marks that Rael was given by the ET's that abducted him to show he wasn't dreaming.*
>
> *They were a set of 3 dots set out in a triangle. When this guy sat down, he glanced at my desktop as I finished what I was working on and asked me if I believed in UFOs?! Out of the blue! I looked up and said yes I do. He proceeded to stand up and pull his pants down and expose some marks on his hip that was nearly identical to the one on my desktop! He then proceeded to tell me that he was an experiencer and ideas came through them to him in different ways, he also told me that his cousin would build things that he didn't even know what they were for. He was also one of the experiencers on that day in July 1974.*

The business investor had one of the units in his office operating, but in the end, the contactee sold his idea to a US firm and requested the unit back.

Matt - Matt was a UFO experiencer I met in Las Vegas. He had attended my lecture and we talked at length the next night at a cocktail party. He had experienced many UFO sightings and downloads. He told me about three key downloads.

It was July 1997. Matt had worked many jobs in Japan and was planning a move to the United States. He had booked himself on Korean Airlines when he suddenly began to get a voice in his head that kept saying "Korean Air crashes…. Korean Air Crashes…Korean Air Crashes." The message continued for weeks.

He knew it would cost hundreds of dollars to change the flight and resisted changing the ticket. Finally, he went to the ticket office and told them to change the ticket. He paid the penalty and left the office feeling good that he had avoided his own death. As he got outside the ticket office, he again heard the voice, "Korean Air Crashes... Korean Air Crashes...Korean Air crashes." He was devastated.

Now resolved to the fact that he would be on a Korean Air flight that would crash, he wrote a letter back to his wife in the United States and his newborn son. Incurring a further expense he sent all his personal possessions that he did not want to lose on the fight. He told his wife that he loved her. He said that if he did not return there was an insurance policy for $800,000 that he had taken out earlier and gave her instructions on where it was. He said that this would help her out, and he wished her a good life. He said nothing about the message he was receiving.

On August 6th just before he left he had an appointment at the dentist. He was just sitting down in the waiting room, and as he sat down, he saw on a small TV screen in the waiting room a news story. Korean flight 801 had just crashed on an approach in Guam. 228 of the 254 people on board were killed.

The voice in Matt's head went silent. (Others had premonitions about this flight.[282])

The second incident happened earlier while working in Japan. Matt had been racing his bike down a road approaching a one-way four-lane highway. It was raining. As he approached the highway, he suddenly experienced a video download from above into the crown of his head. The video, however, was comprised of segments that were not in order. He slowed down to piece together what was happening, and the video had him jumping off his bike but not in time. Both he and the bike were hit by a car from his left, and he was dragged down the highway.

Suddenly from his left there was the sound of a car whose wheels were spinning, and without warning the car cut right in front of his bike turning right onto the four-lane highway. The driver had looked left for traffic but not right where Matt was. It had missed him by inches. The car slammed on his breaks and skidded to a stop.

As Matt got off his bike to go and confront the driver, he heard a voice that was coming from above his head. Matt even looked up to see where it had come from.

The voice said, "It is not intended that you be injured." He is absolutely certain that if he has not slowed down to put together the disjointed video download that he would have been hit by the car.

The third download is a premonition that many UFO experiencers reported to me as also having. It was September 10, 2001, and Matt was in a park in Anthem, Nevada. He was with friends looking down into the valley at Las Vegas. He was suddenly overcome by a great wave of sadness.

His friend, who was with him, noticed his distress. He asked him what was wrong.

Matt replied that he felt soon the state of peace in the world would change. He told his friend that he felt that very soon, nothing would ever be the same again. The next day in New York planes flew into the World Trade Center, and everything changed forever.

Kary Mullis - Mullis won the 1993 Nobel Prize for developing a system to duplicate DNA samples quickly and in great quantities. The *Washington Post* referred to Mullis as "the weirdest person ever to have won. The solution to the problem came in a download as he was driving at night to his cottage. Two years after the download experience Mullis described his encounter with aliens along with similar reports by his daughter. In his 1998 book *Dancing Naked in the Mine Field*, Mullis described an encounter at his cottage:

> *At the far end of the path, under a fir tree, there was something glowing. I pointed my flashlight at it anyhow. It only made it whiter where the beam landed. It seemed to be a raccoon. I wasn't frightened. Later, I wondered if it could have been a hologram, projected from God knows where. The raccoon spoke. 'Good evening, doctor,' it said. I said something back; I don't remember what, probably, 'Hello.' The next thing I remember, it was early in the morning. I was walking along a road uphill from my house."*

Six hours were missing. He was confused and then remembered,

> *All of a sudden it came back to me. The talking glowing raccoon...Yes, I remembered the little bastard and his courteous greeting. I remembered his shifty black eyes. I remembered the way my flashlight had looked on his already glowing face. Where was my flashlight? I walked to the john right away. I wasn't afraid of finding something scary. I wanted that fucking raccoon to be there. He wasn't – and neither was my flashlight."*[283]

Mullis had no idea how he got there, but he was not wet from the extensive early morning dew. His flashlight was missing. He was never able to find it. He had no signs of injury or bruising. The lights of the cabin were still on, along with the groceries on the floor. Some six hours had gone by unaccounted for. Later in the day he found that an area of his property - "the most beautiful part of my woods" - had inexplicably become a place of dread. A year or so later Mullis exorcised this fear John Wayne-style by shooting up the wood. His attempt at psychotherapy proved unsuccessful as it could not help him recall what had happened that summer night in 1985. Mullis would become the only known Nobel Prize laureate to claim an experience of what might be an alien abduction.

Jackie Rhyser - Rhyser is an experiencer who lives just east of Barrie, Ontario, Canada. Among her many bizarre alien experiences was a download experience. It was described by former *Toronto Star* newspaper writer Bob Mitchell.

"One day Jackie was at her desk when an energy field entered her mind. 'I immediately seemed to understand how their spacecraft worked. I sat down and wrote page after page for hours, describing how they worked.' Jackie knew it had something to do with counter rotating electromagnetics that create energy fields. 'It's like they create their own energy field. They're either pushed into it or sucked into it. The faster and bigger they push out this energy field, the greater the distance they can travel'...She had no technological knowledge when she sat down and wrote. 'It was antigravity or negative gravity. It was as if they created a non-existent gravity.'"

Stan Romanek - Like Ramanujan, Stan Romanek received a series of formulas while sleeping or while under hypnosis. Among the formulas he received were one for the element 115 that was not synthesized until long after he received the formula.

Another formula created by Romanek was written backward but can be read in a mirror.

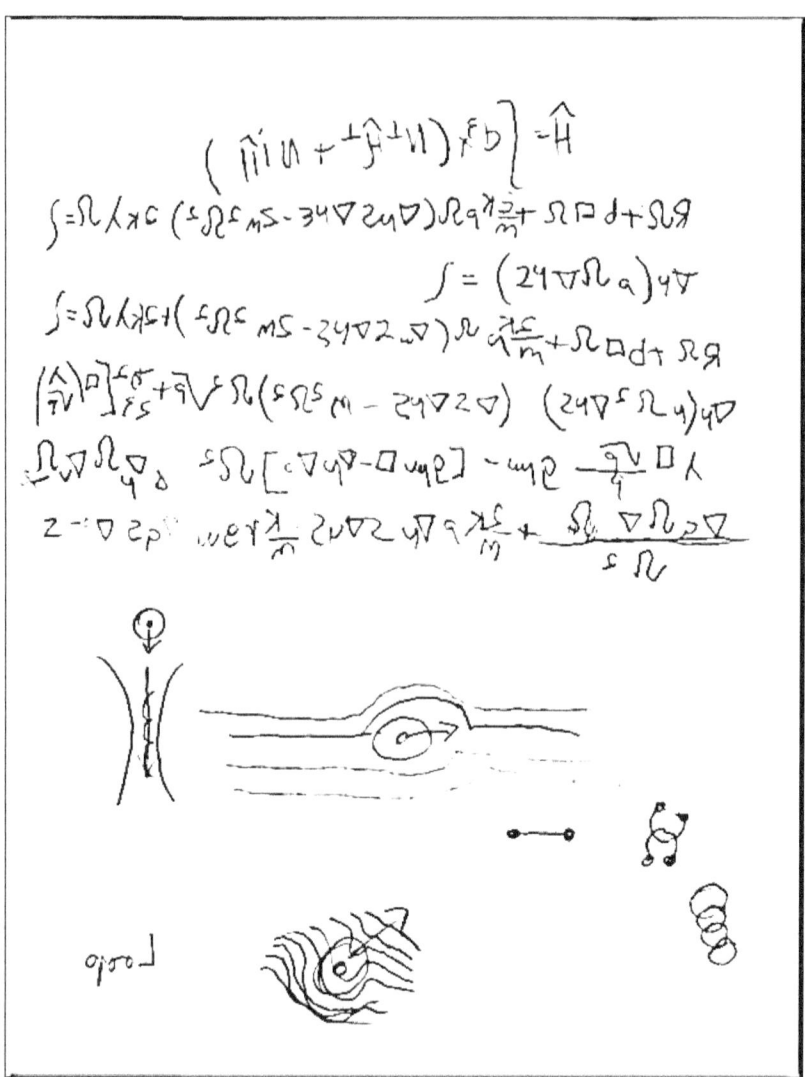

Ralph Steiner - alien - It's interesting to note that we are now getting lots of reports of "physics downloads" from contactees/experiencers. FREE has established a small physics working group to evaluate these reports as they come in. "I myself may have been the recipient of such a 'download' in 1973, although, at that time, I had no knowledge of the UFO phenomenon. I simply thought that I had experienced waking up during a vivid dream borne out of my previous intensive involvement with theoretical physics a decade earlier. But what I experienced perfectly matches the kinds of experiences that people are now reporting while in the presence of non-human intelligence. The content of these experiences seems to have a lot to do with concepts at the root of 'free energy' production; fine-tuning our understanding of the laws of physics to permit humans to access non-polluting sources of electrical power, and to enable anti-gravity tech. I would have to place my own vivid experience into that category as well. Since 1973, I've had several UFO encounters, a number of them involving unequivocal telepathic communication with 'ETs,' and those interactions were of a nature similar in feel to the "download" event that took place during that year. I didn't have any overt UFO contact until 1986, so this vivid physics download event took place 13 years before I knew anything about anything in this subject area."[284]

Implants providing Technology - Through the work of podiatrist and UFO researcher Dr. Roger Leir, there were 17 implants taken from people who showed strong evidence of being abducted by aliens. Two of these experiencers, Alice and Ron, had the objects examined after removal. The work was done by chemist and material scientist, Steve Colbern. The materials were sent to Los Alamos Labs, New Mexico Tech, University of Toronto, and the University of California. The implants provided objects that exhibited advanced technology that if studied may help lead to advanced scientific technologies. These include:

Radio signals (14.749 MHz and 17.686 GHz) were picked up from both devices before removal from the subjects, and they appeared to be transmitting on satellite and aeronautical communication frequencies.

Sophisticated carbon nanotubes which are the strongest known substances in the world with advanced conductive properties made of allotropes of carbon with a cylindrical nanostructure. Colbern claims they are made composed of meteoric iron not found in our solar system because the isotopic ratios are skewed compared to those found on earth or in our own solar neighborhood. Colbern didn't believe we would be able to duplicate.

Colbern stated that the nanotubes had carbon nanotube electronics built right in. We have some nanotube technology since the first patent was filed in 1991, but it is very primitive and could not produce the devices pulled from experiencers. Colbern's best guess is that the objects are probably for the gathering and broadcasting of information - "sensory information - what the subject is seeing and hearing, physiological information, etc." Colbern believed that the objects were at least 100 years ahead of our present capabilities.

Colbern's analysis found that the implants have a sophisticated biological coating that allows our nerve cells to grow into the devices after they're implanted - something that is beyond our technology. Leir believed that this alone could be one of the greatest discoveries ever for its potential to end rejection of organs and objects placed in patients during operations.

Chapter 17 - Inspirations from the Ancients

I keep forgetting, but the people who have gone through the contemplative meditative mystical path got to where I am getting with science thousands of years ago. It's so embarrassing. It like coming on stage and being a toddler and saying "Look mommy it's a tree!" and the audience says "Yes it is a tree." **Neurologist Julia Mossbridge Ph.D. speaking to a conference on science and nonduality**.

What we want is that metaphysical being who uses the brain, that sees and feels, it is the soul (GOD). What we call the "material world" is a group of perceptions viewed by the soul. This is the mystery of life. **St. Francis of Assisi, born 1181 and died 1226, describing an idea that has become part of a prominent modern model of consciousness.**

That's exactly the point of modern quantum theory. So a thirteen-century theologian discovered one of the basic principles of modern physics 700 years ago! **Niels Bohr upon hearing how angels move instantly from one place to another without passing through time and space.**

The modern world paradigm had been influenced heavily by the engineering marvels of the modern world such as cars, planes, computers, and medical developments.

Although most people still buy into the belief of the supremacy of scientific and engineering knowledge, there is a growing movement that began with the counter-culture of the sixties where the nonphysical aspects of life and the true nature of existence have gained a growing number of believers.

Much of what the new beliefs have proposed is what was contained in the writings of ancient societies and spiritual traditions such as Greeks, Romans, Hindus, Buddhists, and aboriginal cultures.

This raises the question - were the ancient mystics correct? Was there a true reality beyond physical toys that was wired into our brains waiting to be revealed by a trigger, such as meditations, psychedelics, dreams, channelers, or psychics?

Aboriginal Culture - Ken Carey in his book *Return of the Bird Tribes* reports having total recall while engaging in an ancient aboriginal practice, attending a sweat lodge. The memories that came to him in the room included having a total recall experience of being born on Earth as part of a mission and that some of the people would deliver trigger melodies that would awaken the consciousness of many.

Archimedes - This Greek polymath (c. 287-212 B.C.) is the originator of the world Eureka, which has long been associated with sudden insight. Archimedes was tasked by the King of Syracuse to determine if his goldsmith had made his crown of pure gold or whether base metals had been added.

Archimedes was bathing and trying to figure out the solution to the king's inquiry. He realized that his body volume could be calculated by measuring the volume of the water that it had displaced. It suddenly occurred to him that the same principle could apply by comparing the displacement of the crown in water, compared to pure gold. As the story goes he left his bath and went running through the streets of Athens naked and yelling "Eureka!" (I found it!).

Buddhist Teachings - In the ancient Buddhist texts there are many indications that they had knowledge that had been developed through some sort of meditative tapping into a universal or collective mind. This same knowledge is being discovered by modern quantum physics, meditation practitioners, lucid dreamers, and users of entheogenic drug compounds tapping into the universal or collective mind.

One example of this comes from *The Flower Ornament Scripture*, written in 100 A.D., which describes precognition and telepathy,

Dr. Targ described what the Buddhists knew and which is now just being rediscovered. "This Buddhist compendium," wrote Targ, "teaches that there is no paradox in precognition or in communicating with the dead, because the past, present, and future are all infinite in extent and independently co-arising. Thus, the future can affect the past...we are also told that telepathy appears as mind-to-mind communication and is to be understood as part of ordinary life; we are just not aware or attentive to its presence. All of the forms of super-knowledge are manifestations of the quiet and spacious mind and should not be expected to appear in our lives as the natural outcome of nonlocal consciousness."[285]

Christian Pantheism - Like the Hindus, the Christians had the idea that the divine is synonymous with the Universe. Acts 17:28 states, "All things live and move and have their being in God." Jesus states in the Gospel of St. Thomas, "I am the light that is over all things. I am all... Split a piece of wood; I am there. Lift up the stone, and you will find me there." With the rising evidence of some conscious element being necessary to collapse the basic wave function to create matter and thus the decline of the solidity of the physical world, this view has gained a foothold again.

Code of Hammurabi - This is the 1754 BC Babylonian law code of ancient Mesopotamia. It is considered to be the first written legal record. It contains 282 laws each with a scaled punishment. He claimed that the laws were dictated to him by the sun God Shamash. He channeled the laws, and this was recorded by scribes in his palace. He could remember nothing of what he had said.

Dowsing - The idea of using a y-shaped metal rod to find metal and water has been used independently by many societies around the world. The USDA reported, "Cave paintings in northwestern Africa that are 6,000-8,000 years old are believed to show a water dowser at work." Divining rods were also used by the Scythians, Persians, and Medes.

As there is no record of technology transfer, it appears that each group may have independently become inspired with the idea of this bizarre tool being used to find buried items. According to George Hansen, dowsing goes way back in history:

> *The first published description of the dowsing rod is probably Georgius Agricola's De re Metallica dated 1556 (translated in 1912 by the then future president of the United States, Herbert Hoover). From an extensive survey of the literature, Barrett and Besterman (1926/1968) found the first unmistakable reference to the dowsing rod was in 1430; although many earlier works have been construed as referring to dowsing. Two major works on the history of dowsing are by Barrett and Besterman (1926/1968) and by Bird (1979).* [286]

Despite the standard claim by materialist scientists, the use and study of dowsing have continued unabated ever since an indication that there is some sort of effect that refuses to disappear when tested. The effects were never explainable by a physical mechanism, and this was enough reason to drop serious work on the subject.

However, it was reported by *The New York Times* that the US military used dowsing in Vietnam. More than one attempt was made to test dowsing at Duke University. British Army and Ministry of Defense did dowsing tests when looking for buried mines, Soviets did many tests, and Mr. P.A. Ongley, a New Zealand research chemist, tested the claims of 75 dowsers.

Even my father, who in public always played the skeptic on paranormal subjects, was very vocal about the power of the dowsing rods which he witnessed when someone in his government aviation office showed him. He was very puzzled by the apparent power of his rods to find stuff and made everyone take a try with the rods so they too could experience the feel of the rods pulling to the middle when water of metal was passed over.

Dr. A. P. Elkin - In his book *The Aboriginal Men of High Degree: Initiation and Sorcery in the World's Oldest Tradition* Sydney University anthropologist Elkin was forced to consider that the bushmen that he was studying had psychic knowledge of when he was arriving. This was despite the fact his arrival was never announced by messenger, drums, or smoke signals. Yet each village was prepared for his arrival, knew where he had just come from and was aware of the purpose of his wilderness trek. Further evidence of this psychic ability by the bushmen came when Elkin studied cases of the high degree karadji and wiringins within tribes who exhibited all manner of psychic abilities such as claims to gain magical personal information telepathically from a faraway village. His investigation showed that the natives were able to predict whether a parent was dying, a nephew was being born, or the victory of a successful hunt.[287]

Greeks - The Greeks believed that new songs, stories and ideas came from the spirit of a muse that entered the author, artist, or thinker. That person was only a channel for the muse to present the new idea. The person became inspired or in spirit.

Hindu Teaching - Like Buddhist teaching the ancient Hindus appeared to have knowledge of reality that we are now only beginning to reveal through quantum physics. One of the main Hindu texts that contain the knowledge is the Yoga Sutras of Patanjali. Erwin Schrodinger, who was one of the key architects of theory and the mathematics of quantum mechanics, realized this as he was a lifelong student of Vedanta.

In addition, the Hindu Vedas from thirty-five hundred years ago spelled out that our awareness (self or *Atman*) is one. Dr. Russell Targ stated that the atman was "unseparated from ultimate transcendent reality, the reality, and nonphysical universe or *Brahman*. We need not experience separation from any aspect of the universe in consciousness. More recently, the great (Nobel Prize winning) physicist Erwin Schrodinger, who perfected quantum mechanics, has written in his thoughtful monograph *What is Life* that the teaching Atman = Braham is the greatest of all metaphysical principles. He went on to write about non-separation: 'Consciousness is a singular of which the plural is unknown. There is only one thing, and that which seems to be a plurality is simply a series of different aspects of that one thing produced by a deception (the Indian Maya). The same illusion is produced in a gallery of mirrors.'"[288]

Toward the end of his life, 1963 physics Nobel Prize winner Eugene Wigner became interested in the Vedanta philosophy of Hinduism. He realized that this ancient knowledge was closely describing discoveries in modern quantum physics. Michio Kaku described the connection:

> *In this Vedanta approach, God or some eternal consciousness watches over all of us, collapsing our wavefunctions so that we can say we are alive. This interpretation yields the same physical results as the Copenhagen interpretation, so this theory cannot be disproven. But the implication is that consciousness is the fundamental entity in the universe, more fundamental than atoms. The material world may come and go, but consciousness remains as the defining element, which means that consciousness, in some sense, creates reality. The very existence of the atoms we see around us is based on our ability to see and touch them.*

Finally, we have the writings of the metaphor of Indra's Net written in 200 A.D., which describes the modern day theory of an infinite holographic universe and quantum interconnectedness developed by scientists like David Bohm and Dr. Karl Pribram. In the Indra story, we read:

> *Far away in the heavenly abode of the great God Indra, there is a wonderful net which has been hung so that it stretches our indefinitely in all directions. In accordance with the extravagant tastes of the deities there has been hung a single glittering jewel at the net's every juncture and since the net itself is infinite in dimension, the jewels are infinite in number. If we now select any one of those jewels for inspection, we will discover that in its polished surface there are reflected all other jewels in the net, infinite in number. Not only that but each of the jewels reflected in this one jewel is also reflecting all the other jewels so that the process of reflection is infinite.*[289]

Lucid Dreaming - Tibetan Buddhism lucid dreaming or "dream yoga" has been a practiced tradition for over 1,000 years. Modern science rejected the concept until 1968 when Celia Green collated lucid dreams accounts identifying it as a unique state of consciousness and 1975 when Keith Hearn proved lucid dreaming through tracking rapid eye movements.

Hippocrates, in ancient Greece, also believed that dreams contained wisdom and trained in dream interpretation. In ancient Greece "dream temples made up the single most popular spiritual healing institution in the Mediterranean world. These restful sanctuaries were designed to produce dreams that provided healing wisdom - and also instant cures - if we are to believe the boasts of ancient graffiti."[290]

The dream temples, built to Aesclepius, the Greek god of healing, had clients sleep on beds with stone headrests which caused people to sleep on their back. We now know that this caused longer REM sleep a more awakenings which are amenable to lucid dreaming.

Moses - In the Old Testament Moses claimed to have received The Ten Commandments after talking with God, who spoke from a burning bush. The Ten Commandments still form the basic principles of modern western law. Others such as Abraham, Jesus, and his disciples also claimed to have received divine inspiration, and these inspirations make up many of the ideas that underpin modern legal and religious thought.

Oracle of Delphi - Young virgin Greek women would be selected to become the Pythia or the Oracle of Delphi at the Apollo Temple. The oracle would receive prophecies from Apollo while sitting on a tall chair over a chasm in the rock where pneuma fumes were rising. Some now believe that the ethylene or methane gas caused the Pythia's state of inspiration. The predictions were only made on the nine warmest days of the year. The Pythias produced prophecies for hundreds of years before and after Christ, and the Pythia shows many traits like the shamanistic practices of using chemically induced dissociated states.

Pumapunku - in the highlands of Bolivia there is a stone slab 7.81 meters long, 5.17 meters wide and averages 1.07 meters thick. Based on the specific gravity of the red sandstone from which it was carved, this stone slab has been estimated to weigh 131 metric tons or 286,000 lbs.[291] This is one of the best stories of huge stone slabs being moved as 286,000 lbs is the amount of thrust used to get Apollo 11 off the ground and on the way to the moon. The explanation that people used ropes and logs to move a stone of such immense weight is unreasonable.

Pre-Columbians and Mexican Culture - priestess - One element of worship and shamanism in these cultures centered on the narcotic mushroom which was known in the native Nahuatl as teonanacatl. Or "God's flesh." A 16th century Franciscan friar Bernard de Sahagun described the effect of teonanactl:

> *Some saw a vision that they would die in war. Some saw in a vision that they would be devoured by wild beasts...some saw in a vision that they would become rich and wealthy. Some saw in a vision that they would buy slaves.*[292]

Later research indicated that there was an actual worship of the mushroom for its ability to bring in higher orders of reality.

Shamanic Traditions - Probably the main inspiration of the shaman knowledge comes from Ayahuasca, witnessed by the Jesuits during their early travels in the Amazon, and described in a report from 1737. The 'diabolical potion' is found in currently Panama, Brazil, Ecuador, Venezuela, Colombia, Peru and Bolivia, and among at least seventy different indigenous peoples of the Americas. In addition to Ayahuasca, other native names include yajé, caapi, natema, pindé, kahi, mihi, dápa and bejuco de oro, the last meaning 'vine of gold'.[293]

Sadus are Indian holy men or wandering monks who take ganja (marijuana) which makes them feel at one with the universe and helps them achieve "moksha" or "nirvana."

Ur Traditions - The Ur religious traditions of Indo-European, pre-modern tribal societies were believed by researchers Gordon and Valentine Wason to have been influenced by the psychedelic mushroom - the fly amanita. This mushroom was described already in 1862 as a species that could cause delirium where anyone eating it would "prophesy wildly, engage in feats of prodigious exertion, and enjoy illusions of miraculous mobility and metamorphosis."[294]

Chapter 18 Inspirations from Channeled Entities

The story I would like to tell is when my father was writing for Edgar Bergen and the Charlie McCarthy Show. One time my father and I came into Edgar's room. He didn't know that we were watching him. Edgar was talking to Charlie, and we thought he was rehearsing, but he was not rehearsing. He was asking Charlie questions: "Charlie, what is the nature of life, what is the nature of love?" And this wooden dummy was answering quite unlike the being I knew on the radio. A regular Socrates, he was. It was the ventriloquist's voice, but the information coming out was very different altogether. Bergen would get fascinated and say, "Well, Charlie, what is the nature of true virtue?" and the dummy would just pour out this stuff: beauty, elegance, brilliance. And then we got embarrassed and coughed. Bergen turned beet red and said, "Oh, hello, you caught us." And my father said, "What were you doing?" And he said, "Oh I was just talking to Charlie. He's the wisest person I know." And my father said, "But that's your mind; that's your voice coming through that wooden creature." And Ed said, "Well, I guess ultimately it is, but I ask Charlie these questions, and he answers, and I haven't the faintest idea of what he is going to say and I am astounded by his brilliance – so much more than I know. To me, that was a classic channeling instance where the dummy was used as amanuensis of depth structures of Bergen's mind." **Jean Houston philosopher and former spiritual advisor to Hillary Clinton**.

He spoke in perfect, publishable sentences, without pause or haste, and in a flat monotone. He used complex theological terminology and told me; it seemed everything there was to know. As I listened, astonished, the hair rose on my neck; I felt goose bumps, and, finally, tears streamed down my face. I was in the midst of the uncanny, the inexplicable. My son's ride to kindergarten arrived, horn blowing, and he got up and left. I was unnerved and arrived late to my class. What I had heard was awesome, but too vast and far beyond any concept I had had to that point. The gap was so great I could remember almost no details and little of the broad panorama he had presented. My son had no recollection of the event. **Developmental psychologist Joseph Chilton Pearce recounting a visit from his five-year-old son and his 20-minute discourse on the nature of God and man before leaving for kindergarten.**

When we talk to God, we are praying. When God talks to us, we're schizophrenic. **Actress Lily Tomlin**

On September 8, 2013, *The Wall Street Journal* published an article titled "Elizabeth Holmes: The Breakthrough of Instant Diagnosis." In the article, reporter Joseph Rago interviewed Elizabeth Holmes, a 29-year-old chemical and electrical engineer and entrepreneur, about Theranos, a company she founded in 2003. Theranos was developing an instrument that could diagnose any illness by processing more than 1,000 laboratory tests on a single raindrop of blood. As revolutionary as it sounds, psychic Edgar Cayce had predicted exactly that ability 85 years earlier in one of his channeled medical readings. At the time of the reading, no diagnostic tests were being done on blood. Modern clinical labs did not arise till the 1960s. In 1927 Cayce made the following prediction about how blood would be used to diagnose disease:

> *Hence, there is ever seen in the blood stream the reflections or evidences of that condition being carried on in the physical body. The day may yet arrive when one may take a drop of blood and diagnose the condition of any physical body..."* Edgar Cayce (Reading 283-2)

Channeled material has been around for a very long time and seems to cross the boundaries of different paranormal experiences. Dr. Jon Klimo, who is perhaps the foremost authority on the subject, described channeling as follows:

> *Channeling is receiving information from some other level of reality than the physical as we currently understand it, and coming from other than the individual self as current psychology would understand the notion of the self. And so that presupposes a multidimensional framework of reality in which the communication is taking place that goes beyond the physical, the three dimensions of space and the one of time as we understand it, and it also presupposes that the self is more permeable, the membrane separating self from other has more influx of information or information-carrying energy, than the ego, as we currently understand it.* [295]

J.Z. Knight, who channels the entity of Ramtha, and who actually came up with the "channeling" term stated that channeling is when the person is out of the body, and another entity takes over the body to communicate. "My job," said Knight, "is to get out of the way and to be gone when another being for reasons of destiny uses my body and uses my body in a mindful way to perform extraordinary phenomena."[296]

As common as channeling is the idea of channeled material, which has been greeted mostly with skepticism and derision in the UFO and metaphysical research communities. Many in the UFO research community are very adverse to even considering the material received from channeling

167

as worthy of any study. This is because it challenges established belief systems.

The reality seems to be that channeling is probably the same dissociative process used by psychics, mediums, meditators, people tripping on psychedelics, or people reporting out of body encounters with aliens. The left brain conscious ego mind has been shut off which allows the material to be gathered by the right brain from the collective unconscious, akashic record, or nonlocal field of consciousness.

Darryl Anka, who channels the extraterrestrial Bashar stated, "Many who have had contact with UFOs do find that their consciousness expands and opens up in a variety of ways after that experience and channeling is certainly one of the ways that seem to be common in terms of expressing that expansion that they feel. Most people have a misconception. Channeling is a very natural state, and everyone can do it. From time to time, everyone does do it. It is just sort of getting into that focused state where you are doing what you love to do. You are focused on something to the point where you are not paying attention to the passage of time. You are flowing energy and information and creativity through you. After it becomes the character – a singer that is lost in the song is channeling but I think that people are starting to discover that when you are in that natural altered state you can access not only other aspects of your own consciousness, that you might not on a daily basis access, but that it is also possible to make contact with other levels, other dimensions, other entities, or expressing consciousness in a different way if you just train yourself to focus in that direction."[297]

A final point on channeling is that with many channels the process often started with Ouija boards like Jane Roberts with Seth or through automatic writing, such as Francis Swan, who channeled AFFA. They usually moved quickly to direct channeling without aid. In the example of Seth, Jane Roberts, and her husband used a Ouija board as an experiment after Roberts had her first dissociated experience where she received information from the Seth entity. After one month, Roberts was doing direct channeling and resulted in thousands of pages over the next 20 years until her death.

The following are only a small sample of what would be thousands of channeled entities who have come through various people over the years.

Abraham - (group of entities) channeled by Esther Hicks.
AFFA - An alien channeled by housewife Francis Swan in New Hampshire. AFFA was also in contact with Wilbert Smith, who was the head of the Canadian flying saucer investigation from 1950-1954. Smith contacted AFFA through a radio device he had built. A Navy intelligence officer was also taught to make contact with AFFA, and there was also a blind telex operator in the Ottawa area who was receiving phone calls from AFFA. George Hunt Williamson, one of the first contactees to come forward in the 50s also claimed to be in contact with AFFA. Smith wrote an entire book *The*

New Science that he claimed had been given by "beings more advanced that we are."[298]

Mrs. Swan, who was a main channel, started receiving messages through automatic writing, but this was quickly dropped as she learned to receive the messages directly in her mind.

Aiwass - Aiwass was channeled by Aleister Crowley. Crowley ascribed that name to a being he encountered in 1904, who dictated to him *The Book of the Law* in a contactee-like experience. Crowley also eventually came to view Aiwass as his own Holy Guardian Angel. According to one Crowley student, Kenneth Grant, Aiwass was an extraterrestrial from Sirius. Crowley stated that Aiwass first appeared to him as a voice while in a temple. "The voice," said Crowley, "was of deep timbre, musical and expressive, its tones solemn, voluptuous, tender, fierce or aught else as suited the moods of the message. Not bass - perhaps a rich tenor or baritone... He seemed to be a tall, dark man in his thirties, well-knit, active and strong, with the face of a savage king... The dress was not Arab; it suggested Assyria or Persia, but very vaguely."[299]

Alexander - Alexander was channeled by Ramon Stevens.

Jane Allyson - A singer who produced many albums with her band Shanghai Lily Dublin stated she started to channel messages that ended up in her music after she experienced a dramatic UFO sighting while sitting on a New York City rooftop. "I have also begun to do 'Space Channeling,' which while being so utterly fantastic to believe, is the communication of someone from another planet, speaking through me, while I am in a trance to one or more people who are desiring a certain type of information. To this date, 7 communications have come through. All of them are documented on tape. A being named CYTRON speaks and gives information concerning the planet, the trip to Arizona and information which is in general of a protective nature. These events have been occurring with increased frequency..."[300]

Aridif - Atridif claimed to be sixth density being. He was channeled by Rob Gauthier through Tbeb (lower than sixth density). He lived 1700 lights years from Earth.

Arigo - Arigo was a Brazilian psychic surgeon who claimed to work as a channel for deceased surgeons. There are many of these psychic surgeons over the years.

Ashtar (extraterrestrial being) - Communicated telepathically to George Van Tassel, who was one of the first UFO contactees in 1952. Prior to Adamski no one publically claimed to have been talking with aliens. Ashtar was also channeled by UFO contactee, Lady Ethel P. Hill, through automatic writing, and in 1957 this material was published as the book *In Days to Come*. In modern times, Ashtar is channeled through Elizabeth Trutwin.

Bashar - Bashar is one of the most popular channels in the UFO world. He is a hybrid alien from the future channeled by former Canadian, Darryl Anka. His experience started in 1973 in Los Angeles when he and two friends sighted black, triangle shaped objects, which were approximately 75-150 feet away. This awakened Anka's interest and he began reading about UFOs and psychic phenomena. Ten years later he attended a course where it was claimed people could learn to channel. Anka was interested in how channeling was taught. During the course, Anka received a flash that he had volunteered to channel because of a past agreement with someone. The flash included the question whether or not he was still willing to do it, now that he had remembered. He thought he might be imagining things except that the entity coming through the instructor stopped at the same time, and the instructor looked at Anka said, "Someone is here for you if you are ready to begin." Also at the same time, one of the other students in the room was getting an impression and was drawing the entity that Anka was seeing in his head. That provided Anka some validation that something real was happening.

After the course was over, Anka decided to try channeling and volunteered to be a subject in a Ph.D. study being conducted by a woman who was looking into the connection between psychology and channeling. He initially channeled in her living room in front or 5 people, 10 the following week, 20 the week after that, started making tapes, and now channels worldwide to huge audiences. The movie *First Contact*, which is based on Anka, will be released in the fall of 2016 and will be hosted by actor James Woods.

Rosemary Brown - Brown was a British housewife who exhibited an impressive skill to produce compositions that she claimed she had created by channeling the spirits of composers such as Claude Debussy, Edvard Grieg, Franz Liszt, Franz Schubert, Frédéric Chopin, Igor Stravinsky**,** Johann Sebastian Bach, Johannes Brahms, Ludwig van Beethoven, Robert Schumann and Sergei Rachmaninoff. Her first encounter with Franz Liszt was in 1923 at the age of 7. She composed in excess of 500 pieces with very little musical training.

The Cassiopaeans - A series of questions and answers were channeled by Laura Knight-Jadczyk with consciousness from beings from the Cassiopaean system that exist in the sixth dimension. The sessions started in 1994 after two years of experimental work and continued until 2002. The Cassiopaeans claim "we are you in the future." According to Jadczyk, the Cassiopaean material was "closely aligned with the teachings of the great Sufi master, Ibn Al-'Arabi, the Fourth Way Teachings of Gurdjieff, Castaneda, with the Esoteric Christianity of Boris Mouravieff, and even ancient Altaic Shamanism."

The Echo - channeled by Clifford Preston.

Edgar Cayce - Cayce was known as the sleeping prophet. He developed his talent after experiencing two separate traumatic events. One was being hit in the head with a baseball after which he developed the ability to diagnose ailments in people. The second trauma involved his father knocking him to the floor on more than one occasion. His father felt exasperated with him during homework assignments. Cayce heard a voice tell him that if he slept, they would help him. He fell asleep on top of the book, and when he woke up, he knew word for word the contents of the book. From that point on, he could the same thing with any other book he slept on.

Cayce did thousands of trance readings over many decades. The material he produced has inspired hundreds of books, and the Association for Research and Enlightenment still houses his material in Virginia Beach, Virginia.

The Galactic Federation of Light - These are alien beings that are being channeled by various mediums. The most prolific is SaLuSa channeled by Mike Quinsey. Quinsey started channeling only after he had retired from the business world. He met several cosmic beings from various star groups. The key group that he had contact with was SaLaSu from the star Sirius. Quinsey stated he had a connection to Sirius in an earlier incarnation.

God - Channeled by Barbara Rose, who began to "bring through" information from God in 1994. She has written twenty-eight books.

God - Channeled by Eileen Caddy, who lived in Scotland and died in 2006. She described how her material began to flow, "One day I went into a room known as a shrine to pray in silence. I was in the midst of my serious monolog when suddenly, I clearly heard a voice speak to me and tell me 'Be still and know that I am God.'"

God - Channeled by Neale Donald Walsch, who published the material he received in a series of books called *Conversations with God*. Walsch maintains his books are not channeled, but rather "inspired" by God.

God, Jesus Christ and Moroni - Encountered by Joseph Smith, as later recounted by him, and other Mormon leaders. Moroni physically appeared to Smith, initially three times the first night, followed by many more visits, eventually leading Smith to the location of buried golden plates in New York. Smith then translated the plates, published as the *The Book of Mormon - Another Testament of Jesus Christ*, which includes a historical account of the indigenous people's encounters with Chris in the Americas. Mormon was Moroni's father and had recorded the history of his people on the golden plates, which Smith translated. Oliver Cowdery, David Whitmer and Martin Harris also physically saw the plates, which Moroni later took back. Part of Mormon scripture includes *The Pearl of Great Price*, which includes the *Book of Moses*, which recounts Enoch and his people suddenly disappearing because they were so righteous, God took them. This is interesting because in Genesis, we are told God took Enoch at the age of 365, but the *Book of Moses* states he and his people were taken.

The Guide - The Guide was channeled by Eva Pierrakos, the daughter of the well-known Austrian novelist, Jakob Wasserman. She began through automatic writing and later spoke in trance states. Pierrakos died in 1979 leaving behind more than two hundred lectures based on the channeled material, which became known as the *Pathwork Guide*.

The Hathors - Tom Kenyon, who channels the Hathors states that they are a group of interdimensional, intergalactic beings who were connected with ancient Egypt and other cultures through Temples dedicated to the goddess, Hathor. In the late 1980s, he was "contacted by them during meditation, and they began to instruct me in the vibratory nature of the cosmos, the use of sacred geometry as a means to stimulate brain performance, and in the use of sound to activate psycho-spiritual experiences."[301]

Frederica Hauffe - Hauffe taught spiritual concepts while in a trance state such as the triune doctrine of body, soul, and spirit. She taught that the ethereal body surrounds the soul, and carries on the vital processes when the body is in a trance and the soul wanders about. Hauffe said it decays after death freeing the soul.

According to Gales Encyclopedia, three volumes of her material were released starting three years after her death:

> *The unique part of the spiritual revelations of the Seeress of Prevorst consisted of her description of systems of circles - sun circles and life circles - corresponding to spiritual conditions and the passage of time. They were illustrated by amazing diagrams. The interpretation was furnished partly by ciphers, partly by words of a primeval language written in primitive ideographs. On the basis of these revelations, a mystic circle was founded, and members claimed that the teachings disclose analogies with the philosophical ideas of Pythagoras, Plato, and others. They issued a journal, Blätter aus Prevorst, 12 volumes of which were published from 1832 to 1839.*

Debbie Hewins - Hewins is the sister of Audrey Hewins, who started the Starborn support network for UFO experiencers and the yearly Starborn Experiencers Conference in Maine. Debbie got a channeled message through automatic writing that said in part that 11:11 is the number for the journey to oneness. She later discovered the message had come from an alien named Setterell. Debbie filled 7 notebooks with automatic writing messages until Setterell said he would teach her to channel with her voice.

Jehovah - In the 19th century, John Ballou Newbrough used automatic writing to produce the *New Bible in the Words of Jehovah and His Angel Ambassadors*.

Jeshua (Jesus) - Channeled by Jaytem, resulting in the "Way of Mastery."

Jesus - The book *A Course in Miracles* was channeled by Dr. Helen Schucman, a psychologist at Columbia University. This is considered by many to be a key channeled work. Schucman, who started out as an atheist, came to believe that Jesus, as an inner voice, had guided the writing. On October 21, 1965, the inner voice stated: "This is a Course in Miracles, please take notes...It made no sound but seemed to be giving me a rapid kind of internal dictation. The dictation continued for seven years, and the 1500 pages were then hidden away in a filing cabinet."

In 1975, Schucman and a colleague Dr. William Thetford, who had typed out the dictation notes, were meeting with Judith Skutch, a parapsychology researcher, to discuss holistic healing. Skutch had a feeling of "unfulfillment" and a couple days before the meeting with Shad a dream where she was looking for "her map home." She asked the universe for help.

At the same time, in early 1975, the voice in Schucman's head was saying a woman would appear who would know what to do with the manuscript. When the three met, Skutch felt inclined to ask Schucman if she had ever "heard a voice in her head." Schucman revealed what had happened ten years earlier and showed Skutch the hidden manuscript.

Kirael - Kirael is a 7th Dimension Master Guide channeled by Fred Sterling, who describes himself as a medium, minister, messenger, and shaman of Native American ancestry.

Kryon - Kryon is an angelic entity or spiritual master who has never been incarnate on this planet. The entity is channeled by Lee Carroll. The channeling began in 1989 after Carroll received messages from two channels, twenty years apart, who told him the same thing. The message from both was that there was an entity named Kryon that Carroll was supposed to get a hold of. 16 books worth of material have been produced. There is a free website that hosts hundreds of hours of audios of channeling sessions. Of special interest is the fact that the term "Indigo Children" used in many places was first used by Kryon in 1999.

Semjase - Semjase is an alien contact who provided information given to Eduard Albert ("Billy") Meier, and his contact is probably one of the most controversial cases in the UFO research community. Interestingly, in 1973 Enoch warned JJ Hurtak who published *The Book of Knowledge: The Keys of Enoch* against the Semjase message. Semjase's message was published by Billy Meier as *The Talmud of Jmmanuel* and in that book Semjase states that Jesus did not resurrect. Interestingly, in the book of Enoch, copies of which have been found among the Dead Sea Scrolls, the Nag Hammadi Library and in Ethiopia, Enoch gives the names of the "Watchers" who negatively interfered with Man's development, and the name of their rebel leader was Semjaza, also known as Samyaza.

Lazaris - Channeled by Jach Purcel since 1974. The website that hosts the channeling material described Lazaris, as follows, "Lazaris is a nonphysical entity. He is a consciousness without form - a Spark of Light, a Spark of Love - an energy that has never chosen to take human form. He is most frequently known as the "vertical elliptic of light who waits for us at the edge of our reality."

Mary Magdalene - Channeled by Mercedes Kirkel, beginning in 2010, when Mary Magdalene gave twenty-five extraordinary messages of spiritual instruction, resulting in Kirkel's book *called Mary Magdalene Beckons: Join the River of Love.*

Barbara Marciniak - Marciniak authored *The Bringers of the Dawn* and three other books with material she channeled coming from the Pleiadians. Some have identified this material as being in the same quality league as *The Ra Material* from The Law of One.

Master Ophanim Enoch - Enoch physically took Dr. James J. Hurtak, on January 2 and 3, 1973, after being surrounded by a vehicle made of white light referred to Hurtak as the Merkabah vehicle of ascension. (Hurtak does not consider his expeience a channeling, but a very real physical event). Hurtak described it as the opening of a morphogenetic door, into a multidimensional reality beyond words. Enoch took him through the lower realms and then to Metatron, who can apparently withstand the higher light, and who was described to Hurtak as the creator of light in the outer universe (and also creator of the electron), an angel of the highest level. Metatron took him to the throne of the Father where he saw Jesus seated to his right, along with 24 Elohim, who create worlds "without end." The material gathered by Hurtak in the two days was published as *The Book of Knowledge: The Keys of Enoch.* When he returned, his students reported that he had light around his body. According to Hurtak the Keys of Enoch are to prepare everyone, including the leading thinkers and scientists of the modern world, for contact and for the return of Jesus.

Melchizedek - Melchizedek is an entity channeled by Kathryn E Cole. The messages were gathered in a book called *Messages from Melchizedek* which is a diary of channeled information on the nature of mankind's' transition into the next dimension - the fourth dimension. Melchizedek identified himself in the messages as "the guardian of the fourth door." In Hebrews 7:3, we read that Melchizedek was without father, without mother, without genealogy, having no beginning of days or end of life, "resembling the Son of God, he remains a priest forever." James J. Hurtak in *The Overself Awakening* has a depiction of Melchizedek (which also includes Metatron and Yeshua), whom, as stated earlier, he also met, while traveling with Enoch.

Maitreya - Maitreya is channeled by Margaret McElroy. According to her website, "In 1992, after channeling an energy known as Argos for 5 years, Margaret began channeling Maitreya. Upon his instructions, she developed a website to allow Maitreya to share his teachings with the world."

Michael (The Michael Teachings) - In 1979 Chelsea Quinn Yarbro and her friends started channeling a group of entities collectively referred to as Michael. The gathered information was published as *Messages From Michael* with *More Messages From Michael* shortly thereafter in 1986, followed by *Michael's People* in 1988, and *Michael For the Millennium* in 1995.

Oahspe - John Ballou Newbrough, a New York Medium, channeled *Oahspe, A Kosmon Bible in the Words of Jehovih and his Angel Ambassadors,* which was considered a "New Bible." The channeling was done by request on the typewriter which had just been invented and which Newbrough had to learn to use. It took fifty weeks to complete, with Newbrough working half an hour each morning. [302]

He stated that the information had come from the higher heavens and was directed by God,

> "I was crying for the light of Heaven. I did not desire communication for friends or relatives or information about earthly things; I wished to learn something about the spirit world; what the angels did, how they traveled, and the general plan of the universe.... I was directed to get a typewriter which writes by keys, like a piano. This I did, and I applied myself industriously to learn it, but with only indifferent success. For two years more the angels propounded to me questions relative to heaven and earth, which no mortal could answer very intelligently....
>
> One morning the light struck both hands on the back, and they went for the typewriter for some fifteen minutes very vigorously. I was told not to read what was printed, and I have worked myself into such a religious fear of losing this new power that I obeyed reverently. The next morning, also before sunrise, the same power came and wrote (or printed rather) again. Again I laid the matter away very religiously, saying little about it to anybody. One morning I accidentally (seemed accidental to me) looked out of the window and beheld the line of light that rested on my hands extending heavenward like a telegraph wire towards the sky. Over my head were three pairs of hands, fully materialized; behind me stood another angel with her hands on my shoulders. My looking did not disturb the scene; my hands kept right on printing ... printing. For 50 weeks this continued, every morning, half an hour or so before sunrise, and then it ceased, and I was told to read and publish the book 'Oahspe.' The peculiar drawings in Oahspe were made with a pencil in the same way."[303]

Orin and DuBen - First channeled by Sanaya Roman using an Ouija board in 1977. Orin declared himself to be a master teacher. After a car accident, Sanaya Roman was able to channel directly without a board. Later in 1982, she did a reading for Duane Packer, who ended up channeling an entity named DuBen. Orin and DuBen seemed to know each other, and a joint channeling started.

Oth - Oth is a guide channeled by Ellen Rauh for the past 10 years.

Pleiadian Collective (9th Dimensional) - The Pleiadian Collection is a group of entities from the future channeled by Wendy Kennedy. Kennedy reported that she always received support from friends after she began channeling, and even told her employers.

Ra - Entity channeled by Carla Rueckert, Don Elkins, and Jim McCarty between 1981 and 1984. The books are known as *The Ra Material* by The Law of One. A Relistening Project was set up to study the material.

Ramtha - Ramtha is an ascended Master, channeled by JZ Knight. Ramtha claimed to have been a Lemurian warrior who fought the Atlanteans over 35,000 years ago. A psychic told her the 'Enlightened One' would appear to her in the future, and the first encounter took place in 1977. Shirley MacLaine was a big supporter. Ramtha's School of Enlightenment headed up by Knight has put out 120 books and 40 DVDs.

Under controlled conditions, noted parapsychologists Ian Wickramasekera and Stanley Krippner of Saybrook Graduate School, using a sophisticated polygraph to show repeatedly that while Knight is channeling Ramtha, the readings of her brain-wave activity shift to delta, and that the lower cerebellum operates her body which talks, walks, eats, drinks and dances while Ramtha teaches the mysteries of mind over matter. Krippner reported that some of the needles on the polygraph were going right of the paper, "The needles went wild. I have never seen anything like it. Some of them actually jumped off the pages, and then she came back and went back to an ordinary state of consciousness...the state of activation that she was in affected six different areas of the polygraph."

The Amazing Randi was publicly asked about this and his comment was, "Well this isn't so surprising. Anyone can do this by breathing deeply."

Knight issued a challenge to Randi, who is always issuing challenges to everybody else, suggesting, "Let's get a polygraph and get a volunteer to come up out of the audience and breathe rapidly and see if the volunteer can do any of the things I did." Randi has not yet accepted the challenge. This doesn't mean that Knight is channeling Ramtha, but she is not role playing, nor is she doing what she does via volitional control. Maybe this is a sub-personality. It can't be dissociative identity disorder because she has control over it, decides when the channeling starts and when it ends. Knight is very clairvoyant, open to research, and she and her group are doing remarkable healings as a result of the meditation that Ramtha teaches.[304]

Seth - Jane Roberts channeled an extremely popular entity known as Seth from 1963 till her death in 1984. It all started with what Roberts described as her psychic initiation. She wrote, "Suddenly my consciousness left my body and my mind was barraged with ideas that were astonishing and new to me at the time." The Wikipedia entry describes the Seth material "as one of the cornerstones of New Age philosophy, and the most influential channeled text of the post-World War II 'New Age' movement (other than *A Course in Miracles*). Jon Klimo writes that the Seth books were instrumental in bringing the idea of channeling to a broad public audience.

Speakers of the Sirian High Council - 6th dimension beings, channeled by Patricia Cori.

Daniel Tammet - Tammet is one of the most famous prodigious savants in the world and not usually seen as a channeller. Tammet, however, in his book *Born on a Blue Day* describes an event that appears as classic channeling. Tammet describes writing stories in school as a young boy:

> *The stories that I wrote, from what I can remember of them, were descriptively dense – a whole page might be taken up by describing the details of a single place or location, its colors, shapes, and textures. There was no dialogue, no emotions. Instead, I wrote of long weaving tunnels far underneath, vast shimmering oceans, of cragged rock caves and towers climbing into the sky. I didn't have to think about my writing; the words just seemed to flow out of my head. Even without conscious planning, the stories were always comprehensible. When I showed them to my teacher, she liked it enough to read out parts of it to the class. My compulsion to write soon disappeared as suddenly as it had first visited me."*[305]

Thoth - Thoth is channeled by Drunvalo Melchizedek. He is reportedly a "specific historical man who went through ascension 52,000 years ago. For 16,000 years he was the king of Atlantis, where his name was Chiquetet Arlich Vomalites. Throughout Egypt, he was known as Thoth. Later he became Hermes of Greece. He remained on Earth in the same body until May 4, 1991."

Tobias - Tobias was a nonphysical entity channeled by businessman Geoffrey Hoppe. Tobias claimed to have had many lifetimes on earth. Hoppe channels ascended masters Adamus St. Germain, and Kuthumi. The first time Hoppe encountered Tobias was on a plane flight in 1997. He kept the fact that this had happened from everyone including his wife for an entire year.

Tom - Gene Roddenberry, creator of Star Trek, channeled Tom, a spokesman for The Council of Nine.

Torah - Torah is an androgynous multidimensional consciousness channeled by Shawn Randall. She learned the ability to channel Torah in a class where they were being taught to create "an inter-psychic bride to other intelligence."

Treb Bor yit-NE - Treb is a seven and a half feet blue-green reptilian channeled by Rob Gauthier. Treb is referred to as a benevolent reptilian hybrid. He is from Capella. According to Gauthier, his ability to channel came from experiments he was doing using the Monroe Institute's Hemi-Sync program, developed to create "complex, multilayered audio signals, which act together to create a resonance that is reflected in unique brain wave forms characteristic of specific states of consciousness." Gauthier stated:

"I had great success in going out-of-body using a program called 'Hemi-Sync' by The Monroe Institute. One night I had this urge to go deeper than the normal out-of-body state I was used to. This is where I met the being I now channel. I was not frightened as you might think seeing a different type of human. This sense of pure love and an overwhelming sense of great joy was felt. He spoke of my mistaken views of reality and that I had achieved a greater ability through meditation. I connected again, this time, I was unsure if this was real or just a creation of my own mind and the long hours of meditation. I wanted something to prove to me that this was actually another being I was speaking to. I was unaware of channeling or any contact of this nature. I was led to a friend who sent me a link to a video on the Seth Material. This book 'Seth Speaks' by Jane Roberts ran almost parallel to what was spoken. I began to understand what was happening and continued to open up to communication." [306]

Neil Walsh - Walsh, who wrote the *Conversations with God* series of books stated, "I do not feel that I wrote them. I just feel that I was a scribe."

YHWH - Channeled by Arthur Fanning (he also channels the being Jehovah).

Zoosh - Zoosh is a great being who has been inspiring and guiding humanity for "about a trillion years." Zoosh is channeled by Robert Shapiro who has produced a series of 13 books called *The Explorer Race*.

Chapter 19 Inspirations through Automatic Writing

I was just sitting there with Pagey in front of a fire at Headley Grange. Pagey had written the chords and played them for me. I was holding a paper and pencil, and for some reason, I was in a very bad mood. Then all of a sudden my hand was writing out words. 'There's a lady who's sure, all that glitters is gold, and she's buying a stairway to heaven.' I just sat there and looked at the words and then I almost leaped out of my seat. **Robert Plant of Led Zeppelin.**

Automatic writing is a practice where a person's hand just writes out messages without any influence from the person holding the pen. The claim is usually made that the message is coming from some nonlocal entity. Many musicians have used this technique and most channelers start their careers off with automatic writing which evolves into direct mental connection to the entity without the use of a pen. The Ouija automatic writing board dates way back to *The Song Dynasty*, 1100 A.D., China, and was known as fuji (扶乩) or "planchette writing."

Assunta Erolano - Automatic Writing - Erolano was an opera singer who obtained a degree in voice performance from the Boston Conservatory. In 1977, while on tour with an opera company, she was asked to try automatic writing by another singer who couldn't do it. Erolano tried and got a short message.

Through the years, as she continued to do it, the messages got longer and longer. Most of them came from her two spirit guides. She also received one message from her mother who had crossed over.

In 1995 and 1996, Erolano started receiving lyrics. She filed them away and then started to hear the music. She fit the first lyric to the music she had heard, and it fit perfectly. Erolano now produces the songs she has been given, such as "Choose Love," "Transformation," and "A Gift from the Heart."

The basic message of all the automatic writing she has received is about the journey to the light. That God is Love and without God, there is no Love. The most common message according to Erolano is that "Love heals it All."

John Lennon - Merrell Fankhauser is a legendary musician from the 1960s whose surf band wrote and produced the famous song *Wipe Out*. Fankhauser has had many experiences that he referred to as a channeling-like an experience where he received music or lyrics. He recalled one meeting he had with Lennon where he played a song *On Our Way to Hana*, inspired by a UFO sighting in Hawaii. Lennon asked him what inspired the song, and they talked about where music came from. Lennon used the word "channeled" and said he himself had received a lot of music that way and that he considered himself to be a medium for the music to make its way into the world. He warned Fankhauser to "record the music when it is fresh" because otherwise it, would be lost. He lamented that some Beatles songs suffered because sometimes weeks or months would pass till they could make into the recording studio.

Grant Morrison - Morrison is a noted Scottish writer who authored The DC Universe comics, Animal Man, Batman, JLA, Action Comics, All-Star Superman, Vertigo's The Invisibles, Marvel Comics' New X-Men, Fantastic Four, Marvel UK's Spider-Man and Zoids and Fleetway's 2000 AD. Morrison is famous for using automatic writing and psychedelic experiences to create his comics. He stated in one interview, "And I've done automatic writing, trance writing, and I always write down my dreams," he adds. "But I don't do it as much now. I think I've just gotten better at shutting down the conscious personality and letting the comics write themselves, so it's become even more fun for me. I can take a backseat and know that this stuff generates itself almost. I've been doing it long enough now that it's kinda easy."[307]

Francis Swan - Francis Swan, was a homemaker in Eliot, Maine who in 1953 started receiving messages through automatic writing. She believed the messages were coming from AFFA and TYLA, who were aliens commanding craft orbiting the earth. Most of the messages came from AFFA (described as a normal and handsome looking human). Swan believed that she had a short encounter with him in October 1953.

Strangely, the USAF picked up two satellites revolving the earth at the same time. They claimed the satellites were "natural satellites."

Swan would hear a tone in her left ear, and that would signal a message was coming through. The message was standard for the 1950s. We needed to stop our testing nuclear weapons and mend our ways. The automatic writing went on until later when Swan was able to receive messages without the use of pencil and paper. The USAF, CIA, US Navy Intelligence, Secret Service, and the Canadian government all were interested and maintained files on Swan. A very interesting article about Swan and the CIA titled "The CIA Channels an Alien" appeared in *Exopolitics Magazine*, Issue No. 2, Autumn 2014.

William Wilkinson - Wilkinson was one of the pioneers of English spiritualism. Although he could paint and compose music without effort, he had tried in vain for weeks to learn the technique of automatic writing. He was unsuccessful until one day, as Wilkinson states, "after waiting less than five minutes it [the pencil] began to move, at first slowly, but presently with increased speed, till in less than a quarter-of-an-hour it moved with such velocity as I had never seen in a hand and arm before, or since. It literally ran away in spiral forms; and I can compare it to nothing else than the fly-wheel of an engine when it was run away. This lasted until a gentleman present touched my arm, when suddenly it fell like an infant's as it goes to sleep, and the pencil dropped out of my hand. I had, however, acquired the power. The consequences of the violent motion of the muscles of the arm were so apparent that I could not for several days lift it without pain."[308] His wife could draw, paint, and play music without effort, but she could not succeed with automatic writing.

W.B. Yeats - As mentioned in the Nobel Prize section, Yeats wrote a metaphysical book called *The Vision* that came from experiments he did with his wife dealing with automatic writing. Dreams and meditations were also used in a process that was carefully documented as to date, questions asked, and material received.

Chapter 20 Inspirations through Meditation

If you just sit and observe, you will see how restless your mind is. If you try to calm it, it only makes it worse, but over time it does calm, and when it does, there's room to hear more subtle things - that's when your intuition starts to blossom and you start to see things more clearly and be in the present more. Your mind just slows down, and you see a tremendous expanse in the moment. You see so much more than you could see before. It's a discipline; you have to practice it. **Steve Jobs, Apple Computers**

Shut down the left logical thinking side of your brain, the side that we use to organize our lives and work etc., while significantly increasing Alpha and Beta activity in the right, which is essential to effective meditation. **Carol Everett, whose meditative brain state, Hi-Energy healing and Medical Intuitive ability, was tested at Tokyo's Denki University.**

Meditation plays a critical role in the inspiration download process. It is meditation that stops the mental chatter and allows the creative right side to link into the universal mind where inspiration and download can take place. In the end, all nonlocal abilities appear to be linked with being able to shut down the ego mind.

Meditation also gives intensity to our thoughts. The word itself is from the Latin "meditari," which means to contemplate. This meditation process can be seen in many of the inventions and scientific discoveries that were addressed in previous chapters. First, hours were spent meditating on a problem. Then those who made the discoveries got lost in their work forgetting about their ego and everything else around them.

It has been reported a certain scientist or inventor worked for years, and then in a moment of silence, sitting on a park bench or while sleeping, a flash of inspiration struck.

Edward Thompson who authored *How to Make Inventions: Or Inventing as a Science and an Art* stated, "discovery like invention is mental before real in many instances." Franklin, Columbus, Priestly (discoverer of oxygen) and Kepler (discoverer of astronomical laws) meditated upon and conjectured (i.e., mentally conceived) the discoveries in advance of the actual results. Meditation or systematic and enthusiastic thought upon a single subject ripens the mind to be influenced by new facts. By meditation, the problem to be solved becomes gradually as clear as an "example" in mathematics. James Nasmith, improver of the early steam engine, was advised thus by his employer, Henry Maudsley: "First, get a clear notion of what you desire to accomplish, and then in all probability you will succeed in doing it." Lombroso says, "Nearly all great intellectual creations and all discoveries of modern physics are the results of the slow and continuous meditations of men of science and their predecessors."[309]

Following are some examples of meditations that led to inspirations and downloads in various fields.

CSETI - The Center for the Search for Extraterrestrial Intelligence was started and directed for many years by Dr. Steven Greer. Greer has been involved in many aspects of the UFO phenomena including his famous CE5 protocol, which is a way to make contact with extraterrestrials. In 1992, when the organization was still called Project Starlight, Greer had gathered after sunset with eight other researchers in the grain fields near Woodborough Hill near the village of Alton Barnes, England to create "a new crop circle symbol for a genuine circle creating intelligence, or intelligences, to make." Greer held a twenty-minute meditation where the group was to visualize a pattern. Seven of the nine people came up with the same symbol – three circles held together one the points of an equilateral triangle. They all meditated the pattern, and hours later a crop circle with that exact pattern was discovered in a wheat field near the village of 'Roundway.'

Steve Jobs - Jobs believed that much of his inspiration came from meditation, and he spent much time at the Tassajara Zen Meditation Center outside of San Francisco. "Your mind just slows down, and you see a tremendous expanse at the moment. You see so much more than you could see before," said Jobs.[310]

Sir Isaac Newton - Newton spoke of originating: "I keep the subject constantly before me, and wait till the first dawnings open by little and little, into a full and clear light."[311]

Laurie Rosenfield - Rosenfield with her family traveled to the UK in June 2006. She was to attend a retreat in Scotland late in the month and like many others had become interested in crop circles. She had hoped to see crop circles in England where she had lived in the past and also "came up with the idea of meditating on and 'asking' the 'circle makers' to have an 'Emissary Wheel' (a 12 pointed star of sacred geometry) circle appear."

She began her meditation on the Emissary Wheel two weeks before the trip. As the family flew over the ocean from Canada on June 21/22, Rosenfield led her three sons in a meditation on the circle creation.

Laurie saw no crop circles while in England and had no internet connection while there. As it was early in the crop circle season, she was not even aware that any had appeared. She returned to Canada in early July. "It was only on my return home," Laurie wrote me, "that I discovered that an 'Emissary Wheel' like circle had indeed appeared. And as a special gift of connection, it arrived on my birthday (June 24)."[312] The crop circle appeared on what is known as "Pilgrims Way" in Kent.

Carlos Santana - Musical inspirations come to Santana as he meditates facing the wall in his house with candles lit and a yellow legal pad waiting for inspiration. He refers to the download process that is about to happen as "kind of like a fax machine."[313]

Dr. Neil Theise - Theise is Professor of Pathology and Medicine at the Albert Einstein College of Medicine at Beth Israel Medical Center, and also involved in stem cell research. He stated, "Without exception - my best research ideas - the kind I know are right even before I confirm them experimentally - have come to me when I am meditating."[314]

Robert Waggoner - Waggoner is one of the leading authorities in the world on lucid dreaming which is the ability to become aware in the dream state. He has practiced this for over thirty years. Waggoner is also able to get to the inner self for direct communication. In one meditation he showed that various nonlocal phenomena could be connected.

He described how in one meditation he got an instruction to send $10,000 to his friend Paul who lived eight hours away in the town where Wagoner grew up. The next day's meditation brought the same message along with Paul's deceased mother.

Waggoner discussed this bizarre situation with his wife, and she suggested sending $1,000 with a note that if he needed help they were willing to do what they could.

Four days later a "blubbering" Paul phoned saying that he had been at his mother's grave the week before and told his deceased mother that he was going to kill himself if he did not get help. He wanted to build a handicap washroom for his father who had broken his hip and was now in a nursing home.

Waggoner provided the $10,000 needed, and Paul's father lived with him for the next six years.[315]

World Consciousness Project - Roger Nelson described the data behind a meditation group that was attempting to influence the consciousness of social change. Groups would gather and meditate to try and change the environment of the city they were in to make it more peaceful. Nelson said, "I was impressed with the literature...as a completely independent outside measure not looking at the social outcome, but only looking at the behavior of our random event generators, what we saw was a rather striking effect exactly during the time that the people were gathering and sitting in meditation. In 2006 they spent time gathering every day. I didn't look at all of that data, but I took a sample of all the Saturdays, put them together, and there was a very striking result."

Chapter 21 Inspirations for the Dying and the Grieving

OH WOW. OH WOW. OH WOW. **Apple Founder Steve Jobs last words.**

It is very beautiful over there. **Thomas Edison last words as he woke from a coma just before his death.**

Still another man, this one blind from birth, found himself in an enormous library during the transcendental phase of his NDE and saw "thousands and millions and billions of books, as far as you could see." Asked if he saw them visually, he said, "Oh, yes!" Did he see them clearly? "No problem." Was he surprised at being able to see thus? "Not in the least. I said, 'Hey, you can't see,' and I said, 'well, of course, I can see. Look at those books. That's ample proof that I can see.'" **One of 31 people who were part of a study into NDEs and OBEs reported by blind people.**

Inspirations for the dying and grieving is a topic that has been covered by perhaps thousands of books that have been written since near death experiences (NDE) exploded on the modern consciousness scene following the popularity of cardiopulmonary resuscitation (CPR) techniques and training provided to the general public in the late 1960s. This is impressive in light of the fact that the term near-death experience (NDE) was coined in 1975.

I researched the visions of dying patients and wrote a lengthy, detailed paper that while attending college in the early 1970s after the first books on near-death studies hit bookstores.

The stories I collected are probably very similar to those many have heard within their own family. The person that's dying is visited by a deceased relative a day or two before death, who comes to comfort the person and prepare them for death.

My own father, who had been interested in my paranormal research, but always played the skeptic, stated he was an agnostic because there were always many more questions than answers. However, in 2006, two days before he died, he relayed to my mother that his father, who had died in the 1950s, came for a visit. My mother asked what, if anything, his father had said, to which my father replied, "He was just here. That's all you need to know."

Before my father crossed, he did relay to me the story of his grandmother coming down to breakfast during World War I and announcing that her son Kenny had come to her in the night to say he had been killed on the battlefield in Europe. A couple days later, a military official appeared at the door with the news that Kenny had died in battle. My father told the story with great reverence, as his grandmother would never lie.

Even in the 1970s when I was doing the research paper, as earlier discussed, I was told by chaplains in Winnipeg hospitals that when the dying were reporting something weird, staff were directed to not ignore or argue with the patients but to immediately call the chaplain.

This is a very popular phenomenon going back a long way and at times has been reported by famous people, such as Serbian inventor, Nikola Tesla, who reported being away from his mother as she was nearing death, but feeling assured that if she did die, she would give him some sort of indication. He spoke of the moment when she died:

> *During the whole night, every fiber in my brain was strained in expectancy, but nothing happened until early the next morning. (Awakening in) a swoon (I) saw a cloud carrying angelic figures of marvelous beauty, one of whom gazed upon me lovingly and gradually assumed the features of my mother. The appearance slowly floated across the room and vanished, and I was awakened by an indescribably sweet song of many voices. In that instant (or) certitude, (I knew) that my mother had just died. And that was true.*[316]

Surveys confirm people believe they have being visited by loved ones who have crossed. This "sense of presence" is almost identical to the "third man factor" earlier discussed. People have sensed an unseen presence, such as a "spirit" who provides comfort or support during a traumatic experience or in situations of danger where they are not even tuned in to an approaching danger.

Often these appearances occur near the time of loss, but this is not always the case suggesting that the state of mind of the surviving partner is not always a factor. Some of these paranormal occurrences take place many years later when the person is no longer being thought of, such as the case of a woman who reported, "My husband died in June 1945, and 26 years afterward when I was at Church, I felt him standing beside me during the singing of a hymn. I felt I would see him if I turned my head. The feeling was so strong I was reduced to tears. I had not been thinking of him before I felt his presence. I had not had this feeling before that day, neither has it happened since then." [317]

Following are results of studies conducted, which include:
- University of Arizona - Of 500 widows over 65 years of age, over half reported experiencing the presence of their deceased partner.
- Of 222 Widows in Wales, half sensed their deceased spouse and the experience lasted for years.

- Studies reported by Camille Wortman Ph.D - "In a study on reactions to the death of a spouse, 63% of the bereaved indicated that they felt their spouse was with them at times, 47% stated that he or she was watching out for them, and 34% reported that they talked with their spouse regularly. In a study of how children react to the death of a parent, 60% said they had talked with their deceased parent, and 43% indicated that they had received an answer. In a telephone survey, 35% of those contacted reported hearing voices of their deceased loved one, 37% saw a vision or image of the deceased, 55% felt the presence of their loved one, and 69% said they had conversations with the deceased. Some of these studies were conducted shortly after the death, while others were conducted months or years later."[318]
- Another Wales study of 293 widowed people found that 14% of those interviewed reported having had a visual hallucination of their deceased spouse, 13.3% had an auditory one, and 2.7% a tactile one.
- A UK study of 1,603 people of all ages reported 35% experienced the presence of the dead.
- In Japan, one of the earlier peer-reviewed studies showed 90% of Japanese widows reported sensing their deceased spouse.[319]

Although there are formal studies, my work with UFO contactees shows that a great number of them at one point or another have relayed sensing someone had died, which was later confirmed. This seems to be part of the sensitivity of contactees. For example, I reviewed two cases reported by Kelly Gessner, who sensed two unexpected deaths within 24 hours of the events. Both were absolutely accurate. In one of two, her prediction was so shocking that the daughter of the victim later believed Kelly had some influence on the event taking place.

Those who have been near death have also received inspirations or knowledge previously unknown to them. Most describe the experiences as life-altering. Those describing near death experiences (NDEs), which are now well-known, report increased psychic occurrences, similar to those who report alien abductions/encounters. Commonalities include telepathic communication, Out-of-Body Experiences (OBEs), being out of one's body, being at one with the Universe, feeling unconditional love, blinding lights, and encounters with deceased relatives. It is almost as if UFO abduction/encounters and NDEs are parallel mystical experiences with differing triggers.

Lorraine Davis, a lecturer and writer on consciousness, conducted a study of 93 people who reported consistent contact with UFOs. Their attitudes towards themselves and others became less egocentric, and their personal religious beliefs moved from atheism or sectarianism to a kind of universal spirituality. Those in the study also reported that their psychic abilities had notably increased.[320]

One letter written to the International Association for Near-Death Studies contained a description of the ability to see into the future, similar to what UFO experiencers have reported.

> One thing that I have noticed since the NDE is that I have many instances of precognition. I had very clear recognition before my father died 10 years ago. Two days before he suddenly died, I had a dream that I would get a phone call saying that a male member of the family has died. The day before he died I was filled with a tremendous sense of dread and fear. The next morning my mother called to tell me that he had died. I have had several other precognitive experiences, including dreams of plane crashes and traumatic events the night before they happen; a dream of a highway collapsing a few days before it occurs; and fairly accurate dreams before family members pass away.[321]

The other thing reported by people experiencing NDEs and OBEs is an innate, instinctive "knowing" of things they had never learned, such as hearing a song in a dream or dreaming or suddenly having an idea worth of a Nobel Prize. These people are receiving inspirations without having ever rationalized the process. Following are examples of four such people.

Eben Alexander - Alexander is a neurosurgeon and author of the book *Proof of Heaven*, dealing with his personal NDE, and in which he describes how he was adopted and later discovered that the girl he met in his NDE turned out to be his sister Betsy, who had died before Alexander ever found his biological mother.

Julia Assante - Assante is a social historian of the ancient Near East who received her Ph.D. from Columbia University. She reported that she had an NDE at the age of seven, which involved being "swept up in a kind of vortex. "As I was whirling upward, I instantaneously understood everything and felt the indescribable love that is at the foundation of reality." This sudden download of everything in the universe is often reported as "indescribable love." Unfortunately, like others who have reported this download of everything, once the experience ended, Assante could not remember a thing that she was given.[322]

Colton Burpo - A similar story involves a four-year-old boy Colton Burpo, who during his NDE, met his sister who died in the womb and further describes knowing that she had not been given a name, neither of which Colton knew prior to the NDE.

Hella Hammid - Hammid was a control subject in the research done by the CIA into psi phenomena at the Stanford Research Institute. One of the experiments she was involved with concerned observing distant targets while out of her body.[323]

In one of the target experiments Hella did for the CIA, she targeted Mikhail Gorbachev's office at the Kremlin, with Russell Targ as the control. She spent one hour walking around the inside of the Kremlin. She reported back the fact that Gorbachev's office door was covered with red leather and brass upholstery tacks holding it on. She also reported Gorbachev's desk had a glass top and that it faced out the window overlooking Red Square. On the wall of the office was a door that led down to a room with computer equipment in it. Targ reported that later he was actually able to tour the inside of the Kremlin and was able to confirm what Hammid had seen.

Dr. Yvonne Kason - Like people who report UFO abduction/visitation, many near death experiencers report picking up paranormal talents. Kason was a doctor who experienced a NDE after a plane crash. After recovery, she began having visions, including one of a friend who had meningitis. She advised her friend who got checked out, and the diagnosis turned out to be correct. Her visions continue.

Dr. Kenneth Ring - Ring, along with Sharon Cooper M.A., at the University of Connecticut, did a two-year study on thirty-one blind people who had either a NDE or an OBE or both. Of the total, 14 had been blind from birth.

Of significance, there was no difference in what was being reported by patients who had been blind from birth, lost vision later in life or were just legally blind. Ring was hoping to verify one way or the other anecdotal cases reported by NDE researchers such as Kubler-Ross in 1983, Fred Schoonmaker of Denver's St. Luke's Hospital, Larry Dossey in 1989 in his book *Recovering the Soul*, and Moody and Perry in 1988.

"Our research," the final paper concluded, "revealed that blind people, including those from birth, do report classic NDEs of the kind common sighted people claim to see during NDE and OBEs, and that occasionally claims of visually-based knowledge which could not have been obtained by normal means can be independently corroborated."[324]

In addition, a very important finding in the study is that "the number of persons who indicated they had some kind of vision, either during an NDE or OBE, was 25, which was 80 percent of our entire sample. Even for those blind from birth, 9 of 14 or 64 percent likewise reported sight."

A prime example of a person from birth reporting the same thing in an NDE as a sighted person was the case of Vicki, who "never been able to understand even the concept of light." Vicki's story:

> *In early 1973, Vicki, then 22, was working as an occasional singer in a nightclub in Seattle. One night, at closing time, she was unable to call for a taxi to drive her*

home and circumstances forced her to take the only other option: a ride with a couple of inebriated patrons.

Not surprisingly, a serious accident ensued during which Vicki was thrown out of their van. Her injuries were extensive and life-threatening and included a skull fracture and concussion, and damage to her neck, back, and one leg. In fact, it took her a full year after being released from the hospital before she could stand upright without the risk of fainting.

Vicki clearly remembers the frightening prelude to the crash itself, but she has only a hazy recall of finding herself alternately out of her body and then back inside of it at the accident scene. Her only definite recollection of anything external to herself while out-of-body is a very brief glimpse of the crumpled vehicle. Although this aspect of her experience was confusing, she does claim that while in her out-of-body state she was aware of being in a nonphysical body that had a distinct form and that was, as she put it, "like it was made of light."

She has no memory of her trip to Harborview Hospital in the ambulance, but after she had arrived at the emergency room, she came again to awareness when she found herself up on the ceiling watching a male doctor and a woman - she is not sure whether the woman was another physician or a nurse - working on her body. She could overhear their conversation, too, which had to do with their fear that because of possible damage to Vicki's eardrum, she could become deaf as well as blind. Vicki tried desperately to communicate to them that she was fine but naturally drew no response. She was also aware of seeing her body below her, which she recognized by certain identifying features, such as a distinctive wedding ring she was wearing.

According to her testimony, Vicki first had a very fleeting image of herself lying on the metal table, and she was sure, she said, that "it was me," although it took her a moment to register that fact with certainty. As she later told us:

I knew it was me. ... I was pretty thin then. I was quite tall and thin at that point. And I recognized at first that it was a body, but I didn't even know that it was mine initially. Then I perceived that I was up on the ceiling, and I thought, "Well, that's kind of weird.

What am I doing up here?" I thought, "Well, this must be me. Am I dead?. ..." I just briefly saw this body, and ... I knew

190

that it was mine because I wasn't in mine. Then I was just away from it.

It was that quick. Almost immediately after that, as she recalls, she found herself going up through the ceilings of the hospital until she was above the roof of the building itself, during which time she had a brief panoramic view of her surroundings. She felt very exhilarated during this ascension and enjoyed tremendously the freedom of movement she was experiencing. She also began to hear sublimely beautiful and exquisitely harmonious music akin to the sound of wind chimes.

With scarcely a noticeable transition, she then discovered she had been sucked head-first into a tube and felt that she was being pulled up into it. The enclosure itself was dark, Vicki said, yet she was aware that she was moving toward the light. As she reached the opening of the tube, the music that she had heard earlier seemed to be transformed into hymns, similar to those she heard during her previous NDE, and she then "rolled out" to find herself lying on grass...

Vicki then became aware of five specific persons she knew in life who were welcoming her to this place. Debby and Diane were Vicki's blind schoolmates, who had died years before, at ages 11 and 6, respectively.

In life, they had both been profoundly retarded as well as blind, but here they appeared bright and beautiful, healthy and vitally alive, and no longer children, but, as Vicki phrased it, "in their prime." In addition, Vicki reports seeing two of her childhood caretakers, a couple named Mr. and Mrs. Zilk, both of whom had also previously died. Finally, there was Vicki's grandmother, who had essentially raised Vicki and who had died just two years before this incident...

People blind from birth reporting sight the same NDE elements as sighted people is significant. As the final paper pointed out, events like these have "far-reaching and possibly baleful consequences for a conventional materialist view of science. By the same reasoning, empirical support for sight in the blind would be consistent with various 'New Paradigm' visions of science that are rooted in nonlocal, nondual or holonomic perspectives in which consciousness is the primary reality. Furthermore, such findings would raise profound questions, from any scientific perspective, about mind/body relationships, the role of the brain in vision, and indeed the very mechanisms of sight."

Kimberly Sharp - Sharp was one of many NDE experiencers who have reported being given knowledge.

> *The light gave me knowledge, though I heard no words. We did not communicate in English or in any other language. This was discourse clearer and easier than the clumsy medium of language. It was something like understanding math or music - nonverbal knowledge, but knowledge no less profound. I was learning the answers to the eternal questions of life - questions so old we laugh them off as cliches. "Why are we here?" To learn. "What's the purpose of our life?" To love. I felt as if I was re-remembering things I had once known but somehow forgotten, and it seemed incredible that I had not figured out these things before now.*

Of importance, this NDE story parallels stories of alien experiencers. In November 2014, I was attending a UFO experiencer support group where a very prominent blind ufologist showed up with his cousin and the cousin's son. Each related their experiences.

The blind researcher told a story of flying to Philadelphia with his wife to look at an experimental procedure for blindness which he had had for twenty-five years. Nothing came of it. While in a restaurant in Philadelphia, the man stated that he could suddenly see, and very clearly. Sitting in the restaurant was a reptilian alien who said to him something to the effect of "Now you can see me, so tell someone."

The man told his wife that he could see, and she didn't believe him, so he insisted describing what the waitress was wearing and what was in the restaurant. He stated that the sight remained until they had left the restaurant and were going into the hotel, at which point he was again blind.

He stated that the sight returned again at the airport as they were waiting to board the plane. Again he described to his wife what he could see. Part of what he described was a bizarre situation where all the people coming off the plane were dressed as if they were in a state of disorder (as if everyone on the plane had been through something traumatic). His wife reported that she could see this as well, but it did not appear that others around them noticed this.

Minutes later he was blind again, and as far as I know, his sight has not returned.

Mellen Thomas-Benedict - Benedict had an NDE in 1982 after dying from terminal brain cancer. After returning, he relayed having direct access to Universal Intelligence, which he can still access. He has filed a number of patents technologies for health and wellness.[325]

Chapter 22 Inspiration through Psychedelic Compounds

I didn't have one whiff of God until I took psychedelics. **Harvard Professor Dr. Ram Dass**

It is not that the psychedelics magically invoke God. Rather it seems that if the setting supports it, the psychedelic compounds somehow act to thin or lift the normally thick veil between normal consciousness and the spiritual dimension, allowing the spiritual dimension to be revealed. The psychedelic experience poses a serious challenge to the dominant materialistic, scientific worldview... It shatters the materialistic paradigm. While it may seem paradoxical that a completely material substance opens to the spiritual realm, it is also part of the larger Mystery that no opening to the Divine is excluded by Spirit. **Brant Cortright, Professor of Psychology and Director of the Integral Counseling Psychology program at the California Institute of Integral Studies in San Francisco.**

I understand from media accounts that you feel LSD helped you creatively in your development of Apple computers and your personal spiritual quest. I'm interested in learning more about how LSD was useful to you. **Albert Hofmann, inventor of LSD, in a letter to Apple Chairman Steve Jobs.**

Something was coursing through every cell in my body - like an intelligence searching everything . And I am wired to the entire cosmos! I look at the ground, and I see a crack in the ground and inside that crack I see a little flower growing...it's my brother - Everything! And I realize for the first time this is the only genuine, religious experience I've ever had! It is this direct access to the Godhead or whatever you think that is. I have no idea what it is, but there is definitely an intelligence - a higher intelligence - at work in you during this experience. **Musician Sting, who starts the Rain Forest Foundation, after ingesting Ayahuasca.**

    The use of psychedelics and other mind-altering components has been a part of man's history, whether recorded in writing or recounted orally. The psychedelic trip has also been recounted in modern rock and roll such as in the Beatles' lyrics, "The deeper you go, the higher you fly. The higher you fly the deeper you go."
    The word psychedelic means "mind-manifesting." Unlike heroin or cocaine, psychedelics such as LSD**,** mescaline, psilocybin, ibogaine, and dimethyltryptamine are neither physically harmful nor habit-forming.

Prior to the discovery of LSD during World War II, nonlocal experiences were reported. William James, the great American philosopher/psychologist, wrote about mind altering components in his 1902 book *The Varieties of Religious Experience*. Speaking of what he called the Anaesthetic Revelation he wrote, "Nitrous oxide and ether, especially nitrous oxide, when sufficiently diluted with air, stimulate the mystical consciousness in an extraordinary way. Depth beyond depth seems revealed to the inhaler...I know of more than one person who is persuaded that in the nitrous oxide trance we have a genuine metaphysical experience."[326]

In 1966 John Lennon wrote a song called *Tomorrow Never Knows* which talked about his first experience with LSD. The lyrics were a message to the youth of the sixties to turn off, surrender and bring in the idea of love as the dominant emotion. The words included,

> Turn off your mind relax and float down stream
> It is not dying; it is not dying
> Lay down all thoughts, surrender to the void,
> It is shining, it is shining.
> Yet you may see the meaning of within
> It is being, it is being
> Love is all and love is everyone
> It is knowing, it is knowing

The expression "turn off your mind...and float downstream" was a line about psychedelics that Lennon borrowed from the book *The Psychedelic Experience: A Manual Based on the Tibetan Book of The Dead* written by Harvard professor and LSD guru Timothy Leary. Lennon had purchased the book in April 1966 just before writing the song.

Lennon's lyrics shared with the youth of the sixties the information found by Leary in the ancient *Tibetan Book of the Dead*. The Tibetans had been referring to meditation and Lennon had raised the modern pharmaceutical equivalent – acid. Lennon proposed having 1,000 monks chanting in the background to "the first acid song: 'Lay down all thoughts surrender to the void, and all that shit which Leary had pinched from The Book of the Dead."

Despite all the bad publicity that psychedelics have received over the years, inspiration through psychedelic components is a critical area where inspirations and downloads can be evaluated under somewhat repeatable and controlled conditions. The three true psychedelics have been identified as LSD, mescaline, and psilocybin.

Time magazine reported that a "new study published last...found that people who took magic mushrooms (psilocybin) had long-term personality changes, becoming more open, more curious, more intellectually engaged and more creative. These personality shifts persisted more than a year after taking the drugs."[327]

Those who led the psychedelic revolution like Aldous Huxley, a writer widely acknowledged as one of the pre-eminent intellectuals of his time went through his progression of psychedelics, and many followed.

Huxley started with mescaline which evolved to LSD which he described as "the most extraordinary and significant experience available to a human being this side of the Beatific Vision."

He wrote the book "Doors of Perception" to describe the power and beneficial nature of these drugs or as he described it a "way to change the way the monkey perceives reality." He had proposed calling psychedelics "phanerothymes," meaning to make the soul visible.

The final step in his evolution of psychedelic awakening came when he tried DMT for the first time. This led him to "break through the visionary layers into the realm of pure oneness."

Prominent people who have reported inspiration and spiritual experiences through psychedelics include the following:

Tori Amos - Amos is an American singer-songwriter, pianist, and composer who also tried Ayahuasca. She said of the experience, "..the most influential journeys I have had have been with Ayahuasca, the vine from the Amazon, the combination of that and mushrooms. It's very much a medicine woman, medicine man's journey drug, where you go inside. It's not a social thing. It's an internal experience. I experiment with things that are usually an internal experience because that's just what excites me. And yes, it does sometimes give me visions. But my intention when I am doing it is very different than recreational. I don't do it recreationally. I do it to go do inner work, and I'm very clear before I do it what I'm searching for. That way, there's no abuse suffered, and I don't rely on it. It's just one more tool that I use sometimes."

Penn Badgley - Badgley *The Gossip Girl* actor tried Ayahuasca with a tribe in the Colombian rainforest and stated about the experience, "these ceremonies seemed to melt away and all melt into one gleaming psychic arrow pointing towards my heart. ... And that was the simplest but, to this day, the most profound moment of my life."[328]

Syd Barrett - Barrett, who had studied art for many years in London and who is recognized as the genius who inspired Pink Floyd's beginnings, spiraled into dark seclusion by the age of 25, due to what other band members, such as David Gilmour, describe as "a sad story romanticized by people who don't know anything about it." Barrett's downfall is said to have taken place after a kamikaze consumption of LSD. His descent was so severe that in June, 1975, nearly four years after his final public interview in December, 1971, he walked into Pink Floyd's recording studio and the rest of the guys didn't even recognize him. He wasn't even 30 years old then, but Roger Waters later broke down in tears remembering how Barrett looked nearly twice that age that day in the recording studio, with shaven head and eyebrows. In 2005, during a unique performance by Pink Floyd, Roger Waters stated, "It's actually quite emotional standing up here with these three guys after all these years…we are doing this for everyone who's not here, but particular, of course, for Syd." Then they played "Wish You Were Here."

Deepak Chopra - Even Deepak Chopra, author of 60+ books on consciousness, brain chemistry, and spirituality, has tried LSD. "My first experience with spirituality was with LSD when I was 17," he said. "It was my first excursion into other dimensions. I do not recommend recreational drugs because they can damage the nervous system, and yet there are traditions around the world, particularly American Indians, and also traditions with the aborigines in Australia and also traditions in India." [329]

Brant Cortright - After a number of studies and evaluations, Cortright, concluded:

> *Psychedelics are important in transpersonal psychology for several reasons, but the chief one is because with proper preparation these substances can reliably produce transpersonal and spiritual experiences of profound intensity and power. A psychedelic journey can open consciousness to vast new dimensions of experience, shattering previous conceptions of reality and revealing a new world of perception where the spirit is no longer an abstract concept but a living, vivid actuality... Most all of the founders of transpersonal psychology have been influenced by psychedelics or originally became interested in spirituality as a result of psychedelic experiences. It may be no accident that the Journal of Transpersonal Psychology was born shortly after 1967's Summer of Love, a period of great psychedelic experimentation in virtually every part of society.* [330]

Dr. Ram Dass - Dass, a Harvard professor and American contemporary spiritual teacher and the author of the seminal 1971 book *Be Here Now*, has told the story of asking his Hindu guru Neem Karoli Baba what the significance of LSD was. His guru replied that the West was so materialistic that God had to take a material form to be revealed here.

Walt Disney - Disney took Disney Mescaline (Peyote) starting in 1936 after visiting Black Mountain College in North Carolina in 1935. The result was the 1941 movie Fantasia.

Doug Engelbart - Engelbart was the visionary behind the 1968 demo in San Francisco of a new powerful computer system complete with modem, monitor, keyboard and mouse and experimented with LSD. He stated, "It must be changing something about the internal communication in my brain. Whatever my inner process is that lets me solve problems, it works differently, or maybe different parts of my brain are used. When I'm on LSD and hearing something that's pure rhythm, it takes me to another world and into another brain state where I've stopped thinking and started knowing." [331]

Paul Erdos - Erdos was a Hungarian mathematician who was known for his prolific authorship (most mathematical papers ever) and his social practice of mathematics (more than 500 collaborators). He worked 19 hour days. One of the reasons he was so prolific was that he took amphetamines regularly, after 1971. A friend bet him $500 he couldn't go a month without, and Erdos took him up on the bet. After the month was over, Erdos had won the bet, but during the month he complained that he had been unable to do any work and that mathematics had been set back: "Before, when I looked at a piece of blank paper my mind was filled with ideas. Now all I see is a blank piece of paper." When the bet was over Erdos continued his amphetamine use and prolific pace of work.[332]

Jerry Garcia - "Psychedelics were probably the single most significant experience in my life. Otherwise, I think I would be going along believing that this visible reality here is all that there is. Psychedelics didn't give me any answers. What I have are a lot of questions. One thing I'm certain of; the mind is an incredible thing, and there are levels of organizations of consciousness that are way beyond what people are fooling with in day to day reality... I've been spoken to by a higher order of intelligence - I thought it was God. It was a very personal God in that it had exactly the same sense of humor that I have [laughter]. I interpret that as being the next level of consciousness, but maybe there's a hierarchical set of consciousness. My experience is that there is one smarter than me, which can talk to me, and there's also the biological one that I spoke about."[333]

John Gilmore - Gilmore was the first employee at Sun Microsystems stated that most of his colleagues in the sixties and seventies used psychedelics drugs. Stated psychedelics taught that life was not rational, and that is why IBM was overtaken by Apple and other such upstarts. IBM was "very rational." Gilmore also stated that those who developed the internet were interested in the same thing as consciousness researchers – creating new ways of storing and sharing knowledge. Those who are tripping do come to conclusions and experience revelations, some of which may have turned up in programming code.[334]

Roland Richard Griffiths - The Pahnke experiment, which involved the use of psilocybin, was reproduced in 2002 by Griffiths at John Hopkins University (and published in 2006) under more rigorous and controlled conditions. It yielded similar results, validating Pahnke's conclusions.

Later in a 14-month follow-up study, "over half of the participants rated the experience among the top five most meaningful spiritual experiences in their lives, and considered the experience to have increased their personal well-being and life satisfaction."[335]

Dr. Stanislav Grof, M.D. - Grof first started working with LSD when he volunteered as a subject for LSD testing in Czechoslovakia in 1954. Grof stated, "It was such a powerful opening of my own unconscious that I temporarily became more interested in psychedelics than in psychoanalysis.

In the middle of my first LSD experiment, when I watched the flashing stroboscopic light, the nature of it all changed and what happened was that I was catapulted out of my body. I first lost the laboratory, then I lost the clinic, then Prague, and then the planet. I had the sense that I was a disembodied consciousness of universal cosmic dimensions. I witnessed things that I would describe today as pulsars, quasars, the Big Bang, and expanding galaxies." [336]

The initial experience led him to author over ninety related professional articles and six books.

Presently because of the ban on LSD testing, Grof uses non-drug methods for deep psycho-spiritual work. The system used is called Holotropic Breathwork, which produces deeper, states through specialized breathing techniques, in conjunction with specially chosen music. This produces what Grof calls a "psychospiritual crisis" or "spiritual emergency."

In speaking about the 60 years of research he has done on non-ordinary states of consciousness, Grof states, "I have had many mystical experiences and transpersonal experiences in general - experiences of identification with other people and other species, psychospiritual death and rebirth, encounters with archetypal beings and visits to various archetypal realms (heavens, hells, and paradises of different cultures), past life experiences, experiences of cosmic unity, powerful visions of the source of creation that I perceived as God, experience of the Supracosmic and Metacosmic Void, and so on. I have experienced most of the types of experiences that I have been writing about in my books, many of them in my psychedelic sessions, others during spiritual practice, Holotropic Breathwork, or in the sensory isolation tank designed by my friend John Lilly. They had a very profound influence on me and radically changed my worldview – from a monistic materialistic Newtonian-Cartesian one, imparted on me by my academic training, to an essentially mystical or transpersonal one."[337]

Michael Harner - Harner is the founder of the "Foundation for Shamanic Studies." He stated of his experience with Ayahuasca, "For several hours after drinking the brew, I found myself, although awake, in a world literally beyond my wildest dreams. I met bird-headed people, as well as dragon-like creatures who explained that they were the true gods of this world. I enlisted the services of other spirit helpers in attempting to fly through the far reaches of the Galaxy. Transported into a trance where the supernatural seemed natural, I realized that anthropologists, including myself, had profoundly underestimated the importance of the drug in affecting native ideology."[338]

Kevin Herbert - Herbert developed software that runs millions of routers worldwide. He spoke of his own use of psychedelics, "From my personal experience, psychedelics have helped me to get past some of my most challenging problems. Overall, I feel like it's affected the development of my ideas about what our responsibility is to society of the kinds of technologies that we develop. I think that it also has given me insight into how to create technology. So, extrapolating from there, I think that many technical people have been exposed to LSD - although, it's hard to say just how many people. This is because engineers working in corporate situations don't want to get into trouble.

Psychedelics are especially helpful with the development of new computer technologies because recent developments have shifted toward more open technology, and an increased reliance on software, as opposed to reliance on machines and mechanisms. I think the fact that everything in the world has become more and more flexible, and more programmable, is a result of people taking LSD at early times in their life, like in high school or college. It changes one's vision of the kinds of technology that one can build. It encourages a departure from things being rigid and imposing."[339]

Dr. Oscar Janigan - Another set of experiments on psychedelic components was done by Dr. Oscar Janigan at UC Davis. The research involved 900 subjects and started in 1954 till it was shut down in 1962. Following the shut down, 200 of the participants were given questionnaires.

The results were significant in that 24% of the participants reported a spiritual experience, which is particularly significant as the subjects Janigan chose strenuously avoided providing any religious or mystical information at the inception of the research. There were absolutely no expectations of spiritual experiences when the research began. In fact, when Janigan wrote up the results, he considered the spiritual experiences as an anomaly despite the high number.

Steve Jobs - Jobs was the force behind Apple Computers. He credited his inventiveness to taking LSD up to 15 times between 1972 and 1974.

Steve Jobs considered his experimenting with LSD "one of the two or three most important things he had done in his life." Jobs stated, "Taking LSD was a profound experience, one of the most important things in my life. LSD shows you that there's another side to the coin, and you can't remember it when it wears off, but you know it. It reinforced my sense of what was important - creating great things instead of making money, putting things back into the stream of history and of human consciousness as much as I could."[340]

He further claimed that Bill Gates "is basically unimaginative and has never invented anything, which is why I think he's more comfortable now in philanthropy than technology. He just shamelessly ripped off other people's ideas."

Olivia-Newton John - Olivia tried Ayahuasca in June 2007 and experienced "an astral journey," as she recounted on Peruvian TV.

Terence McKenna - McKenna and Timothy Leary were two of the most outspoken men in favor psychedelics. McKenna believed strongly psychedelics were tied to spiritual qualities. "Psychedelics are illegal," wrote McKenna, "not because a loving government is concerned that you may jump out of a third-story window. Psychedelics are illegal because they dissolve opinion structure and culturally laid down models of behavior and information processing. They open you up to the possibility that everything you know is wrong."

"The 'Stoned Ape' Theory of Human Evolution" proposed by McKenna detailed how magic psilocybin mushrooms could have created the first psychedelic experiences engendering a deep connectivity with the universe at large creating what could be called religious experiences.

The first person to take the mushrooms would share his enlightenment with the other in the tribe who would make him the shaman for his great insights into the mysteries of the universe. This would lead to attempts to express the psychedelic visions which would turn into rituals eventually growing into worship and then religion.

In a wiki article dealing with McKenna's Stoned Ape theory, there was a discussion of two studies that were done on spiritual experience and psilocybin:

> *In 2006, the United States government funded a randomized and double-blinded study by Johns Hopkins University, which studied the spiritual effects of psilocybin in particular. That is, they did not use mushrooms specifically (in fact, each individual mushroom piece can vary wildly in psilocybin and psilocin content. The study involved 36 college-educated adults (average age of 46) who had never tried psilocybin nor had a history of drug use, and who had religious or spiritual interests. The participants were closely observed for eight-hour intervals in a laboratory while under the influence of psilocybin mushrooms.*
>
> *One-third of the participants reported that the experience was the single most spiritually significant moment of their lives and more than two-thirds reported it was among the top five most spiritually significant experiences. Two months after the study, 79% of the participants reported increased well-being or satisfaction; friends, relatives, and associates confirmed this. They also reported anxiety and depression symptoms to be decreased or completely gone. Despite highly controlled conditions to minimize adverse effects, 22% of subjects (8 of 36) had notable experiences of fear, some with paranoia. The authors, however, reported that all these instances were "readily managed with reassurance."*
>
> *Roland Griffiths has conducted pioneering research at John Hopkins University showing that the correct dose of psilocybin mushrooms can cause mystical-type experiences that have substantial and sustained personal meaning and spiritual significance. At 2 months, the volunteers rated the*

psilocybin experience as having substantial personal meaning and spiritual significance and attributed to the experience sustained positive changes in attitudes and behavior consistent with changes rated by community observers. These effects were still apparent even 14 months after taking the ingesting the psilocybin.[341]

Kary Mullis - Mullis won the Nobel Prize for the development of the polymerase chain reaction (PCR), the lab technique that can turn a single segment of DNA into millions of identical copies. He did a lot of LSD during the 60s and 70s while going to school and said the "mind-opening" experiences were much more important than any of his courses. He told the 3rd International Conference on Entheobotany, "I was at Berkeley and taking acid every week. That's what people did for entertainment: drink beer or to out into Tilden Park and take 500 micrograms of LSD and sit all day thinking about the universe, time going backward and forward…"

During a BBC's Psychedelic Science documentary, Mullis mused aloud: "What if I had not taken LSD ever; would I have still invented PCR?" To which he replied, "I don't know. I doubt it. I seriously doubt it."[342]

John McCarthy - McCarthy was an artificial intelligence pioneer who coined the term "artificial intelligence" and headed Stanford's Artificial Intelligence Lab (SAIL), where LSD was taken both as serious experimentation and recreationally.[343]

Walter Pahnke - Harvard Doctoral Candidate Walter Pahnke conducted an experiment in 1962 with psilocybin in a double-blind experiment with 20 graduate divinity student volunteers, and it came to be known as the "Good Friday Experiment." At the time, Timothy Leary was the academic advisor. Half of the students received psilocybin. A control group received an active placebo consisting of a large dose of niacin which causes produces clear physiological changes such as face flushing and feeling hot and tingly.

The results were clear. Almost all of the members of the experimental group reported profound religious experiences "indistinguishable from mystical experiences described in the cross-cultural literature." Those having the experience included religious scholar Huston Smith, who would go on to write many books on comparative religion. Smith described his psilocybin experience as "The most powerful cosmic homecoming I have ever experienced."

25 years later, in a follow-up to the study, "all of the subjects given psilocybin described their experience as having elements of "a genuine mystical nature and characterized it as one of the high points of their spiritual life."

Mark Pesce - Pesce co-invented the virtual reality coding language VRML. He stated, "To a man and a woman, the people behind (virtual reality) were acidheads."[344]

Carl Sagan - Sagan spoke of smoking pot in an article he wrote under the name Mr. X in 1971. "I do not consider myself a religious person in the usual sense, but there is a religious aspect to some highs. The heightened sensitivity in all areas gives me a feeling of communion with my surroundings, both animate and inanimate. Sometimes a kind of existential perception of the absurd comes over me, and I see with awful certainty the hypocrisies and posturing of myself and my fellow men."[345] Speaking of the ability of pot to inspire ideas, Sagan said, "the devastating insights achieved when high are real insights; the main problem is putting these insights in a form acceptable to the quite different self that we are when we're down the next day."[346]

Paul Simon - Simon also tried Ayahuasca. He wrote a song about it called Spirit Voices.

Sting - Sting, lead singer for the band, The Police, became involved with Ayahuasca, the drug most significantly associated with inspirations and downloads. It is brewed from two ingredients: Banisteriopsis caapi and Psychotria viridis. It is usually found and used in Brazil, which is where Sting found it.

Sting states he discovered it in 1987. "...It's not a frivolous pursuit... there's a certain amount of dread attached to taking it - you have a hallucinogenic trip that deals with death and your mortality. So it's quite an ordeal. It's not something you're going to score, and a have a great time on." Others have described it in similar ways. It is said that people's hands and knees shake just before taking it.

"I realized for the first time that this is the only genuine religious experience I have ever had," Sting said in the 2010 documentary *2012: Time for Change*. "There is definitely a higher intelligence at work in you during this experience."

Dr. Rick Strassman - Another psychedelic study that was done involved 400 doses of N,N-dimethyltryptamine, or DMT, now known in the popular discussion as the "spirit molecule." It is an extremely short-acting (15 minutes or less) and powerful psychedelic; that was administered to 60 test subjects. The research began in Albuquerque in 1990 at the University of New Mexico's School of Medicine.

DMT is produced by the tiny pineal gland organ situated in the center of the brain. This organ has long been associated with "metaphysical" history. Western and Eastern religions place the pineal as the center of religious experiences. Even Descartes centuries ago believed the pineal was "the seat of the soul."

The New Mexico experiment was headed by tenured Associate Professor of Psychiatry, Dr. Rick Strassman. Some conclusions reached in the DMT study included:

Spiritual states can be accessed, and mystical information gained with DMT.

DMT is intimately involved in "alien abduction" events. There was a close correlation between the reports of DMT experiencers and abduction experiences. This relationship extended to the description, what the being was doing, their messages for the future, and the lack of emotions in the beings.

There is a pineal DMT release at forty-nine days after conception marking the entrance of the spirit into the fetus. This is when the pineal gland first makes its appearance in the body. According to the Tibetan Book of the Dead, 49 days is the estimated time it takes for the spirit to move through the three bardos after death and be reborn into a new life.

When Strassman shut the research down in 1995, he felt discomfort because he could not explain what was going on. It began to dawn on him after he ended the study was that he might be dealing with a spiritual phenomenon.

Phil Tippet - Tippet, who won the 1984 Oscar for his animation effects on "Return of the Jedi", stated during an interview with Vice that he took LSD while working on the movie.[347]

Bob Wallace - Wallace, who was the ninth employee of Microsoft, now runs Mind Books, devoted to psychedelic and alternative consciousness. Wallace is the creator of the word processing program PC-Write, and founder of the software company Quicksoft. He is the man who came up with the word shareware. He stated that his conception of shareware as a formal business application was psychedelically inspired.

Brian Wilson - Wilson wrote most of the big songs for the 12th largest selling rock band in history, The Beach Boys. He wrote, "Good Vibrations" calling it "the summation of my musical vision. It was a harmonic convergence of imagination and talent, production values, and craft, songwriting, and spirituality." Wilson wrote it while on LSD and stated that when he took LSD his fingers flew across the keys like you wouldn't believe, but that LSD also messed up his mind.

Bill Wilson - Wilson was the co-founder of the Alcoholics Anonymous program. He used and promoted LSD as a tool for alcoholics to shake their addiction. Wilson was closely associated with others conducting early experiments with LSD. In recent years, LSD has again been promoted as a treatment for alcoholism.

Chapter 23 What is the Main Message?

Many of the messages that come across in the lyrics of the musicians mentioned in Chapter 3 are the same messages that are found in many of the other types of inspirations and downloads. The messages seem to be positive in nature centering around what could be considered key life lessons.

Below are the key messages and a listing of examples of the different types of inspirations which shows this particular message.

Oneness

The Oneness message is that everything in the universe is connected and thus One. This is what the ancients referred to as the nirvikalpa samadhi experience. Each person is part of the whole, and the whole is made up of the parts, similar to a tree where all the leaves are different in shape, size, and fractal vane patterns, but where they are all an essential part of the tree and its mission. This is what Einstein's intellectual successor David Bohm called the Implicate Order.

Aliens

George Adamski, the first reported alien contactee relayed a message he received from the aliens - there is a Basic Universal Law: all things are connected; there is a Oneness of consciousness throughout the cosmos. An alien referred to as a "master" told Adamski, "You must impress, as best you can, understanding in the minds of your brothers on Earth that knowledge of themselves is the first requisite. And the first questions: 'Who am I? Through what avenues can, I express in order to return to the Oneness from which I have fallen?'"

Betty Andreasson, an experiencer, who has been the subject of five books by Raymond Fowler documenting his research into her lifelong experiences, described what she was told, "I understand that everything is one. Everything fits together. Everything is one. It's beautiful! No matter what it is!"

Bashar, a multi-dimensional, extra-terrestrial being who speaks through channel Darryl Anka, stated there are only four laws in the universe, and the main one is, "The One is the all, and the all are the One."

Tina Marie Caoette, an experiencer, Caouette was told by the alien elder, "There is no difference between that chair, that planet and you. You are all energy just vibrating at a different frequency."[348]

Audrey Hewins, who received the vision to start Starborn Support and the Experiencers Conference held in Maine each year got a Oneness message which stated, "AFTER DEEP COVER AND GREAT DISC EYES WE

WILL RECOGNIZE THE ONENESS IN EACH OTHER. THE CREATOR RETURNS WHEN THE ONENESS IS RECOGNIZED BY ALL WHICH WAS CREATED."

John - Regressionist Yvonne Smith had a client named John who described the Oneness idea he had been given by the aliens, "Part of it was through the experiences themselves that I don't want to say [was] conditioning, but them helping me acknowledge that we are all connected and that I am part of them and they are part of me…"[349]

Bret Oldham, an experiencer, was told by the aliens in reply to a question about God, "We are all one with the one who is all."

Sherry Wilde, an experiencer, spoke of three main lessons she learned from the aliens. The first was that we are all one. To illustrate the point they took her and showed her father sitting at the kitchen table by himself. Just As she was wondering why they were showing her this, she stated that her father suddenly picked up his fork and drove it into his left hand spraying blood everywhere. At that point, she was told that this illustrates we are all one and what we do to others we do to ourselves.[350]

Art

Akeane Kramarik - Artistic Savant - "If we really look at it everything is connected. Everything is one. Even all the emotions are one."

Books

Grant Morrison - Famous DC Comics cartoonist and UFO experiencer, Morrison said he was told by the aliens, "I was told that our universe is a living single entity, the larval form of beings who inhabit what felt like an infinite, yet enclosed 'ocean' of living information."[351]

Channeling

Edgar Cayce - Cayce, the Sleeping Prophet, stated, "The first lesson for six months should be One-One-One-One; Oneness of God, Oneness of man's relation, Oneness of force, Oneness of time, Oneness of purpose, Oneness in every effort-Oneness- Oneness!"[352]

Lazarus - A spirit that never came into the physical, Lazarus stated, "Sense the Oneness and the Power of One. Connect with the ethers and surrender your sense, your pretense, of separateness."[353]

Ramtha - One of the key messages of Ramtha's teachings encompasses the internalization of divinity meaning God is in Us, You are God. Therefore, all is one.

Helen Schucman - In the channeled book *A Course in Miracles,* Schucman states, "All things that come from God are one. They come from Oneness, and must be received as one."

Patience Worth - One of the many poems channeled by Worth was Oneness. "I have said 'Thou art sprung from my side, Rooted in my substance' ...Without thee I am nothing.'" [354]

Music

Led Zeppelin in the lyrics for "Stairway to Heaven," which came through automatic writing, stated, "'Cause you know sometimes words have two meanings...And if you listen very hard the answer will come to you at last. When all are, one and one is all."

John Lennon - "I am he as you are he as you are me, and we are all together."

John Denver - Denver in his last song *The Wandering Soul*, which was never recorded or released, talked of Oneness and love being the key, "Within each part, and in the whole. Love is the answer; love is the way."

Sting - Lead singer for The Police, Sting described his feelings following an Ayahuasca experience in Brazil, "When we walk out into the cool of the evening, the jungle is vibrantly alive, in fact disarmingly alive, and I have never felt so connected before. I may be out of my gourd, but I seem to be perceiving the world on a molecular level, where the normal barriers that separate 'me' from everything else have been removed, as if every leaf, every blade of grass, every nodding flower is reaching out, every insect calling to me, every star in the clear sky sending a direct beam to the top of my head. This sensation of connectedness is overwhelming."[355]

Chris Robinson - Front man for the group The Black Crowes, Robinson spoke about the Oneness he experienced ingesting Ayahuasca. "I was very lucky, eight or nine years ago, to have an Ayahuasca experience... that was the literal opening up of all my minds and hearts. Where my mind and heart and soul all coalesce of having at least the initial understanding of the interconnectedness of all living entities in the universe."[356]

Movies

Gene Roddenberry - Creator of Star Trek, Roddenberry channeled Tom, a spokesman for The Council of Nine. "But we would say to you, yes, we are in connection with one that is higher, but in totality together we are one, as all the universe is one.... We wish you to know that we are not God. We are collective and become one. We wish you to know that we are you as you are we. You created us, and out of that creation, you were created."[357]

Near Death Experiences (NDEs)

Penny Sartori's research on NDEs showed that "during the experiences some people feel a great sense of unity and interconnectivity between all people."[358]

Anthony - A gentleman who had an NDE as a result of an asthma attack. The experience lasted 8 minutes but Anthony maintained he had lived 2,500 years in that alternate timeline. Oneness was the message that was part of that experience. Anthony states he learned that "... everyone in the world [is] interconnected on these lines and I felt love and empathy..."[359]

78% of all people who have near death experiences describe Oneness or cosmic unity as part of the experience.[360]

Psychedelic Components

DMT - One test subject in the SRI DMT experiments conducted by Rick Strassman described his experience this way, "So I went right into this white light. When I went into it, I lost any sense of being, any sense of what I was doing, any sense of past, any sense of future. It was absolutely blissful and euphoric. I just felt like it wasn't I. I was everything. I was the light. There is no sense of separation, no past, no future, all present, and white-yellow light." As he fell out of the light, he could immediately feel this sense of separation.[361]

Another person in the study talked about how all ego was peeled away like skins of an onion, "There is that last level that defines you as a human being, and it goes.... you are no longer a human being. In fact, you are no longer anything that you can identify."

Scientific Discoveries

Fritjof Capra, a physicist, believes quantum theory reveals a basic Oneness of the universe. It shows that we cannot decompose the world into independently existing smallest units. As we penetrate into matter, nature does not show us any isolated "building blocks," but rather appears as a complicated web of relations between the various parts of the whole. These relations always include the observer in an essential way. The human observer constitutes the final link in the chain of observational processes, and the properties of any atomic object can be understood only regarding the object's interaction with the observer.

Shan Gao, a physicist, developed the quantum theory of discontinuous electron motion and held Oneness as part of a vision that led to his discovery, "In the early morning of 12 October 1993, I experienced a sudden enlightenment. At that moment, I felt that my body permeated the whole universe, and I was united with it ..."[362]

Edgar Mitchell, the sixth man to walk on the moon, experienced an instantaneous Oneness inspiration on his return trip from the moon on Apollo 14:

> *And suddenly it settled in a visceral moment of knowing that the molecules in my body, the molecules in the spacecraft, and the molecules in my partners had been prototyped and manufactured in an ancient generation of stars. It was not an intellectual realization, but a deep knowing that was accompanied by a feeling of ecstasy and oneness that I had never experienced in that way before.*
>
> *In that instant, I knew for certain that what I was seeing was no accident. That it did not occur randomly and without order. That life did not, by accident, arise from the primordial earthly sea. It was as though my awareness reached out to touch the farthest star and I was aware of being an integral part of the entire universe, for one brief instance. Any questions that my curious mind might have had about our progress, about our destiny, about the nature of the universe, suddenly melted away as I experienced that oneness. I could reach out and touch the furthest parts and experience the vast reaches of the universe. It was clear that those tiny pinpoints of light in such brilliant profusion were a unity. They were linked together as part of the whole as they framed and formed a backdrop for this view of planet Earth. I knew we are not alone in this universe that Earth was one of the millions, perhaps billions, of planets like our own with intelligent life, all playing a role in the great creative plan for the evolution of life.*[363]

Andrew Newberg, a neuroscientist at the University of Pennsylvania, has been scanning the brains of religious people for more than a decade. He has found that people who meditate, from Franciscan nuns to Tibetan Buddhists, go dark in the parietal lobe - the area of the brain that is related to sensory information and helps us to form our sense of self. Newberg found that the various religious groups (praying or meditating more than one hour a day) all felt the same Oneness with the universe. "There is no Christian. There is no Jew; There is no Muslim. There is just all one."[364]

Erwin Schrodinger, a physicist, wrote, "The earliest records, to my knowledge, date back some 2500 years or more... the recognition ATMAN = BRAHMAN (the personal self equals the omnipresent, all-comprehending eternal self) was in Indian thought considered, far from being blasphemous, to represent the quintessence of deepest insight into the happenings of the world." He also stated, "Deep down the consciousness of mankind is one. This is a virtual certainty because even in the vacuum matter is one; and if we don't see this, it's because we are blinding ourselves to it." [365]

Rusty Schweikart, an astronaut, had a Oneness experience on a March 6, 1969, during a spacewalk outside Apollo 9, "When you go around the Earth in an hour and a half, you begin to recognize that your identity is with that whole thing. That makes a change...it comes through to you so powerfully that you're the sensing element for Man."

Jill Bolte Taylor, a neuroanatomist, talked about the brain and Oneness. "The present time is a time when everything and everyone is connected together as ONE. As a result, our right mind perceives each of us as equal members of the human family. It identifies our similarities and recognizes our relationship with this marvelous planet, which sustains our life. It perceives the big picture, how everything is related, and how we all join together to make up the whole." [366]

Fear/Love

Another message that is brought back by many experiencers, NDEers, and other having NF is that there is no time, space, gravity, good, or evil. All that there is fear and love, and we evolve by moving from fear to love. Following are some examples.

Aliens

Mike Maloney - Maloney remembering his abduction experience stated, "While my mind was still pulling away, she surrounded me with an overwhelming feeling of unconditional love and contained within that was a message that said, 'We are here to help you...during my initial physical contact experience in Winnipeg, the overpowering love that radiated from the being I was interacting with was unlike anything that I have experienced in human life. It was all-encompassing as if it came from God.'"[367]

Sara - experiencer - John Mack quoted Sara, one of his subjects, as saying, "The context is almost 100% emotional...it's all about...the emotion of love is the most...unconditional supportive love...not the human love...but creativeness...growth-affirming kind of love. It bowls you over. When you feel that and when you feel that connection to that, the love feeling is so tremendous."[368]

Randy Kitchur - experiencer - Kitchur stated, "I witnessed a UFO only a couple of hundred feet away in August of 1981 twenty-five miles NW of Winnipeg late at night. I could see its occupants silhouetted against its portals on the top deck through three portals which were lit; the rest of the body of the object was dark. I waved at it, and it signaled back with flashing lights, and also sent me a telepathic message which brought me great peace and joy. It was the most profoundly intense spiritual experience of my life. I would never exchange it for a billion dollars.[369] A new person showed up at the Winnipeg Experiencer Anonymous meeting. When asked why she had attended she said, "I was abducted." She spoke of the difficulties that came with the experience. When one person asked her if there was a main message that the aliens were giving her, she stated, "Yes, love." Short and simple - the message was love.

In the final FREE Phase 2 survey 66.70% of all experiencers felt a sense of love from the aliens, 54.6% were given a message of love or Oneness.[370]

James J. Hurtak - social scientist, linguist, futurist, and author with Ph.D. in History and Oriental Studies and Social Sciences and Linguistics, had a two-day experience starting on January 2, 1973 where he interacted with Enoch and divine intelligences as recounted in *The Book of Knowledge: The Keys of Enoch*. During that experience, Hurtak experienced "unconditional love, supreme love that I cannot explain…the whole body began to vibrate with love….The body begins to vibrate with love abstracts connected to other. There is nothing you can do wrong. If I had to boil this entire message down to one sentence, it would run this way: You are loved. And if I had to boil it down further, to just one word, it would (of course) be, simply: Love."[371]

Art

Akeane Kramarik, an artist, states that the main message of her paintings and poetry is love.

Music

Jon Anderson, who has had many UFO experiences, including getting information from an alien that came through the wall into his Las Vegas Caesar's Palace Hotel room, co-wrote the song "Madrigal" about "celestial travelers." Part of the lyrics included the lines, "Sacred ships do sail the seventh age. Cast off your garments of fear, and replace them with love."

John Lennon - When it comes to music there are many songs about love. The key one may have been "All You need is Love" which was written by Lennon for "Our World" project, the first worldwide TV special.[372] "It was an inspired song, and they really wanted to give the world a message," said former Beatle manager Brian Epstein. "The nice thing about it is that it cannot be misinterpreted. It is a clear message saying that love is everything."[373] The song was intended that the song is understood by people of all nations. Its simple message was love. It was released in 1967 during the Summer of Love, and it embraced the feeling of the world's youth during that period. The words "all you need is love" became a slogan of the anti-Vietnam war movement. Lennon stated, "It matters not who you love, where you love, why you love, when you love or how you love, it matters only that you love" and "Love, Love, Love. All you need is love. Love is all you need." and "Love is the Answer. What was the Question?"

Reg Presley - Member of the British band The Troggs, Presley wrote the song *Love is all Around* which was a hit in the late 60s and became a hit again when featured in the movies *Three Weddings and a Funeral* and also *Love Actually*. Presley reported UFO experiences and stated he "had a profound experience in constructing, writing, releasing and influencing the world by *Love is All Around*.

Carlos Santana, who claims to get his musical inspiration from the Archangel Metatron stated, "If you take one thing from this interview, just one thing alone, this is it: There's only two energies in this planet, love, and fear."

Near Death Experiences (NDEs)

Eben Alexander - Neurologist - In Alexander's book *Proof of Heaven*, we see the main message,

> But none of that mattered because I had already been taught the one thing - the only thing - that, in the last analysis, truly matters. I had initially received this piece of knowledge from my lovely companion on the butterfly wing upon my first entrance into the Gateway. It came in three parts, and to take one more shot at putting it into words (because of course it was initially delivered wordlessly), it would run something like this: You are loved and cherished. You have nothing to fear.
>
> If I had to boil this entire message down to one sentence, it would run this way: You are loved.
>
> And if I had to boil it down further, to just one word, it would (of course) be, simply: Love.[374]

Joe McMoneagle - Remote Viewer - McMoneagle experienced an NDE prior to becoming one of the key remote viewers for the US Army. After going through the tunnel reported by many who have had NDEs, he found himself "enveloped in a very soft but intense white light… swimming in endless unconditional love, totally whole totally complete, totally loved. It's really hard to describe because I don't think there are any words that can describe it. I knew at this time that this must be what God is."[375] 72% of people experiencing near death experiences report feeling unconditional love.[376]

Vicki - Vicki is a girl blind from birth who had two NDEs. "She was surrounded by trees and flowers and a vast number of people. She was in a place of tremendous light, and the light, Vicki said, was something you could feel as well as see. What the light conveyed was love. Even the people she saw were bright and reflected the light of this love. "Everybody there was made of light. And I was made of light. There was love everywhere. It was like love came from the grass, love came from the birds, love came from the trees."[377]

Savants

Dr. Diane Powell did work with non-verbal savants who had been able to communicate with a computer keyboard. Powell stated "they talked about love. They talked about peace. They talked about compassion. I was very interesting. Very spiritual children."[378]

Scientific Discoveries

Andrew Newberg described the effect of the meditation in love and fear on the brain: "Indeed, meditating on any form of love, including God's love, appears to strengthen the same neurological circuits that allow us to feel compassion towards others. In contrast, the religious activities that focus on fear may damage the anterior cingulate, and when this happens, a person will lose interest in other people's concerns or act aggressively against them."[379]

The Environment

The general idea of the environment in the western hemisphere has been influenced by the evolutionary model put forward by Darwin which is that we are nothing more than random particles colliding with each other in space. Allegedly, the interaction of these particles after the Big Bang has led to the world we see today, and the driving force inside evolution is a genetic mutation that allows the fittest to survive and create succeeding generations with better genes. It is a world premised on the survival of the fittest.

In such a model the rule is "every man for himself." Everyone grabs what they can because if they don't, they won't make it. The world is therefore just another object up for grabs. Humans descended, in the words of quantum physicist David Bohm, like a swarm of locusts on the earth. The earth has been divided up like a real estate subdivision, and the only remaining struggle is to fight others around us for our piece of the pie.

The alien message is completely the opposite. In the visions shown to experiencers, the aliens have shown a multiverse based on Oneness. The message is clear that we do not own the earth like we think we do. The earth and everything around it is entangled and whatever we do affects the boundless whole comprised of worlds without end.

For this reason, the aliens show experiencers pictures of economic disaster and how if we do not reverse our thinking or how we live, we are headed for an ecological disaster.

Aliens

Yvonne Smith - Alien experiencers who recall their experiences or who have been hypnotically regressed often recall what seems like their involuntary genetic participation in the grey aliens' hybrid program. What many may not know is that experiencers are shown screens or 3-D images of earth's destruction or the earth following a great cataclysm. They are told that we are destroying the planet and that we must do something to stop it before it is too late. Yvonne Smith, who is one of the main regression therapists in the field of ufology stated: "Every case that I have had over the last 23 years has had that message." This is a very important and dire fact and indicates that the aliens are giving us a helpful warning, as opposed to the notion pushed by many that the aliens are here to enslave us, steal our gold, or take over our planet.

John Mack - In his 1994 book *Human Encounters with Aliens*, Harvard psychiatrist Dr. John Mack suggested that the aliens seem to be warning us of possible planetary destruction, and their message to experiencers was to "a commitment to changing their relationship to the earth, of living more gently on it or in greater harmony with other creatures that live here."[380]

In 1994, 62 children at the Ariel school close to Ruwa, Zimbabwe had a close encounter with a UFO that landed in the schoolyard as they played. Even though the aliens did not touch the children, and the aliens remained near the landed flying saucer, many of the children reported receiving telepathic messages and later recounted them to John Mack, who investigated the case. The messages were ecological in nature.

One girl, who was very young at the time, received a message which she described, "I think they want people to know that we are actually creating harm on this world and we must not get too technoliged [that was the term she used since she didn't know 'technologized' at the time of the incident]."

Another other girl reported the message she received from the creature around the craft, "The world is going to end. I thought maybe they were telling us the world was going to end."

She was asked by Mack, "Why do you think they might want you to be scared?" The young girl replied, "Maybe because we don't look after the planet – the area properly. I had this horrible feeling. All the trees would go down, and there would be no air, and the people would be dying."

"How did that message get communicated to you?" asked Mack.

"They didn't say anything. It was just the face – the eyes. They looked horrible," the girl replied.

"The horrible look in their eyes had that information in them?" Mack asked.

"Yes," she replied.

Finally, a young boy who was in the school yard watching the landed aliens said, "I think something is going to happen."

"How did that get communicated to you?" asked Mack.

"I don't know, the boy replied. "It just popped up in my head."

Music

Olivia Newton-John - Had a very close UFO experience as a teenager and had a mystical Ayahuasca experience in 2007. Olivia is very involved in environmental and animal rights causes. She is United Nation's Goodwill Ambassador for the Environment.

Neil Young - Young produced a song in 1968 called *After the Gold Rush*. Asked later by Dolly Parton what the song meant Young stated that he didn't know, admitting that he was high when he wrote it (pointing to a possible download experience). The song bears a very clear message, which is that we are treating the world like a gold rush and that after the gold is gone, the world will become a ghost town. At that point, the aliens will come down and pick up the chosen survivors and seed them on another planet: "There were children crying and colors flying all around the chosen ones, all in a dream…the loading had begun, they were flying Mother Nature's Silver seed to a new home in the sun." Young is extremely active in bringing awareness to environmental issues and supports the aboriginals in Canada, fighting the Alberta oil sands development.

Sting - So affected was Sting by his Brazilian Ayahuasca experience, where all the plants were talking to him, that he created the Rainforest Foundation to save the Brazilian rainforest. Since then, millions of acres have been saved.

Near Death Experiences (NDE)

Penny Sartori - NDE researcher Penny Sartori reported, "Many NDErs recognize the importance of the ecological issues and the impact that humans are having on the planet."[381]

Psychedelic Compounds

Dennis McKenna - An ethnopharmacologist who researched Ayahuasca for his Ph.D. dissertation, McKenna spoke about one clear experience he had with Ayahuasca. It involved a direct environmental message, similar to those received by many UFO experiencers who report seeing these messages on huge screens while on board UFOs:

> *Suddenly I was wracked with a sense of overwhelming sadness, sadness mixed with fear for the delicate balance of life on this planet, the fragile processes that drive and sustain life, sadness for the fate of our planet and its precious cargo. "What will happen if we destroy the Amazon," I thought to myself, "what will become of us, what will become of life itself if we allow this destruction to continue? We cannot let this happen. It must be stopped, at any cost." I was weeping. I felt miserable; I felt anger and rage toward my own rapacious, destructive species, scarcely aware of its own devastating power, a species that cares little about the swath of destruction it leaves in its wake as it thoughtlessly decimates ecosystems and burns thousands of acres of rainforest. I was filled with loathing and shame.*
>
> *Suddenly again from behind my left shoulder, came a quiet voice. "You monkeys only think you're running things," it said. "You don't think we would really allow this to happen, do you?" and somehow, I knew that the "we" in that statement was the entire community of species that constitute the planetary biosphere. I knew that I had been given an inestimable gift, a piece of gnosis and wisdom straight from the heart/mind of planetary intelligence, conveyed in visions and thought by an infinitely wise, incredibly ancient, and enormously compassionate "ambassador" to the human community. A sense of relief, tempered with hope, washed over me.*[382]

Summation

The final word on the message involves Dr. Russell Targ, who helped run the initial research into remote viewing for the CIA. He was asked on a radio talk show: How shall we live?

He replied with a two-part answer. The first thing we should do is find out who we are - find out our true nature as psychic beings as extended in space and time and our awareness extended in space and time. As Ramada Harshi would say, "Who we are is a flow of loving awareness." That the love we have is within us, not outside of ourselves.

"So you discover that who you are is a being of love which extends through all space-time. Some people would call that your divine nature. The Ramada Maharshi is a teacher of the Vichada Vedanta - that is, veda not divided, not separated. You discover your own divine loving nature and your nonlocal awareness, and you teach that.

The idea of your life is first to discover who you are as a divine being and then teach that. That helps you diminish the suffering in the world.

What you want to do with your life is be helpful. We are here to be helpful. To be helpful first, you have to discover who you are, and then you can share that awareness.

Do a little meditation and quiet the chatter…you see, what causes suffering is what you believe you see in the mirror in the morning. If you go downstairs in the morning and look in the mirror and say that is who I am, that is the source of suffering, or if you spend time defending the story."

Chapter 24 What is the Mechanism?

Spirit is the Life, Mind is the Builder, and the Physical is the Result. **Edgar Cayce**

In itself, the insight is not new. The earliest records, to my knowledge, date back some 2500 years or more... the recognition ATMAN = BRAHMAN (the personal self-equals the omnipresent, all-comprehending eternal self) was in Indian thought considered, far from being blasphemous, to represent the quintessence of deepest insight into the happenings of the world.

Erwin Schrodinger

Modern quantum theory, the overarching principles of 20th Century physics leads to quite a different view of reality, a view that man, or intelligent life, or communicating observer participators are the whole means by which the very universe is created: without them, nothing. **John Wheeler**

There are five key elements that seem to direct us towards a possible hypothesis for understanding what might be going on.

- The brain appears to be some receiver in the process of inspirations and downloads much like radio or TV.
- The evidence seems to point towards some sort of nonlocal reality field attached to, but outside of, the physical brain.
- Consciousness appears to be primary, and the physical in reality is secondary. Physical reality appears as vibration or noise in what would otherwise be a pure, quiet signal.
- There appear to be two distinct minds comprised of the two hemispheres in the brain. There may be a second sub-conscious inside the left-brain, and an undiscovered sub-conscious inside the right-brain.
- There appears to be a consciousness or entities of some sort outside the physical brain aiding the process.
- We move in and out of right-brain states many times a day. We simply do not know this because we have no awareness. Once a person learns mindful awareness, he/she will recognize the nonlocal state of consciousness.

The Brain

In 1996 Dr. Jill Bolte Taylor, a Harvard-trained neuroanatomist experienced a severe hemorrhage in the left hemisphere of her brain. In what could be considered first-hand expert witness testimony, she described the experience in an 18 minute TED talk which has become the second most viewed TED talk ever.[383] She wrote a book called *My Stroke of Insight* and also talked at length in an interview with Oprah Winfrey about what she learned after losing her rational, analytical left hemisphere for five weeks.

Based on her experience and her neurological training, Taylor importantly points out that our brains have two hemispheres which "are completely separate from one another," as opposed to a single unified brain. Taylor pointed out, as many other neurologists have, that the two brain hemispheres perform different tasks.

It is when we make this distinction that there are two brains, as opposed to one, that a model for understanding inspirations and downloads starts to emerge. We are forced to stop talking about the "brain" and "mind" and realize that like nature, they are probably multi-layered and very complex.

The left brain is the analytical, rational, and linear side. It comprises the ego, which helps us to operate in the physical world. It gathers details, more details, and then details about the details. It talks to us constantly about its concerns with the past and future. As pointed out by Taylor, the left hemisphere functions like a serial processor, only able to process one piece of information at a time.

The right hemisphere of the brain operates like a parallel processor, able to process lots of information simultaneously. It is intuitive and holistic. It is the non-verbal brain interested in the HERE and NOW. It thinks in pictures and is the dominant hemisphere of creative and artistic individuals.

The Nonlocal Field

If you want to find the secrets of the universe, think in terms of energy, frequency, and vibration. **Nikola Tesla**

We can all see matter, but we cannot see what IS the matter. **John Lloyd**

Five centuries ago when man thought he was living on a flat earth and that he was the sole intelligent life at the center of the universe, the idea of fields was totally unknown.

Now as we have unraveled some of the secrets of the universe, many fields have been discovered and explored. Scientists have discovered the electric field, the magnetic field, the gravitational field, the nuclear fields, the quantum field, and most recently the Higgs field. Each of these fields is considered to be consistent throughout the universe and elegantly defined by mathematics.

There are other fields that have been proposed, but like the ideas of the round earth and earth not being the center of the universe, these new fields have met intellectual resistance. The knowledge of these fields has effectively challenged the standard physical worldview because it shows that the electron, proton, and neutron are not particles but fields.[384]

Another field that is still challenged but which may be significant is the morphic field. According to Dr. Rupert Sheldrake, who first proposed it, the morphic field links to consciousness and gives habit to things in the universe. "Morphic fields," wrote Sheldrake, "underlie the organization of proteins, cells, crystals, plants, animals, brains, and minds. They help to explain habits, memories, instincts, telepathy, and the sense of direction. They have an inherent memory and imply that many of the so-called laws of nature are more like habits."[385]

A number of observations support the idea of a field such as a morphic field to explain memory, instincts, inspirations, and downloads. Inspirations and downloads, for example, seem to occur outside the physical Newtonian space-time world. They are nonlocal in nature indicating that there is something outside the localized physical brain involved.

In the 1950s, Dr. Karl Pribrum and Dr. David Bohm did work leading to holonomic brain theory, where the brain acts like a holographic storage network. Their work led to the hypothesis that there is no memory storage in any particular part of the brain, but rather memory is stored nonlocally like a hologram. In such a holographic system, all memory can be contained in any part of the brain. This radical idea in turn was supported by the work of Dr. Karl Lasher, who cut out parts of a rat brain but failed to find a particular memory center.

The idea that memory is in a nonlocal field begins to provide a model for how savants produce music, mathematics, calendaring calculations, and other information which they had absolutely no prior knowledge of. It begins to explain how musicians can receive entire songs in dreams and also explains remote viewing and telepathy, where people gather information with no physical connection to the information.

The field provides an explanation of "multiple independent discoveries" (discussed in Chapter 6), where major inventions end up being invented at the same time by various people in different locations who have no communication with each other, as if the invention is in a field and at a particular point in time the inventors are tapping in.

This idea of multiple inventors coming up with the same invention is even supported by the Nobel Prize committee, which more and more awards prizes to more than one researcher for coming up with the same idea or advancement. Columbia sociologist and winner of the National Medal of Science, Robert King Merton, states that the multiple discoveries are now becoming the rule. [386]

People like Edison, Salvador Dali, and others discussed in Chapter 2, understood that there was a field outside of themselves and they used various techniques to enter into the hypnagogic state between sleep and wakefulness in order to tap into it.

There is support for the theory of a memory field via experiments conducted at Harvard in the 1920s by psychologist William McDougall.[387] His rat experiments showed that a field may exist or extend outside the brain and may be intrinsic to the universe. If this field exists, then all the inspirations and downloads discussed in this book are easily explained. An individual can access the inspiration or download or as in McDougall's experiments, rats tapped into a universal field of information. Putting it another way, the individual's mind would be like a computer, whereas the universal mind would be the internet. All that would be required is learning how to log in.

The experiments conducted by McDougall spanned a 15-year period and involved 22 generations of rats learning how to escape a water maze. The researchers bred each generation of rats from the rats that had already learned the task.

The first generation of rats averaged 200 mistakes before they learned the way out of the maze; the last generation made 20 mistakes. Even when McDougall bred the slowest rats, there was a marked increase in the next generation for learning the maze. Genetic memory theory would predict that the rats should have gotten slower, not faster, since the slower rats had been bred.

The mind-blowing revelation came when experiments similar to McDougall's (involving rats which were not genetically related to McDougall's rats) were conducted in Edinburgh, Scotland and Melbourne Australia, and showed that those rats made fewer mistakes right from the start. One of the first rats studied in Edinburgh made zero mistakes during the experiment. All the rats in the later experiments did better, even though they were not genetic descendants of the rats in McDougall's experiments.

The results indicated the Scottish and Australian rats seem to have obtained what the Harvard rats had learned in the 1920s, as if that knowledge had been stored in some morphic resonance field, and had been accessed by the rats in the later experiments despite that they were in completely different locations and had never physically met. Dr. Rupert Sheldrake, who has conducted advanced morphic resonance and morphic field research, documented many other examples of this kind. [388]

Support for the idea of a field comes from the writings of Douglas Engelbart and J.C.R. Linklater who perhaps were two key individuals behind the invention of the modern computer. Both men talked about how the right-brain concept of unity, as opposed to left-brain concept of individuality, was critical to creating a platform for intelligence in the form of a computer platform. Engelbart, who received the idea for the personal computer in a 1950 inspirational download, wrote in 1962:

> *If we then ask ourselves where that intelligence is embodied, we are forced to conclude that it is elusively distributed throughout a hierarchy of functional processes – a hierarchy whose foundation extends down into natural processes below the depth of our comprehension. It there is one thing upon which this "intelligence" depends, it would seem to be organization. The biologists and psychologists use the term "synergism" to designate (from Webster's Dictionary) as "cooperative action of discrete agencies such that the total effect is greater than the sums of the two effects taken independently."*[389]

In the same way, Licklider in 1960 was calling the future computer the "intergalactic communications network" and was proposing a "man-computer symbiosis" as if the computer were alive and acted as a part of the human. This "intergalactic communications network" is only one step removed from what Dr. Max Planck, the father of quantum physics, called the matrix field. It has also been called the divine field, akashic record, noosphere, all self, zero point energy field, universal hologram and scores of other things.

One of the more popular descriptions is a field of consciousness. The idea is that consciousness is the basic field of the universe and the mechanism that brings the physical world into existence. In the words of Art Hobson, "electrons, photons, and so forth are merely excitations (waves) in the fundamental fields."[390]

Within the consciousness field, there are other sub-fields such the magnetic field, electromagnetic field, quantum field, the morphogenetic field proposed by Dr. Rupert Sheldrake in his 1981 book *A New Science of Life,* and the astral field that has been proposed as surrounding the physical body.

These sub-fields may simply be characteristics of the pure field of consciousness, which means everything will be uniform across the universe. In every corner of the universe and at every level of physical reality we will find life, consciousness, gravity, electromagnetic fields, strong and weak nuclear forces, galaxies, stars, planets, and morphogenetic fields. At no point in the universe will one of these elements be missing. There will be no separate individual situations where "the earth is the only place in the universe with intelligent life" or "only human beings have consciousness."

It is apparent that we are surrounded by fields and are just not aware of all of them yet. This ignorance was the case with the magnetic field before 1840, the electromagnetic field before 1890, and the quantum field before the

1920s. Because people did not know about them, it didn't mean that they didn't exist.

Finally, the field concept provides a replacement for the genetic memory as a theory for complex structure in the world such as the brain or the human body. The gene explanation ran into trouble after the discovery that genes provide a blueprint for proteins and have little to do with memory. Moreover, the gene theory fails to explain who is reading the blueprint and who is building the structure.

Take the example of the simplest of human structures – the cell. In the human embryo division will take about 12-15 hours and will continue until there are 10 trillion cells plus 100 trillion cells that will symbiotically work in cooperation with the body to create a fully functioning individual. The cell and the second cell it builds in 15 hours will both contain 100 trillion atoms.

Therefore, in one 15-hour period the first cell will find the 100 trillion atoms or atomic fields required, put them all in the right positions to form a second cell, by day five it will have built one hundred 100 trillion atom cells with a fluid filled cavity. There clearly seems to be something unseen that is quickly and accurately building in a very orderly fashion according to some set plan.

A second problem occurred once the Human Genome Project was completed. It became apparent that there would only be 19,000 genes in the human body to explain everything as opposed to some predictions that there would be up to 150,000 genes to explain all the amazing human features. Corn and rice had more genes than humans, and things like fruit flies and wolves had just as many.

The idea that only 19,000 genes could explain millions of complex human functions became a real stretch.

Consciousness is Primary

The reductionist materialistic paradigm is that there is nothing beyond a universe made of small particles. In such a universe the left brain analyses the situation using the five senses to gather and measure input. Whatever can't be measured or observed does not exist. Local causation rules govern anything that happens. There must be a force involved, and it happens within time and space.

In this worldview consciousness cannot be measured and has therefore been called "the hard problem." That has led many scientists to conclude that consciousness is an illusion. Reports of nonlocal consciousness like inspirations and downloads coming in from outside the five senses and reason or outside physical time and space rules are interpreted as nothing more than misinterpretations, fantasies, hoaxes, or pseudoscientific claims.

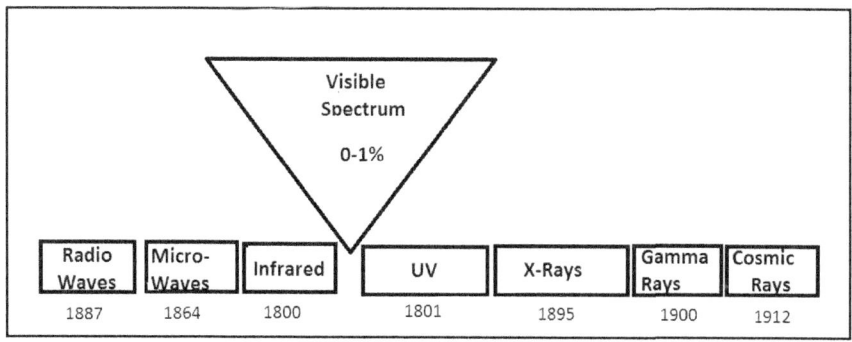

Figure 1 - Physically visible spectrum in a larger spectrum of unknown electromagnetic waves in 1800.

This view is somewhat similar to the situation that existed in 1800 before wavelengths outside the visual electromagnetic spectrum were discovered. At that time, it was believed that 100% of reality existed in what we know as the visible spectrum. If someone, at that time, proposed the idea of infrared, ultraviolet, radio, TV, and Wi-Fi signals, it would have been flatly rejected as paranormal experiences are today.

The paradigm in 1800 would have been that the physical spectrum represented 100% of reality. Today because we can measure other parts of the electromagnetic we know that what we see is 1% or less. (In reality the figure will be actually closer to 0% because the electromagnetic spectrum will go on to infinity in both directions with longer and longer wavelengths on one end and smaller and smaller wavelengths on the other end. The small section we see in relationship to an infinite spectrum will be very small.)

In the same way, the evidence presented by inspiration and download stories tends to indicate the conscious mind of the five senses is only a small segment of the entire consciousness spectrum.

Frederic Myers, the first head of the Society for Psychical Research, was one of the first in the late 19th century to propose that the model of matter and mind was changing quickly, and therefore the standard materialistic model on the relationship between mind and matter would also change. He wrote, "I venture to affirm, beyond each end of our conscious spectrum extends a range of faculty and perception, exceeding the known range but as yet indistinctly guessed."

Myers was also one of the first to point out the efforts by science to shut the door on this new idea of consciousness. He wrote, "Popular science sometimes speaks as though nearly everything in human nature has been observed already! As though normality had been defined, aberrations classified, a mass of experience which our successors will only have to work out the details! A vain conceit! A monstrous prematurity!" [391]

Philosopher, psychologist and physician Williams James also pointed in 1902 that the waking consciousness has a limited ability to see:

... our normal waking consciousness, rational consciousness as we call it, is but one special type of consciousness, whilst all about it, parted from it by the filmiest of screens, there lie potential forms of consciousness entirely different. We may go through life without suspecting their existence; but apply the requisite stimulus, and at a touch they are there in all their completeness, definite types of mentality which probably somewhere have their field of application and adaptation. No account of the universe in its totality can be final which leaves these other forms of consciousness quite disregarded. How to regard them is the question,-for they are so discontinuous with ordinary consciousness. Yet they may determine attitudes though they cannot furnish formulas, and open a region though they fail to give a map. At any rate, they forbid a premature closing of our accounts with reality. Looking back on my own experiences, they all converge toward a kind of insight to which I cannot help ascribing some metaphysical significance.[392]

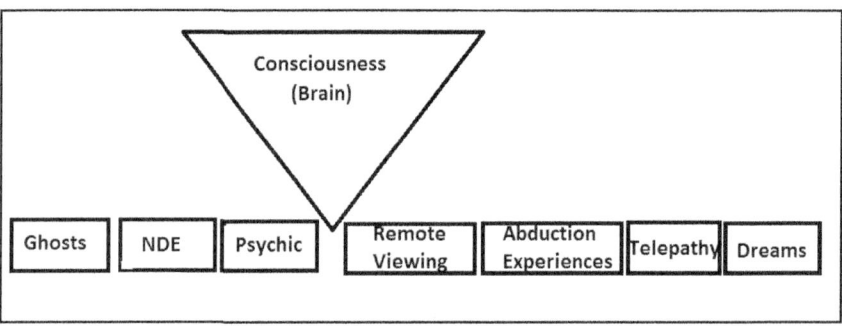

Figure 2 Left physical brain consciousness in a spectrum of other reported types of consciousness.

The modern scientific hierarchy would argue that this is not so. The argument is that none of these claimed states of consciousness outside the five senses consciousness is measurable and reproducible. Anything claiming to be outside of random chemical brain consciousness must be therefore be rejected, and any attempt to change the model must be met with crushing resistance.

The 2015 model for consciousness is stuck like the 1800 model of the electromagnetic spectrum believing what we can see and measure is the only reality. The model presented is a physical brain in which chemicals and random neuronal interactions produce consciousness. The model, however, is now being re-assessed as inadequate, unable to explain many consciousness phenomena.

Modern quantum research has also done much to challenge the idea that physical matter is at the basis of everything in the universe. Quantum physics now speaks of the fact that when the physical world is broken down into its base constituents, we are left with is a field of wave potentials. The particles that make up physical matter in actuality are a result of consciousness acting upon wave potentials.

Danish physicist Neils Bohr was the first to propose this theory. He was experimenting with quantum systems that seemed to remain in superposition until the moment they were measured or observed, which then led to the collapse to one possible state versus the other. To proceed with experiments, Bohr just said that the conscious observer caused collapse - the "Copenhagen interpretation." Bohr explained, "consciousness must be part of nature, or, more generally, of reality, which means that, quite apart from the laws of physics and chemistry, as laid down in quantum theory, we must also consider laws of a quite different type."[393]

Bohr was supported years later by Nobel Prize physicist John Archibald Wheeler, "The universe does not exist 'out there,' independent of us. We are inescapably involved in bringing about that which appears to be happening. We are not only observers. We are participators. In some strange sense, this is a participatory universe." He proposed a participatory anthropic principle saying that consciousness plays some role in bringing the universe into existence - the entire universe and everything inside it is brought into existence by innumerable acts of observation, by all the observers that have ever existed, exist now, or will ever exist.[394]

Nobel Laureate physicist Eugene Wigner added, "The laws of quantum mechanics itself cannot be formulated ... without recourse to the concept of consciousness." Nobel Laureate Max Planck agreed, "All matter originates and exists only by virtue of a force. We must assume behind this force is the existence of a conscious and intelligent mind."

Others such as Arthur Eddington stated, "The universe is of the nature of a thought or sensation in a universal Mind... To put the conclusion crudely - the stuff of the world is mind-stuff."

The top minds were saying consciousness was primary, and the physical universe was a secondary result. There are no individual personalities. Each person is part of the hologram and everything in the hologram is within and accessible to each individual. The brain becomes part of the inspiration process acting only as a radio/TV/computer type receiver.

Hierarchical science, on the other hand, maintains that the brain is the only component and that there is nothing outside of it. In this "physiology of the mind" model, consciousness and memory are contained in the brain. At death, they disappear.

This brain = mind model, however, has come under serious scrutiny in the last century on a number of fronts. The scrutiny started in the late 1940s and the 1950s with the work of Dr. Karl Pribram and Dr. Karl Lashley. Lashley had tried and failed to find a memory center in the brain. He taught rats to run a maze and then would cut out a section of the rat brain. When he put the rat back in the maze, it still had the memory of how to run the maze. Eventually, Lashley had excised every part of the brain from various rats and the memory of how to run the maze remained. He also realized that patients that had sections of their brain removed had memory that became hazy but did not disappear. He concluded there was no memory center in the brain.

After the discovery of the hologram in the sixties, Pribram realized that both the brain and the hologram used Fourier transform mathematics. This connection showed that brain memory was being stored nonlocally like a hologram. Like a hologram each piece of the brain contained the memory of the whole brain, and therefore the rat could still run the maze despite what piece of the brain it was missing. Pribram later collaborated with physicist David Bohm and came up with the holonomic brain theory.

Two Brains and Two Minds

In the 1960s, the brain = mind theory came up against a new challenge after new research arose involving neurological testing done with split-brain patients.

Starting in the 1940s, it was discovered that it was possible to control epilepsy by cutting the 300 million axonal fibers collectively known as the corpus callosum, which connects the two brain halves. Although the operation did not cause any apparent neurological problems, it resulted in two brains that could no longer communicate with each other. It also produced stunning new empirical evidence that we have two brains each having its own consciousnesses and they are completely different from each other.

Dr. Roger Sperry pioneered the main split brain research. In 1981 he was awarded the Nobel Prize for his discovery of the two brains and their different personalities and roles. According to Sperry,

> *Everything we have seen so far indicates that the surgery has left these people with two separate fields of consciousness. What is experienced in the right hemisphere seems to lie entirely outside the realm of consciousness of the left hemisphere? This mental division has been demonstrated in regard to perception, cognition, volition, learning, and memory...in the right hemisphere...we deal with a second psychic entity...that runs in parallel with the more dominant stream of consciousness in the left hemisphere. Each brain*

half, in other words, seems to have its own largely separate cognitive domain with its own private perception, learning, and memory experiences, all of which are seemingly oblivious to corresponding events in the other hemisphere.[395]

At points, the two brains and their consciousness would even fight with each other.[396] Neuroscientist V.S Ramachandran also pointed out that split-brain patients even had two different views of their origin. When Ramachandran asked one split brain patient, the left brain described itself as an atheist and believed in a meaningless evolutionary random world. The right brain was a theist believing that all things in the universe are connected and work as one.[397]

Left Brain	Right Brain
Separation, Individual	Connected, Oneness
Self – Survival of Fittest	Altruistic
Language Center	Cannot speak
Words and language	Pictures and symbols
Sees details	Sees big picture
Rational, Analytical	Intuitive, Holistic
Uses Logic	Uses feeling
Creates consistent story	Regurgitates event
Past and Future	Here and Now
Cautious and Safe	Adventurous, Risk-taking
Form strategies	Presents possibilities
Academic	Creative
Conscious actions	Unconscious actions
Logical and calculating	Telepathy, psychic, dreams
Math and science	Philosophy and religion
Yang, Masculine	Yin, Feminine

Table 1 - A list of the characteristics of the right and left hemispheres based on split patient research.

The Storyteller – A Third Consciousness?

"The interpreter tells us the lies we need to believe to stay in control." **Dr. Michael Gazzaniga**

The work done by Sperry continued on with one of his students Dr. Michael Gazzaniga, who added new and important aspects to the discovery of the dual consciousness model by working with split brain subjects. The

Gazzaniga work would introduce yet a third consciousness besides the two (right brain, left brain) found by Sperry.

Gazzaniga began by asking his subjects what they were thinking as instructions were being read into the right and left minds. He ended up referring to this third consciousness as "the interpreter." Other neuroscientists who followed Gazzaniga's lead named it "the storyteller."

The intrepreter that Gazzaniga discovered was much more like a pathological liar, or like the silver-tongued used-car salesman who shows up from time to time at a cocktail party. Perhaps that is why it is rarely talked about in neurology despite solid empirical evidence related to its existence and role.

The interpreter was found inside the rational, analytical left brain. It has a role that works with the left hemisphere, but it is independent and does not take instruction from anyone. It role is to keep the story being assembled by the left hemisphere consistent.

With the study of split brain patients, the two brains were not able to talk to each other. Therefore, when researchers fed information to one side of the brain, it was unknown to the other brain. When Gazzaniga started asking the patients what they were experiencing, the storyteller surfaced. If the corpus callosum had not been severed to treat epileptic patients, the storyteller might have stayed hidden forever.

The discovery was made by showing slides like Figure 3.

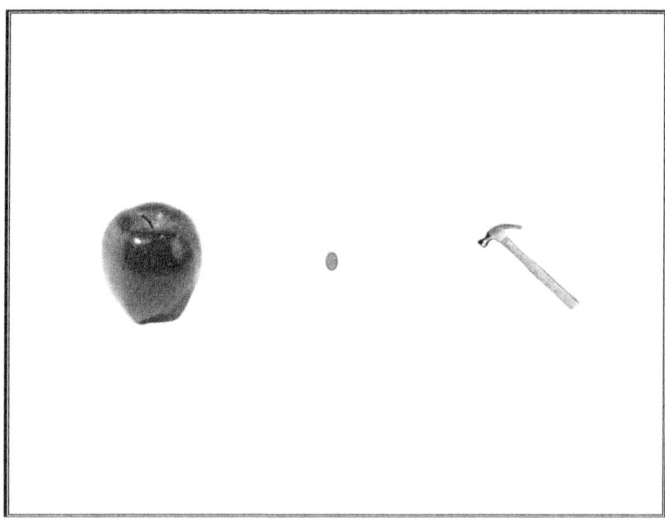

Figure 3 - Information was fed to split brain patients by loading words and images through the field of vision of one eye or the other. Images on the left go to the right brain, while images on the right go to the left brain.

The patients are asked to look at a screen and stare at the dot in the middle. By doing so, anything that appears on the screen to the right of the dot is seen by the right eye and is sent to the left mind. This is because the left brain runs the right side of the body and the right brain runs the left side of the body. In the same way, anything on the left of the dot goes in the left eye and is sent to the right brain. In the above example, the left eye would direct an image of an apple to the right brain, and the right eye would send a picture of a hammer to the left mind.

When researchers ask the left brain what it sees, it will report a hammer as seen through the right eye. The left brain has the verbal center and can easily answer. The right brain cannot talk so the only way the researchers could get a reply for the above example of an apple, seen by the left eye, was to get the left hand (run by the right brain) to draw the object or pick it off a table or out of a bag.

That was all simple enough. When each brain was asked to report what it saw on the other side of the dot, it would see and say nothing. It was at this time that the storyteller surfaced.

Each brain could not tell what the other one saw. What happened is that in the figure above the researcher would ask the non-verbal right brain to pick up what it saw to the left of the dot. The left hand would immediately take the apple. The left brain would have no idea what just happened. The researcher would then ask the patient why he took the apple. As only the left mind could talk, only the left mind could reply why the left hand picked up the apple.

Researchers expected the left mind to say "I have no idea why my left hand picked up an apple." That would be the true and correct answer but in every case, an immediate false reply surfaced as told by the storyteller. It was for this reason that Gazzaniga called the interpreter the "know it all." The answer seemed to be coming from an entirely different consciousness, unrelated to the rational, analytical, literal, and detail oriented left-brain consciousness.

Following are some of the research examples illustrating the left-brain storyteller's habit of fabricating.

- The right brain of a split-brain patient was shown the command for walking. When researchers then asked left brain why he got up and walked, the storyteller replied, "I need to get a drink" – a totally made up answer.
- One female split-brain patient was shown a pinup girl, the photo having been shown to the right brain. She snickered. When the left brain was asked why she snickered, the storyteller replied that it was because the computer was funny and made her laugh.
- One split-brain patient was shown a picture of a chicken, and a shovel. Then they showed an image of a snow scene to his right brain which couldn't communicate what it had seen. When the man's left hand pointed to

the shovel, the man was asked why he picked the shovel. The storyteller replied that he cleaned the chicken coop with a shovel.
- One split brain patient had a message sent to his right brain to laugh. When the researcher asked the research subject why he was laughing his left brain replied: "You guys are funny."

Gazzaniga determined it's the storyteller's job to explain the physical world around it and when necessary make up fictional tales to maintain continuity and fill in any missing or unexplained gaps. Therefore, when there is a presentation of two or more facts to the left brain, it fills in the gap with whatever it can to keep the story consistent.

When researchers present the left brain with something new like the body walking, snickering, or picking up objects for no apparent reason, the storyteller quickly makes up a story to correct the inconsistency that has arisen.

The storyteller syndrome extends beyond split brain patients. Following are stories of patients with right-brain damage where information doesn't transfer to the left brain, and the storyteller is forced to fill in the gap with a fictional tale.

- One a woman suffered from a right-brain condition that caused her to believe she was in her home and not in the hospital. No amount of talk could convince her otherwise. Finally, Gazzaniga said to her "If you are at home, why are there elevators in the hallway?" She quickly replied, "Do you know how much it cost me to put those elevators in?" The left brain interpreter was ready with a story to explain the discrepancy in the tale.
- Gazzaniga also worked with people suffering from anosognosia caused by a stroke in the right parietal cortex, which caused left arm paralysis. As the left arm controls the right brain, the left brain was getting no input that anything was wrong. The interpreter in the left brain had to come up with an explanation of why the arm was not working. As Gazzaniga pointed out, the interpreter took over to make explain the inconsistency, "When patients with this disorder are asked about their arm, and why they can't move it, they will say, 'It's not mine' or 'I just don't feel like moving it.'"[398]
- Dr. Diane Hennacy Powell tells the bizarre story of a man who had suffered a right-brain stroke and kept throwing himself out of bed thinking that the left side of his body was another man trying to sleep with him.[399]

The Source of Skepticism and Debunking

The left-brain storyteller raises an important point. Scientists constantly make the case that the scientific method of rational and analytical inquiry is the way to truth. The fact is those scientists are using the same left-brain mind to gather and evaluate evidence and whenever they encounter something that contradicts the established opinions, the same storyteller surfaces and imposes fictional tales to explain away knew facts.

The storyteller may explain the strong skepticism that ufology and other paranormal research fields encounter from the scientific community. The scientific hierarchy has a paradigm of a world that is strictly physical with no room for aliens, telepathy, ghosts, precognition, and other nonlocal phenomena.

The reason for the skepticism may simply be that those subjects seem inconsistent to the left-brain storyteller and so by labeling those subjects as "paranormal" or as hogwash, the storyteller is able to explain away what appear to be inconsistencies in reality.

The storyteller therefore quickly exclaims hoax, illusion, psychosis, and misidentification to counter the reported experience that is inconsistent with its reality. It goes without saying that the explanations that have been used to explain the paranormal have left-brain storyteller written all over it. They don't make sense and don't have to. They just have to fill the gaps.

The storyteller and the skeptic share one other thing. They are sold on their story no matter how bad it is and no matter who challenges it. Gazzaniga's research showed that "The left-hemisphere interpreter is not only a master of belief creation, but it will stick to its belief system no matter what."[400] Two famous experiments illustrate how unwavering the storyteller is once it has told its tale.

1) In 1931 Norman Maier at the University of Michigan ran an experiment that involved two ropes that were hanging from the ceiling in a room. The goal of the research was for the participants to tie the two ropes together. The problem was that the ropes were too far apart to reach. In the room were some items that participants could use to help. There was a pole, an extension cord and a pair of pliers. People used the pole and the extension cord with success, but no one used the pliers. That is not until Maier walked by one of the ropes making it look like he accidently bumped the rope making it swing.

Within 45 seconds most of the participants had tied the pliers to the rope turning it into a pendulum. They then held the one rope and waited for the other rope to swing over.

Following the experiment, the participants were asked how they had solved the problem. No one mentioned the bumping of the rope because no one remembered it. People said the idea just came to them, or they got a vision of swinging on a rope as children or swinging monkeys. The left-brain storyteller had resolved the inconsistency of how they had figured it out as evidenced by their inability to remember Maier bumping the rope.

When they learned about the bumping of the rope, 2/3 denied that they had been influenced by the event, and for the 1/3 who acknowledged they may have received a prompt, they referred to a second cue that Maier had performed during the experiment that had nothing to do with the solution. No one converted to the truth. No one backed away from their original storyteller's tale.[401]

2) In 1976 researchers R.E. Nisbett and T.D. Wilson set up a table in a mall to ask shoppers to examine four pairs of socks on a table to determine which socks were of the best quality. Even though all four pairs were the same, the experiment indirectly implied there were differences. People examined the four pairs, and the test results reflected the last pair on the far right picked by shoppers were rated the best at a 4 to 1 ratio over the pair on the far left. Asked why they chose the pair on the right, the shoppers stated the pair they picked was the highest quality, nicest feel or best shade of color. The left-brain storyteller, faced with inconsistency, naturally made up a story. None of the shoppers mentioned the location of the socks as a reason for their pick. When Nisbett and Wilson referred to the fact that most people picked the right pair and that all the pair were the same, all the shoppers denied that this had influenced them and stuck with their story. They even produced "an occasional worried glance at the experimenter for asking such an obviously insane question."[402]

The most important observation about the left-brain storyteller is that its very existence counters the arguments poised by established science against ufology and the paranormal. In response to accounts of inspiration, ESP, NDEs, UFOs and other non-material reality phenomena, the usual argument put forward is that the person's naive mind is delusional, untruthful, or suffering from the will to believe.

Evidence would show that the right philosophical brain, which believes in the nonlocality, is the truthful non-delusional side of the brain (perhaps this is where the expression, "You are not in your right mind" comes from). According to Gazzaniga "the right brain, without an interpreter, regurgitates the literal story, not one embellished by the interpreter,"[403] and "problems of false memories come from the interpreter."[404]

More supporting evidence for this model of lie on the left, truth on the right, came from Langone Orrin Devinsky, M.D., head of the NYU Comprehensive Epilepsy Center at NYU Langone Medical Center. Devinsky performed an in-depth analysis of patients with certain delusions and brain disorders and revealed a consistent pattern of injury to the frontal lobe and right hemisphere of the human brain. Devinsky's study showed that it is the left rational, analytical brain and not the right brain that is deluded. His study concluded,

> *Problems caused by these brain injuries include impairment in the monitoring of self, awareness of errors, and incorrectly identifying what is familiar and what is a work of fiction. However, delusions result from the loss of these functions as well as the over-activation of the left*

> *hemisphere and its language structures, that 'create a story', a story which cannot be edited and modified to account for reality. Delusions result from right hemisphere lesions, but it is the left hemisphere that is deluded.*[405]

Even the use of the terms storyteller and interpreter to describe this additional consciousness in the left brain is itself a story. The evidence clearly shows that this element of the rational, analytical mind is more like a pathological liar. The terms storyteller and interpreter, however, were created by left-brain dominated scientists in a world run by science. Calling this additional consciousness a pathological liar, however, would make the entire scientific worldview inconsistent. It would become evident that a lot of what is put out as scientific fact may just be made up. Therefore, when described by left-brain dominant scientists, the additional consciousness is not a pathological liar but something much nobler. It is an interpreter or a prolific storyteller.[406]

Right Brain Gateway to Nonlocal Phenomena

"The intuitive mind is a sacred gift, and the rational mind is a faithful servant. We have created a society that honors the servant and has forgotten the gift." **Albert Einstein**

It comes as no surprise that when it comes to nonlocal phenomena, most psychologists and neurologists divorce themselves from the evidence which firmly shows an inspirational connection with the right brain. Historical talk about inspiration has associated it with delusionary thinking, but empirical evidence shows it is not. The link of nonlocal phenomena to the right brain is clear and unmistakable.

The connection of the nonlocal and the right brain is not talked about much in ufology and parapsychology, but was recognized by Dr. Joseph. He was an internationally recognized expert in the fields of both neuroscience and clinical psychology, "The right brain is responsible for the production of diverse and highly developed forms of mental activity, such as a flash of insight, intuition, creative leaps of the imagination, daydreams, and a variety of images, feelings, and thoughts that seem to envelop the mind, only to disappear as quickly as they arrive."[407]

Brain	Phenomena	Right Brain Characteristics
Right	UFO Experiencers	All right-brained, creative, individuals report image and symbol communication, communication in dreams, and OZ effects
Right	Remote Viewing	Space/time, controller (left) viewer (right) reports images/impressions, warned not to (left brain) guess
Right	Art	Most artists are right-brain creative. Painting done upside down or in dark to block left brain.
Right	Hypnosis	Quiets left the brain, enables the right brain to tap into an eidetic akashic-type memory field resulting in creative ideas.
Right	Psychic phenomena	No sense of space/time, symbols, and images, some initiated by left brain damage.
Right	Precognitive Dream	Dreaming is a result of right-brain activity.
Right	Meditation	Quiets left brain; kills left-brain ego, chatter, and sense of space/time. Individual moves to experience right-brain Oneness, here and now, and Nirvana.
Right	Psychedelics	No space/time, kills left-brain ego, symbols and images, telepathic ability, Oneness and Nirvana.
Right	Religious experience	Comes in dreams, unconscious/altered states. Reports of Oneness and Nirvana.
Right	Savants	Most suffer left-brain damage, some exhibit pure telepathy, and eidetic right-brain memory.
Right	Aliens	Purely telepathic, communication in dreams and symbols, some channelers report voices in left ear (right brain).
Right	Spirit Voices	Hear through left ear (right brain) and messages come through images and pictures.
Right	Inspirations	No space/time, come from unconscious. Occur in quiet moments implying left-brain inactivity.

Brain	Phenomena	Right Brain Characteristics
Right	Energy Healing	Many advocates use prayer and meditation to calm the left conscious ego mind and move conscious attention to right brain. Things like rapid image cycling distract the left brain and improve results.
Right	Dowsing, Tarot, Divining Tool	Way to communicate with the right brain. Requires a quiet left hemisphere.

20th Century Musicians: As author Michael Luckman pointed out in his book *Alien Rock* there is a strong, clear connection between musicians and aliens - especially rock and roll musicians. The interest in musicians by aliens may be due to musicians having a creative dominant right brain, which would make them more receptive to messages from nonlocal entities. Other musicians claim inspirations from angels, spirit guides, or say they don't know where the inspirations originate. It appears that they are able with their dominant right brains to tap into a nonlocal matrix where these inspirations exist. Second, musicians may be picked for the role because of the young people that follow them. The left-brain storytellers in young people have not come up with as many fabrications as older people, and this enables them to be more receptive to the messages the musicians are imparting, regardless of whether they are being given the info or whether they are tapping into a field and downloading.

Savants/Autistics: Savants and autistics suffer from left-brain damage. This damage sends the rational left brain off for coffee, allowing the right brain to do amazing things such as complex math, tapping into an Akashic type memory banks, extraordinary musical abilities, and telepathic abilities.

The ones who have the strongest savant skills tend to be the ones who have the most severe left-brain damage. Dr. Diane Powell reported that autistics with the best telepathic abilities tend to be the non-verbal autistics, indicating severe damage to the left speech centers of the brain. Powell pointed out that once these children are taught to speak, the telepathic abilities fade. Speech, associated with left-brain activity will override the telepathic signal which is associated with the right brain.

The best example of this is ten-year-old Hayley, who Powell worked with in 2014. She was a non-verbal autistic who exhibited pure telepathic ability upon focusing. She has been able to telephatically transmit entire sentences, foreign languages, made up words, and complex mathematical formulas. The most spectacular feat achieved by Hayley was to recite 162 randomly selected numbers in a row on the second try. This ability is beyond normal odds.

Hayley's abilities also support a two brain model, because although she can somehow telepathically transmit the answer to a complex mathematical problem (which points to right-brain tapping into a non-material reality matrix) she is not able to do elementary mathematics, such as multiplying 3 x 5 (which would be a left brain function).

Producing complex calculations in the absence of elementary mathematical ability is very common with autistic savants. This evidences that savants are not calculating like normal people when coming up with complex calculations, whether mathematical or otherwise (like where they can name the day of the week for any date 40,000 years in the past or future). As stated earlier in this book, Dr. Oliver Sacks knew a set of twins who could produce six and seven digit prime numbers in sequence and predict the day of the week for any date in the past or future. Despite this, they were unable to multiply 7 x 4 even though for months it was attempted to teach them simple mathematics. They also did not know how many minutes there were in an hour or seconds in a minute.[408]

Research done at the by Dr. Allan Snyder at the University of Sydney has shown that savant-type abilities are achievable by ordinary people in the lab. This shows that savant ability is not due to chemical imbalances or genetic memory.

The process Snyder used involved low-frequency repetitive transcranial magnetic stimulation (rTMS) to inhibit the left anterior temporal lobe. Shutting down the left side of the brain with stimulation creates savant abilities in ordinary people. Some of the talents included increased ability to draw, and capacity to count numerous dots on a screen with only 1.5 seconds to view it.[409]

This technique to shut down the left brain indicates clearly that every person can tap into these nonlocal states of consciousness via the right brain. The magnetic simulation merely shuts down the left brain in the same way as meditation, brain damage, or psychedelic compounds.

Another technique able to inhibit the left brain, producing savant-like abilities, is hypnosis. It is a well-known fact that the conscious mind can only handle about four new items at a time before it starts to forget. The subconscious mind accessed by quieting the left brain through hypnosis seems to be able to produce memory almost at an eidetic level, where a person can recall events on certain days at any point in their life with great detail. This supports the idea that the brain is simply a cache and that the memory of all things is in a field the right side of the brain can access through the hypnotic process.

Psychic Phenomena - There are many examples in the field of psychic phenomena that show a right brain connection. 1) In the protocols of the successful remote viewing program run by the CIA, Army, and Air Force all used protocols involved an intricate understanding of the left and right hemispheres and their roles. The process involved a remote viewer, who was the controller, and would act as the left brain asking questions and recording the impressions of the other remote viewer, whose job was simply to relax and thus quiet the chatter in the left brain that creates noise in the signal. The subject would remain in right-brain mode and regurgitate images, feelings, sounds, tastes he or she experienced. Even though the target viewed might be in the past of the future, the viewer would stay in the non-linear "here and now," a right hemisphere function. This pivotal role of the right brain in remote viewing was pointed out by the two physicists who were running the RV program at Stanford Research Institute for the CIA.

> *Our experience with the phenomena leads us to believe that at least part of the difference in task performance in task performance may stem from the fundamental difference in cognitive styles between left-brain and right-brain functioning."*[410]

The number one thing told to people in remote viewing training is not to rationalize, analyze the images or guess what the target is. Those are left-brain functions that move the mind out of the right brain and cause loss of the signal. Jack Houck, a systems engineer for Boeing, spelled out what people were told,

> *Another aspect of doing remote viewing is trying not to analyze the data. I think that this is the most difficult part because we all tend to analyze, all the time. It is very natural to do so. You may already know about the right and left brain theory; that the left brain is the analytical side, and the right brain is the creative, imaginative side. So in remote viewing, the analogy is to just use your right brain. It is sometimes nice to have someone there who is asking your left brain questions; we call this person "the interviewer."*[411]

The remote viewer seems to be able to tap into some nonlocal holographic field holding all the information that exists and which coincides with a right brain's Oneness view of reality.

It was for this reason that when remote viewer Dr. Russell Targ later used "associative" remote viewing to play the silver future market in an experiment, right-brain images were used as targets instead of left-brain numbers. The experiment using objects was very successful. The research also made a lot of money for the remote viewers.

Precognitive Dreams - Remote viewers have a great deal of reading. Dreams are an activity of the right unconscious mind. By accessing the future, it lacks the time and space elements of the left brain physical world. One of the tests done by lucid dreamers is to look at their hand and then look at it again. In the dream state the hand will have changed in some way on the second look. The file for detailed pattern recognition is in the left brain, so if the dreamer tried to duplicate the detail of the hand, it would not be present.

Hypnosis - The right brain is clearly evident in hypnosis. To get into the state, there has to be a relaxation which quiets the left brain chatter. When in a deep trance, the left brain ego will remember nothing from the session. The person in the hypnotic state is the non-dominant mind or "hidden self."

Dr. Ernest Hilgard did experimental work into verifying what he called a hidden observer "hidden part of you that knows things that are going on in your body, things that are unknown to the part of you to which I am now talking."[412]

Another indication that hypnosis puts the person activates the right brain is that the subconscious is accessed, which is a right-brain component. The person is then able to access a complete and accurately remember all the events in their life.[413] These memories are stored in the mind field and are obtained via the right brain.

Experiments done by Robert Dave showed that hypnosis can also produce creative problem-solving dreams (dreams are also unconscious right brain). Rave found the technique successful in 75% of the subjects in the experiment.[414]

Meditation - Meditation is the process of creating a state of mind that produces a deep state of a relaxed, tranquil mind. Many also claim to be able to initiate inspirations and creativity through meditation. Everyone who has meditated, however, knows the problem of ongoing brain chatter which distracts the mind away from the required quiet. This chatter is the left ego brain interrupting the right brain attempt to tap into the matrix. Meditation allows us to cut off the conscious mind by cutting off sensory data the left brain thrives on. It gets bored and turns off.

Dr. John Hagelin states, "properly understood meditation is a technique to pull the awareness from the outwardly directed self (left brain) powerfully within to experience deeper levels of mind – simpler, quieter, more unified levels of thinking process (right brain) and then slipping beyond thought (transcendental) to experience this universal unity at the basis of the universe."[415] Neuroscientist Dr. Shanida Nataraja's studies on meditation show that success comes from letting go and reducing left brain activity. The shift is from 'intellectualized' left-brain thinking involving categorizing and analyzing, to a right-brain state, where the ego is dissolved, with increased "activity in the right verbal-conceptual area, leading to an inability to convey the experience efficiently through language."[416]

Aliens - There are many indicators among those who have had alien encounters that the events are associated with right hemi sphere communication.

1.	Dr. Roger Leir, a podiatrist in Hollywood, California who pioneered the removal and analysis of reported alien implants, stated the there was only one common characteristic in his clientele who had encountered aliens and from whom he had removed implants - they were all right-brain, highly creative people. Which came first, the chicken or the egg? Were they visited because they were creative or did they come creative after being visited?

2.	People experimenting with DMT, Ayahuasca, LSD and other psychedelics also report alien-type beings and a complete collapse of the ego or "ego death." As the ego is associated with left hemisphere, this would indicate a shutdown of the left brain. Dr. Rick Strassman's study of DMT found that about 40% of the participants were met by what was described as intelligent "beings," "entities," "aliens," "guides," and "helpers." They exhibited many of the same descriptions, actions, and personalities as those reported by UFO abductees. The DMT subjects also reported strong vibrations or pulses of energy accompanying the onset of the drug, a loss of body awareness and time perception, floating or flying through exotic spaces, and a feeling of Oneness with the universe and of love, joy, and acceptance. All the communication by the entities they perceived was telepathic, like in the people who report alien encounters.

3. Although there are no firm figures, there is a disproportionately high ratio of musicians who report both UFO experiences and alien abduction. Musicians are right-brained creative individuals.

4. Abductees often report their experiences as not involving left-brained spoken language, but rather involving images, telepathic communication, and symbols. Many report the experience to be dreamlike which would point to a right-brain connection.

5. People who have had a close up experience will report what has become known in the UFO world as "the OZ effect." This effect is clearly right-brained in that space and time no longer seem to exist. Events may repeat themselves as if in a loop, and time may go backward. The world perceived by the left brain dissolves as people report all the cars and individuals around them disappearing or being put into a state of suspended animation. 6. Abduction researchers now acknowledge that abductees are "lifers" and their experiences are not random (although once in a while you get a case like that of Travis Walton, who feels he was just at that particular place in time and that their taking him was not intentional, despite the fact that he was gone for five whole days). Most experiencers seem to have been chosen and are first taken by the aliens when they are babies. Regarding split brain theory, this makes total sense as young children are clearly right brained, and the left brain storyteller does not fully come online till the child is about seven. Therefore, the young children present no left brain block to the training they receive as children.

7. Many experiences report having been exposed to the right-brain concept of Oneness. Betty Andreasson Luca had an encounter with "The One"

during an abduction and recalls being in an out-of-body state. Bret Oldham asked the alien in control of his abduction about God and was told, "We are one with the One, who is all."

8. Dr. Leir stated that all the implants he removed were on the left side of the body, and the right brain controls the left side of the body.

Ancient Wisdom - Research was conducted by Drs. Andrew Newberg and Eugene D'Aquili with Tibetan monks and Franciscan nuns who meditated or prayed inside a SPECT machine employing single photon emission computed tomography. The monks or nuns pulled on a cotton twine when they felt they had reached their meditative climax or felt at one with God. A decrease in left brain language center activity was discovered, pointing to the chatter that is so distracting when they try to meditate.

The SPECT also showed a notable decrease in activity in the area responsible for orientation - the parietal lobe in the back of the brain. Dr. Newberg confirmed that that was shown in the scan, "During meditation, people have a loss of the sense of self and frequently experience a sense of no space and time and that was exactly what we saw." [417]

Richard Davidson, who directs the Waisman Laboratory for Brain Imaging and Behavior, did research on Tibetan monks. He showed that the meditating monks produced gamma waves 30 times stronger than students used as control subjects.

The most interesting are descriptions given by a 1) mindfulness meditator - "I am usually aware of the boundary of my body against the skin, and you lose that sense in Dhyana...you become a kind of...field of energy, the boundaries of which are not clearly delineated 2) A TM meditator stated, "Literally as though my arms were extended and they extended to the reaches of the universe...whatever that was...a kind of immeasurable distance...my head would feel incredibly expanded and huge...as if it were capable of being the size that a galaxy could fit into...and so that sense of being enormous and yet not out of my body...but expanding out from there in all directions, infinitely." [418]

Dr. Jill Bolte Taylor experienced an identical thing. She told of her experience living in her right brain for five weeks after she had a hemorrhage which shut down her entire left brain. Taylor felt there was no boundary between her body and the outside world and like a fluid as big as the universe. She did not gain back the feeling of a solid body for seven years. "Everything in my visual world blended together and with every pixel radiating energy we all flowed in mass, together as ONE," said Taylor,[419] and "my conscious mind felt so detached from my physical body that I seriously believed that I would never fit the energy of me back inside this skin.[420]

Channeling - People who channel messages they claim are from nonlocal sources exhibit characteristics that show the left ego mind is being shut down. 1) The channeler is not aware of what they are saying which indicates the shutdown of the conscious mind. 2) The process often involves a tool such as Ouija board or automatic writing associated with right brain unconscious processes.

Religious Experience - As mentioned previously, work by at least one split brain researcher, V.S. Ramachandran, showed that the left brain is an atheist, and the right brain is a theist. Religious experience involving nonlocal elements is therefore associated not with the left brain helping to navigate in the physical world but in the philosophically oriented right brain. Often religious traditions show rhythm has been used in many cultures to induce nonlocal religious states of experience. These seem to shut down the left brain and force people into their right brains through mandalas, dancing, drumming and chanting. According to neuroscientist Dr. Diane Powell "these work because low sound frequencies preferentially activate the right brain."[421]

The physical behavior of the girls to whom the Virgin Mary appeared in San Sebastian de Garabandal, Spain, reportedly from 1961-1965, points to a right-brain connection. The girls while in trance walked backward, never tripping or falling, as if something was in complete control of their bodies, but they were completely unaware. These events were filmed and photographed.

Savants - Savants have left brain damage which will shut down the noisy chatter of the left brain and allow the right brain to access the information or signal. Daniel Tammett, one of the savants who can explain what happens states he receives images (pointing to a right-brain function). When he recited Pi to 22,154 decimal places, he saw the numbers as "complex, multidimensional, colored, and textured shapes." Savants can't do simple mathematics like multiplying 7x4, which is a left brain function, but can calculate the day of the week that any day will fall on 100,000 years in the past or future, or calculate the cube root of a ten-digit number, all indicating a right brain ESP/clairvoyant function.

Dr. Powell did work on non-verbal autistic savants, where the left brain damage was so severe, there was no language. This research shows a high degree of pure telepathy such as with Powell's subject Hayley, who was able to telepathically come up with long strings of numbers, made-up words, sentences, and understand foreign languages. The left brain damage shuts off the noise/chatter completely and allows the right brain to access the nonlocal field.

Psychedelic Drugs - Psychedelics "cause the death of the version of self that depends on upon separation rather than communion; dominion rather than cooperation; and an end to the 'me-an-mine' way of relating to existence."[422] Psychedelic experiencers talk about a feeling of Oneness, associated with the right brain as opposed to the left brain ego, which believes it is separate and distinct. Along this vein, Aldous Huxley found psychedelics turned off the brain's "reducing valve" opening people up to mystical and psychic states. In this book *The Doors of Perception* (1954) Huxley stated that "each person is at each moment capable of remembering all that has ever happened to him and perceiving everything that is happening everywhere in the universe. The function of the brain and nervous system is to protect us from being overwhelmed and confused by this mass of largely useless and irrelevant knowledge, by shutting out most of what we should otherwise perceive or remember at any moment, and leaving only that minuscule and special selection which is likely to be practically useful. According to such a theory, each one of us is potentially Mind at Large."

Even more interesting is the connection between ESP and telepathy and intuitive, holistic right brain.

A simple Google search for "psychedelics and telepathy" will bring up scores of articles and anecdotal accounts showing a healthy relationship between the two. The supporting stories go all the way back to the Oracle of Delphi in Greece. The female oracle, or seer, would prophesize in a delirious, altered state. According to the geographer Strabo (c. 64 B.C.–25 A.D.), "the seat of the oracle is a cavern hollowed down in the depths ... from which arises pneuma [breath, vapor, gas] that inspires a divine state of possession."[423]

Research done by anthropologist William McGovern and reported in his 1927 book *Jungle Paths and Incan Ruins* detailed his encounter with the psychedelic brew called yage as produced by a Peruvian rain forest tribe. During one session, the natives described what was going on at that moment with a tribe hundreds of miles away. McGovern ran a check and found their information to be accurate.

Psychedelic pioneers Timothy Leary and Richard Albert from Harvard traveled to Duke University informal experiments were being conducted on the connection between ESP and psychedelics, and the results of their research found a link.

Research done by David Luke, Ph.D. and Stanley Krippner, Ph.D. indicate that ESP experiences while on psychedelics run as high as 83% but less than 2% with people using psychoactive agents such as alcohol, heroin, and cocaine.[424]

Two examples were related to me personally.

One couple relayed telepathy with one another while under the influence of LSD. She would think targets such as "yellow triangle" which would be called out immediately by her partner.

Two men told me of doing the same sort of experiment while under the influence of the psychedelic, DMT. Like the couple, they both reported an absence of noise and an ability to send and receive messages.

Energy Healing - Most energy healing techniques describe the use of experience, intuition, the big picture, imagination, inspiration, patterns, living in the here and now, all replacing the left-brain approach of quantitative analysis, categorization, study, certainty, results, linear thinking, and research development.

One of the most successful energy healing techniques illustrating a connection to the right brain is the Bengston healing method. Its development came from a psychic, Bennett Mayrick, who exhibited a strong healing ability. Mayrick was discovered by sociologist Dr. William Bengston, who studied him and his technique, then taking what he had learned to the lab. The resulting experiments with mice showed almost a 100% rate of healing for diseases like cancer, by engaging natural energy fields.[425] Bengston conducted ten controlled animal experiments carried out in five university biological and medical laboratories. What resulted was "the first successful full cures (and subsequent immunity to the cancer) of transplanted mammary cancer and methylcholanthrene-induced sarcomas in experimental mice with hands-on techniques."

The results of the tests were dramatic and open for all to see. What is relevant to the left-brain/right-brain argument is a technique known as rapid image cycling that was used to increase the effectiveness of the hands-on healing. This technique is unique to the Bengston method. Student healers in controlled studies were trained to rapidly cycle at least 20 images of things that they would like, such as a new car, a trip to Hawaii. These are images that appeal to the left brain ego of the healer. Altruistic images such as helping others are not allowed. These would interfere with the process.[426]

The healer rotates through the pictures in their mind at a rate of hundreds or thousands a second. At the same time, they use a hands-on method of healing.

According to Bengston, the cycling technique helped to get the healer out of the way of the energy that was healing or restoring balance to the mice. He called it "concentrated detachment."

The Bengston technique represents a dissociation method that blocks, distracts, or quiets the left brain allowing the right brain to channel, access, and direct the energy which heals or restores balance. The technique also supports a right/left brain model when the evidence for what the method does not cure:

1. The Bengston Method is entirely ineffective against things like warts. The reason for this is that, although a wart may be something or left brain ego may not like, there is nothing wrong with the condition except for appearance. The body is still in balance, and therefore, there is nothing to fix.

2. The Bengston technique will not work when radiation and chemotherapy are involved. Both these treatments are modelled on a left brain medical model of individual cells, survival of the fittest, and separation. The belief in separation assumes there are good cells and bad cells. Bad cells must be killed by cutting them out, poisoning them, or radiating them like a war. As with human wars the technique does not work well, and in many cases the opposition gets stronger. The Oneness in the Bengston technique, therefore, cannot counter the war that is killing of cells and upsetting the

balance. The radiation and chemo also destroy the immune response in the body.

3. When healing mice, Bengston stated that heat would come out his left hand and that the mice in the cage (even after he spinned the cage) would press their cancerous tumor against his left hand. The right brain controls the left hand.

4. Maybe most importantly, research done by the Chicago-based Equilibrium Energy + Education group, which does a great deal of Bengston healing, pointed out that the two situations that are the most successful for the technique are Alzheimer's and animals. Bernadette Doran, the director of Equilibrium, hypothesized that these two groups do not have a left brain ego to get in the way of the healing, and the energy flows unhindered.[427]

5. An interesting crossover to the Bengston method is a story told by one UFO experiencer, Suzy Hansen, who stated that the aliens were teaching a similar type of cycling technique. This alien cycling is significant because many UFO experiencers claim aliens healed them, and a high percentage of them state they can heal others.

Hansen reported that 200-250 experiencers were taken to an underground theater and told that they were about to see some images that would be disturbing, but it was necessary to do. Pictures of earthy devastation started to appear on the screen slowly. They increased in speed until there were hundreds of images flashing on the screen at the same time. People were very emotional, and many were crying. It ended, and an alien came over and just by looking out sent a wave of calm over the assembled people. This telepathic demonstration is very right-brained.

Combine this story with the fact that Mayrick claimed he was from the star Alpha Centauri, located in the Centaurus constellation.

The Oneness Ghost in the Machine

On February 26, 2012, I had one of the critical awakening moments of my life. While sitting in a lecture in Phoenix, Arizona, I received a download that we would find that nonlocal consciousness was the answer to the UFO question. It led me to search out others who had had such downloads and record them in this book.

This download would not be my last. I would have at least three more that would spell out other key components of the matrix of nonlocal reality. One occurred January 26, 2015, while in the shower, and then against February 2, 2015, while in the shower again. The third took place during a computer course where I was scanning the internet while listening to the instructor. They happened in moments where my mind was in a state of rest.

My personal downloads led to an obsession with inspirational stories. I had piles of interviews to listen to and books on my desk ready to read. I was moved to search during every waking moment. Suddenly, either because I had learned how to link in or just because I was now on the right road, all the pieces I was finding were no longer puzzle pieces but pieces that fit perfectly into a completed model.

I took to carrying paper and pen with me at all times, as I was always receiving material that I knew was important. I found those who believe in such inspiration were doing the same thing. I learned that John Lennon had a tape recorder by his bed so he could record the magic of inspiration. He told Merrell Fankhauser who started surfer rock with his famous song "Wipeout" that these song inspirations were like channeling and that it was important to document the song before its freshness wore off. Fankhauser told me that he too had a tape recorder beside his bed and also kept a yellow legal pad nearby. This yellow legal pad technique is a habit which musician Carlos Santana also used to record inspirations he was receiving from who he claimed was the archangel Metatron.

Of the inspiration that came after the February 2012 download; the most notable came on January 6, 2015, when I was sitting in a course on the workings of the internet. The course was elementary, and I was spending most of my time reading e-mail and Googling for new stories of inspiration. Suddenly I heard the instructor mention Tim Berners-Lee, who had invented the World Wide Web.

My attention to the statement was immediate. I had never heard the name, despite the fact I had researched quite a bit on the computer and the internet. I knew that the pre-thought to the development of the modern computer and internet had come from a paper written in 1945 by Vannevar Bush. I knew that the modern computer had come in a download to Douglas Engelbart in 1950.

I knew that the modern computer would never have seen the light of day if it had not been for LSD used by all the key players in the area that would later become the Silicon Valley. I knew that the early linked computers in the early 1960s would become the Arpanet and then the internet had been called the Intergalactic Communications Network. I knew that the idea for Google, which would revolutionize the storage and sharing of information on the internet had come to Larry Page in a dream.

Most importantly I realized the concept that the Internet seemed to represent the physical version of the collective unconsciousness. Little did I realize that I was about to get an insight that would clearly show this.

I checked the class notes, and there was Tim Berners-Lee's name. I quickly Googled his name along with "LSD" and "Eureka" to see if he had taken LSD or if he had received the idea for the web in an inspiration or download.

The LSD search did not produce anything. The search for the word Eureka showed that he claimed it had not come in an inspiration either. In fact, Berners-Lee maintained that he did not even believe in Eureka moments by inventors.

Next, I searched his name against quotes to see what insights he may have had, and that is when the key piece of the puzzle popped up. Berners-Lee said this about the brain:

> *There are billions of neurons in our brains, but what are neurons? Just cells. The brain has no knowledge until connections are made between neurons. All that we know, all that we are, comes from the way our neurons are connected.*

Berners-Lee had made an important point. We have 100 billion neurons in our brain, but they are useless unless wired together. They have to be wired in conjunction with a dendrite-axon network to create quadrillion synapse connections. If they are not connected, nothing works.

This connection represents a right-brained concept of Oneness as opposed to the left brained idea of neurons being separate individual cells in an evolutionary battle for survival.

Not only do the 100 billion neurons have to be connected as Berners-Lee pointed out, they all have to be connected and operate together as one unit. If each neuron is doing its own thing, the brain will not work. It is evident that each neuron is performing a defined and assigned task and that all the neurons are working together for a common goal.

This Oneness model extends to the body which a massive feedback loop of trillions of tiny feedback loops. Messages are sent continuously from one part of the body to another as the body unconsciously does things, including regulating heartbeat, blood pressure, breathing, digestion, and a million other tasks.

This team approach where each unit is doing what it is supposed to for the whole is a principle that is followed in most of nature, whether it is a cell, termite mound, beehive, or colony of emperor penguins. Humankind seems to be the exception.

The human body is the best example of this Oneness principle. It consists of 100 trillion cells that all do separate jobs, but all work together to create the human being. Each cell has 100,000 chemical reactions per second. All the cell actions are self-directed. The ego mind is entirely divorced from the process has no idea what is going on. Somehow each cell knows what to do, and the mysterious process is able, in an orderly fashion, to replace 500,000 cells of various kinds that die in the human body each second with 500,000 cells of the same type.

Each of these cells contains 100 trillion atoms that must operate as one to allow the cell to form properly and to do its job. When the cell duplicates, it can source the proper 100 trillion atoms required to make a new cell, gather them together, put them in the right place, in the right order, and do all this in less than a day.[428] There is no indication of a left brained individual working against all the others individuals for survival. Therefore, each atom joins the same pattern to form the cells which in turn fit into a repeating body pattern to form a functioning human body. The same pattern repeats the same way each time for the 7+ billion people on earth.

Most importantly 90% of the cells that make up the body are not human cells but various bacteria. These non-human cells work in a right- brain type of symbiotic Oneness with the human body. They do not operate in a separate left-brain survival mode. Without these cells, the human body would die quickly as these cells help digest food, and fight harmful germs and bacteria.

The evolutionary left brain separation model of the brain says that complexity is what causes consciousness. Therefore, we have consciousness because we have 100 billion neurons. Berners-Lee, however, pointed out that 100 billion separate neurons are just 100 billion cells, and nothing happens until they are connected.

It was at that moment that I had my insight. Berners-Lee was right that the neurons had to be connected, but you needed one more thing. The neurons are just infrastructure like a huge building or the latest TV model. Even when they are connected, they will not produce consciousness.

One millionth of one second after a person dies and consciousness leaves, the neurons are still there along with the dendrites and axons. The infrastructure is still there as the neurons will not die for a couple of hours. People have been brought back hours after being EEG flat-lined.

If the neuron dendrite structure caused consciousness, the consciousness should still be there but clearly is not. The same applies to the unconscious mind which the materialist model insists is a part of the brain and which keeps the heart beating 60 times a minute for 100 years. If the infrastructure of the brain is still there, the unconscious mind should still be there. Why then has the heart stopped?

The same principle applies to the internet where Cisco Systems, which designs, manufactures, and sells Internet networking equipment, believes "internet connected devices reached 8.7 billion in 2012." If complexity and connections were the keys, the 8.7 billion computer internet would be conscious. They are not. They merely represent a very complicated connected infrastructure like the brain. Even when the 8.7 billion computers are wired together and turned on, they still will do nothing.

What is missing is consciousness itself. What is missing when the person dies is the EEG signal which represents consciousness interacting with the brain. When the conscious mind stops its interaction with the brain the brain goes flat line, and the unconscious component of the mind stops its direction to the heart and other organs. The body goes into instant chaos, and physical death begins to take place. It is like Elvis leaving the building. Once he does, the audience isn't far behind.

The 100 billion neuron brain with its trillions of connections can do nothing but begin to die. You can shock the heart. You can continue to supply oxygen to the brain. It is not caused by the complex brain, but by something outside, like TV. When the TV signal stops the TV goes blank and no amount of complexity will put the little football players back inside the TV.

The same rule applies to the internet, and Berners-Lee described that relationship in another quote.

> *The web is more a social creation than a technical one. I designed it for a social effect - to help people work together - and not as a technical toy. The ultimate goal of the Web is to support and improve our weblike existence in the world.*[429]

The internet of 8.7 billion computers is like the brain's 100 billion neurons. They are just computers. They do not create consciousness, and they do not create the internet. They must be connected and work together. The $64,000 question is what does the internet connect?

Like the 100 billion brain neurons the computers just form a complex infrastructure. If the 8.7 billion internet devices are wired together and turned on they will still do nothing. It is still just infrastructure. Even if you put 8.7 billion computers along with 8.7 billion people (along with their 100 billion neuron brains) in front of the computers, nothing will happen. It is still just infrastructure.

Only when there is consciousness interacting with the 8.7 billion computers, and they download their information to their local computer, will an internet be formed that contains accessible information? The internet is a connection of minds and the information produced by those minds.

It is a system to link together the minds of the billions of people who are using it. It is symbolic of the Buddhist concept that small mind = big mind or Nobel Laureate physicist Erwin Schrodinger's who stated, "multiplicity is only apparent, in truth, there is only one mind."

Each of the billions of small minds instructs their 100 billion neuron brains to take the information they have access to and load it into a computer. When the billions of computers are linked, all the information of all the small minds becomes the big mind. It is stored and can is accessible by anyone who has access to the internet. Like the storage of memory in the brain the information becomes stored nonlocally in a big mind, consciousness internet, collective unconscious, akashic record, quantum hologram, or whatever term people want to use.

Downloads and inspirations merely become information from people who have gotten the password to log into the consciousness internet. The password may be a near death experience, a dream, psychedelic experience, meditation session, a channeling, a prayer, or a psychic intuition. Telepathy is getting the password and accessing what another small mind has downloaded to the big mind. It would be like going to the Facebook page of another small mind and reading the information they have stored there.

The quality of the information becomes determined by how clear the signal is and how much noise is in the signal. The left brain creates the noise (ego chatter) which acts as a filter blocking out most of the consciousness signal. This block allows us to live in the physical world. Things like DMT rip open the filter and allow large portions of raw conscious reality data to be perceived.

Those who learn to quiet the left brain reduce the ego chatter and thus the noise. The quite left brain produces a better signal and thus better quality information accessable from the big mind. That is why non-verbal autistic children (like the Dr. Powell's subject Hayley) report not just telepathy but almost pure telepathy. The left brain damage is severe enough to cut out all the chatter and provide a strong signal.

Powell provided more evidence for the idea that the left brain creates noise by pointing out that when non-verbal autistic children are taught language skills, telepathy diminishes. This is the result of the left brain coming back online and causing noise in the signal.

This understanding of inspirations and downloads may also explain why aliens are reported to be purely telepathic and also possess great powers of precognition and other psychic abilities attributed to the right brain. They have learned to shut down the conscious left brain that is blocking the signal.

When the computer is off, the information continues to exist on the internet. Likewise, when a brain shuts off or dies the information remains on the consciousness internet. At death, the consciousness separates from the brain and continues to upload to the big mind. This theory explains how mediums can talk to the dead. The medium simply has developed a technique to get the password and can communicate to the small mind which is alive and well and part of the big mind. As Schrodinger said, "multiplicity is only apparent, in truth, there is only one mind..."

The physical internet and the consciousness internet work on the same principle. The physical internet is a collection of material loaded by all the small minds in a physical form using computers, and the consciousness internet is a compilation of all the information gathered by the small minds throughout eternity.

Inspirations and downloads are simply information moving from the big mind to the small mind that has figured out how to gain access. The quality of the inspiration or download, just like a TV or radio, is proportional to the quality of the signal.

Conclusion

The stream of knowledge is heading toward a non-mechanical reality; the universe begins to look more like a great thought than like a great machine. Mind no longer appears to be an accidental intruder into the realm of matter; we ought to rather hail it as the creator and governor of the realm of matter. Get over it, and accept the inarguable conclusion. The universe is immaterial-mental and spiritual. **Sir James Jeans**

Observations not only disturb what is to be measured, they produce it. **Pascual Jordan**

I regard consciousness as fundamental. I regard matter as a derivative of consciousness. We cannot get behind consciousness. Everything that we talk about, everything that we regard as existing postulates consciousness. **Nobel Laureate and father of quantum physics Max Planck**

If I didn't know better, I would think that memory is stored outside the brain. **Dr. Karl Lashley, who studied brain memory, for 50 years.**

We don't know one-millionth of 1% about anything. **Thomas Edison**

The modern materialistic paradigm is that consciousness is an epiphenomenon produced by the physical brain. Research, however, is slowly changing the paradigm.

Neurological research has started to raise questions about the materialistic concept that brain = mind. We now know that there are two distinct brains, with equal numbers of neurons. It has clearly been shown that severing the corpus callosum (300 million axonal fibers) between the two brains creates two separate brains and minds that are completely different in tasks and beliefs.

The fact that there might be an additional independent "storyteller" in the left brain makes it even more unlikely that the left mind, right mind and storyteller were formed from one set of identical neurons. These facts are ignored as if they didn't exist.

The materialistic interpretation becomes even more difficult when it is observed that there are actually hundreds if not thousands of modules (sight, balance, hearing, etc.) that all work together to produce the experience of qualia consciousness. This is called the binding problem and is ignored by those who view the brain as a randomly created material machine.

To make matters worse for the random model, it is very apparent that the brain is made up of 100,000,000,000 neurons that all work in Oneness to create consciousness. Each stores only three seconds of energy relying on the system to provide the rest.

Also ignored is the fact that there probably is no solid physical brain and no solid physical world, as proposed by Rutherford when he first performed his gold foil experiments over 100 years ago evidencing that matter was almost entirely space. More recent experiments have shown that even the small amount of matter found by Rutherford in the atom is also almost all space. The more one breaks down matter into its primary components, the less physical it becomes. These are facts that no one challenges, and everyone continues to teach the illusion.

The idea of a single consciousness produced by a solid physical brain has become a statement of ontological faith created by the prolific left-brain storyteller. This story, like others generated by the storyteller, is the cement that keeps the materialistic story consistent and holds the bricks of false belief together.

The story that has been developed by the storyteller is that the post big bang world did not contain consciousness. It only appeared when the physical brain became complex enough. According to that view, at some point consciousness was generated by the physical brain.

A second commonly held view by modern science is that the five senses and reason are the only things that can be used by humans to come up with new ideas. This view maintains that there is no Atman = Brahman where the small mind is linked to a bigger universal mind. Humans are merely biological robotic beings struggling to survive in a meaningless, random world.

The End of the Physical World as We Know It

Twentieth-century research into quantum physics has laid waste to classical Newtonian billiard ball physics. It shows a world where awareness and consciousness are the primary forces in the universe, and the material world may just be a product of the conscious mind. In other words, the thought/mind creates the brain and not the other way around (perhaps that is where the expression, "Don't mind me" comes from, implying that if you don't "mind" it will cease to be).

This new paradigm developed from the "dual slit" experiment, which may be the greatest experiment ever conducted. In this experiment, photons were shot through a panel with two slits in it. It left a pattern of wave interference on the back wall. This interference made no sense because if the photons were particles (the classical physics view), then two bands of light should have appeared on the back wall.

The experiment was then done using just one photon at a time so that multiple particles could not be colliding with each other producing a scatter and wave pattern. The wave pattern still appeared indicating that the photon was a wave instead of a particle.

The next step in the experiment is what actually destroyed the idea of a physical world and where consciousness is a late stage emergent phenomenon caused by complexity.

When the scientists tried to observe which slit the single photon had gone through, suddenly a pattern appeared on the back wall that would be created by particles going through the slots. When they stopped observing, it turned back to a wave pattern. Experimenters ran the experiemnet thousands of times, and the result is always the same. The act of observing forces the photon to change from a wave to a particle.

The discussion of this finding began at the 1927 Solvay Conference on Electrons and Photons, where 17 men and women, who had or would win the Nobel Prize, discussed the emerging idea that the physical world as they knew it might be dead.

In 1932 an interpretation of the experiment was proposed by John Von Neumann and Neils Bohr. They concluded that everything exists only as a wave of potential (quantum superposition) and an observer is required to manifest the physical particle (quantum collapse or collapsing the wave function). Werner Heisenberg who developed the uncertainty principle summed up the new model of material reality, "[T]he atoms or elementary particles themselves are not real; they form a world of potentialities or possibilities rather than one of things or facts."[430]

The new idea caused a debate between Bohr and Einstein that went for decades. Einstein defended the Newtonian world of local causation and attacked the quantum idea that a physical particle only became physical when observed. He stated he would like to believe that the moon was still behind him when he was not looking.

Even during the last lecture he gave for a John Wheeler at a Princeton relativity seminar Einstein questioned, "If a person, such as a mouse, looks at the universe, does that change the state of the universe?"[431] He wanted to make the point that he believed the universe was out there and that objects in the universe were separate and measurable. He could not accept non-locality.

In 1982, Alan Aspect ran an experiment[432] proposed by Einstein, and the entangled quantum world created and initiated by consciousness was confirmed. Einstein's world of separate objects in the vacuum of time and space was proved wrong.

Other luminaries in the world of physics have weighed in. Hans-Peter Durr, Professor of Physics at the Max Planck Institute declared, "Matter is not made up of matter. Matter as we know it exists only in the mind."

Michio Kaku wrote, "The implication is that consciousness is the basic entity in the universe, more fundamental than atoms. The material world may come and go, but consciousness remains as the ground of being, which means that consciousness, in some sense, creates reality. The very existence of the atoms we see around us is based on our ability to see and touch them."[433]

John Wheeler, a Nobel Prize winner, who developed the accepted theory on nuclear fission, and the terms "black hole" and wormhole" also spelled out the primary nature of consciousness over matter, "The universe does not exist 'out there,' independent of us. We are inescapably involved in bringing about that which appears to be happening. We are not only observers. We are participators. In some strange sense, this is a participatory universe."[434]

The dual slit clearly shows awareness as the ground of being. Consciousness is a reflection of awareness, and the physical world a manifestation of consciousness. The great answer to the chicken/egg dilemma is that consciousness came first, and matter was secondary.

Nisargadatta Maharaj, an Indian spiritual teacher of nonduality, put it this way:

> *Awareness is primordial. It is the original state, beginningless, endless, uncaused, unsupported without parts, without change.*
>
> *Consciousness is on contact is a reflection against a surface, a state of duality. There can be no consciousness without awareness, but there can be awareness without consciousness as in deep sleep. Awareness is absolute. Consciousness is relative. To its content consciousness is always of something. I am conscious of something. Consciousness is partial and changeable whereas awareness is total and changeless, calm, and silent, and it is the common matrix of every experience.*[435]

The universe operates with downward causation where consciousness forms elementary particles, which form atoms, which form cells, which form entities with brains. The idea of upward causation where elementary particles form atoms, which form cells, which form bodies with brains, and then the brain forms consciousness is falsified.

The dual slit experiment also showed awareness and consciousness at the elementary particle level. There is no doubt that both the wave and the photon were aware of whether or not there was an observer to the experiment. Both were, therefore, aware and conscious.[436]

This evidence for the primacy of consciousness also has great implications for theories like the Big Bang Theory. If consciousness, according to the materialistic model, is nothing more than a late stage evolutionary development caused by a complex brain, then who broke down the quantum wave to form the physical universe before the emergence of consciousness?

Physicist John Von Neumann was clear in his writings that upward causation where simple particles develop into more complex units could not collapse the wave. The universe must be downward causation with consciousness at the top. He posited "that consciousness 'chooses' the actual event of experience from all the quantum possibilities."[437]

The materialistic world model came under further attack with the development of cardiopulmonary resuscitation (CPR) in the 1960s. The moment of death moved from when the heart stopped to perhaps hours later where death[438] can still be reversed.

Like many new ideas in science, the idea of CPR did not gain acceptance until a decade later. Its use brought with it stories that helped Dr. Raymond Moody create his 1975 book *Life after Life* that dealt with strange new reports of near death experiences that appeared anything but physical.

Now, 40 years later, there are hundreds of books on the subject and the number of NDE reports is in the millions.[439] The story is always the same. People claiming their consciousness was no longer attached to their body during flat line EEGs caused by cardiac arrest.

Instead of the darkness predicted by the flat line EEG model, they described being conscious, moving around the room, and were able to accurately describe what people were saying and doing, or off down a tunnel encountering a bright light that exhibited indescribable love and forgiveness.

The left brain storyteller has tried to make the NDE accounts consistent with the materialistic brain=mind worldview, proposing the NDE is a result of oxygen deprivation, hallucination, and bursts of activity by a dying brain. All of these theories, however, have failed to explain the testimonials, and the numbers of NDE reports continue to mount as technology seeks to advance to a point where death can be reversed.

Altruistic Inspirations

The many chapters of this book have shown people aided by their art, music, invention, or life itself, separate from their materialistic five senses and reason, their human minds tapping into something that doesn't fit well with a materialistic world view.

The inspiration and download accounts have shown that there may be nothing new under the sun. Mark Twain summed up this idea in a letter he penned to Helen Keller, "ninety-nine parts of all things that proceed from the intellect are plagiarisms, pure and simple; and the lesson ought to make us modest. But nothing can do that."[440]

Steve Jobs added to this concept saying, "Creativity is just connecting things. When you ask creative people how they did something, they feel a little guilty because they didn't really do it, they just saw something. It seemed obvious to them after a while." [441]

The inspiration and download accounts point to the left brain gathering facts, with the right accessing higher levels of nonlocal consciousness resulting in great advances in human understanding.

Nonlocal consciousness seems to have all knowledge contained in it, but also appears to be altruistic, loving, and there to help, as opposed to the left brained model of individuality, self-preservation, and materiality.

Many have questioned why aliens, spirits, or entities would come to help us or why this higher consciousness would be altruistic. As was pointed out in Chapter 24 all these inspirations and downloads find their access through right brain nonlocal consciousness, and this is the consciousness of Oneness, altruism, and spirituality. Aliens, for example, are purely telepathic and therefore profoundly right-brain dominated. It would make sense that they are here to help.

Empirical evidence supports the theory that nature of the right mind/brain is geared to connectedness/brotherhood/unity. In experiments conducted with split-brain patients, there is clear proof that the right brain tries to help the left brain when the latter becomes confused. However, there is no empirical evidence showing that the ego-oriented left mind/brain of split brain patients tries to help out the right.

A paper by neurologist Dr. Rhawn Joseph described some clear efforts by split-brain patients' right-mind/brains to rescue their left-mind/brains during experiments:

> *In its most subtle manifestations the disconnected right hemisphere may attempt to provide the left with clues when the left (speaking) hemisphere is called upon to describe or guess what type of stimulus has been secretly shown to the right (such as in a T-scope experiment). Because the corpus callosum has been severed transfer and information exchange is not otherwise possible.*
>
> *Hence, when a picture has been shown to the right, and the left has been asked to guess, the right hemisphere may listen and then nod the head or clear the throat so as to give clues or indicate to the left cerebrum that it has guessed incorrectly. In one case the right hemisphere attempted to trace or write an answer on the back of the right hand (e.g. Sperry et al. 1979). For example, after the right hemisphere was selectively shown a picture of Hitler, and then asked to indicate their attitude toward it before verbally describing it, the patient signaled "thumbs down."*
>
> ***Experimenter****: "That's another 'thumbs-down?"*

Left Brain: "Guess I'm antisocial."
Experimenter: "Who is it?"
Left Brain: "GI came to mind, I mean..." *The subject at this point was seen to be tracing letters with the first finger of the left hand on the back of his right hand.*
Experimenter: "You're writing with your left hand; (right brain) let's keep the cues out."
Left Brain: "Sorry about that.[442]*

The right brain/mind was clearly trying to help which is entirely contrary to the evolutionary model that competition for survival is the key.[443]

It seems apparent that inspirations and downloads have aided our evolution through history as a species. If Mark Twain was right that 99% of everything is plagiarism, then all human intellectual evolution may be traceable back to inspirations, downloads, accidents or the copying of nature, rather than the five senses and reason.

Inspirations and downloads are moving humankind from a lef-brained ego-centered world to a right-brained world of connection and Oneness. It represents a movement away from the individual ego mentality to a wholeness mentality.

The new world that is evolving is one where the rights of individuals to pollute are trumped by the collective consciousness seeking protection of the environment. A higher consciousness that wants to protect the planet is replacing the perceived rights of selfish individuals who given the opportunity would clear all the forests to extinction. The new worldview of Oneness is replacing the current and soon to be old world where some feel ethnically, intellectually, or politically superior to others. It is becoming a world where borders are collapsing and everyone is connected via the internet.

This enhanced right-brain consciousness will lead to an increased acceptance that we are all part of the same planet and the damage we do to the environment, and to other beings on the planet, is damage we do to ourselves. We will move from a "survival of the fittest," "killed or be killed" separatist worldview to a Oneness worldview, where we recognize we are all leaves on the same tree, where we need the tree to survive, and the tree, in turn, requires the leaves.

This new model provides a possibility for world peace where everyone changes attitude from seeing themselves separated by religion, race, and nation to a single humanity on Earth existing as part of a mutiverse that includes world without end.

Betty Andreasson described this right brain world during a hypnotic regression, "I understand that everything is one. Everything fits together. Everything is one. It's beautiful! No matter what it is!"[444]

It may have been just this Oneness idea that former President Ronald Reagan was trying to get across when he spoke of his fantasy of an alien invasion. "I have often wondered," said Reagan, "how the world would be united if faced with a threat from an alien invasion. And yet, I ask – is not an alien force already among us? What could be more alien to the universal aspirations of our peoples than war and the threat of war?"[445]

The Oneness model will move the world from a male left-brain dominated world, based on combat and fear, to a female right-brain model involving nurturing and bonding. The world will move away from "us versus them" and "good vs. evil" to a single humanity working together. The world will move from a left-brained society dominated by ego and fear to a right-brain integrated society that "values community, birthing, nurturing, empathy, intuitive intelligence, earth, nature, connection, and interdependence."[446]

The part of the Oneness model that may take the longest to achieve will be the conservative ideal of individuals' rights versus a just and equal society. This change may take a long time because in recent years the wealthy have gained ground on the poor, and the gap has widened, making love, brotherhood and equality more difficult to perceive among the multitudes.

The change to brotherhood may evolve from duress as has occurred with the environment. Even though the rich control the resources, gone are the days when someone could say, "I own 100 acres on the San Andreas fault in downtown San Francisco and I will build a nuclear power plant there if I want to," or "I own 200 feet of frontage on the Hudson River and if I want I will dump my toxic waste into the river." Ecological concerns, consumer protections, and disadvantaged minorities have made great gains in the 20th century, changing the attitude from perceived individual elitism to Oneness.

The chapters of this book have shown that inspirations and downloads are occurring regularly and in all aspects of daily life. The evidence I have cited also shows that the inspiration/download phenomenon has probably occured for as long as man has been recording history. Like gravity and consciousness, the phenomenon exists despite our inability to understand it fully. It appears to be as much a part of the fabric of the matrix of reality as are fractal patterns and elegant mathematics.

The origin of inspirations and downloads lies in the mystery of consciousness which appears to precede creation as we know it. Understanding consciousness is where future research efforts must focus. Despite the failure of science to explore consciousness and its implications, it is apparent that there can be no unified field theory of reality that does not include consciousness.

The neurotheology that investigates the neurobiology of the brain is restricted to description and naming. Machines can record brain waves and measure active regions of the brain while someone is having a mystical experience (meditation, psychedelics, remote viewing). However, these measurements fail to explain the mind that is having the experience, where the experience is, or what the experience means.

The perfect analogy is the TV, radio, or computer. Because we can record and observe what is happening inside, which components are lighting up, does not mean that there is a football game going on inside the unit.

It's All Connected

One of the key messages described in Chapter 23 – What is the Main Message? – is the fact that everything in the universe is in a state of connectedness and Oneness. Could the answer to inspirations and downloads be as simple as patterned evolution where everything is connected, and that part of that pattern may be a unification of both the left and right hemispheres, working together to evolve human beings to the next level of development?

Consciousness is central to the human design and contained in everything, right down to the reality of entangled particles as demonstrated by the Einstein, Podolsky, and Rosen Paradox experiment done in 1982. [447]

In that experiment, Alain Aspect showed when the one particle has its spin changed, its opposing entangled particle, even if it is at the other end of the universe, will change its spin to balance. It is aware of what happened to its partner cell. The particles clearly exhibit awareness and consciousness. The effect was instantaneous and nonlocal. This finding is completely opposite to the physical space/time beliefs of the left brain. It indicates the entire universe may be made up of nonlocal consciousness and that the concepts of time, space, and physicality are illusions.

Materialists will argue that this is not what the entanglement experiment means. However, the research shows otherwise.

The idea of the conscious entangled particle gained ground in the mid-1940s when physicist David Bohm did his pioneering work on plasmas and began a direct discussion of consciousness as a part of the scientific worldview.

It was during these plasma experiments that Bohm began to have his doubts about the random unintelligent unconscious nature of particles. He even began to wonder if the electrons in the plasma were alive. That is because Bohm observed the electrons acting like they were part of a larger interconnected whole rather than acting as individuals, which was expected. Bohm began to see the Oneness of the world which he called the implicate order and undivided wholeness.

He gave the analogy that physical forms are like whirlpools that form in a river of consciousness. Although they are describable and distinctive, they are intricately part of and connected to the river. "We have to regard the universe as an undivided and unbroken whole," wrote Bohm. "Division...is only a crude abstraction and approximation."

Oneness also exhibited itself in the Toshiyuki Nakagaki slime mold experiment done in 2000 at Hokkaido University in Japan.[448] Nakagaki chopped up pieces of a single physarum polycephalum, and scattered the pieces throughout a plastic maze. The mold began to grow and filled every corner of the maze. Then Nakagaki placed food at the two entrances to the maze. Within four hours the slime had retreated from all the dead end corridors. With intelligence that outperforms the best robots man has created, it formed a thin tube-like structure that ran with maximum efficiency from one entrance to the other by the shortest path possible. It was consciousness of the situation and had the intelligence to find the most efficient way to gather its food.

There is the plant Daughter (Cuscuta) which like the entangled particle and slime mold does not have a brain which many maintain is a requirement of consciousness. The Cuscuta plant has no root system, and yet it can move around and live off other plants apparently exhibiting awareness of its surroundings, and thus consciousness.

David Bohm added the idea of the holographic universe field which has become an essential component to many discussions and theories about how nonlocal phenomena work. In such a universe, like a physical hologram, each piece of the holographic field contains all the information of the whole. Therefore, humans who learn the technique can tap into the hologram and access the information contained within. The universe appears ordered instead of random, and time and space play no role.

A similar analogy is a human fertilized cell that contains all the information of the entire body. Within hours of its beginning, it will have sourced 100 trillion atoms required to build a second cell. It will then place those atoms in the right place in the correct order and then gives the second cell life (however that is defined). It will do this all in 15 to 24 hours.

In nine months it will have built 100 trillion of these cells to create a human being. All 100 trillion cells are self-organized, and they will work together as a team for up to a hundred years.

Every cell will be in its right place, and it will be cooperating with other cells like itself to build structures like the heart, the brain, the nervous system and a million other systems that required for the healthy baby hoped for by every parent. 90% of the cells will not even be human cells, but outside viruses and bacteria that will work symbiotically with the body.

In addition to this, it will create a system for replacing 500,000 cells of various types that will die every minute in the body. It will provide at least two distinct brains that will work together to live in the physical world.

When cells no longer cooperate, such as in the case of cancer cells that become independent, duplicating in an out of control fashion like a booming capitalist economy, the imbalance is recognized as a disease. With enough disease, the body dies.

How can such a small cell contain so much information and the ability to assemble a body with such precision in nine months? This information complexity is where the ideas of the field and the hologram provide a plausible explanation.

The cell itself is like a piece of the universal hologram. Like a physical hologram where the whole it is cut into pieces, each piece has the information of the whole. The cell therefore does not store the knowledge but accesses it from the nonlocal holographic repository.

The final assessment of downloads and inspirations is that we live in a reality that is consciousness. The physical world is only one facet of that consciousness, like water which can also transform into steam or ice.

Our consciousness has the same structure as the consciousness of the universal reality. We have pure consciousness and various purities of consciousness down to our conscious mind which is entirely unaware.

Inspirations and downloads are not a talent. They are innate to everyone. Inspirations and downloads arise when the ego mind is quietened or shut down. The ego mind is no longer able to block the nonlocal consciousness. The better the noise of is blocked the better the signal will be.

A good analogy to illustrate this is the stars we view every night. During the day, we do not see them even though their light still enters our eyes. They have gone nowhere. The reason we cannot see them is that the light of the sun creates noise that overruns the star's light.

In the same way, a bee can smell 100 times better than a human. Because we cannot smell what bees do, does not mean that bees are hallucinating. We just cannot perceive it. We are simply unaware.

Consciousness is just awareness. Everything is visible to us if we tune into the right station.

By this understanding, there is no unconscious mind, no subconscious mind, and no super conscious mind. There is just consciousness with various levels of noise in it. In human beings the noise is provided by the left brain which acts like the sun blocking out starlight during the day.

If we could block out all the noise we could experience the quiet of pure awareness, the Oneness, and the nirvana described by so many. We are conscious of everything in the universe but don't know it because of the noise of the physical world.

Meditation, psychedelics, holotropic breath work, sensory deprivation tanks, near death experiences, magnetic brain stimulation, alien encounters, dreams, rhythmic drumming, fasting, pain, and other inspirational techniques are methods used to reduce some or all of the noise. The better the technique, the more noise can be cut out and the better the signal to pure consciousness.

Those who have had downloads and inspirations have not traveled anywhere to get them. There is no space. There is just a hologram of information that is accessible to the proper understanding and technique. Those who have reported inspirations and downloads have not gone into the future or past because there is no time. There is only now.

There is only localized consciousness (our physical awareness) in a sea of nonlocal consciousness. It is all the same consciousness. It is all connected.

A Final Note

The idea of downloads and inspirations is still generally rejected by the scientific community. This rejection occurs because science has a belief structure that rivals the greatest religion traditions. The central belief that dominates the scientific community is reductionistic materialism. Like religious hierarchies new ideas that challenge the present scientific paradigm meet derision and exclusion.

If you are a scientist who rejects the materialistic model of reality you will not get published, promoted, or funded. You will probably not have a job for long. That keeps scientists in line, and the dogma of materialism stays pure.

Ironically, however, there is a good chance that the left brain that supports the idea of survival of the fittest, individuality, and rationality will, in the end, make itself extinct.

That is because the left brain believes in self, getting ahead, and materialism. Inspirations and downloads can mean money. No good business person really cares where it comes from or what it means. All that matters is can we make money at it. Nature has produced many Velcro-type discoveries, and any of them can make you a million.

That is why biomimicry spends millions of dollars of an investment each year. The idea that the universe has immense intelligence will, if researched, will be worth a lot of money.

A crude example of this is the 1982 associated remote viewing (ARV) experiment that was conducted to try and make money in the silver futures market. The effort netted a $250,000 profit betting on whether or not the price would go up, down, or remain the same.

ARV techniques are now employed by people doing sports betting. Now even the attention of academia is looking at this predictive ability of remote viewing to predict the Dow Jones. Researchers at the University of Colorado have just published their results which were very positive.[449] People and companies that want to make money can't be far behind, so the technique will become much more well-known along with the theories of how nonlocal consciousness works to achieve such results.

There is a lot of evidence to back up the claim that the use of LSD helped built Silicon Valley and the modern computer industry. This discovery led many to ignore the legality issue and look to using psychedelics for ideas inspirations that will add to the bottom line.

Even the weird stories of alien experiencers are getting serious behind the scenes attention, although this idea is in its infancy. I personally know four major business people who are looking to abductees realizing they have valuable information in their heads.

Some businesspeople have caught on and in time, this will become an industry. Business will not care about anyone's belief system. The only thing that will count is the technology and the money it will make.

Inspirations and downloads will become more and more accepted. With that acceptance will come the idea that there is a consciousness beyond the brain=mind dogma. It will open up the field to more research money. The left brained mechanical worldview will change to one where the idea of a universal conscious become well accepted.

The greed of capitalism will ensure it. It is a matter of time.

Appendix 1- Songs That Were Inspired by Dreams

A Soldier's Tale - Stravinsky
A Tout Le Monde - Megadeth
Across The Night - Silverchair
All Night Cinema - Just Jack
All You Had To Do Was Stay - Taylor Swift
Andelman's Yard - Mike Gordon
Angel - Jimi Hendrix
Awake - Devin Townsend Project
Bang the Drum All Day - Todd Rundgren
Black Out the Sun - Sevendust
Blade - Third Eye Blind
Blunderbuss - Jack White
Burning House - Cam
Carousel - Vanessa Carlton
Counteract - Islander
Dreamember - Twin Atlantic
Dream Divison – Kevin Estrella
Dreaming - System of a Down
Dreaming of Houses - Nina Persson
Dreams - Fleetwood Mac
Drops Of Jupiter (Tell Me) - Train
Electron Blue - R.E.M.
Elevator - David Archuleta
Enterlude - The Killers
Every Breath You Take – The Police
Fireflies - Faith Hill
Fireworks - Drake
Five Years - David Bowie
Florence and the Machine - If Only For a Night
Frankie - Sister Sledge
Free Radicals (A Hallucination Of The Christmas Sky) - The Flaming Lips
Grown Ocean - Fleet Foxes
Gust of Wind - Pharrell Williams
Hand Me Down Your Love - Hot Chip
Have I Run Out? - Secret Machines
Here Comes The Flood - Peter Gabriel

Honey are You Straight or Are You Blind - Elvis Costello
Horse and I - Bat for Lashes
How To Disappear Completely - Radiohead
Huey Newton - St. Vincent
Hurdy Gurdy Man - Donovan
I Can Feel a Hot One - Manchester Orchestra
(I Can't Get No) Satisfaction - The Rolling Stones
I Gotta Feelin' - The Black Eyed Peas
I Want Your Love - Chic
I Wouldn't Believe Your Radio - Stereophonics.
If I Could Divide the Smell of Flowers - Catman Cohen
In Dreams - Roy Orbison
Infinity - Rickie Lee Jones
It's the End of the World As We Know It (And I Feel Fine) - R.E.M.
Josef's Train - Thea Gilmore
Just The Way You Are - Billy Joel
Knife Going In - Tegan and Sara
La Villa Strangiato - Rush
Leaky Little Boat - Roger Clyne & the Peacemakers
Leap of Faith - Kenny Loggins
Leave - Barenaked Ladies
Leaving Your Body Map is maudlin of the Well's
Let It Be - Paul McCartney
Lifeboats - Snow Patrol
Lighters - Gloriana
Like I'm Gonna Lose You - Meghan Trainor
Love Is All Around - Reg Presley
Lucid Dreams - SOJA
New Perspective - Panic! at the Disco
No Regrets - Paul McCartney
O'er - Jon Anderson

One Voice - Barry Manilow
Only If for A Night - Florence + the Machine
Only In Dreams - Weezer
Paul McCartney - Scissor Sisters
Peter and the Gun - Palma Violets
Photographs (You Are Taking Now) - Damon Albarn The Sweeper Of Dreams
Purple Haze - Jimi Hendrix
Red Rain - Peter Gabriel
Riding With The King - B.B. King
Selected Ambient Works Volume II - Aphex Twin
Sharing a Gibson with Martin Luther King Jr. - Lambchop
Sign Your Name - Terence Trent D'Arby
Silent Lucidity - Queensrÿche
Single File to Dehumanization - Whitechapel
Sleep Alone - Two Door Cinema Club
Solemn Skies - Childhood
Stop The Clocks - Noel Gallagher's High Flying Birds
Sun King - The Beatles
Sweet Home Alabama - Ed King
Symphony No 7, 1st movement - Anton Bruckner
Take It Out on Me - Chairlift
That's Showbiz - The Reverend Horton Heat
The Crow And The Butterfly - Shinedown
(This Is) The Dream of Evan and Chan - Dntel
The Grave - Don McLean
The Green Manalishi - Fleetwood Mac
The Highwayman - Jimmy Webb
The Killers - Enterlude
The Lost Chord - Arthur Sullivan
The Man Comes Around - Johnny Cash
The Rifle - Alela Diane
The River of Dreams - Billy Joel
- Alma Deutscher
There's A Key - M. Ward
This Tornado Loves You - Neko Case
Torture - Danny Brown
Tourniquet - Marilyn Manson
The Prophet's Song - Queen
Wait and Bleed - Slipknot
Where We Gonna Go - Jon and Roy
Wired For Light - School of Seven Bells
Word of God Speak - MercyMe
Yesterday - Paul McCartney
You Could Be Different - Childhood
You Found Me - The Fray

Index

1927 Solvay Conference, 5, 252
Adams
John Couch, 60
Adamski, George, 169, 204
AFFA, 168, 180
Agassiz
Louis, 82
Agre Peter, 54
Aiwass, 169
Alanis Morissette, 29
Alexander Eban, 188, 211
Allende
Isabel, 88
Alleyne John, 130
Allyson
Jane, 169
Amos Tori, 195
Amos, Tori, 23, 195
Ampere
Andre, 82
Anderson Jon, 263
Anderson, Jon, 24, 75, 143
Andreasson, Betty, 204, 239, 256
Anka Darryl, 150, 168, 169, 170, 204
Anton
Florencio, 107
Aridif, 169
Arigo, 169
Armstrong Neil, 10
Assante
Julia, 188
Atwater P.M.H., 90
Auld Doug, 42
Ayahuasca, 8, 165, 193, 195, 198, 199, 202, 206, 214

Bach Johann, 29, 90, 170
Badgley Penn, 195
Baez, Joan, 24
Banting
Frederick, 73
Barnsley
Michael, 64
Bartlett
John, 108
Bashar, 24, 150, 168, 169, 204
Baum L. Frank, 91
Baur Fred, 54
Beatles, 2, 29, 30
Becquerel
Henri, 60
Beethoven Ludwig, 36
Beethoven, Ludwig, 20, 33, 115, 170
Bell
Alexander, 50
Graham, 65, 66, 67, 68, 69, 70
Jocelyn, 46, 60, 115
Benedict
Thomas, 192
Bergen Edgar, 166
Bergman Ingmar, 103
Berkowitz
Rita, 108
Berlin, Irving, 141
Berlioz Louis, 36
Beveridge W.I.B., 45
Billy Joel, 115
Biomatrica, 54
Birdseye Clarence, 55
Birnat-Provins
Marguerite, 112

Blake
William, 107, 108
Bob Dylan, 72, 115
Bohm, David, 128, 141, 164, 204, 212, 219, 258, 259
Bohr Neils, 5, 73, 74, 160, 225, 252, 258
Bolyai, Farfas, 59
Bond
Fredrick Bligh, 130
Bond Fredrick, 130
Boudreaux Ellen, 44, 119
Bowie, David, 24
Brad Steiger, 2, 92, 98
Brahms Johannes, 37, 170
Braude
Stephen, 92
Brennan Allison, 91
Breton
Andre, 107
Bronte Charlotte, 91
Bruckner Anton, 37
Bunyan John, 91
Burpo
Colton, 188
Calvin
Melvin, 73
Cameron
James, 104
Campobasso Craig, 103
Canning
Lloyd, 108
Capra, Fritjof, 205, 207, 208, 209
Carl Perkins, 30
Carliner Paul, 48
Carlos Santana
Santana, 211
Carlson
Chester, 65

Carroll Judy, 91
Carter Jimmy, 135, 136
Cassiopaeans, 170
Cayce, Edgar, 23, 123, 131, 137, 167, 170, 171, 217
channeling, 2, 34, 92, 109, 137, 166, 167, 168, 170, 171, 173, 174, 175, 176, 177, 178
Chopra Deepak, 196
Chris Bledsoe, 42, 76, 108, 121, 138
Christensen
Daniel, 114
Cicoria Anthony, 41, 116, 119
Clapton, Eric, 23
Clarke Sazanne, 91
Clemons
Alonzo, 119, 127
Clinton
Hillary, 166
Cohen
Leonard, 23
Morris, 79
Colburn
Zerah, 114
Collins, Phil, 23
Colquhoun
Ithell, 108
Cooley
Anne, 144
Coover
Harry, 47
Corbain, Kurt, 23
Cortazzo Jeff, **42**
Cortright Brant, 193, 196
Cottrell, Douglas, 131
Coumadin, 55
Courtois
Bernard, 47

266

Cox, Bradford, 24
Crick Francis, 8, 9, 10, 12, 74, 276
Crisis, Karyn, 24, 92
Crowley Aleister, 113, 169
Crum
George, 47
CSETI, 183
Cuccia Maria, 41, 42
Cumming, Burton, **25**
Curran Pearl, 92, 131
Daguerre
Louis, 47, 63
Dali, Salvador, 20, 220
Darwin
Charles, 81, 115
Dass Ram, 193, 196
Davids Paul, 104
Davidson
Cindy, 109
Richard, 240
Dawkins, Richard, 14
Dee
John, 131
Delius Frederick, 37
Denver John, 115, 206
Descartes
Rene, 83
Devi
Shakuntala, 127
Dick Philip, 92
DiFrancesco
Ron, 144
Disney, Walt, 104, 196
DMT, 195, 202, 203, 207, 209, 210, 211, 212, 239, 242
Donovan, 25
Dotter
Charles, 47
Doudna

Jennifer, 47
Duckett
Jane, 114
Dylan, Bob, 23, 28, 72
Eastgate Centre, 55
Eckemoff Yelema, 25
Edison
Thomas, 20, 48, 60, 61, 115, 185, 220, 250
Edison, Thomas, 19
Edwards, Henry, 23
Einstein, Albert, 1, 5, 8, 17, 53, 60, 71, 73, 79, 115, 184, 204, 233, 258
Elfman Danny, 23
Elgar Edward, 37
Elijah, 41, 42, 98
Emerson
J. Norman, 83
Engelbart, Douglas, 59, 196, 220, 221, 245
Enoch
Ophanim, 174
Epperson Frank, 48
Erdos Paul, 197
Erolano
Assunta, 179
Estrella Kevin, 25, 263
Evans
Mary Ann, 93
Everett
Carol, 182
Eysenck
Hans, 129
Fahlberg Constantin, 48
Fankhauser
Merrell, 179
Fanning
Arthur, 178

Farnsworth
Philo, 65
Ferrell Vance, 8
Feynman
Richard, 71, 115
Fish Frank, 55
Fleming Alexander, 48
Flory
Paul, 45
Fodo, Jerry, 21
Fothergill
William, 60
Freud, Sigmund, 4, 79, 80
Gabor
Dennis, 74
Galactic Federation of Light, 171
Galileo
Galilei, 66
Gamwell
L., 107
Gao, Shan, 207
Garcia, Jerry, 23
Garcia,Jerry, 62, 197
Gasparetto
Luiz, 109
Gates Bill, 115, 199
Gauss
Carl, 83
Gay Leslie, 48
Gaye, Marvin, 23
Gazzaniga Michael, 6, 7, 227, 228, 229, 230, 231, 232, 276
Geckskin, 55
Gershwin George, 37
Gessner
Kelly, 187
Gilbert Elizabeth, 18, 33, 88, 93, 99
Gilmore John, 197

Gleason, Jackie, 23
Glidden
Joseph, 56
Global Consciousness Project, 140, 141
Gonzalez.
Santiago, 135
Gorbachev
Mikhail, 189
Gould
Gordon, 66
GQ magazine, 135
Graham, 65
Gratzel Michael, 56
Greenburg, Jay, **26**
GreenShield, 56
Griffin, Patty, **26**
Griffiths Richard, 197
Grof Stanislav, 197
Gruzewski
Marjan, 109
Hadamard
Jacques, 83
Hagelin
John, 238
Halsted William Stewart, 48
Hammeroff, Stuart, 21
Hammid Hella, 129, 140, 189
Handel George Frideric, 38
Harner, Michael, 198
Harris
Susannah, 109
Haston
Douglas, 146
Hathor, 172
Hauffe Frederica, 109, 172
Hawking Stephen, 9, 10, 276
Hayley, 235
Heisenberg

Werner, 74
Heisenberg Werner, 5
Heller-
Joseph, 93
Hendrix, Jimi, 23, **26**, **93**, 263, 264
Herbert Kevin, 198
Hertwig
Oskar, 61
Hewins Debbie, 172
Hill Julian, 48
Hillary
Peter, 144
Hippopotamus Sweat, 56
Hoffman
Dustin, 115
Hoffman Albert, 49
Hofmann Albert, 193
Holotropic Breathwork, 198
Honegger Arthur, 38
Houck
Jack, 237
Houdin Paul Robert, 56
Hough Peter, 138
Houston Jean, 91, 166
Howard, Harlan, **26**, **64**, **115**
Howe
Elias, 66
Howe Julie, 35
Hoyle
Fred, 71
Hoyle, Fred, 9
Huang
Alan, 66
Huggins
David, 109
Hurkos Peter, 116, 136, 137
Huxley
Aldous, 195
Ionni, Tony, 23

Isaac Newton, 20, 62, 80, 115, 183
Jackson, Michael, 23, **26**
James
William, 223
James Richard, 49
Janigan Oscar, 199
Jeans James, 250
Jeffreys Alex, 49
Jehovih, 172
Jenner Edward, 56
Jeshua, 172
Jimmy Page, 30, 113
Jobs, 183
Steve, 183
Jobs Steve, 182, 185, 193, 199, 254
Joel, Billy, **26**, **115**
John Lennon, 27, 28, 194, 206, 207, 208, 210
John of God, 132
Jon Anderson, 210
Jones
Earnest, 80
Elvis, 115
Jones Jones, 31
Joni Mitchell, 29
Joseph Rhawn, 60, 61, 63, 114, 166, 171, 233, 255
Judith Orloff, 133
Jung
Carl, 132
Jung Carl, 94, 115, 139
Jung Karl, 4
Kaku Michio, 86, 163, 252
Kason
Yvonne, 189
Katie Perry, 276
Kekule

Friedrich, 83
Kellogg Will Keith, 49
Kelly
Edward, 131
Kerner
Justinus, 109
Kerouac Jack, 94
Kerr, Jim, **115**
King Steven, 94, 95
King, BB, 23, 27, 94, 95, 160, 220, 264
King, Kaki, 115
Kipling
Rudyard, 74
Kirael, 173
Kitchur
Randy, 209
Klimo, Jon, 167, 176
Knight
JZ, 176
Knight-Jadczyk Laura, 170
Kramarik, Akeane, 94, 109, 121, 205, 210
Krippner Stanley, 19, 35, 176, 242
Kryon, 173
Kubler-Ross
Elizabeth, 189
Kurtyka
Voytek, 144
Lanigan
Catherine, 102
Lanigan Catherine, 102, 142
Lapseritis Kewaunee, 95
Lasher
Karl, 219
Lashley Karl, 226
Lawrence D.H., 95
Lazaris, 173
Lazarus, 205

Leadbeater
Charles, 132, 133
Leary Leary, 194, 199, 201, 242
Led Zeppelin, 2, 34, 72, 179
Leir
Roger, 239
Lemke Leslie, 43, 121
Lennon, John, **27**, **179**, **180**, **194**, **245**
Lesage
Augustine, 111
Light emitting diodes, 56
Lindbergh
Charles, 145
Linklater
Richard, 104
Lloyd
John, 218
Loewi
Otto, 75
Love
Dianna, 95
Lovecraft H.P., 95, 105
LSD, 45, 49, 74, 75, 77, 193, 194, 195, 196, 197, 198, 199, 201, 239, 242, 245, 262
Luckman, Michael, 235
Lutyens Elisabeth, 38
Mack John, 106, 209, 213
MacLaine Shirley, 96, 176
Mahler Gustav, 38, 115
Maitreya, 174
Manning
Matthew, 111
Marciniak Barbara, 174
marijuana, 165
Marks, Doug, 22
Martens
Phil, 67

270

Mary Magdalene, 174
Massey, Irving, 22
Matsuura Reiko, 95
May Pang, 27
Mayrick Bennett, 133
McCarthy John, 201
McDougall William, 220
McKenna Dennis, 214
McKenna Terence, 11, 199
McLuhan Marshall, 96
McMoneagle Joe, 137
McMonteagle Joe, 211
Medrado Jose, 112
Melchizedek, 174
Drunvalo, 177
Melchizedek., 46
Mendeleyev Dimitri, 84
Merton Robert, 59
Mescaline, 104, 195, 196
Mestral George de, 56
Metatron, 174, 211, 245
Meucci Antonio, 49
Meyer Stehanie, 96
Michael Jackson, 21, 26
Michelangelo, 115
Mike Pinder, 30
Mike Reno, 30
Miles Mark, 57
Millikan Robert, 81
Mitchell, Edgar, 29, 63, 152, 157, 208

Monroe, Bob, 23, 178
Montgolfier Joseph, 57
Moody Raymond, 30, 189, 254
Morrison, Grant, 28, 96, 149, 180, 205
Mother Teresa, 75, 76
Mozart Wolfgang, 29, 35, 38, 115, 119
MUFON, 2, 138
Mullis Kary, 75, 156, 201
Music in Dreams, 20
musician, 21, 23, 28, 32, 37, 42
Muybridge Eadweard, 85
Myers Morton, 45, 223
Nakatsu Eiji, 57
Nasmith James, 182
Nataraja Shanida, 238
Near Death Experience, 206, 214, 215
Newberg, Andrew, 208, 240
Newbrough John Ballou, 112, 175
Newton John, Olivia, 199, 214
Nietzsche Frederich, 96
nitinol, 81
Nobel, Alfred, 9, 12, 45, 50, 71, 74, 115, 156, 163, 181, 188, 201, 248, 252, 253
Nolan Chris, 104
Nusslein Heinrich, 112
Obermeyer Ken, 67

Oneness, 1, 91, 172, 195, 204, 205, 206, 207, 208, 209, 210, 227, 234, 237, 239, 241, 243, 246, 247, 257, 258, 259, 260
Orin and DuBen, 175
Oth, 175
Page
Jimmy, 245
Larry, 67
Page, Jimmy, 23, 67
Papanicolaou, George, 50
Paravicini Derek, 44
Parkinson
David, 68
Paul McCartney, 28
Pauli Wolfgang, 5
Paxton Joseph, 57
Pearce
Chilton, 114, 166
Pemberton, John, 50
Penzias, Arno, 52, 60
Pesce, Mark, 201
Pessoa Fernando, 97
Pfizer, 51
Planck Max, 7, 81, 221, 225, 250, 252
Plant
Robert, 179
Pleiadian Collection, 175
Plunkett, Roy, 50
Podolsky Boris, 258
Poe Edgar Allan, 97
Poe, Edgar Allen, 20
Poincare
Henri, 85
Polge
Coral, 112
Post Wiley, 58

Powell Diane, 114, 116, 124, 128, 134, 212, 235, 241
Presley, Elvis, 2, 23, 30, 211, 263
Pribrum
Karl, 219
Prignon, Don Pierre, 50
Ptaszynska Marta, 38
Puccini Giacomo, 38
Puharich
Andrija, 68
Puthoff Hal, 129, 130, 140
Quinsey Mike, 171
Ra, 176
Ragsdale
Floyd, 68
Ramachandran
V.S., 227, 241
Ramachandran, V.S., 6
Ramanujan
Srinivasa, 85, 86
Ramtha, 176
Raphael
Sanzio da Urbino, 107
Ray Manzarek, 28
Reg Presley, 30, 211
Rich
Ben, 81
Richard
Diane, 146
Richard Rodgers, 31
Richards, Keith, 23, 31, 32
Ring
Kenneth, 189
Roberts Jane, 168, 176, 178
Robinson, Chris, 206
Roddenberry, Gene, 177, 206
Roentgen, Wilhelm, 51
Rosales, Albert, 13
Rosemary Brown, 170

Rosen Nathan, 258
Rosenfield, 183
Rowling J.K., 97
Rumball
Alma, 112
Rutherford Ernest, 4
Sacks Oliver, 121, 122, 123, 236
Sagan, Carl, 12, 202
Sanders Rw, 42
Santana
Carlos, 183
Sartori, Penny, 207, 214
Schauer
Robert, 145
Schmidt
Gerhard Carl, 61
Schoenberg Arnold, 22, 39
Schoonmaker
Fred, 189
Schrodinge
Erwin, 217
Schroedinger, Erwin, 208
Schubert Franz, 170
Schumann Robert, 39, 170
Schwabe
Stephanie, 147
Schwartz
Charles, 139
Schweikart, Rusty, 209
Scott
Doug, 146
Scott Mike, 31
Semjase, 173
Seth, 168, 176, 178
Sevigny
James, 146
Shackleton
Ernest, 147
Shapiro

Robert, 178
Sharp
Kimberly, 191
Sheldrake
Rupert, 219, 220, 221
Shelley Mary, 104
Sherman Patsy, 51
Sherr
Elliot, 126
Shklovskii
S., 12
Shostakovich Dmitri, 39
Sibelius Jean, 39
Silver,Spencer, 51, 261
Simon, Paul, 63, 202
Smith
Craig F, 115, 138, 171, 201, 205, 213
Wilbert, 97, 168
Smith, Adrian, 23
Smythe
Frank, 147
Snyder
Allan, 236
Allen, 114
Soupault
Breton and Philippe, 89
Spare
Austin, 113
Sparks Kerrelyn, 98
Speakers of the Sirian High
Council, 177
Spencer Percy, 51
Sperry
Roger, 226, 227, 228, 255
Stanford
Ray, 69
Stars and Stripes, 57
Steiger

Brad, 92
Stereophonics, 31, 263
Sternbach, Leo, 51
Stevenson Robert Louis, 105
Stiles
Kristine, 107
Sting, 193, 202
Stinnett David, 44
Stoker
Henry, 148
Stone Ruth, 99
Stones, 2, 28, 31, 32, 102
Storace
Marc, 32
storyteller, 276
Storyteller, 6, 228, 229, 230, 231, 232, 233, 239, 250, 251, 254, 276
Strassman, Rick, 202, 207, 239
Strauss Richard, 39
Stravinsky Igor, 39, 170
Streisand, Barbra, 23
Strieber Whitley, 99
Stripe
Michael, 32
Styron William, 105
Swan Frances, 168, 180
Swedenborg, Emanuel, 19
Szent-Györgyi
Albert, 45
Taff
Barry, 81
Talpazan
Ionel, 113
Tammet
Daniel, 124, 128, 177
Targ Russell, 90, 129, 140, 189, 215, 237
Taylor, Jill Bolte, 6, 91, 209, 218, 240

Tchaikovsky
Pyotr, 40, 43, 121
Tchaikovsky Pyotr, 40
Tesla, Nikola, 59, 61, 69, 79, 86, 115, 119, 186, 218
The Guide, 171
The Michael Teachings, 174
Theise
Neil, 184
Thompson
Edward, 182
Thor Val, 103, 104
Thoth, 177
Tobias, 177
Tom, 177
Tomlin Lily, 166
Torah, 177
Townes
Charles, 17, 77
Townsend, Peter, 23, 263
Treb Bor yit-NE, 177
Treffert,
Darold, 43, 114, 125, 133
Twain, Mark, 53, 115, 254, 256
Ueland Brenda, 90
Unnikrishnan Nadana, 133
Urantia book, 100
Vallee Jacques, 46
Van Halen, Eddie, 23, 115
Vaughan, Stevie Ray, 23
Vile, Kurt, 23
Von Neumann
John, 125, 254
Von Neumann John, 252
Von-Neumann
John, 87
Wachowski Andy and Lana, 105
Waggoner
Robert, 184

Wagner Richard, 40
Waits Tom, 33, 88
Wakeman, Rick, 24
Wald
George, 88
Wallace
Alfred, 79, 80
Bob, 62, 203
Wallas
Graham, 89
Walpole
Horace, 45
Walsch Neale Donald, 171
Walsh
Neil, 178
Walter Pahnke Study, 201
Wang
Ryan, 33, 125
Ward
Bill, 33
Warren, J. Robin, 77
Watson
James, 77
Watt
James, 69
Watts
William, 70
Weiss, Brian, 19
Wells H.G., 100
West, Kanye, 23, 93, 138, 196
Wheeler
John, 217
White E.B., 100

White Sasha, 89
Whitney
Eli, 70
Wilkinson
William, 180
Williams
Hank, 34
Robin, 115
Williams Denise, 106
Wilson
Bill, 203
Brian, 203
William, 100
Wilson, Robert, 48, 52, 60, 232
Wiltshire
Steven, 125
Winfrey Oprah, 97, 218
World Consciousness Project, 184
Worth, Patience, 92, 131, 206
Wortman
Camille, 187
Wright
Gary, 34
Xavier Francisco, 100
Yeats
W.B., 181
William, 77
YHWH, 178
Yoko Ono, 29
Yorke, Thom, 23
Young, Angus, 23, 34, 164, 214
Zeppelin, Led, 35, 113, 206
Zoosh, 178

Footnotes

[1] An experiencer is a person who claims to have had interaction with non-human beings or consciousness. It is a wider term than the term abductee which has been implied to be a person taken against their will by aliens.

[2] The music of Katie Perry is the main music that seems to have inspired this idea that the Devil co-producers some modern music. I have even pulled her songs from my aliens and modern musician lecture, as it almost always motivates from people who seem to believe that Perry is a devil worshipper.

[3] Brad Steiger, Sherry Hansen Steiger, "Real Encounters, Different Dimensions and Otherworldy Beings," page xiii

[4] Bill Nye debates Ken Ham on Creationism, https://www.youtube.com/watch?v=ekse95-owyo

[5] Bruce Lipton, "A Romp Through the Quantum Field," February 2012, https://www.brucelipton.com/resource/interview/romp-through-the-quantum-field

[6] Dr. Quantum, "Double Slit Experiment," https://www.youtube.com/watch?v=fwXQjRBLwsQ

[7] Geoff, "The Mystics and Realists of Quantum Physics," http://www.gmilburn.ca/2009/06/15/the-mystics-and-realists-of-quantum-physics/

[8] "Werner Heisenberg Quotes", *Goodreads*, https://www.goodreads.com/author/quotes/64309.Werner_Heisenberg

[9] EPR Paradox, http://en.wikipedia.org/wiki/EPR_paradox

[10] In the experiment when two entangled particles are sent in opposite directions, when one particles spin is affected the other particle will change its spin to balance no even if it is on the other side of the universe. The particle is therefore aware of what was done to its buddy. Awareness is consciousness. If the particle was aware of what was done it has consciousness.

[11] Michael Gazzaniga, "The Ethical Brain," http://www.press.uchicago.edu/Misc/Chicago/1932594019.html

[12] Stephen Hawking and Leonard Mlodinow, "The Grand Design"

[13] David Deutsch Quotes, https://www.goodreads.com/quotes/862111-as-the-physicist-stephen-hawking-put-it-humans-are-just

[14] Fred Hoyle(1983): "The Intelligent Universe," page 19.

[15] Francis Crick, "Life Itself: Its Origin and Nature," London Futura 1982, p. 88.

[16] The process is actually explained in modern neurology by what had been identified as the storyteller or interpreter. This independent consciousness is found in the left brain. Its role is to make the story consistent. When an idea is presented to the brain that challenges what is normal an inconsistency arises, and the storyteller instantly presents the mind a made up story that makes the held paradigm consistent again. Much of this fascinating research what done by Gazzaniga at the University of California, Santa Barbara.

[17] "Chapter 6 – Research with Psychic Pets," http://www.bibliotecapleyades.net/ciencia/ciencia_morphic03e.htm

[18] John Carl Villanueva, "Atoms in the Universe," *Universe Today*, http://www.universetoday.com/36302/atoms-in-the-universe/#ixzz387Vtvqiv

[19] Fred Hoyle and N. Chandra Wickramasinghe, "Evolution from Space" [Aldine House, 33 Welbeck Street, London W1M 8LX: J.M. Dent & Sons, 1981), page 148, 24,150,30,31).
[20] Chandra Wickramasinghe, Fred Hoyle, "Panspermia and the Black Death," https://sebastianhayes.info/2014/10/13/panspermia-and-the-black-death/
[21] Research calculation done by Rick Ramashing and Sir Fred Hoyle. https://mrayton.wordpress.com/2011/03/12/1-in-10-to-the-40000th-power/
[22] http://www.ufoinfo.com/humanoid/
[23] "Humans Have Ten Times More Bacteria Than Human Cells: How Do Microbial Communities Affect Human Health?" Science Daily, June 5, 2008, http://www.sciencedaily.com/releases/2008/06/080603085914.htm
[24] Clara Moskowitz, "Mind's Limit Found: 4 Things at Once" April 27, 2008, http://www.livescience.com/2493-mind-limit-4.html
[25] Jim Elvidge, "Intuition & Innovation in the Age of Uncertainty" March 19, 2013, http://www.bigvisible.com/2013/03/intuition_innovation_uncertainty/
[26] "Dreams and Music" –Radio New Zealand, http://www.radionz.co.nz/concert/programmes/music-and-dreams
[27] Charles G. Sampas Readers Digest 1945.
[28] Morton A. Myers, "Happy Accidents: Serendipity in Modern Medical Breakthroughs,"Arcade Publishing, 2007, page xiii.
[29] Gijs van Wulfen, "Top Eureka Moments: Women Drive Men Shower," https://www.linkedin.com/today/post/article/20131227083932-206580-top-eureka-moments-women-drive-and-men-shower
[30] Elizabeth Gilbert: "Your elusive creative genius," TED talk 2009.
[31] Ibid.
[32] Stanley Krippner, "Susan Powers Broken Images Broken Selves: Dissociative Narratives in Clinical Practice," page 92.
[33] Brian Weiss, "Through Time into Healing," 1992 page 26.
[34] Mavromatis, Andreas (1987). Hypnagogia: the Unique State of Consciousness Between Wakefulness and Sleep. London: Routledge and Kegan Paul. page 4.
[35] Music in Dreams, http://www.brams.umontreal.ca/cours/files/PSY-6441/Musique%20et%20reves/Uga_2006_Music%20in%20dreams.pdf
[36] Larry Dossey, "Why Consciousness is not the Brain," - See more at: http://www.superconsciousness.com/topics/science/why-consciousness-not-brain#sthash.wEkHnhOH.dpuf
[37] "consciousness & quantum physics ~ Reality is an illusion," https://www.youtube.com/watch?v=gUyqfUut8lA
[38] Michael Jackson Quotes, http://www.truemichaeljackson.com/on-music/
[39] Sterling Whitaker, "Unsung Heroes of Rock Guitar: 15 Great Rock Guitarists in Their Own Words," page 199.
[40] Arnold Schroenberg, "Style and Idea," trans. D. Newlin, London, Williams and Norgate, 1951, page 108
[41] Jon Anderson interviewed by Suzanne Chancellor, Random Alien Brain Droppings Radio Show, May 2014

[42] Best Songwriting Quotes, http://jeanettearsenault.ca/2010/06/best-songwriting-quotes/
[43] Matthew Perpetua, "Bradford Cox Talks Nervous Breakdown, New Atlas Sound Album," http://www.rollingstone.com/music/news/bradford-cox-talks-nervous-breakdown-new-atlas-sound-album-20111107#ixzz353b4gAeq
[44] Interview with Karyn Crisis on Podcast "Where did the Road Go," October 26, 2013
[45] Cummings, Burton (July 23, 2013). The Guess Who legend reveals true origin of "American Woman". Examiner.com.
[46] Interview with Burton Cummings, "Burton Cummings: The Guess Who legend reveals true origin of American Woman" http://www.examiner.com/article/burton-cummings-the-guess-who-legend-reveals-true-origin-of-american-woman
[47] Carol Weber, "What dreams May come: Songwriters muse on nocturnal inspirations" http://www.axs.com/what-dreams-may-come-songwriters-muse-on-nocturnal-inspirations-35518
[48] E-mail, Estrella to Cameron, July 4, 2015.
[49] Patty Griffin – An "American Kid" Interview, Posted by Folk Villager on May 10, 2013, http://www.nodepression.com/profiles/blogs/patty-griffin-an-american-kid-interview
[50] Frank C. Tribbe, "Research report –Musical Composers," Spiritual Frontiers, Spring 1985, page 83
[51] Michael Jackson, online audio chat, October 21st, 2001
[52] Derrell Treffert, "'Ancestral' or 'Genetic' Memory: Factory Installed Software," https://www.wisconsinmedicalsociety.org/professional/savant-syndrome/resources/articles/ancestral-or-genetic-memory-factory-installed-software/
[53] Carol Weber, "What dreams May Come: Songwriters muse on nocturnal inspirations" http://www.axs.com/what-dreams-may-come-songwriters-muse-on-nocturnal-inspirations-35518
[54] Maris Popova, "Legendary Songwriter Carole King on Inspiration vs. Perspiration and How to Overcome Creative Block," https://www.brainpickings.org/2014/06/26/carole-king-creativity-interview/
[55] "The Gibson Classic Interview: Lynyrd Skynyrd's Ed King," http://www2.gibson.com/News-Lifestyle/Features/en-us/Lynyrd-Skynyrds-Ed-King-913.aspx
[56] John Lennon quotes, http://www.johnlennon.it/john-lennon-quotes-it.htm
[57] John Lennon, People Magazine, Aug. 22, 1988, page 70
[58] The Playboy Interview with John Lennon and Yoko Ono (Berkeley, 1982), page 169
[59] Jerry Hopkins and Daniel Sugerman, No One Here Gets Out Alive (Warner Books, 1980), pages 158-60.
[60] "12 Famous Dreams of Creativity and Inventions", Mind Power News, http://www.mindpowernews.com/BrilliantDreams.htm
[61] Barry Miles, "Paul McCartney: Many Years From Now," Vintage 1998
[62] Time magazine, December, 16, 1974, page 63
[63] Why Knock Rock? p. 112, citing Time magazine, Dec. 16, 1974, page 39.

[64] Eric Holmberg, Hells Bells2
[65] The Playboy Interview: John and Yoko Ono,
http://www.recmusicbeatles.com/public/files/bbs/jl_yo.playboy/lennon3.html
[66] The Scotsman "Interview: Guitarist Jimmy Page,"
http://www.scotsman.com/what-s-on/music/interview-guitarist-jimmy-page-1-473048
[67] http://www.lauriloewenberg.com/5-iconic-rock-and-roll-songs-that-were-inspired-by-dreams-4428#sthash.Hjj9oqLb.dpuf
[68] Statement made to Colin Andrews and related in an interview with podcast host Mike Clelland.
[69] Dr. Synthia Andrews and Colin Andrews, "The Complete Idiot's Guide to the Akashic Record," Penguin 2010.
[70] Loverboy's Mike Reno Dreams Up a Song,
http://www.lisashea.com/lisabase/dreams/inspirations/mikereno.html
[71] Bill DeMain, "In their Own Words : Songwriters Talk about the Creative Process," Greenfield Publishing Group 2004, page 89
[72] Songfacts, "I wouldn't believe your Radio"
http://www.songfacts.com/detail.php?id=5185
[73] "Mike Scott: Adventures of a Waterboy," http://www.amazon.com/Mike-Scott-Adventures-Waterboy/dp/1908279249
[74] "Rain," Rolling Stone, Dec. 9, 2004
[75] http://www.lauriloewenberg.com/5-iconic-rock-and-roll-songs-that-were-inspired-by-dreams-4428#sthash.Hjj9oqLb.dpuf
[76] Circus, January 31, 1984, page 70.
[77] Pete Townshend from the band The Who, taken from his book "Who Am I: A Memoir."
[78] Elizabeth Gilbert, "Your Elusive Creative Genius,"
https://www.ted.com/talks/elizabeth_gilbert_on_genius?language=en
[79] "Ryan Wang, Piano Prodigy, plays for 'Ellen,'" Huffington Post,
http://www.huffingtonpost.ca/2013/05/30/ryan-wang-piano-prodigy-ellen-video_n_3363518.html
[80] Black Sabbath An Oral History, page 7
[81] Best Songwriting Quotes, http://jeanettearsenault.ca/2010/06/best-songwriting-quotes/
[82] Hit Parader, July 1985, page 60.
[83] Davin Seay, Stairway to Heaven, page 249.
[84] Stanley Krippner and Susan Marie Powers, "Broken Images, Broken Selves: Dissociative Narratives in Clinical Practice," page 184
[85] Kelly L. Stone, "Thinking Write: The Secret Freeing of your Creative Mind," pages 65-66.
[86] Note in a sketch-book of 1810, containing studies for the music to "Egmont" and the great Trio in B-flat, op. 97. H. E. K.
[87] http://www.brainyquote.com/quotes/authors/l/ludwig_van_beethoven.html
[88] ibid
[89] ibid

[90] Louis Berlioz, "Memories," https://groups.google.com/forum/#!msg/alt.quotations/UUPsvkBWvbM/w0sug_PTwz8J

[91] Willis Harman and Howard Rheingold, Higher Creativity, (Jeremy P. Tarcher, 1984), pp. 46-47; cited in Klimo, Channeling, page 314.

[92] Jane Piirto, "Creativity for 21st Century Skills: How to Embed Creativity Into the Curriculum" page 57.

[93] ibid

[94] Glavin Dixon, "Classical Music and Dreams," July 25, 2012 http://www.limelightmagazine.com.au/Article/308213,classical-music-anddreams.aspx/0

[95] Jonathan Harvey, "Music and Inspiration," Faber and Faber New York, 1999, page 3.

[96] The Most Bizarre Composer Facts, http://www.classicfm.com/discover/music/bizarre-composer-facts/edward-elgar/

[97] Frank C. Tribbe, "Research report –Musical Composers," Spiritual Frontiers, Spring 1985, page 83

[98] Jon Klimo, "Channeling: Investigations on Receiving Information from Paranormal Sources" page 315

[99] Famous Quotes from Famous Composers, http://musiced.about.com/od/beginnersguide/a/bg.htm

[100] "Music and Inspiration" page 4

[101] "Music and Inspiration," page 7

[102] "Music and Inspiration" page 10

[103] Goodreads Mozart Quotes, https://www.goodreads.com/author/quotes/22051.Wolfgang_Amadeus_Mozart

[104] Exploring the Sources of Musical Creativity, University of Chicago, http://www.uchicago.edu/features/exploring_the_sources_of_musical_creativity/

[105] Klimo, "Channeling: Investigations on Receiving Information from Paranormal Sources," page 314

[106] Lucy Adams, "Oh Little Town of Bethlehem," http://www.wyll.com/spirituallife/1457973/

[107] "Music and Inspiration," page 13.

[108] Philosophy of Dreams and Sleeping (lecture course slides ... www.academia.edu/.../Philosophy_of_Dreams_and_Sleeping_lecture_co.

[109] "Music and Inspiration," page 6.

[110] "Channeling," Klimo 314

[111] Richard Strauss, "Recollections and Reflections," Boosey and Hawkes, London, 1953, p.114.

[112] Igor Stravinsky Octet for Winds, https://www.boosey.com/cr/music/Igor-Stravinsky-Octet-for-Wind-Instruments/826

[113] Goodreads, Pyotr Ilyich Tchaikovsky > Quotes, https://www.goodreads.com/author/quotes/1672211.Pyotr_Ilyich_Tchaikovsky

[114] Modesta Tchaikovsky, "The Life & Letters of Peter Ilich Tchaikovsky."

[115] "Music and Inspiration," page 5

[116] Jonathan Harvey, "Music and Inspiration," page 82.

[117] Richard Leppert, "Paradise, Nature, and Reconciliation," *Echo* Volume 4 Issue 1, http://www.echo.ucla.edu/Volume4-issue1/leppert/index.html

[118] Interview with Maria Cuccia, Frontiers of Faith, http://www.thecursednet.net/radio/FOF2gregandmaria.mp3

[119] Dr. Darold Treffert, "The Case of 'Sudden' Savant," https://www.wisconsinmedicalsociety.org/professional/savant-syndrome/resources/articles/the-case-of-the-sudden-savant/

[120] Morton A. Meyers M.D. described the situation in his book Happy Accidents: Serendipity in Modern Medical Breakthroughs, Accidental Discoveries. page 245

[121] . Meyers, page xiii.

[122] H. Peter Alesso, Craig F. Smith, "Connections: Patterns of Discovery," John Wiley and Sons, 2008, page 6.

[123] Melissa Pandika, "Jennifer Doudna, CRISPR Code Killer," http://www.ozy.com/rising-stars-and-provocateurs/jennifer-doudna-crispr-code-killer/4690

[124] Meyers, page 288.

[125] "History of Genetic Fingerprinting," http://www2.le.ac.uk/departments/genetics/jeffreys/history-gf

[126] Richard Platt "Eureka: Great Inventions and How they Happened," Kingfisher, Boston, 2003, pages 67-68.

[127] Meyers, page 282.

[128] Evolution in Truth, "The Technology of Nature" http://evolutionoftruth.com/msc/beenther.htm

[129] Meyer, page 3.

[130] Jonas Salomansen, "Top 10: The best copies of Nature (Part 1)" *ScienceNordic,* http://sciencenordic.com/top-10-best-copies-nature-part-1

[131] Jan Harman, "The Shark's Paintbrush: Biomimicry and How Nature is Inspiring Innovation," White Cloud Press, Ashland Oregon, 2013, page 1.

[132] Richard Platt "Eureka: Great Inventions and How they Happened," Kingfisher, page 19.

[133] Tom Vanderbilt "How Biomimicry is Inspiring Human Innovation" http://www.smithsonianmag.com/science-nature/how-biomimicry-is-inspiring-human-innovation-17924040/#3qrsbb62bRwXJe7j.99

[134] Richard Platt "Eureka: Great Inventions and How they Happened," page 21

[135] William F. Ogburn and Dorthy Thomas, "Are Inventions Inevitable? A Note of Social Evolution," http://www.jstor.org/stable/2142320?seq=3

[136] Dream Interpretation: Everything about Dreams, http://dreamtraining.blogspot.ca/2010/12/inventions-that-came-in-dreams-largest.html

[137] "Philo Taylor Farnsworth," http://www.byhigh.org/History/Farnsworth/PhiloT1924.html

[138] Leslie Horvitz, "Eureka: Scientific Breakthroughs that Changed the World," page 143.

[139] Robert Crease, "Alan Huang Lights Up Bell's Computers," The Scientist, January 9, 1989
[140] "How information in a dream lead to a medical breakthrough," http://www.silvamethodlife.com/invention-in-a-dream/
[141] Larry Page's University of Michigan Commencement Address May 2009, http://googlepress.blogspot.ca/2009/05/larry-pages-university-of-michigan.html
[142] George Schindler's "Dreaming of Victory" in New Scientist, p. 53, May 31, 1997
[143] Of Sewing Machines and other Dreams, http://jackiewhiting.net/Psychology/Sleep/DreamInvent.htm
[144] Jon Klimo, "Channeling" page 166
[145] William Rosen, "The Most Useful Man Who Ever Lived," http://www.thenewatlantis.com/publications/the-most-useful-man-who-ever-lived
[146] "Richard Feynman and Fred Hoyle discussing their Moments of Revelation," https://www.youtube.com/watch?v=n9KeIXhj62U
[147] Bob Dylan, Blowing in the Wind Song Facts, http://www.songfacts.com/detail.php?id=1669
[148] Conversation with Mike Maloney, •Encounters ,Global Radio Alliance, 7 Oct. 2012
[149] 60 Minutes Interview, http://www.youtube.com/watch?v=3cM6M2FRoJU
[150] Dylan Looks Back, *60 Minutes,* December 5, 2004, http://www.cbsnews.com/news/dylan-looks-back/
[151] Einstein: My Entire Career has Been a Mediation on my Dream," http://jungcurrents.com/einstein-dream/
[152] Jungcurrents.com, http://jungcurrents.com/einstein-dream
[153] Alun Rees, "Nobel Prize genius Crick was high on LSD when he discovered the secret of life," Mail on Sunday August 8, 2004.
[154] *Something of Myself for My Friends Known and Unknown,* Chapter 8 (1937)
[155] http://www.unmeditation.org/intuitionQuotations.cfm?subject=4
[156] Kary Mullis, "The Unusual Origin of the Polymerase Chain Reaction," *Scientific American,* April 1990, page 56
[157] "Mother Teresa: In the Shadow of Our Lady" by Joseph Langford, Our Sunday Visitor, 2007
[158] "Newly released letters tell of Jesus calling Mother Teresa 'my little wife'," The Scotsman, http://www.scotsman.com/news/world/newly-released-letters-tell-of-jesus-calling-mother-teresa-my-little-wife-1-1380060
[159] No retirement for 95 year old inventor of Laser – "Science is so much fun…" http://www.skeptical-science.com/science/retirement-95-year-inventor-laser-science-fun/
[160] "Automatism And the Occult," http://www.ithellcolquhoun.co.uk/988/
[161] Ellmann, Richard (1948). "Yeats: The Man and the Masks." (New York) Macmillan. p.94.
[162] 10.Letters from Darwin to Wallace, March 1869.
[163] "Telepathy" http://www.unexplainedstuff.com/Mysteries-of-the-Mind/ESP-Researchers-Telepathy.html

[164] Amanda Gefter, "Newton's Apple: The Real Story," January 18, 2010, http://www.newscientist.com/blogs/culturelab/2010/01/newtons-apple-the-real-story.html
[165] Russell Grigg, "Alfred Russel Wallace - 'co-inventor' of Darwinism" http://creation.com/alfred-russel-wallace-co-inventor-of-darwinism
[166] Roy Davies, "The Darwin Conspiracy: Origins of a Scientific Crime" Golden Square Books 2008.
[167] "Lord William Kelvin", http://scienceworld.wolfram.com/biography/Kelvin.html
[168] A.A. Michelson, "Light Waves and Their Uses," The University of Chicago Press, Chicago 1903.
[169] Leslie Alan Horvitz, "Eureka: Scientific Breakthroughs that Changed the World," John Wiley and Sons, 2002, page 3.
[170] "Louis Agassiz: His Life and Correspondence" Edited by E.C. Agassiz, volume 1., pages 181-183
[171] Stephan Schwartz, "The Secret Vaults of Time," Grossett and Dunlap, 1978, page 136
[172] "Eureka: Scientific Breakthroughs that Changed the World,"p.2.
[173] Ibid. page 1.
[174] Leslie Alan Horvitz, "Eureka: Scientific Breakthroughs that Changed the World" John Willet and Sons, 2002, page 29.
[175] B.M Kedrov, "On the Question of Scientific Creativity."
[176] Ibid. page 1
[177] Hasan Suroor, "American mathematicians solve Ramanujan's "Deathbed" Puzzle," http://www.thehindu.com/news/american-mathematicians-solve-ramanujans-deathbed-puzzle/article4253593.ece
[178] Michio Kaka, "Hyperspace: A Scientific Odyssey through Parallel Universes, Time Warps, and the Tenth Dimension." http://www.famousscientists.org/7-great-examples-of-scientific-discoveries-made-in-dreams/
[179] The Doc, "7 Great Examples of Scientific Discoveries Made in Dreams,"
[180] Neville, Eric Harold (March 1942). "Srinivasa Ramanujan." Nature 149 (3776): 293.
[181] Kenneth Ring and Sharon Cooper, "Near-Death and Out-of-Body Experiences in the Blind: A Study of Apparent Eyeless Vision," Journal of Near Death Studies 16(2) Winter 1997.
[182] Norman Macrae, "John Von Neumann: The Scientific Genius who Pioneered the Modern Computer," page 153.
[183] Jean Houston inter with Lisa Zimmer, *Unlimited Realities Podcast*, March 28, 2013.
[184] Matilda Josyln Gage, "The Unlikely Inspiration for the Wizard of Oz," http://www.historynet.com/matilda-josyln-gage-the-unlikely-inspiration-for-the-wizard-of-oz.htm
[185] L. Frank Baum, "The Real Wizard of Oz," http://www.telegraph.co.uk/culture/5949617/L-Frank-Baum-the-real-Wizard-of-Oz.html

[186] Kelly Stone, "Thinking Write: The Secret to Freeing Your Creative Mind," Adams Media, 2009, page 60.
[187] Lev Grossman, "Of Magic and Men," Time (8 August 2004). Retrieved 5 January 2009.
[188] The Zeta Message: Connecting all Beings in Oneness," by Judy Carol and Helen Kaye, 2011
[189] "Karen Crisis on Mediumship, Channeling, and Energy - 10-26-13," Where did the Road Go? Radio, https://www.youtube.com/watch?v=26KFHjDPjcU
[190] W.F. Prince "The Case of Patience Worth," New York, University Books, 1964 page 487
[191] Gioia Diliberto "Patience Worth: The Author from the Great Beyond" http://www.smithsonianmag.com/arts-culture/patience-worth-author-from-the-great-beyond-54333749/#fTqJa7e2gJkjo3CY.99
[192] K.K. Collin, "George Eliot: Interviews and Recollections," page 221
[193] Elizabeth Gilbert, "Your elusive Creative Genius,' TED Talk, February 2009.
[194] 10 Great Stories Inspired by Dreams, http://www.pastemagazine.com/blogs/lists/2013/10/10-great-stories-inspired-by-dreams-and-visions.html
[195] Kelly Stone, "Thinking Write: The Secret Freeing Your Creative Mind," page 66.
[196] Carl Jung, "Memories, Dreams, Reflections," page 190-.1.
[197] Akiane Kramarik about her art and the inspiration from God, http://www.youtube.com/watch?v=C5H3V4BZCZw
[198] Mike Clelland Interview of Kewaunee Lapseritis, June 10, 2014, http://hiddenexperience.blogspot.ca/
[199] Philip Marshand, Marshall McLuhan: The messenger and the Messenger: A Biography, page 51
[200] Stevan J. Thayer, "Interview with an Angel," Random House Publishing Group, 2009, page 11.
[201] Five Famous Books inspired by Dreams, http://listverse.com/2011/02/26/5-famous-books-inspired-by-dreams/
[202] Grant Morrison, "DinInfo.com lecture," https://vimeo.com/65180541
[203] Ghiselin B., The Creative Process, Mnetor, New York, 1952, page 202
[204] Laura Lee McKay, "Write Fantasy Fiction in 5 Simple Steps," Enslow Publishers, Inc., Aug 1, 2012 page 5.
[205] J.K. Rowling interview with Oprah Winfrey, October 2010.
[206] Wilbert B. Smith, "The New Science," Fenn-Graphic Publishing 1978.
[207] Kelly L. Stone, "Thinking Write: The Secret Freeing of your Creative Mind," Adams Media, Sep 18, 2009, page 65.
[208] Elizabeth Gilbert, " Your Elusive Creative Genius," TED Talk Transcript, https://www.ted.com/talks/elizabeth_gilbert_on_genius/transcript?language=en
[209] "Who Wrote the Urantia Book," http://www.urantiabook.org/archive/mjs_archive/who-wrote-urantia-book.htm
[210] "My Word Like Fire," http://mywordlikefire.com/2008/09/24/seances-spirits-and-12-steps/
[211] "Pass it On," Alcoholics Anonymous World Services, Inc., pg. 278-79.

[212] Robert Fitzgerald, S.J., "The Soul of Sponsorship," page 59
[213] Catherine Lanigan, "Devine Nudges: Tales of Angelic Intervention," Health Communications, 2006, page 212.
[214] Jane Piirto, "Creativity for 21st Century Skills: How to Embed Creativity Into the Curriculum," page 68.
[215] Galactic Connection, "Craig Campobasso and Alexandra Meadors Transcription for October 8, 2013," http://galacticconnection.com/craig-campobasso-and-alexandra-meadors-trasncription-for-october-8-2013/
[216] Ibid.
[217] Rebecca Turner, "Famous Lucid Dreamers: 10 Celebrities Who Lucid Dream," http://www.world-of-lucid-dreaming.com/famous-lucid-dreamers.html
[218] Carolyn Gregoire. "Eight Famous Ideas that Came from Dreams –Literally," http://www.huffingtonpost.com/2013/11/16/famous-ideas-from-dreams_n_4276838.html
[219] Mary Wollstonecraft Shelley, from her introduction to Frankenstein.
[220] Stanley Krippner and Susan Powers, "Broken Images, Broken Selves," page 5
[221] Willis Harman and Howard Rheingold, "Higher Creativity: Liberating the Unconscious for Breakthrough Insights," Jeremy Tarcher, 1984, page 37.
[222] Gamwell, L. (Ed). (2000). Dreams 1900-2000: Science, art, and the unconscious mind. New York, NY: Cornell University Press.
[223] Kristine Stiles, "Parallel Worlds: Representing Consciousness at the Intersection of Art, Dissociation and Multidimensional Awareness," from the boos Reframing Consciousness by Roy Ascott.
[224] Stanley Krippner and Susan Powers, "Broken Images, Broken Selves," page 183
[225] Hayley Coyle, "British Artist Claims to Have Been Visited by Aliens SIX Times in 10 years," *Mirror Newspaper*, December 27, 2014.
[226] "Luiz Gasparetto from UFOs and Channeling, part 1," https://www.youtube.com/watch?v=4x3QnnwdPXM
[227] Gale Encyclopedia of Occultism & Parapsychology: Frederica Hauffe, http://www.answers.com/topic/frederica-hauffe#ixzz35WQJlDsw
[228] Akiane Kramarik about her art and the inspiration from God, http://www.youtube.com/watch?v=C5H3V4BZCZw
[229] Gale Encyclopedia of Occultism & Parapsychology: Matthew Manninghttp://www.answers.com/topic/matthew-manning
[230] "Gale Encyclopedia of Occultism & Parapsychology: John Ballou Newbrough, http://www.answers.com/topic/john-newbrough#ixzz35Cxlfzcl
[231] http://www.galerie-zander.de/artist.php?lang=en&a=heinrich_nuesslein
[232] Daniel Wojcik, "Ionel Talpazan's Mysterious Technology," *Raw Vision Magazine*, http://rawvision.com/articles/ionel-talpazans-mysterious-technology
[233] Dr. Diane Powell Newsletter and Research Update, December 18, 2014.
[234] Lawrence Osborne, "Savant for a Day," *New York Times*, June 22, 2003, http://www.nytimes.com/2003/06/22/magazine/22SAVANT.html?ex=1371614400&en=0497e5b30fc4a9d8&ei=5007&

[235] William Stillman, "The Soul of Autism: Looking Beyond Labels to Unveil Spiritual Secrets of the Human Savants," page 95.
[236] Oliver Sacks, " Musicophilia:Tales of Music and the Brian," Alfed Knopf, 2007 pages 5-6
[237] E W Scripture, Arithmetical Prodigies, The American Journal of Psychology 4 (1) (1891), 1-59.
[238] Oliver Sacks, "The Man Who Mistook His Wife For A Hat: And Other Clinical Tales," Simon and Schuster, 1998, page 199.
[239] 60 Minutes, "USA's Musically Gifted Youths: JAY GREENBERG at age 12" https://www.youtube.com/watch?v=DT94FGBj2FU
[240] Oliver Sacks, page 199.
[241] Calendar calculations involve being able to quickly determine what day of the week for any date in the past.
[242] Dr. Diane Powell in conversation with Alex Tsakiris, host of the Skeptiko.com podcast, October 28, 2014.
[243] Kevin T. Dann, "Bright Colors Falsely Seen: Synesthesia and the Search for Transcendental Knowledge," page 183
[244] Darold Treffert, "Islands of Genius," Jessica Kingsley Publications, 2010, page 59
[245] This research was written up by Peon K. Miller in "Musical Savants: Exceptional Skill in the Mentally Retarded."
[246] Miller, page 9.
[247] The Real Rain Man Documentary, https://www.youtube.com/watch?v=4wjgMtNF3Ms
[248] Diane Powell interview with Alex Tsakiris, Skeptiko Podcast, January 3, 2013.
[249] Russell Targ, "The Reality of ESP," Quest Books 2011, page 1.
[250] Russell Targ, "The Reality of ESP" p. 134.
[251] "The Ghosts of Glastonbury," https://www.youtube.com/watch?v=Is5W-_dGNIM
[252] CoasttoCoastAM interview with Richard Syrett, December 13, 2014.
[253] Stanley Krippner and Susan Marie Powers, "Broken Images, Broken Selves: Dissociative Narratives in Clinical Practice," page 187
[254] Richard Evans, "Conversation with Carl Jung," 1957, http://gnosis.org/Evans-Jung-Interview/evans3.html
[255] Russell Targ, "The Reality of ESP," page 198.
[256] Bill Bengston, "The Energy Cure," Sounds True Inc., 2010, page 259
[257] Sajila Saseendran , "Mind reading Sharjah Girl 'exceedingly rare' savant," Khaleeg Times, April 2, 2013
[258] Sajila Saseendran, "Miracle Girl: Nandana has access to mother's memory," Khaleej Times, March 25, 2013.
[259] Diane Powell, "The ESP Enigma: The Scientific Case for Psychic Phenomena," Boomsbury Publishing, 2009, page 144.
[260] Jimmy Carter, "White House Diary", Page 313.
[261] "Dreams and Creativity," http://www.lanesarasohn.com/templeofdreams/creative.html
[262] Oalexa's Blog "Carl Jung," https://oalexa.files.wordpress.com/2012/05/carl-jung1.pdf

[263] "The Global Consciousness Website," http://noosphere.princeton.edu/
[264] Interview of Roger Nelson by Dean Radin, April 7, 2010, http://noetic.org/directory/person/roger-nelson/
[265] Johanna Sänger*, Viktor Müller and Ulman Lindenberger, "Intra- and interbrain synchronization and network properties when playing guitar in duets," Frontiers Journal," http://journal.frontiersin.org/Journal/10.3389/fnhum.2012.00312/full
[266] Catherine Lanigan, "My Guardian Angel," Hay House 2008, Page 69. London page 211.
[267] Catherine Lanigan "Devine Nudges" Health Communications 2006 pages 36,52, and 136.
[268] Ibid page 90.
[269] Doreen Virtue, "My Guardian Angel," Hay House Inc., 2008, page 10.
[270] Nicholas O'Connell, "Beyond Risk: Conversations with Climbers," The *Mountaineers 1993*,
[271] Charles Lindburgh, The Spirit of St. Louis", Page 353.
[272] John Geiger, "The Third Man Factor," Penquin Canada 2009, page 280.
[273] Doreen Virtue, "My Guardian Angel," page 6.
[274] John Blake, "Near death, aided by Ghostly Companion" CNN Living, http://www.cnn.com/2009/LIVING/wayoflife/11/08/third.man/index.html?iref=nextin
[275] Sarah Chalmers, "The Third Man Factor: How those in dire peril have felt a sudden presence at their side, inspiring them to survive" http://www.dailymail.co.uk/news/article-1197394/The-Third-Man-Factor-How-dire-peril-felt-sudden-presence-inspiring-survive.html#ixzz31SWnQCad
[276] Shackleton, Ernest Henry (1914). South: The Endurance Expedition. Frank Hurley, Fergus Fleming. Penguin Classics, page 204.
[277] Sarah Chalmers, "The Third Man Factor: How those in dire peril have felt a sudden presence at their side, inspiring them to survive" http://www.dailymail.co.uk/news/article-1197394/The-Third-Man-Factor-How-dire-peril-felt-sudden-presence-inspiring-survive.html#ixzz31SWnQCad
[278] FREE Phase 1 Survey results, September 15, 2015
[279] "Walking Universe with Darryl Anka" video https://www.youtube.com/watch?v=DyNwxRMgJbY
[280] E-mail from Gabrielle Giet to Grant Cameron June 15, 2015.
[281] Interview of Rey Hernandez by Joanne Summerscales, The AMMACH files radio podcast, October 6, 2014
[282] http://www.abovetopsecret.com/forum/thread666085/pg
[283] Kary Mullis, "Dancing Naked in the Mine Field," Knopf Doubleday Publishing Group, 2010 page 132.
[284] Ralph Steiner – E-mail to board members of FREE group.
[285] Russell Targ, "The Reality of ESP," Theosophical Publishing, 2012, page 246.
[286] George Hansen, "Dowsing: A review of Experimental Research," http://www.tricksterbook.com/ArticlesOnline/Dowsing.htm
[287] A.P. Elkin, "Aboriginal Men of High Degree: Initiation and Sorcery in the World's Oldest Tradition" Inner Traditions 1993.

[288] Erwin Scgrodinger, "My View of the World," Woodridge Ct. Ox Bow Press, 1983, pages 87-89.
[289] Francis H. Cook, trans., "The Jewel Net of Indra: The Avatamsaka Sutra" Philadelphia: University of Pennsylvania 1977.
[290] Ryan Hurd, "5 Aspects of Ancient Dream Technology That Boost Lucid Dreaming," http://dreamstudies.org/2011/12/04/5-aspects-of-ancient-dream-technology-that-boost-lucid-dreaming/
[291] Ponce Sanginés, C. and G. M. Terrazas, 1970, Acerca De La Procedencia Del Material Lítico De Los Monumentos De Tiwanaku. Publication no. 21. Academia Nacional de Ciencias de Bolivia.
[292] Jay Stevens, :Storming Heaven," Harper and Row, 1988 page 76
[293] Richard Rudgley, "The Encyclopedia of Psychoactive Substances," Little, Brown and Company (1998)
[294] Jay Stevens, :Storming Heaven," Harper and Row, 1988 page 75
[295] Dr. Jon Klimo interview with Michael Mishlove, http://www.intuition.org/txt/klimo.htm
[296] "What the Bleep Interview 06 JZ Knight ON Creating Reality," https://www.youtube.com/watch?v=AyTFo5Mt1Cg
[297] Mike Clelland Interview of Darryl Anka, February 16, 2012, Hiddenexperience.com.
[298] Wilbert B. Smith, "The New Science," Fenn-Graphic Publishing, 1978
[299] Lucem Portabo "Misconceptions About Aleister Crowley, LAM, AIWASS and Alien Contact," http://www.blastedtower.com/misconceptions-about-aleister-crowley-lam-aiwass-and-alien-contact/
[300] Jane Allyson, "Diary: October 27, 1979 The Introduction."
[301] Tom Kenyon, "Who are the Hathors," http://tomkenyon.com/who-are-the-hathors
[302] Raymond Buckland, "The Spirit Book: The Encyclopedia of Clairvoyance, Channeling, and Spirit ..." page 282 and http://www.answers.com/topic/oahspe-1#ixzz35D1wTkzZ
[303] "Gale Encyclopedia of Occultism & Parapsychology: John Ballou Newbrough" http://www.answers.com/topic/john-newbrough#ixzz35D4xE0DM
[304] "Varieties of Dissociation Experience" with Stanley Krippner (part 1 of 2), IONS Institute, 2010, http://www.noetic.org/library/audio-lectures/varieties-of-dissociation-experience-with-stanley/
[305] Daniel Tammet, "Born on a Blue Day," page 74-75.
[306] Rob Gauthier, "Treb Bor yit-NE," *Inward Quest*, March 19,2011, http://www.inwardquest.com/users/1326/treb-bor-yit-ne
[307] Grant Morrison – 1996 Interview, http://arthurmag.com/2008/06/17/grant-morrison-1996-interview/
[308] "Gale Encyclopedia of Occultism & Parapsychology: Automatic Drawing and Painting" http://www.answers.com/topic/automatic-drawing-and-painting#ixzz35Cc7GGvV
[309] Edward P. Thompson "How to Make Inventions: Or, Inventing as a Science and an Art," D. Van Nostrand Company, 1893 page 171

[310] "Steve Job Quotes; The Ultimate Collection," http://www.applegazette.com/steve-jobs/steve-jobs-quotes-the-ultimate-collection/16/#qAMlziBTaqXpLPU0.99
[311] Ibid page 170.
[312] E-mail - Laurie Rosenfield to Grant Cameron December 4, 2014.
[313] The Epic Life of Carlos Santana, http://www.rollingstone.com/music/news/the-epic-life-of-carlos-santana-20000316
[314] Jason Padgett, "Struck by Genius: How a Brain injury Made me a Mathematical Marvel,"Harper Collins, 2011, page 174
[315] Interview of Robert Waggoner by Iain McNay at Consciousness TV.
[316] Marc Seifer, "The life and Times of Nikola Tesla," Citadel 1998, page 94.
[317] Green and McCreery, Apparitions, p.118.
[318] Camille Wortman Ph.D. "Communicating with Deceased," http://www.pbs.org/thisemotionallife/blogs/communicating-deceased
[319] Yamamoto, J., Okonogi, K., I wasaki, T., & Yoshimura, S. (1969). Mourning in Japan. American Journal of Psychiatry, 125, pages 1660-1665.
[320] Lorraine Davis, "A comparison of UFO and near-death experiences as vehicles for the evolution of human consciousness," http://www.newdualism.org/nde-papers/Davis/Davis-Journal%20of%20Near-Death%20Studies_1988-6-240-257.pdf
[321] Precognition after NDE, http://iands.org/experiences/nde-accounts/564-precognition-since-nde.html
[322] Michael Tymn, ""The Last Frontier": An Interview with author Julia Assante, Ph.D." November 7, 2012, http://whitecrowbooks.com/michaeltymn/entry/the_last_frontier_an_interview_with_author_julia_assante_ph.d
[323] Dr. Targ described the fact that there is a difference between remote viewing and near death experience. He wrote, "Basically, there is a continuum from remote viewing to full out-of- body experience with no discrete break between one and the other. In an out-of-body experience, you generally bring along with you emotionality, sensitivity, and sexuality…in a out-of-body you have mobility of your point of view at the distant target beyond what you would experience in remote viewing."
[324] Kenneth Ring and Sharon Cooper, "Near-Death and Out-of-Body Experiences in the Blind: A Study of Apparent Eyeless Vision," Journal of Near Death Studies 16(2) Winter 1997.
[325] A list of Thomas-Benedict's patents are listed on the web at http://patents.justia.com/inventor/mellen-thomas-benedict
[326] William James, "Varieties of Religious Experience," 1902, page 283
[327] Maia Szalavitz, "Steve Jobs Had LSD. We Have the iPhone," *Time Magazine*, October 6, 2011.
[328] Katie Bain, "Ten Celebrity Ayahuasca Users," http://www.laweekly.com/westcoastsound/2013/11/22/ten-celebrity-ayahuasca-users
[329] Deepak Chopra, October 22, 2009, Commonwealth Club of California, Santa Clara.
[330] Thomas B. Roberts, Ph.D. and Paula Jo Hruby, Ed.D., " Psychotherapy and Spirit: Theory and Practice in Transpersonal Psychotherapy" 1997.

[331] Inventions Inspired by Inventors Who Used LSD, Drug Forums, http://www.drugs-orum.com/forum/showthread.php?t=206788#ixzz37Z1WuJHK
[332] Hill, J. Paul Erdos, "Mathematical Genius, Human" http://www.untruth.org/~josh/math/Paul%20Erd%F6s%20bio-rev2.pdf
[333] "Interview with Jerry Garcia," http://malfalfa1.tripod.com/garciainterview.htm
[334] Ryan Grim, "This Is Your Country on Drugs: The Secret History of Getting High in America," page 228.
By Ryan Grim
[335] Griffiths R, Richards W, Johnson M, McCann U, Jesse R. (2008). "Mystical-type experiences occasioned by psilocybin mediate the attribution of personal meaning and spiritual significance 14 months later" (PDF). Journal of Psychopharmacology 22 (6): 621–32.
[336] Daniel Redwood "Frontiers of the Mind': Interview with © Stanislav Grof MD," http://www.healthy.net/scr/interview.aspx?Id=200
[337] "Interview with Dr. Stanislav Grof for "The Empire of the Spirit" – April 2010," http://www.stanislavgrof.com/pdf/Russian%20Journal_Empire%20of%20the%20Spirit.pdf
[338] "A General Introduction to Ayahuasca," http://www.ayahuasca-info.com/quotes/
[339] The peculiar relationship between genius, intelligence and psychedelic drug use," https://www.facebook.com/notes/mushrooms-are-awesome/the-peculiar-relationship-between-genius-intelligence-and-psychedelic-drug-use/516519355074296/
[340] Inventions Inspired by Inventors Who Used LSD, Drug Forums, http://www.drugs-orum.com/forum/showthread.php?t=206788#ixzz37Z1WuJHK
[341] Drugs Forum, "Stoned Ape Theory," http://www.drugs-forum.com/forum/showwiki.php?title=Stoned_Ape_Theory#ixzz362JKDsuI
[342] Drug Forums opinion, https://www.drugs-forum.com/forum/showthread.php?t=206788
[343] Amazon.ca book review, "What the Dormouse Said: How the Sixties Counterculture Shaped the Personal Computer Industry Paperback " http://www.amazon.ca/What-Dormouse-Said-Counterculture-ComputerIndustry/dp/0143036769"
[344] Ryan Grim, "This Is Your Country on Drugs: The Secret History of Getting High in America," page 228.
[345] Account was written in 1969 for publication in Marihuana Reconsidered (1971) http://marijuana-uses.com/mr-x/
[346] "The peculiar relationship between genius, intelligence and psychedelic drug use," https://www.facebook.com/notes/mushrooms-are-awesome/the-peculiar-relationship-between-genius-intelligence-and-psychedelic-drug-use/516519355074296/
[347] "Oscar Winning Animator Admits He Took LSD While Working on Return of the Jedi," The Mind Unleashed, http://themindunleashed.org/2015/12/oscar-winning-star-wars-animator-admits-he-took-lsd-while-working-on-return-of-the-jedi.html
[348] Facebook message to Grant Cameron, December 18, 2015.

[349] Yvonne Smith, "Chosen: Recollections of Abductions Through Hypnotherapy," Backstage Entertainment, 2008, page 88.
[350] Sherry Wilde in her May 30, 2015 presentation made at the Contact in the Desert conference in Joshua Tree, California.
[351] Jonathan Ellis, "Pop Will Shit Itself with Grant Morrison," http://www.popimage.com/profile/morrison/012501_grant6.html
[352] Edgar Cayce Reading 900-429.
[353] Lazarus: Dealing with Troubled Times," http://www.lazaris.com/publibrary/RespondingtoTheseTimes.cfm
[354] Patience Worth, "Oneness," http://www.inspirationalstories.com/poems/oneness-patience-worth-poems/
[355] Sting (musician) " Broken Music: A Memoir" Cambridge University Press, 2003, page 46.
[356] "10 Celebrity Ayahuasca Users," http://www.laweekly.com/westcoastsound/2013/11/22/ten-celebrity-ayahuasca-users?page=3
[357] Phyllis V. Schlemmer, "The Only Planet of Choice: Essential Briefings from Deep Space," Gateway Books, 1993, pages 6-7.
[358] Penny Sartori, "Wisdom of Near Death Experiences: How Understanding NDEs Can Help us Live."
[359] Near Death Experience Research Foundation, "100 Experiences," http://neardeathexperiences.podomatic.com/entry/2014-06-09T09_46_51-07_00
[360] Bruce Greyson, "Does Consciousness need a Brain? - Evidence for Reincarnation," https://www.youtube.com/watch?v=yosn_GHYiR4
[361] "DMT: The Spirit Molecule Full Documentary" http://www.suspicious0bserverscollective.org/the-blog/dmt-the-reality-molecule-space-weather-effects
[362] Gary Bekkum, "Kit Green's Mindtap: The Experiment," http://www.starpod.us/2013/01/17/kit-greens-mindtap-the-experiment/
[363] Stephen Martin, "A View from Space: An Interview with Edgar Mitchell," http://www.motorcityfreegeek.net/index.php?option=com_content&view=article&id=107&Itemid=108
[364] Barbara Bradley Hagerty, "Prayer May Reshape Your Brain: And Your Reality," *National Public Radio*, http://www.npr.org/templates/story/story.php?storyId=104310443
[365] Statement of 1986, as quoted in "Towards a Theory of Transpersonal Decision-Making in Human-Systems" (2007) by Joseph Riggio, p. 66
[366] Jill Taylor, "My Stroke of Insight: A Brain Scientist's Personal Journey."
[367] Mike Maloney, "The Extraterrestrial Answer Book: UFOs, Alien Abductions, and the Coming ET ..."
[368] John Mack, "Abduction: Human Encounters with Aliens"
[369] Email to Grant Cameron from Randy Kitchur March 26, 2014.
[370] Phase 2, English, Summary Data, PDF Pie Charts, December 9, 2015 Cutoff Date.

[371] Alan Steinfeld, *New Realities*, "Exclusive Interview with Dr. J.J. Hurtak on the 40th Anniversary of The Keys of Enoch - Part 1" January 2, 2013, https://www.youtube.com/watch?v=PQw4DHVfjDw

[372] "Songfacts – All You Need is Love" http://www.songfacts.com/detail.php?id=130

[373] Jade Wright "Rock of Ages – 1967 The Beatles- All you Need is Love," http://www.liverpoolecho.co.uk/news/nostalgia/rock-ages-1967-beatles--3450666

[374] Eben Alexander, "Proof of Heaven: A Neurosurgeon's Journey into the Afterlife," https://mygov.in/sites/default/files/user_comments/Proof_of_Heaven__A_Neurosurgeon_s_Journe_-_Eben_Alexander.pdf

[375] Joe McMonteagle Interview with Skeptiko podcaster Alex Tsakiris, April 3, 2012. http://www.skeptiko.com/psychic-spy-joe-mcmoneagle-near-death-experience-led-to-remote-viewing/

[376] Bruce Greyson, "Does Consciousness need a Brain? - Evidence for Reincarnation," https://www.youtube.com/watch?v=yosn_GHYiR4

[377] Kenneth Ring and Sharon Cooper, "Near-Death and Out-of-Body Experiences in the Blind: A Study of Apparent Eyeless Vision," page 111

[378] Dr. Diane Powell "Traveling Psychic Supper Club live radio interview : Host Deborah Antich" June 12, 2014

[379] Andrew Newberg, M.D., Mark Robert Waldman, "How God Changes Your Brain: Breakthrough Findings from a Leading Neuroscientist," Random House Publishing Group, 2009, page 53.

[380] John Mack, "Human Encounters with Aliens," page 398.

[381] Penny Sartori, "Wisdom of Near Death Experiences: How Understanding NDEs Can Help us Live." Kindle version.

[382] "Dennis McKenna- ayahuasca and human destiny.. and a tale of experiencing photosynthesis," https://www.dmt-nexus.me/forum/default.aspx?g=posts&t=27058

[383] Jill Bolte Taylor, "My Stroke of Insight" *TED Talk* February 2008, http://www.ted.com/talks/jill_bolte_taylor_s_powerful_stroke_of_insight?language=en

[384] Art Hobson, "There are No Particles, there are only fields," http://arxiv.org/ftp/arxiv/papers/1204/1204.4616.pdf

[385] Rupert Sheldrake, "Morphic Fields and Morphic Resonance," http://www.noetic.org/directory/person/rupert-sheldrake/

[386] Merton, Robert K. (1963). "Resistance to the Systematic Study of Multiple Discoveries in Science." European Journal of Sociology 4 (2): 237–282.

[387] Rupert Sheldrake, "Rat Learning and Morphic Resonance," http://www.sheldrake.org/about-rupert-sheldrake/blog/rat-learning-and-morphic-resonance

[388] Rupert Sheldrake, http://www.sheldrake.org/Articles&Papers/papers/morphic/morphic_intro.html

[389] Douglas Engelbart, "Augmenting Human Intelligence," 1962 page 18.

[390] Art Hobson, "There are No Particles, there are only fields," http://arxiv.org/ftp/arxiv/papers/1204/1204.4616.pdf

[391] Hereward Carrington, "Psychic Science and Survival," Health Research Books, 1993, page 17.

[392] William James, Varieties of Religious Experience, 1902, p. 283.
[393] Bernard Haisch, "The God Theory: Universes, Zero-Point Fields, and What's Behind It All," page 130.
[394] Abc.net.au. 2006-02-18. Retrieved 2011-01-24., http://www.abc.net.au/rn/scienceshow/stories/2006/1572643.htm.
[395] Rhawn Joseph "The Split Brain: Two Brains- Two Minds," Journal of Cosmology, 2011, Vol. 14. Journal of Cosmology.com, 2011.
[396] Split brain research tells many funny stories where the two non-communicating brains would fight for control such as one story told were both hands (right brain controls the left hand and the left brain controls the right hand) would both try and open a car door at the same time. The hands would actually fight with the other hand to stop it from opening the door. In another account the left hand (right brain) was unbuttoning a particular shirt and trying to pull it off while the right hand (left brain) tried to keep it on. In another story the left brain wanted to smoke but the left hand (controlled by the right brain) kept pulling the cigarette out of the mouth.
[397] V.S. Ramachandran "Split brain with one half atheist and one half Theist," https://www.youtube.com/watch?v=PFJPtVRlI64
[398] Michael Gazzaniga, "An Excerpt from the Ethical Brain," http://www.press.uchicago.edu/Misc/Chicago/1932594019.html
[399] Diane Hennacy Powell M.D., "The ESP Enigma," Walker and Company New York, 2009, page 276.
[400] Ibid.
[401] Maria Konnikova, "Our Storytelling Minds: Do We Ever Really Know What's Going on Inside?," *Scientific American*, March 8, 2012
[402] Nisbett RE, Wilson TD. "Telling more than we can know: verbal reports on mental processes." *Psychological Review* 1977; 84: 231-259
[403] "The Neuronal Platonist,"Michael Gazzaniga in conversation with Shaun Gallagher, *Journal of Consciousness Studies*, 5, No. 5–6, 1998, pp. 706–17
[404] Michael Gazzaniga, "The Mind's Past," page 145.
[405] NYU Langone Medical Center, "Delusions Associated with Consistent Pattern of Brain Injury," http://communications.med.nyu.edu/media-relations/news/delusions-associated-consistent-pattern-brain-injury
[406] The characterization of the actions of the left brain as just a storyteller is equivalent to describing Nixon and his Watergate associates as just good storytellers.
[407] R. Joseph, "The Right Brain and the Unconscious: Discovering the Stranger Within," Basic Book, 2001, page 96.
[408] A video of the Sacks Twins doing calendar counting but being unable to do complex multiplication can be see on YouTube at https://www.youtube.com/watch?v=YuhTFsiEcMU
[409] This ability was shown in the movie "Rain Man" where 246 toothpicks falling on the floor are counted almost instantly. This story was pulled from a true story involving the Salk's twins, John and Michael, who instantly counted 111 matchsticks that had fallen on the floor.
[410] Russell Targ and Harold Puthoff, "Mind Reach Scientists Look at Psychic Abilities," Hampton Roads Publishing, 2005,

[411] Jack Houck, "Instructions for Conducting a Remote-Viewing Experiment," in ARTIFEX, 4, 1 (Spring 1985), 4.
[412] http://www.oxfordreference.com/view/10.1093/oi/authority.20110803095935377
[413] http://www.macmillanhighered.com/Catalog/uploadedFiles/Content/Worth/Product/About/Look_Inside/Revlin,_Cognition_1e/Revlin1e_Chapter%205.pdf
[414] Stanley Krippner, Fariba Bogzaran, Andre Percia de Carvalho ,"Extraordinary Dreams and How to Work with Them," page 25.
[415] "Russell Brand Interview of Quantum Physicist Dr John Hagelin," https://www.youtube.com/watch?v=WjTHpVfaDiA&spfreload=1
[416] Mindfulnet.org, "The neuroscience of mindfulness," http://www.mindfulnet.org/page25.htm
[417] "Biology Brain," http://www.bibliotecapleyades.net/ciencia/ciencia_brain01.htm
[418] Bryan Williams, "A Glimpse into the Meditating Brain," http://earthvision.info/meditatingbrain.html
[419] Taylor, "Stroke of Insight," page 116.
[420] Ibid page 121.
[421] Dr. Diane Powell, "The ESP Enigma" Walker Publishing, 2009, page 160
[422] Rick Straussman, Slawek Wojtowicz, Luis Eduardo Luna, and Ede Frecska" "Inner Path to Outer Space," Park Street Press, 2008, page 58.
[423] Lisa Karrer, "The Phenomenology of the Pythia and the Metaphysical as Industry in Ancient Greece," http://www.academia.edu/5899461/The_Phenomenology_of_the_Pythia_and_the_Metaphysical_as_Industry_in_Ancient_Greece
[424] David Luke, Ph.D., and Stanley Krippner, Ph.D., "Psi-chedelic Science: An Approach to Understanding Exceptional Human Experiences," http://www.maps.org/news-letters/v21n1/v21n1-59to60.pdf
[425] William F. Bengston Homepage, http://www.bengstonresearch.com/
[426] The idea that right brain ideas negatively affecting the shutting down the left brain with ego images is similar to the situation that was clearly established in remote viewing. Viewers were asked to simple describe what they were seeing, sensing, tasting, and a perceiving. This would be a right brain process. They were told not to try and guess the target. The analytical process is left brain process and caused what was called "analytical overlay." Once the left brain was allowed into the viewing session it was over and the target usually missed.
[427] This was reported by Bernadette Doran at a Bengston training session. November 12, 2015.
[428] It should be noted that human knowledge could not source, gather, and arrange even the first 10 atoms in the new 100 trillion atom cell.
[429] Christian Crumlish, Erin Malone , "Designing Social Interfaces: Principles, Patterns, and Practices for Improving the User Experience," 2009 page 15.
[430] Quantum Quotables, http://gardenoflifetemple.com/WordPlay/QuantumQuotables.html
[431] "Quantum theory poses reality's deepest mystery." Obituary of John A. Wheeler by Tom Siegfried. Science News, 173, 17. May 24th 2008, p.32.

[432] The Aspect experiment is described in Wikipedia as follows, "he performed the elusive "Bell test experiments" that showed that Albert Einstein, Boris Podolsky and Nathan Rosen's reductio ad absurdum of quantum mechanics, namely that it implied 'ghostly action at a distance', did in fact appear to be realized when two particles were separated by an arbitrarily large distance (see EPR paradox). A correlation between their wave functions remained, as they were once part of the same wavefunction that was not disturbed before one of the child particles was measured."

[433] "Future of Mind Quotes," https://www.goodreads.com/work/quotes/25207078-the-future-of-the-mind

[434] Orest Bedrij, "The Greatest Achievement," Xlibris Corporation, 2013, page 84

[435] Nisargadatta Maharaj Quotes, https://en.wikiquote.org/wiki/Nisargadatta_Maharaj

[436] Double slit experiments have been run with objects as big as molecules that contain 810 atoms. The results were the same.

[437] "God is Not Dead," *Resurgence and Ecologist*. http://www.resurgence.org/magazine/article2894-God-is-not-Dead.html

[438] Sam Parnia, M.D. describes in his book *Erasing Death: The Science that is Rewriting the Boundaries between Life and Death* states that neuron cells can be taken from a patient who has been dead for four hours and regrow in a laboratory.

[439] A 1992 Roper Poll indicated a figure of 5% which would be 20 million Americans.

[440] Mark Twain, "Mark Twain's Essays, Letters, and Speeches," B&R Samizdat Express, Feb 6, 2012.

[441] Steve Job Quotes, http://www.brainyquote.com/quotes/quotes/s/stevejobs416925.html

[442] Rhawn Joseph, "The Split Brain: Two Brains - Two Minds," http://journalofcosmology.com/Consciousness163.html

[443] There is also a video on the internet that shows the left brain of a split brain patient trying to do a simple children's puzzle. It is unable to do it. The right brain does the puzzle in seconds. The video shows that as the right hand, controlled by the left brain, struggles to do the puzzle, the left hand, controlled by the right brain, keeps trying to help do the puzzle and at one point had to be tied down by the researchers to stop it. "Early Split Brain Research Gazzaniga" https://www.youtube.com/watch?v=0lmfxQ-HK7Y

[444] Ascension Earth, "Betty Andreasson's Remarkable Alien Abductions & Out of Body Experiences," http://www.ascensionearth2012.org/2014/06/betty-andreassons-remarkable-alien.html

[445] Grant Cameron, "Reagan UFO Story," http://www.presidentialufo.com/ronald-reagan/99-reagan-ufo-story

[446] "Left Brain/Right Brain Matters," Women Waking the World, http://www.womenwakingtheworld.com/right-brainleft-brain-matters/

[447] For a review of the experiments done in this area see https://en.wikipedia.org/wiki/Quantum_entanglement

[448] "'Intelligent' Slime Mold able to Navigate its Way out of Mold," http://www.telegraph.co.uk/news/worldnews/asia/japan/8982310/Intelligent-slime-able-to-navigate-its-way-out-of-maze.html

[449] Garrett Moddell, Darrell Lanham, Christopher Smith, "Stock Market Prediction Using Associated Remote Viewing by Inexperienced Remote Viewers," 12/7/13, http://psiphen.colorado.edu/Pubs/Smith14.pdf

Printed in Great Britain
by Amazon